With all blessing

Israel

9/1/20.

The Greatest Act of Faith

The Greatest Act of Faith

The First Organic Union
of the Church of South India

Israel Selvanayagam

Christian World Imprints

© Israel Selvanayagam

First Published in 2019 by

Christian World Imprints
Christian Publishing & Books from India
C-3, Shop No. 14, Ground Floor
Wazirpur Industrial Area, **Delhi-110052**
cwidelhi2017@gmail.com
www.ChristianWorldImprints.com
Phone: +91 11 41526079

ISBN: 978-93-5148-392-2 (HB)
ISBN: 978-93-5148-393-9 (PB)

Printed in India.

TO
Those Persons of Great Faith
Who Participated in the Negotiations for
the Formation of the Church of South India

Contents

Foreword-I

Israel Selvanayagam, who I count as a dear friend, has contributed so much to contemporary Mission Studies and to Ecumenical and Inter-faith relations. As a teacher and pastor, both in India and in the U.K, he has influenced many hundreds of pupils and colleagues including myself. His many published books contain at least one masterpiece. I refer to *Kristu Bhakti and Krishnu Bhakti* (2017); an extraordinarily original and daring exploration of the devotion found in St John's Gospel and the dance or play of divine love in the '*Rāsalīlā*' section of the *Bhāgavata Purāṇa*. Whether in the formal rôle of teacher, preacher and pastor or as a smiling host welcoming the visitor to his home or radiating joy in accompanying worship songs on his Indian accordion Israel evidences the presence within of the Spirit.

This new book is deeply rooted in my friend's pride and affection for the Church which nurtured his faith and of which he is a Presbyter of several years standing. This book is, at one level, both a history and a celebration of the Church of South India (CSI). The story should be so much better known than it is. It's a wonderful story. In these pages, Israel rescues from comparative obscurity those whose vision, perseverance and moral courage brought the first United Church into existence. They are the heroes of his book. Israel hails them as stars in dark clouds! They are.

Nevertheless, this is a troubled book. It arises from a deep disquiet, an awareness, on Israel's part, that somewhere along the way distortions have arisen within CSI which now threaten it's integrity and authenticity. These misgivings become focussed in his chapter about relations with the Anglican Communion and CSI's apparent acceptance as a Province within the Anglican Communion. As an Anglican myself, a priest within the Church of England, what Israel has to say makes for some uncomfortable reading. He and I have also had some painful conversations. Suffice to say I tend to be ready, too ready no doubt, to interpret Anglican approaches and overtures to CSI as well meaning attempts to repent of past wrongs and redeem past hurt rather than as a new, creeping neo-colonialism.

Israel, though, is too exact a scholar and too stern a seeker after truth to let me get away with very much revealing how often urbane smiles and courtesy reveal either an implicit arrogance or simple ignorance of what is at stake. He is a great teacher. The difficulties he has encountered in getting 'answers' from Church leaders in both the U.K. and South India, I would scarcely have believed possible if I hadn't shared in them myself. For sure some of our correspondents have been generous in their thoughtful and honest responses and we are grateful. But, the failure of many senior players even to acknowledge correspondence is disquieting and disappointing. Important decisions affecting both CSI and the Anglican Communion have been made. The absence of any documentation or inability to produce any record of how those decisions were made is a cause for real concern.

Michael Hollis, the first CSI Bishop of Madras and first Moderator, saw the creation of CSI as a United Church as the thrilling and wonderful achievement of the Spirit. He characterised it as nothing less than 'the most important event since Pentecost'. He and other founders hoped and prayed that the same Spirit would inspire others to follow in their footsteps, to really feel the unhappiness of the Lord at the divisions within His Church and find the courage to die that 'they be one' as the churches that came together as CSI had done.

We must not lose that hope.

Rather than dismissing Israel's book as negative or judgemental I invite the reader to take utterly seriously his strictures, acknowledge the past errors of judgement and ignorance we have all made but then find in his writing, as I have done, an electrifying call to let the Spirit once again lead us forward and re-energise our limping efforts towards organic Union in order that, as Israel himself puts it, we can become what at root we already are: 'children of God and disciples of Jesus'.

Owain Bell
Worcester, UK
Ascension Day, 30 May 2019

Foreword-II

I am honoured by the invitation to write a foreword to the monograph by Dr. Israel Selvnanaygm. It is providential that it is being published on the 100th anniversary of the Tranquebar Manifesto, a statement signed in May 1919 by 7 Anglican Ministers and 26 representatives of the South India United Church, a union of non-episcopal Churches in South India. They looked forward to a union of the two churches which will respect the Congregational, Presbyterian and Episcopal elements, which they asserted, no one of which is absolute or sufficient without the other. When, after prolonged negotiations, the union became a reality in the year 1947, these three elements were recognized in the Basis of Union, as the necessary elements in the life of the United Church, exercising responsibility and authority in their several spheres. The Constitution of the Church of South India contains a Chapter on the Governing Principles of the Church in which this principle is incorporated giving it a legal status.

It is tragic that over the years the Episcopal element has become more and more dominant in the life and administration of the CSI sidelining the other two elements. Many in the CSI today consider it a breach of the solemn assurance given to the non-episcopal churches at the time of Union that the Episcopacy in CSI would be in a constitutional form. There are several reasons for this deplorable state of affairs. One is the role played by vested interests that can benefit from the centralization of powers in the hands of the bishop. Another is the apathy and the indifference of ordinary members who, due to their ignorance of the history of the process that led to the unique organic union of the Episcopal and non-episcopal churches, are content to accept the *status quo* and do not have the motivation to question the state of affairs. Most of the bishops are happy with the development and seek ways and means of increasing their stranglehold on the administration. Three years ago, a set of amendments was forced on the people which made further increased the authority of the bishops. Consequently, one can say that today, a bishop of the CSI enjoys more power than his counterpart in the Church of England.

The situation in the CSI has been aggravated by the decision to make the CSI as one of the Provinces of the Anglican Communion. The CSI Bishops who are now invited by the Archbishop of Canterbury to attend the decennial Lambeth Conference with their spouses are euphoric and the next issue of CSI Life, the official magazine of the CSI would contain a number of pictures highlighting the visit. One can tolerate this state of affairs except for the fact it has contributed to an alarming increase in the already bloated self importance of the bishops. More importantly, the strange and untenable claim that the CSI is the legal successor of the Church of England has totally subverted the historic importance of the union which sought to create a unique Church in South India which is autonomous and distinct from the uniting churches.

Many persons like me in the CSI who are perturbed at the turn of events would joyfully welcome the well researched monograph of Dr. Israel Selvanayagam, who has painstakingly identified the serious issues that are lurking behind the seemingly innocuous decision to declare the CSI as a Province of the Anglican Communion. He rightly points out that it is a process of 'absorption' by a historically powerful and traditional church, a new movement or new reality, made unilaterally without consulting the other churches which were involved in the union. Whether the action was deliberate or unintentional arising out of a well-meaning attempt at partnership in ecumenical context is a moot point. The fact, however, is indisputable that there has been no consultation with the official machinery of the Church, which has been so 'honoured', like the Synod of the CSI. Had that been done, perhaps some discerning voices might have been raised regarding the danger it posed to the self identity of the United Church.

Dr. Israel Selvanayagam does not propose his thesis either lightly or superficially. He has unfolded the main thrust of the monograph from his own personal perception and struggle to understand the phenomenon, through historical snapshots outlining the process that led to the formation of the CSI. The chapter on brief biographical notes on many players in the whole fascinating journey towards union is very valuable since it indicates how a large number of persons from different denominational backgrounds played critical roles in the process. There is an element of poignancy in his narration of his futile attempts to get a healthy conversation going among persons of significance on this issue.

It is my hope that the publication of this monograph would challenge the leaders of not only the Anglican Communion and the CSI but also the Methodist and Reformed Churches who were the 'mother churches' in the process of the Union, who, so far, have not raised any question about this obvious 'absorption'. Those of us who have been advocating a reform of the CSI would be in great debt to Dr. Israel Selvanayagam if this helps not only to reclaim the uniqueness of the CSI but also provide impetus for further growth in the organic union.

R. Jayakaran Isaac
Vellore, India
The centenary of the release of the
Tranquebar Manifesto, 2 May 2019

Acknowledgements

Owain Bell, a senior priest of the CofE retired as Rector few years ago. He is well-known for working ecumenically and inter-religiously. He was the chairman of the Advisory Committee in the United College of the Ascension, Birmingham where I was the Principal (2001 Jan-2006 July). I excited him about South Indian life and the life of the CSI and he, along with his wife Kim, visited India. On return he asked questions and then such visits have been a regular feature of his life. When I shared the concern of this book, he became enthusiastic for the sake of finding out the truth. He introduced me to a few people and himself corresponded with a number of leaders, particularly former bishops and archbishops. Above all he has graced the project with a foreword.

An Indian foreword has come from Jeyakaran Isaac, a former principal of the Voorheese College, Vellore and former Lay Secretary, CSI Diocese of Vellore, Tamil Nadu. He has been involved in reforming the CSI through public protests and publications. He has argued that the CSI bishops' association with the Anglican Communion and Lambeth Conference has given them a false prestige and honour which has covered up corruption and hampered reform. Somehow, I tend to compare him to K.T. Paul about whom we will study. Isaac sent some materials and information and has strengthened the appeal of this book.

William Allberry, another senior priest in the CofE, regular visiting teacher of English at the Tamilnadu Theological Seminary Madurai, apart from checking the language as usual for nearly two years, has picked up issues that needed refinement and even softening.

Mary Tanner, a biblical scholar who has taught in universities in England and outside, has been involved in various ecumenical conversations on behalf of the CofE. She kindly and patiently guided me to important resources, both printed materials and websites.

Stephanie Taylor, the Executive Officer & Information Manager of the Anglican Communion Office, London, was engaged in a helpful correspondence about possible records in the AC's record library about the process of the CSI being incorporated into the AC.

Apart from Bell, the following read the seventh chapter and made comments: Andrew Wingate, an educational missionary in TTS and my predecessor at UCA (along with general support), Arthur Jayakumar, a church historian, and O.V. Jathanna, eminent theologian and former Principal of the United Theological College Bangalore, who sent elaborate comments with critical questions; also he sent important details about the Basel Mission

As I have already noted, to get the biographical details of those who were associated with the negotiations for CSI was most tedious. In this process the help, little and great, of the following persons are noteworthy: Lance Martin, Archivist, Special Collection in the School of Oriental and African Studies of the London University; John Lenton and Peter Forsaith of the Wesley Historical Society, Oxford; Sheila Himsworth, Archivist, Stratford & Evesham Circuit of the Methodist Church; James Steele, a local preacher of the same circuit who was instructed by Hooper and who guided me to his last house and the crematorium where his name has been inscribed in the Book of Remembrance; Kanagu Nelson of TTS; Babu Jeyaraj of the Evangelical Church of India Chennai; and Vincent Robert, Densingh Oliver and Jebin Paul of Kanyakumari Diocese.

Those who corresponded with me with a spirit of dialogue gave the most authentic opinions. I have mentioned most of them and for good reasons I have not given their names. I had brief conversations with a number of persons of whom most remarkable are Eric Lott, my teacher at UTC Bangalore, and Frank Bentley, a retired Archdeacon.

I have been privileged to live at a manageable distance from Birmingham. The staff of the Orchard Learning and Resource Centre in Selly Oak helped to locate old issues of the *South India Churchman* and to photocopy rare materials. The staff of the Cadbury Research Library in the main campus of the University of Birmingham were courteous and helpful. The one day visit to the Library of the Church Mission Society Oxford was fruitful.

Repeating thanks will take much space. Let me just record the fact that the limited language I have is incapable of conveying the unstoppable springs of gratitude gushing out from a source within for which I have no proper name.

Though I have unearthed findings of others' work I do not claim that all the contents of this book are fruits of my own research. Presenting the biographical sketches of those 71 persons who participated in the negotiations for about 28 years to achieve the first organic union is a matter of joy though it was hard work. At times I was thrilled and excited about their commitment and determination and for that reason I may have slightly exaggerated certain cases.

The most useful resource is the classical study by Bengt Sundkler, a Swedish mission historian, the fruit of which is *Church of South India: The Movement Towards Union – 1900-1947* (1954). However, today an average reader will find the book complex and the language rather old-fashioned. I have tried to simplify, summarise and make its contents orderly. It is unbelievable that no one has thought of bringing out a new edition of this resourceful book. K.M. George's book *Church of South India: Life in Union (1947-1997)*, 1999 is a good update with a critical appraisal. *Christianity A Complete Guide* (ed. by John Bowden, 2005) is an invaluable reference book on the history and issues in the life of the Church. On several matters I have checked Wikipedia, but I have not given references for just checking dates and facts.

A note on the style of writing is in order. I am fully aware of gender biases in certain materials I have used and reproduced. I have not changed them nor given '*sic* notes'. The reader may be fully assured of my disagreement on any bias and prejudice of that kind.

There are many abbreviations in the text. For easy reference a list with expansion is separately given. In every chapter when an acronym occurs for the first time the full form is given in brackets. If the full form occurs in quotations it has not been changed.

Finally thanks are due to publishers, i.e., Christian World Imprints. They are the delight for any serious (even stressful) author to work with. Their commitment to prompt communication, precision and perfection is admirable indeed.

It is my sincere wish and hope that those who love the Church and the truth will find this book informing and motivating for action.

Evesham, UK
Pentecost, 9 June 2019

Preface

The original stimulus for working on this book was the question 'Is CSI Anglican?' found on the cover page of an issue of the *Pilgrim*, the magazine of the Friends of Church in India (based in UK), in 2002. It was heartening to know that FCI was a fellowship of returned missionaries from India and Indian Christians living in the UK. It was the continuation of the Church of South India Council in Great Britain founded in 1953 with J.S.M. Hooper, as the Chairperson. He was the architect of the CSI union, convener of the JC (Joint Committee) during the most crucial years towards the consummation of the union and preacher at the inaugural service. The main purpose was to celebrate and share the achievement of the formation of the CSI in 1947 constituted by five denominations – Anglican, Congregational, Presbyterian, Methodist and Basel Mission (Reformed-Lutheran). The members of these denominations, with prayer and evangelistic commitment, came forward for Christ's sake, to die from their old denominational selves and rise to a new identity of organic union taking the name of the area or region as was the practice of the early Church.

It was a painful realisation that most of those denominations persist in the UK and USA while the membership (particularly in the UK) is fast declining. Equally painful, not unrelated to the above, was the sheer ignorance about the formation of the CSI as a unique expression of the organic unity of its kind, 'a miracle next to the Pentecost' (according to Michael Hollis, ex-Anglican from England, church historian and the first Moderator of the CSI). However, the Anglo-Catholic wing of the Church of England and those influenced by them, protested against this unity, stopped support, refused to recognise it, but ridiculed its existence. This attitude and approach continued until the late 1980s. The growth of the CSI could not be damped by this attitude and in fact, with different factors contributing, it grew about fourfold. There was an apparent conversion in the Anglican ranks when six bishops were invited as guests for the Lambeth Conference (1988), all the bishops as full members in the next conference (1998) and accompanied by their spouses in the following conference (2008). Most remarkably, without any prior information or consultation in the CSI circle, at the end of the 1988 Conference, the CSI was declared as a Province of the

Anglican Communion. The question 'Is the CSI Anglican?' was raised in this context by informed persons while those unaware of the history and significance of the CSI took it as *fait accompli*.

A number of important questions arise in the whole episode. For example, what were the reasons for the AC (Anglican Communion) and its mother CofE (Church of England) suddenly recognising the CSI? Was it an embrace with respect or a tight embrace that killed its unique identity? What was the process of consultation both in London and Chennai, and what were the conditions of mutual recognition? Has the Anglican Communion recognised and regarded the ministry of the CSI as the Methodist and Reformed Churches have done? Is there an anomaly of absorbing the CSI while the Church of England was not in full communion with the non-Anglican constituents (mainly URC – United Reformed Church – and Methodist)? When declaring the CSI as a Province of the Anglican Communion, were those constituents consulted and if so, what was their response? Those who do not know the history of the formation and birth-pangs of the CSI may allow it to pass, and with noble slogans such as tolerance, status-quo, decency, etc., they might want to move on. But, those who know the history, particularly the hurdles put up on the way by Anglican structures, particularly on the issues such as inter-communion and apostolic succession that delayed the achievement, naturally agonise when they see the power of a neo-colonial intrusion through the church doors on the part of Church of England and the weakness of a continuing colonised psyche on the part of the CSI leaders and people. What this study aims to achieve is to remind the present generation of the Anglican Communion and the Church of South India about the story of the CSI, to point out an ecumenical tragedy and to warn the worldwide ecumenical movement which once celebrated in jubilation the birth of the CSI as a great event in the history of Christianity.

Let ignorance not be taken as pride and advantage! Ignorance about the unique nature of the CSI has been often taken advantage of twisting the facts and maintaining a wrong understanding. Most significantly, the CSI is not simply a communion of certain denominational churches, as many in the Anglican circle say. As we pointed out earlier, it represented a dying to denominations and rising to be a new organic union. Further, an empirical study will reveal how many Anglican leaders know that great leaders such as William Temple, the then Archbishop of Canterbury, stated clearly that the CSI would never be a Province of Anglican Communion. Today in conversations and communications the argument often goes to the extent of claiming the 'ex-Anglicans' who in effect asking for a very late post-mortem and a share of a decomposed body! On the CSI side, the ignorance is taken advantage of not by people but the bishops, who seem to regard being part of the Anglican Communion is a privilege and prestige. As they are full members of the Lambeth Conference, they enjoy the colourful company of bishops from all over the world. I hope that this book will reveal the complex realities that have perpetuated the ignorance on both sides.

I have good Anglican friends and had close colleagues and I greatly admire the life-style, speeches and writings of many leaders. They would encourage the removal of ignorance and rectifying distortions. I have come across inspiring leaders and lay thinkers who played their role in the formation of the CSI, but I am not sure if their memory is kept and their legacy maintained. The research for this book was very hazardous and challenging. Personally, I do not have any other interest than 'speaking the truth in love', challenging the stubborn to be led from ignorance to truth, encourage unity efforts all over the world and regain the gospel nerve 'that the world may believe'.

Let me admit that I am not a church historian and I wish that a historian might undertake such research. Mostly I have relied on the research of others though I have not found anything untrustworthy in their information. Given the peculiar nature of this writing, I am in a dilemma about the proper approach in communication. I abhor perpetuating contradiction in the name of plurality and tolerance. Having fifty years' experience of ministry, pastoral and teaching, I feel it is my Christian obligation to leave this piece of work as a resource for the present and future generations. I wish that I am able communicate in Jesus' way and style using stories, anecdotes and exhortations and, if necessary, caricaturing certain persons and tell them 'woe unto you' and calling some fools, hypocrites and foxes, with indignation. Though such persons will come to mind, readers will realise that I have failed to follow Jesus closely in this matter because I too have been influenced by what is considered as polished and decent. If 'greatest truths are the simplest', truth-lovers appreciate however simple are the contents of this book.

The first chapter sets out my personal experience and questions both in South India and in England. This may explain the limitation and particular flavour of this book.

The second chapter is an outline of church history leading up to the rise of major denominations, especially those who constituted the organic union of the CSI.

The third chapter introduces all the major players in the union talks, both Western and Indian. This book is dedicated to them whom I call persons of great faith (who had the capacity to transcend, to move on, to try the impossible, to cross boundaries and transgress cultural norms, to persist as will be explained in chapter 5). The hardest part of the research was to get basic biographical details though, sadly, a few have passed on without any recognition. In order to show the pluralistic nature of their personalities, denominational loyalties and theological/spiritual positions, after biographical notes, I have quoted their words. It has been thrilling to note that some of them were open to change their positions, even to go through a conversion experience. Their prayer as well as humour have not been concealed.

The fourth chapter gives snapshots of a long journey of forming the CSI, from 1919 to 1947. The purpose is to inform and educate those who are ignorant of what exactly happened during those years but in a nutshell. Perhaps, the exercise and achievement of the first organic unity may inspire the present and future generations to work out similar unity.

The fifth chapter deals with the basic issues such as understanding the Bible, the place of creed(s), doctrines, apostolic succession, definition of episcopacy, faith, spirituality, signs & symbols and so on.

The sixth chapter presents the story of the CSI forging partnerships with their mother and other churches.

Chapter seventh's title is self-explanatory: Distortion of Organic Union by Absorption into the Anglican Communion. As we have already noted, this is the burden of the whole research and of this book; hence more detailed than any other chapter.

The eighth chapter briefly explains what I call the true 'ever reforming evangelical and ecumenical church'. The terminological confusion about 'evangelical' will be exposed and explained. Thus, those who are truly committed to a living outreach, an ongoing transformation with openness to change, cannot but be one in spite of all complementary and comprehensive differences.

Abbreviations

AC	Anglican Communion
ACC	Anglican Consultative Council
BCC	British Council of Churches
CC	Continuation Committee
CIBC	Church of India, Burma, Ceylon
CMS	Church Missionary Society (now Church Mission Society)
CNI	Church of North India
CofE	Church of England
CSI	Church of South India
CSIPS	CSI People's Synod
CSITA	Church of South India Trust Association
CISRS	Christian Institute for the Study of Religion and Society
CTBI	Churches Together in Britain and Ireland
CTE	Churches Together in England
FCI	Friends of Church in India
FELC	Federation of Evangelical Lutheran Churches
LC	Lambeth Conference
LEP	Local Ecumenical Partnership
LMS	London Missionary Society
LWF	Lutheran World Federation
JC	Joint Committee

MCC   Madras Christian College

MMRC   The Movement for the Renewal and Reformation of Churches

MMS   Methodist Missionary Society

NCCI   National Council of Churches in India

NMS   National Missionary Society

PFLWC   The Prophetic Forum for the Life and Witness of Churches

PMR-CSI   People's Movement for the Reformation of the CSI

SCM   Student Christian Movement

SICman   South India Churchman

SIUC   South India United Church

SPCK   Society for Propagating Christian Knowledge

SPG   Society for the Propagation of the Gospel (now the United Society)

TDTA   Thirunelveli Diocesan Trust Association

TTS   Tamilnadu Theological Seminary (Madurai)

UCA   United College of the Ascension

UELCI   United Evangelical Lutheran Churches in India

URC   United Reformed Church

USPG   United Society for the Propagation of the Gospel

WMMS   Wesleyan Methodist Missionary Society

UTC   United Theological College (Bangalore)

WCC   World Council of Churches

YMCA   Young Men's Christian Association

WCRC   World Council of Reformed Churches

WMC   World Methodist Council

Chapter 1

Background:
A Personal Journey

Simple Beginning

A simple church building, a mile inland from the shores of the Indian Ocean. There were a few benches, and most members squatted on mats on the floor. The focal points were a wooden table and a pulpit behind which had railings on both sides. The deacons sat on the side benches and the harmonist nearby. There was no candle or flower. The church hand-bell was rung two times before the start of a service. A group of youngsters went to the church on Sundays well before the actual start of service and sang songs with the accompaniment of drums, hand drum and harmonium. The lay catechist conducted the service and he did everything. He was clad with a white *veshti/doti* (one piece with border lines wrapped around from the waist), a white shirt tucked in and an open coat. Usual prayers were offered, all extemporary, lesson (s) read and hymns and lyrics announced. The intercessory prayer was long, as long as over fifteen minutes, covering all people and all issues. There was regular notice for giving, giving in kind (jaggery, coconuts, banana bunches) and in lives (chicken and goats). There was a short mid-week service on Wednesday evening.

Usually the lay catechist was on a part time arrangement, and the stipend was very meagre. People shared their first fruits of the field with him. There was a paid or honorary sexton to assist the catechist. The higher structure was the pastorate, and the pastorate chairman was an ordained pastor. He visited the branch churches for baptisms, communion and weddings. Higher still are the districts and there were seven in those days (the late 1960s). The district chairmen were invited to visit the pastorate as well as branch churches on special occasions. The highest in the order was the diocese and the bishop. The bishop visited churches on the inauguration of buildings and projects and confirmations. Invariably the concerned district chairman and pastorate chairman were present when the bishop came to a church.

Then as a teenager I did not know that I was worshipping in a congregation of the Congregational tradition, one of the components of the South India United Church, the other being the Presbyterian. The SIUC was formed in 1908 with a view to being effective in mission. Simplicity, spiritual equality, self-governance of every local congregation (even in the appointment of their church worker or catechist and pastor) and deciding on local mission basics. However, there were regional federations such as Councils with Superintendents and Presidents. Later, I realised that SIUC was part of the CSI (Church of South India, along with Anglican, Methodist and Basel Mission Churches) that was formed in 1947 as the first united church of its kind in the history of the Christian Church. Since 1947 there have been changes with dioceses and bishops.

At a young age, I joined the ministry as catechist of a small congregation, ten miles away from my home village. The selection was done by the bishop in a brief meeting. There was no training, and the expectation was that through my involvement in the Sunday school and youth fellowship and training by the catechist of my home church I should acquire basic skills. While in the service I attended the church workers' bible class. Apart from colleagues of my diocese I had chances to meet priests of the Roman Catholic Church, ministers of the Salvation Army and pastors of the Indian Evangelical Lutheran Church. Pentecostal churches were slowly spreading and growing, often with people having joined from the CSI churches. There was often tension with accusations of sheep-stealing and safeguarding unsaved souls. Apart from this, there were independent preachers preaching at gospel conventions of the CSI churches. Some of them with their charismatic appeal and media glamour became exceedingly popular and rich. They promoted sectarianism, and the mainline churches were not able to do anything about their growth. There was even suspicion that some western forces instigated some popular preachers with a view to disintegrating the CSI as they could not stomach the success of CSI's organic unity.

Surprises and Challenges in Seminary/College

After four years of church work, in 1973 I joined TTS (Tamilnadu Theological Seminary in Madurai, a temple town, 145 miles away from my village) for theological education and ministerial training. This was an ecumenical seminary that came into existence in 1969 combining a Lutheran seminary in the east and a CSI seminary in the south. It was the outcome of the Lutheran-CSI dialogue to train their ministers together, with a view to moving closer in church union. For me it was the first experience to see candles used in the worship service, and often they were replaced by the Indian brass lamp. Along with the organ there were all types of Indian musical instruments including different types of drums, harmoniums and flutes. There were sung liturgies in Tamil and sometimes liturgical dance too. The traditional Lutheran sung liturgies had their own flavour while the Tamil classical forms appeared to be more natural. When the ex-Anglicans of the CSI used collects, I was moved by the distilled wisdom and spirit embodied in them. Only later I realised that many of them were incorporated in the CSI's Book of Common Worship which had yet to become popular as former denominational liturgies continued to hold sway. From time to time students with charismatic lenience introduced lively songs which we were encouraged to sing, clapping hands and moving bodies. All these were startling and, admittedly, at the beginning I had moments of intense struggle to appreciate and appropriate different styles of worship and I longed for the simple worship form of my diocese and village. But, in due course, for both students and the staff, such worship life with variety and richness of sources, was truly ideal and enriching. The key was the ability to move on from what was familiar and to be open to accept the gifts of others with a spirit of unity.

Teaching in TTS was based to a great extent on a syllabus prescribed by the Senate of Serampore College (University), founded by the famous Baptist missionary William Carey and his two colleagues, in the State of West Bengal. The broad subject areas were Old Testament, New Testament, History of Christianity, Theology, Ministry (with the branches of Pastoralia, Counselling and Christian Education) and Religions. The advantage of training in an ecumenical seminary was that we were exposed to different views though the scripture was the touching stone. Even in Theology, though the title 'doctrines' was used, as far as I remember, finally the bible was used as the primary point of reference. There were moments to struggle to reconcile different views of the bible itself and perceptions of scholars. I felt that our knowledge of the bible was admirable; but our lack of clarity to approach and appropriate its message and apply its appeal to our life today, was miserable. In the context of literalist approach, scientific approach, doctrinal approach, etc., I was searching for a method which would be helpful to discover the gospel, the pearl in deep sea or the treasure in a bewildering forest. At some point in TTS the Lutherans felt that the Lutheran heritage including their doctrines were not adequately dealt with. Consequently, separate sessions were arranged for Lutheran students. This was not an issue for the CSI students as their new united church did not sign up for any doctrines. The basic requirement was to hold on two Testaments, two Creeds, two Sacraments and episcopacy in a constitutional form. And I was not convinced that apart from the above and the two Catechisms of Luther, there were indispensable doctrines that were important for a Lutheran identity! In any case, the 'Lutheran Hall' in the seminary was established to assert the Lutheran identity.

Lessons from a Pioneering Ministry

It was a deliberate choice to situate the new seminary in Madurai, one of the prominent temple towns of South India. Apart from the magnificent Meenakshi Temple (Saiva) and Perumal Temple (Vaishanava), there are hundreds of temples and thousands of shrines in the relatively small city of Madurai. Apart from the study of Hinduism, there was the intensive practical exposure that made a group of staff and students to encounter Hindus face to face. After my training, while preparing to go back to my church, my mentors in the seminary persuaded me to stay on and take up the pioneering ministry of interfaith dialogue. Some of the questions the Hindu friends posed were piercing. 'You criticise that we worship many gods and goddesses although we hold that Reality is One and the wise call it differently. In spite of a variety and multiplicity of cultures, languages and traditions, more than 82% of about 1. 2 billion people share the common identity as Hindus. But you say that you worship one God, follow one Jesus and belong to one Church, yet you are so divided with confusing labels? Are you bankrupt of any unified vision, teachings and structures? You seem to be self-deceiving and confusing.' Some informed Hindus pointed out in meetings that the kind of interreligious wars and conflicts within Christianity in Europe was unheard of in India. It is true that sometimes they exaggerated, but there was no reason to ignore their challenge. I tried to explain the pioneering achievement of the CSI. But since the ex-denominations continue to keep their structures (including the buildings) and styles of worship and functioning it was not easy to explain the history.

Starting from the time of my initial ministry as church worker, I was attracted by the life and ministry of Sadhu Sunder Singh (1889-1929). He was a Sikh convert, the greatest lay theologian and preacher in India, who was perceived by some theologians and scholars of Europe to be the embodiment of the living Jesus of Nazareth. He was baptised in St. John's parish church in Shimla, but soon he left the church and declared that he belonged to the universal body of Christ. He was open to worship and preach at any church and believed in the transforming power of the divine word operating beyond denominations. His free movement among monks of other faiths helped to understand what others thought about the churches in India with conflicting claims denominational divisions.

The ministry of interfaith dialogue in Madurai brought me in contact with Catholic friends. It was in Madurai that the Jesuit missionary Robert de Nobili arrived in 1905 and established a mission. Observing the reality of the Christian converts being from the low caste and untouchable communities, he wanted to make the Christian message appealing to the high castes. He mastered the Sanskrit language and read the Hindu scriptures. He lived like a Brahmin teacher, eating vegetarian food cooked by a Brahmin and was carried in a palanquin. He preached the Christian doctrines in Hindu terms, but the response was disappointing.

Since the Second Vatican Council (1962-65) a different kind of interfaith approach was initiated by the Catholic Church in India. In every diocese there was someone in charge of organising programmes on interfaith dialogue. As far as Madurai was concerned, what TTS initiated was pioneering. Some Catholic priests attended our meetings and their presence was encouraging as the Protestant churches were very suspicious of interfaith dialogue. Another major area of Catholic-Protestant collaboration was inter-confessional bible translation in Tamil. After about twenty-five years of sustained work, the new Bible was released in 1995. It was both a privilege and challenge for me to be part of the team of translators. We, the Protestants and Catholics had many opportunities to pray together and to say 'Amen' together. But it was intriguing to hear the notice in some service, 'non-Catholics are not welcome to receive the Communion.' Actually, I had once received the Communion innocently in a Catholic mass, and I felt no discomfort in my body and mind! Should we distinguish between speaking to God and hearing the divine word from receiving his body and blood? In what way the latter was superior to the former? I have been searching for a convincing answer.

To further my understanding of Hinduism and Hindu-Christian dialogue, I joined UTC (the United Theological College), Bangalore in 1981. Founded in 1910 it was the first united college of its kind. It attracted candidates for ministry and scholars for specialization from all over the world. Later I came to know that a bishop in Iran had been trained in UTC. He gave his testimony that it was a life-changing experience to study and share fellowship and eucharist with colleagues from different parts of India and world. The church traditions represented were vast, ranging from the Orthodox Churches in Kerala to the Pentecostal Churches of various names. It was not insignificant that the first World Missionary Conference, Edinburgh 1910, was held in the same year as UTC was established. This college's contribution to the unity talks in South India and in the ecumenical movement has been consistent. It had creative relationship with the Catholic theological colleges/seminaries in Bangalore and from time to time Catholic theologians were on the faculty.

First Exposure to the United Kingdom

Already I had been taught by and had worked with missionary educators from the UK, especially from the Anglican and Methodist Churches of Britain, but only later I came to know about their denominations. Working in the atmosphere of the Church of South India, no one dared to talk about their denominational identity. Some of them enjoyed dual identity as they were ordained in the CSI. From their life-style I could not see any difference between them. And I am aware that after their return to their home church, some of them have been nostalgic about South India and its ecumenical aroma.

It was in 1988 I was sent to Cambridge (UK) for 10 months of special research as part of my doctoral programme at UTC. My programme was administered by Wesley House. After a month, my family and I were accommodated in the Curate's house of the Church of the Good Shepherd. The vicar encouraged me to share in the service but realised that I needed a licence to function. The licence came just before I left, and I was able to celebrate Communion only once. For the final four weeks our accommodation was arranged in Westcott House of the Anglo-Catholic orientation, just across Jesus Lane opposite Wesley House. Apart from these two colleges there were Westminster College of the URC (United Reformed Church) and Ridley Hall of the low or charismatically leaning Anglican tradition. All of them were parts of the Cambridge Federation of Theological Education where one can do the Tripos, the basic theological degree programme, while doing the ministerial training in their respective colleges. Periodically, they came together for common worship services including the Holy Communion. I felt like a fish out of water. I could not help asking myself when these colleges and their denominational churches would grow to maturity as to train their candidates together as in TTS and UTC in India. Even in small conversations I realised that there was no one aware of the CSI and the united theological colleges in India. When I walked through these four colleges, I could sense different sub-cultures and ethos. This was because of their orientation. For example, I was told that the majority of the students of Westcott had studied in Grammar schools while the majority of Wesley House in Comprehensive schools! But I did not have a chance to find out whether this had any bearing on their theology, spirituality, understanding of ministry and urge for unity of churches and cooperation in theological education and ministerial training.

Of course, there was certain pride about each one's denomination, history, heritage and physical expressions. The Anglican cathedrals and church buildings with Gothic architecture, spires, etc., were widespread and impressive. However, coming from India where Hindu temples with intricate and colourful structures with beautiful paintings, and intense devotional activities, they were not particularly impressive. Also, I had the practice of questioning the economic sources of such buildings. The temple of Jerusalem, built by King Solomon with forced labour, heavy tax and unjust dealing with the king of Tyre, for me sends a stark warning. However great its beauty, sacredness and centrality of a religious community, I cannot ignore Jesus' words against it. For him the sanctity of a fellowship (church) was the unity of the people, not spectacular buildings with amazing architecture.

As Mission Partner in Britain

I returned to Britain in 1996, this time as a mission partner, under the World Church in Britain Partnership of the Methodist Church. I joined Wesley College, Bristol, as the World Church Tutor, teaching one day a week at Queen's College,

Birmingham. The same year, at the beginning of the first term, the Bristol Theological Federation was formed, bringing together the Wesley College, Trinity College (Anglican), Baptist College and South West Ministerial Training Course (ecumenical). I was excited about the prospect of working with colleagues of different denominations. I thought it would function almost like the Cambridge Federation. But planning to work together to share the resources across the federation proved to be very difficult. I was made the Dean of Research and I started to prepare materials on research methodology. However, things did not move forward. It met with a natural death without a decent funeral! I heard that for some time the Baptist College and Trinity worked together while Wesley College was heading towards its closure.

It took a long time for me and my family to settle in Wesley College. On the one hand, though a Methodist foundation, Wesley had an ecumenical outlook. Apart from me from a united church, the Dean of the Academic Studies was a Catholic lay man. The chaplain had interesting transitions, from a Methodist, to Anglican and to a Catholic nun. On the other hand, I and the Methodist Community took each other for granted, and no orientation was given either side about our church backgrounds. To start with, certain names and acronyms, were not familiar. For the Methodists it was tutors, not lecturers, ministers, not pastors or presbyters, manse, not mission house, circuit, not pastorate, District Chairs, not bishops (District Chair in my diocese is a category in between bishop and pastorate chairman), and so on. 'MLA' was used for Minister in Local Appointment, whereas for Indians it is Member of the Legislature Assembly.

I was astonished that no student was aware of the CSI. One or two said that their parents knew about the achievement and were even excited. Should they not know when they had a tutor from CSI, that that knowledge might inspire them to work for a similar united church in the UK? Was it not important to know what were the issues to deal with, the hurdles to overcome and the birth pangs too reckon with? One related pitfall I noticed was that the students and the staff had nursed a negative attitude towards the missions and missionaries who went overseas. After watching the film 'The Mission' which exposes the destruction of cultures in South America by some Catholic missionaries from Spain, they generalised that all missions had the same approach. They were not taking seriously the British missionaries' contributions to education, health, alleviation of poverty, linguistic renaissance, etc., in countries like India. For me from South India, knowing the continuing divisions in UK and lack of confidence in gospel and mission, the achievement of a group of the missionaries in collaboration with the American and Indian colleagues in forming the CSI, the first organic union in the history of the Christian church, was great indeed. Wesley College compared well to Queen's College Birmingham, although I breathed fresh ecumenical air in Queen's because of the unique combination of the community there, including staff and students from the URC, Anglican and Methodist.

I was encountering strange behaviour among the ministerial candidates. As orientated in South India, my family and I attended the nearest local CSI or other Protestant church. But even after three or four months the students were not able to settle in a church in Bristol. They were still 'shopping around' as someone hinted. The bottom line was that the congregations they did not return to were not interesting. Probably the particular day of their going or the particular church had difficulties in having a full audience, lively preaching, pleasant door stewards and Sunday School. They appeared to be the victims of a consumerist culture searching for the best choice. Perhaps to their displeasure or even indignation I commented that even if the concerned congregation was dull it should be our responsibility to join and infuse some life. And this would match all we talk about dynamic discipleship and generosity of the spirit in the chapel and class rooms.

Oral sharing of the unity story of South India was felt to be not enough. I encouraged individuals and small groups to have placements in South India. They returned with exuberant joy and enthusiasm, and organised sessions to share their experience with pictures to the community. I was particularly keen to know their experience of the united Church of South India. No one had felt it strange, and they appreciated that Christians had forgotten their original denominations, although church buildings and liturgies of the ex-Anglicans often betrayed their original identity.

Because, of the ignorance of the resources in the world church and the history of the 'Third Church', Wesley College's curriculum was framed in such a way that biblical scholarship was European, history of Christianity proper was European, theology proper ws European and so on. Therefore, consequently, world church and interfaith formed the last tiny basket as an exotic optional extra. My colleagues were kind and understanding when I pointed out, but even then it was impossible to study interfaith experiences and achievements of various combinations of church unions in the 'Third Church'. Also, I objected when categorizations such as gospel and culture (meaning cultures of the third world), and British Church and World Church (as if BC is not part of WC) was made!

On my part, through conversation and reading, I was eager to understand the origins of the Methodist movement. I had to change my view that Methodism was a monochromic discipline with devotional songs such as 'Jesu lover of my soul'. John Wesley was a 'reasonable enthusiast'. He and his brother Charles, after they failed as priests and missionaries in America, were open to new conversion with their hearts strangely warmed. On the one hand, John and his brother Charles experienced God's prior acceptance of sinners by grace in Christ, and the Wesleyan hymns celebrate this. On the other hand, he declared 'the world is my parish' and he travelled more than 250,000 miles on horseback, inviting all people to a new orientation in life. He preached to the miners and pointed out how their drunkenness affected the family economy. He declared slavery inhuman and supported the anti-slavery campaign of William Wilberforce. He was open to use any new device to alleviate physical pain. His first open-air preaching (1739) was based on the Nazareth Manifesto (Lk. 4: 18f), the total liberation offered by Jesus. It was not without reason that the following saying became proverbial: 'The labour movement owes more to Methodism than Marxism.' Equally important was that he inculcated a Catholic Spirit based on affinity of hearts. Bristol was the most suitable place to imbibe the spirit of Methodism. The archives in Wesley College held handwritten and printed manuscripts of the Wesleys. In Bristol we find the New Room (the first chapel established by John Wesley for training lay preachers), Charles Wesley's house, the church in which he and his children played music, the spot (Bread Street) where John Wesley preached his first open air sermon, and so on. Though originally Anglican priests, the extraordinary experiences and achievements of the Wesley brothers should be shared by all true Christians, I was firm. Therefore, I started to share the Methodist stories in South India by speeches and writings. Particularly, the ex-Methodist members of the CSI found them to be new and refreshing.

Opportunities for Interaction

Wesley College had an MA programme. For seminars, Bishop Rowan Williams from Monmouth (Wales) used to come for lectures. Particularly, he expounded the theology of a Russian Orthodox theologian. It warmed my heart to listen to an Anglican bishop passionately expounding the theology of an Orthodox theologian in a Methodist college. Of course, I experienced similar combinations elsewhere as well. When Williams was enthroned as the Archbishop of Canterbury (i.e. of the Church of England, chief priest of the royalty and President of the Anglican Communion) in 2002, there was much expectation for his leadership in promoting ecumenical relations and church union. Of course, this is not the place for assessing his achievements. However, friends of the Church of South India did not fail to point out his special relationship with that Church as his father-in-law worked in South India as a missionary. Jane Williams, a distant colleague in Bristol, a daughter of that missionary, declared to the church press that she came to faith because of the CSI. She also reminisced that when she came to England on furlough, she was shocked to see notices in certain churches that members of the CSI were not welcome!

However, such good will and maturity could not be seen in different denominations who could do things together while almost each denominational church was declining, locally and nationally. Whether documents on human sexuality, interfaith dialogue or environmental care and eco-spirituality, Anglicans, Methodists, URC, Baptists, etc., prepared and published their own documents. As an outsider, reading them with a certain amount of objectivity, I found considerable duplication. It was clear that what one hand did the other hand did not know. When I pointed this out to friends, they found it perfectly normal and no one needed to feel guilty. Besides, each major Church had its hymn book.

As a special independent effort there appeared a beautiful hymn book with the title *Anglican Hymns, Old and New* and immediately another came with the title *Methodist Hymns, Old and New*.

Methodist Sacramental Fellowship since the 1930s exists 'to affirm the catholic and universal tradition of Christianity within Methodism. It also seeks to promote the sacramental faith and practice which John and Charles Wesley drew from scripture and Christian tradition.' It reaffirms the historic creeds and the doctrine of Trinity and 'encourages a pattern of Christian discipleship rooted in Holy Communion'. It promotes a eucharistic way of life which inspires us to work for a church 'that is diverse, hospitable and inclusive'. It is committed to unity with other Christians in life and worship and in a common programme for justice and peace. As far as I could observe, there were some remarkable people whose spirituality and life transcended narrow denominational bounds.

On the whole, the Methodist Church in Britain is open to the united churches such as the CSI. In a form I had to fill in when I joined them in 1996 and one question was about the doctrines I held. I wrote that my Christian faith was not guided by any set of doctrines but biblical insights. There was no comment. In actual fact, the Methodist movement and latter Church was not bound by doctrines, but as if there can be no Church without fixed doctrines, perhaps in order to look standard, Methodists use the word 'doctrine.' I will explain this in the fifth chapter. But at the same time, Methodists seem to have a particular ethos, method and dedication for church union movements. In the context of being a member of the ongoing project of the History of Methodism (under the leadership of Andrew Walls), I produced and published an essay entitled 'The Catholic Spirit in Action! – Methodists and the Formation of the Church of South India' (2006). In Britain also, the Methodists are in the forefront in forging relationships or unions with other Churches. Moreover, they recognised and regarded me as a presbyter.

Cry for Mission while Maintaining Divisions

For me, coming from lively and thriving congregations of a minority Church in India, the situation in the UK has been intriguing. Three or four churches around a corner of a town, each struggling to survive at a great cost of maintaining a building and a minister, appeared to challenge common sense. The experiment of LEPs (Local Ecumenical Partnerships) was not spreading as fast as once thought. The difficulties include complex legal arrangements, each partner church having to maintain their connection with the headquarters of their denomination and having to be sensitive to each other's liturgies and ministerial patterns.

The steady decline of church attendance in Britain has been a growing concern. According to statistics around 1998, 78% of the British people believed in God but only about 8% worshipped in a church. Then the phrase 'believing, not belonging' was widely shared. As a coincidence, two popular events happened.

Princess Diana was killed in a car accident in Paris on 31 August 1997. It was a national shock to lose such a charming member of the royal family, a kind-hearted person who associated herself with a number of charities. More remarkable was the swell of crowds who filled the churches with candles in hands and sobbing in prayer. This happened all of a sudden in a country where knowing was claimed with pride over feeling. Moreover, J.K. Rowling's bestselling Harry Potter series of seven books (published between 1997 and 2007) and the films that followed presented the spectacular show of a mytho-technic manipulation that appeared to kindle the dormant religiosity of the people.

The above phenomena and others were hot subjects of study and research in the Centre for the Study of Implicit Religion and Contemporary Spirituality. This had been founded by Edward Bailey (1935-2015), the longest standing Rector of St Michael's Winterbourne, a suburb of Bristol. I happened to meet him in the seminars of the Bristol Theological Society. He had a striking memory of spending two years in UTC in Bangalore and its neighbour CSIRS (the Christian Institute for the Study of Religion and Society) in Bangalore (1959-61) where he met the pioneering leaders P.D. Devanandan and M.M. Thomas, as part of his priestly training. The formation and life of CSI was one of his attractions and, of course, the unique kind of secularism in India, the other. My continued association with his CSIRCS included the regular participation in their annual international conference in Denton, west of Leeds, and being one of the trustees. Statistics of church life in Britain, topics such as the religion of football in England and of Glastonbury festival raised questions within me about what went wrong in a Christian country while new expressions of religion were flourishing. Will church unity turn the table around?

Friends of the Church in India: Sharing in Mission while Raising Alarming Questions

The formation of the CSI in 1947 sent waves of church unity through the whole of India as well as South Asia. The Church of North India, on the same principles, was born in 1970 but apart from the CSI components it included the Baptists of British origin, the Church of the Brethren and the Disciples of Christ. The Church of Pakistan and Bangladesh, born at the same time had almost the same components, with the addition of the Lutherans. From the beginning of the formation of the CSI the British missionaries in India felt obliged with certain sense of excitement to share the story of the first organic unity with their home churches. The returning missionaries formed a fellowship, celebrated the Holy Communion using the Indian liturgies and writing about the effect of the union on their spiritual life and mission. The fellowship had its own story of development with names. Finally, they settled with the name 'Friends of the Church in India' with a half yearly magazine *Pilgrim* and annual gathering in London on the first Saturday of October. The St. Thomas Unity Lecture (originally established by

Scottish friends) became part of the FCI's programme, once every four years, with an Indian speaker.

It was my privilege to be invited to give the third Unity Lecture in 1997, the Jubilee year when the CSI rather elaborately celebrated its 50th anniversary. The preceding lecturers were Christopher Duraising and Thomas Thangaraj and both had used memorable images. Duraising distinguished between curried chicken (the spread of a few spices on the chicken) which was the ecumenism in the West and chicken curry (spices and chicken blended together to give a unique taste) which was the formation of the CSI. Thangaraj observed in the light of church relations that in the West it was 'courtship first and marriage next', whereas in India it was 'marriage first and courtship next', which was strong and stable as the CSI has exemplified. The title of my lecture was 'A Mission Spirituality for a United Church – Reflections from fifty years of experience of the Church of South India'. I illustrated it with fruits of effective mission of an organic union without hiding the pitfalls. I delivered this lecture in four places: Aberystwyth (Wales), Belfast (Northern Ireland), Edinburgh (Scotland) and London (England) during April-September, 1997. The audiences were enthusiastic to know about mission initiative and church growth though a few asked, 'Does the united church CSI continue without challenge for its historic unity?' In one place the host leader responded emotionally that what South India achieved his country could not, i.e. organic unity and vibrant mission. More than everything else, the experience motivated people to read in more detail and patience the story of the CSI, its vision, wise coordination, hurdles and the way they were overcome, friendships etc. Interestingly, the resources of the history and development of the CSI including the journal *South India Church man* (later *CSI Church Life*) were kept in better order in some of the libraries in England than in India! There were moments of being thrilled by the quality of behaviour of missionaries and their Indian colleagues with catholic spirit and persistence to achieve the desired unity for the sake of mission, without compromising the truth. The CSI members have been witnesses to the inextricable connection between mission and church unity.

The Challenges of the Anglicans

The way the CSI was absorbed by the Anglican Communion will be dealt with in detail in the seventh chapter. Back in India, I observed first hand a process of anglicisation in non-Anglican areas of the CSI, particularly the areas of Congregationalist origin. For example, my home diocese in casual manner started a process of anglicisation in the 1980s which has continued to the present day. Clericalization of ministry with every lay church worker aspiring to appear in white cassock, the use of liturgical colours without awareness of actual seasons, building altars, towers, memorial arches, spires and belfries and so on could not go unnoticed. The simplified CSI form of episcopacy has been developing almost medieval glamour. Using the 'watchdog magazines' in the diocese some of us have expressed our cry against the new wave; a few dissertations also have been written. The silence of the bishops and pastors seemed to suggest that they did enjoy the new wave, and the theological awareness of laity has been at its lowest. Ironically, on the other hand, elections for bishops and various other positions are fought with party politics and vigorous campaigns, not bothering about the way it is done in the original parent churches including the CofE.

As I noted in the 'preface' the FCI's magazine *Pilgrim* raised the question, 'Is CSI Anglican?' Among the articles in response was one by Victor Premasagar, a former Moderator of the CSI. He mentioned stories of initial Anglican opposition to the extent of not allowing Michael Hollis, the first Moderator of the CSI, to solemnize Holy Communion in an Anglican Seminary in Cambridge without conditions. He then affirmed that the CSI was not Anglican but a united church. He stated his experience in the first Primates' Meeting he attended. When the Archbishop addressed the members 'Bishops and Archbishops', he and his South Asian colleagues protested, saying 'We, the Moderators of united churches, must be addressed by that title.' But any informed reader would ask the question, 'Why did they agree to sit in the exclusively Anglican Primates' meeting in the first place?' No doubt, the reasonable FCI were perplexed and agonising. The Methodist and URC members have been conspicuously silent!

An International Mission Community

Before completing my term in Bristol, I was invited to be the Principal of the United College of the Ascension, one of the Selly Oak Colleges for mission education and training in Birmingham. I started my work in January 2001. Built in 1926 by the Society for the Propagation of the Gospel (SPG - USPG from 1978) with the name College of the Ascension, it became united when the Methodists closed their college Kingsmead and joined with the Anglican College of the Ascension in 1996. Roughly there were three categories of students – missionaries or mission partners in training to go overseas, study partners for higher studies in the local universities from overseas, and those who came for short, specific courses. The community including staff and students were international and ecumenical and very few wanted to show their denominational identity. It was so multi-cultural that in certain terms as many as twenty-five countries were represented. It was a vibrant community with worship and Eucharist in the chapel at the centre. There was a weekly service and other events that we shared with the other colleges in Selly Oak, including Crowther Hall, belonging to the CMS (Church Missionary Society). 'Mission from everywhere to everywhere' was the slogan being propagated.

The original Anglican chapel was three-tiered. Before my arrival there had been a decision to modify it in order to make it world-Church friendly at great cost. During my time the work was completed, and it turned out to be a fascinating chapel with creative arts, paintings and a glass enclosure Emmaus

Chapel. There were visitors to see the chapel and feel the bondedness of an international community. There was the Anglican Communion Studies Course, sponsored by the USPG and CMS and held alternatively in UCA and Crowther Hall. From time to time I was invited to resource sessions and I was keen to bring in views from other churches, particularly CSI. Moreover, I was invited to be part of the Secretaries Group (later changed as Directors), the main decision-making body of the USPG (for policy making there were Trustees). It was housed in Partnership House on Waterloo Road in London where I travelled at least once a month to attend USPG's Secretaries'/Directors' meetings. CMS and some other organisations also had their offices in this building. In the first floor, just outside the chapel, on the way to the USPG block of offices, there were stained glasses of the portraits of the first two non-white Anglican bishops (S. Crowther of Nigeria and V.S. Azariah of South India, the pioneer of the formation of the CSI). Quoting Azariah, an international spokesman of church unity and mission, I suggested collaboration between USPG and CMS in certain projects of common concern. We had one or two meetings, but nothing happened. I was aware that a few voices were vociferous for union of these two societies. I was told that theologically these two Anglican societies (there were nine more) were poles apart. I was genuinely open to learn the differences and contribute to a discussion if I could, but they were best kept secrets!

The Anglican-Methodist partnership in running the UCA warmed my heart. I took a group of students from the college to Lincoln Cathedral (with a guided tour of John Wesley's birth place in Epworth inbuilt) to attend the 300th birth anniversary of Wesley in 2001. As an Anglican priest and missionary John Wesley went to the New World, and this was highlighted. A facsimile of his appointment order was released by the USPG. And following the narrow failure of the unity vote in 1972, about fifty years of conversation culminated in the signing of 'An Anglican-Methodist Covenant' in November 2003. While affirming the shared history, beliefs, and views on the validity of the ministry of each other, the purpose has been clearly stated as visible unity. But the excitement of this great step appeared to be fading away when I read later that leaders of these two bodies acted as if the Covenant never existed.

The situation in Selly Oak was fast changing. Colleges were being closed, combined or moved. UCA's time came quite unexpectedly. With the new chapel and ideas for the future, USPG, the owner of the College of the Ascension (known as the 'jewel in the crown'), with the inevitable consent of the Methodists, decided to close the UCA and move it to the Queen's Ecumenical Foundation for Theological Education (College) with the new name 'Selly Oak Centre for Mission Studies.' The last service in May 2006 held in the local St. Mary's Church was a most poignant moment. For me it turned out to be a particular anti-climax. I suggested con-celebration of the Eucharist with an Anglican and Methodist along with me. But there was an Anglican No from the USPG headquarters, and without understanding the reason I was left with celebrating with inner brokenness and bleeding.

I moved to the Birmingham District of the Methodist Church with two part-time jobs – the interfaith Consultant and preaching minister of two congregations in East Birmingham. On the one hand, I was part of the local ecumenical fellowship. It included the bishop of the Free Church of England, which I came to know for the first time. I had been exposed to the Free Church of Scotland before. On the other hand, I moved closely with colleagues of the ministry of interfaith dialogue from different denominations. The tone of conversations suggested that some of them were willing to move closer to people other faiths than to members of other denominations!

Newer Experiences and Challenges

If I was inherently disturbed by denominational persistence in the midst of the steady decline of most of the churches, my sanity was restored when I returned to South India. Following a year of being the Principal of the UTC, Bangalore (after a period of illness and recuperation) I joined the Gurukul Lutheran Theological College and Research Institute, Chennai (Madras). Though a Lutheran foundation, Gurukul was ecumenical in its outlook and ethos. Churches represented were 11 Lutheran Churches in India, CSI, CNI, Baptist and Presbyterian Churches of the North East, Mar Thoma and Orthodox Churches of Kerala, Pentecostal Churches and the Evangelical Church of India, which shares all the beliefs and practices of the CSI except child baptism. From an open and friendly Pentecostal pastor, a postgraduate student, I learned about plurality among the Pentecostal churches and that in and around Chennai some Pentecostal Churches are Unitarian, and that divorce is one of the important issues that need pastoral care and counselling.

Though the Lutheran Churches pulled out from the negotiations for the formation of the CSI, later there was conversation for some time, and though it ended, the decision to train ministers of these two Churches together has continued. There are eleven Lutheran Churches (plus one in Nepal) as members of the United Lutheran Church of India, headquartered in Gurukul. Interestingly, betraying a conflict around the matter, on the above name printed outside the building with capital letters, two letters in small size (ES) have been inserted. I have a desire to find out from the European and American sponsors or partners of these churches about their position and policy on these churches, and on negotiations for unity in their local areas. Many have informally said that there are no serious theological differences (though some leaders mention 'doctrines') but that there are property, power and proprietorship issues. Of course, this is not the Lutheran cases only. The Methodists of American origin refused to join the CSI for the same reasons. When CNI was formed in 1970, American Methodists, one of the negotiating partners withdrew at the last moment for the same reason.

It was customary for me to ask Lutheran friends if there was any scope for reviving negotiations with the CSI. Almost all of them said that the leadership situation in CSI was not encouraging. Was the condition in their own churches different? Another excuse was 'doctrines', but I could not see anyone speaking about this topic clearly and confidently. In Gurukul I had the chance to discuss with one or two senior colleagues who attended meetings of the Lutheran World Federation. Documents were shared with me which reported and reflected various negotiations. One was on Catholic-Lutheran discussion. Very significantly, it was acknowledged that in fundamental issues the differences are not as vast as we earlier thought. This confirmed my feeling when I had read earlier ecumenical documents. Also, I came to the conclusion that heaps of documents produced by the Faith and Order groups have been hardly helpful for forging actual church unity and being effective in mission.

One reasonable question is whether this development has anything to do with the process of the Anglicization of the CSI churches and its transformation as a Province of the AC (Anglican Communion) that facilitated the CSI bishops to attend the LC (Lambeth Conference) as full members from 1998. An empirical study alone can answer.

Rowan Williams' visit to the CSI in October 2010 was national news. It was reported that it was 'on the invitation of the Communion of Churches in India'. Earlier, during my long stay in England I was roped in to be part of the preparing team. I attended two meetings held in Lambeth Palace, and my special input was in the area of interfaith relations. In Chennai I attended the grand reception accorded to the 'Chief Shepherd of the CSI' in the premises of the St. George's cathedral where the CSI was inaugurated in 1947. There was speech after speech by the CSI leaders about the greatness of their Church and its historical connection with the Anglican Church. Fortunately, a veteran journalist, a Hindu, spoke having done adequate homework about Rowan's theological position and commitment to interfaith dialogue. Finally, the chief guest was left with a short time which he used most wisely, stressing the graciousness, humility and openness of God. Knowing a bit about Rowan, for him it should have been a depressing experience! No wonder, then, that the highlights of his visit, according to reports were his engagement with members of the church in a slum in Chennai and discussion with a group of interreligious leaders in Bangalore.

Initiating Conversations

In the spring of 2015 I was in England and I started conversations with some Anglican friends about what I viewed an ecclesial injustice, i.e. the Anglican Communion's unilateral absorption of the CSI as a Province (united). The responses varied: 'What is wrong in this, because Anglicans are the majority in the CSI communion?' 'This is partnership, and how is it wrong?' 'It is good for CSI to get respect and support in this way.' 'What form would it take if the Methodist

Church or the United Reformed Church incorporated CSI into their families and structures?' Obviously, such responses were not convincing, and I was appalled to find the level of ignorance about the history and nature of CSI in England (as well as India). In the formation of the CSI the three major Churches and five traditions were seen as dying to denominations and rising to a new church, an organic union.

On the other end, what was the CSI Synod doing? Apart from bishops rushing to attend the Lambeth Conference, was there any discussion and decision made about being incorporated as a Province of the Anglican Communion? The Synod office was unaware of anything like that. I wrote a long letter to all the bishops of the CSI with a copy to the Archbishop of Canterbury, and there was no response! I came to the conclusion that on both sides there is so much of ignorance about the history and nature of CSI.

In September 2016 I came to Evesham, a country town thirty miles south of Birmingham, as a minister of the Methodist Church. Unexpectedly, new knowledge and contacts revived my ecumenical spirit to work for church union for the sake of mission and to tell the story of CSI. I came to know that the Methodist missionary to South India, J.S.M. Hooper, the convener of the Coordination Committee of the CSI formation, who preached the inaugural sermon in 1947, had retired in nearby Stratford and continued his teaching and preaching ministry. More details could be gathered about Michael Hollis, the first Moderator of CSI, who returned to Sheffield as a vicar. New studies about Lesslie Newbigin, the youngest new bishop, have shed important insights into the profound significance of CSI not only for South India but also for Britain. In the special worship services in connection with the 70th Anniversary of CSI which I have organised or preached in, these great persons were remembered.

I am fortunate to have some friends who are willing to support my research. Some senior church leaders expose their ignorance about the CSI, the first and unique union. Those who are aware of the changing attitudes of Anglicans towards the CSI admit saying, 'first we opposed and then patronised'.

Continuing church decline is a growing concern of the sensitive minds of all Churches in the UK. For example, with alarming awareness the Methodist Conference (2017) has noted a 35 per cent decline in the last decade. Its membership is now less than two million. In all churches there is a cry for mission with desperation introducing new programmes and recycling ideas but without any effort to come together as one church. Most churches content themselves by doing charitable work. Christian Aid, the leading charity in the UK, introduced a slogan some years ago: 'We believe in life before death', as if the majority of the people in the UK believe in life after death and that such belief cannot care about the present worldly life. Hence the dominant mindset is to do something to help others (coffee mornings, eating fellowships, assisting drunken young women if they stumble, welcoming refugees, caring for the environment, supporting a project overseas, etc). There is no doubt that these are noble activities, often supplementing the government's schemes, but the question is: is there still a place for sharing the liberating 'Eternal I am' and the need of breaking the inner chains? The dominant pattern of preaching sounds like a 'love lullaby', and is there a place for a new orientation in life by responding to God's grace and love by worship and service? Rethinking preaching for new life and bearing the good news should be the priority, and in this connection unity among the followers of Jesus becomes indispensable to make the message credible.

There seems to be apathy about studying the history of the missionary movement and the theology of transforming mission. As far as I know, 'Churches Together' carries the irony of 'Together in Division', and apart from some services and events, there is no fellowship, no studying of the Bible together and no sharing of each other's traditions and experiences. I think the annual routine of observing the 'Week of Prayer for Christian Unity' without action, ritual acts of walk of witness on Good Friday, and one joint service at Pentecost do not express the desire of moving towards organic union. I will explain later.

Chapter 2

Roots and Branches:
An Outline of the Church's Story

It Began with Liberation and Covenant

The liberation story of the Hebrew community started with the Yahweh God's declaration, 'I have indeed seen the misery of *my people* in Egypt' (*italics* added; Ex. 3:7). Behind many symbolic titles such as vine and sheep, the most significant title the Israelites were given was 'God's people'. As a covenanted community they were expected to be a 'kingdom of priests and a holy nation' (Ex. 19:6). Commandments were given as part of the covenant, and by observing them they would surprise the neighbouring nations with their wisdom and intimacy with God (Deut. 4:6-8). Essentially, the twin commandments of loving God with their whole being and loving their neighbours as themselves were both fascinating and challenging (6:5; Lev. 19: 18). Those who loved God found the laws and commandments most refreshing, enlightening, precious treasures and sweet (Ps. 19:8-11).

The people of God had their Lord as the unrivalled leader and select human leaders as servants who could judge and protect from enemies while being simple. Later when they asked for a king with pomp and glamour as in the case of the kings of other nations the ideal vision got blurred. The first king, Saul, was found to be humble and weak and there were plots to oust him. David was projected as going to establish a glorious kingdom. His initiatives on unifying the Israelite tribes, on conquering the enemies and urbanisation and centralising Jerusalem as God's city as well as David's city, gave the impression that he was an ideal king. But his personal life and family life with several sex scandals and conflicts betrayed him as an atrocious and cruel king with blood on his hands. His 'scandalous son' Solomon went a step further in destroying the ethos of a covenanted community.

His temple building project involved heavy taxes, forced labour and deceptive deals. Provisions for his hundreds of wives and concubines led to depletion of the common treasuries. When he died, people took some courage to raise their concern about heavy taxation with his successor Rehoboam, and his irresponsible and arrogant answer caused the division of the kingdom into north and south, or Israel and Judea. Apart from internal conflicts, there were constant fear and tension due to changing allegiances with the empires and super powers.

The Hebrew prophets reminded the community of their original call as God's people to be a light to the nations. They presented new possibilities for newly anointed figures who would restore the original vision and unite God's people, although the Davidic line and fame was expected to continue by some. For example, because of the disastrous kingship the ideal of the Jubilee year (periodic re-sharing of the land; Lev. 25) was forgotten and there was a possibility to regain the ideal (Is. 61:2). There would be no more war, and people would live in peace (Mic. 4:3-5). Above all, there would be unity among the empires and particularly connected with the Israelite community (Is. 19:23-25). Ezekiel, following his vision of a valley of dry bones, asked to take two sticks signifying the northern and southern kingdoms and join them together 'that they will become one in your hand' (Ez. 37:17). Subsequently, God says that there will be only one kingdom. 'They will be my people, and I will be their God' (37:23). The unified or united people of God was an essential condition for revival and renewal. There were visions with different expectations and details.

Jesus and the Church

Jesus, a multifaceted Jew, found his mission of restoration and unification in continuation of the mission and vision of the Hebrew prophets. As true shepherd with a sacrificial mind, he sought the lost sheep (scattered and victimised) with the hope that 'there shall be one flock and one shepherd' (Jn. 10:16). To be with him and to share in his mission, keeping the numerical significance of the Hebrew/ Jewish tribes, he chose twelve disciples. They were dull-headed, quarrelsome, power-mongering and thoughtless. However, Jesus did not want to replace them with a group of high intellectuals or a small army. Presumably he was aware of the significance of the Yahweh God choosing numerically insignificant people (Deut. 7 :7f). He taught them the power of powerlessness, of being a minority as salt and light, and the authority of serving others like slaves. His encouraging words to his disciples were, 'Do not be afraid, little flock, for your Father has been pleased to give you the kingdom' (Lk. 12:32). It was a prolonged struggle to establish and project the new kingdom over against the kingdoms and empires which they and their later generations had to face.

It is still debated by scholars whether Jesus established a church. We need not rehearse the arguments here. We continue from the premise that anyhow the church happened and has made a great impact on the world history. From the clues we have in the New Testament, we can conclude that for Jesus the sanctity of the church rested on the reconciliation and unity of the people. Particularly, the Gospel of Matthew has recorded the most important teaching. When a person was offering his/her gift at the altar, and if he/she had something against his brother, they should leave the gift there and go and get reconciled. It is profitable and honourable to settle matters before the adversary took it to the law court (Mt. 5:23-26). There was a severe warning to those who refused to get reconciled by direct negotiation, mediation of two or three witnesses and finally the involvement of the church: 'Treat them as you would a pagan or a tax collector.' The concluding words are very profound:

> Again, truly I tell you that if two of you on earth agree about anything they ask for, it will be done for them by my Father in heaven. For where two or three gather in my name, there I am with them (18:19-20).

In response to Jesus' question, 'Who do you say I am?' Peter replied, 'You are the Messiah, the Son of the living God' (16:15-16). Declaring that this confession was from the Father in heaven, Jesus said, 'I tell you that you are Peter (= *rock*), and on this rock I will build my church. And the gates of Hades (=*the realm of the dead*) will not overcome it. I will give you the keys of the kingdom of heaven; whatever you bind on earth will be bound in heaven. Then he ordered his disciples not to tell anyone' (16: 18-20). Obviously, there was no indication of foretelling that Peter was to be the supreme leader. And in fact his confession that Jesus was the Christ (shrouded in mystery) had parochial implication as that title was relevant only to the Jewish community, and when the Jesus movement spread to Hellenistic and Roman contexts there were new confessional titles such as Lord and Saviour. Later in the history of the Church the note about Peter was blown beyond proportion and through him the bishop (pope) in Rome was recognised and regarded as the cardinal link of the apostolic succession. Without reproducing arguments for and against this view, let us point out some facts from the Gospels. First, Jesus' address was to all the disciples, and singling out Peter was accidental. Second, as we have noted above, the confession that Jesus was the Messiah was fundamental in the Jewish context, and titles were attached when the Jewish Jesus was Hellenised and Romanised. Third, that the Heavenly Father revealed this to Peter was not a statement of his infallibility because after a few moments, when Peter tried to thwart the path of suffering that Jesus was determined to be on, Jesus rebuked him saying, 'Get behind me, Satan! You are a stumbling block to me; you do not have in mind the concerns of God, but merely human concerns.' This was followed by the teaching on self-denial, cross bearing and readiness to lose life for God's kingdom (16:22ff). Fourth, in the last section of John's Gospel we read a poignant dialogue between Peter and Jesus in which it is clarified that loving Jesus should find expression in tending and caring for the vulnerable sheep. Fifth, though there are evidences to present the chief apostle, his questionable practices were openly pointed out and recorded (e.g. Paul's opposition to Peter's hypocrisy in eating with Gentiles, Gal. 2:11-14). Sixth, Peter himself has written affirming the Hebrew vision of the royal priesthood of all believers (1 Pet. 2:9). The greatest tragedy of the Christian thought and expression has been forgetting or watering down this glorious vision as part of the original covenant with the people of God.

Towards the end of his earthly life Jesus prayed for the disciples' protection, joy, sanctification and unity. The most important petition was '... that all may be one, Father, just as you are in me and I am in you. May they be also in us so that the world may believe that you have sent me' (Jn. 17:21). Obviously, what is meant here is not forming a social club but living with deep intimacy with the fellowship of the Father-Son-Spirit as well as with a loving unity with fellow believers or disciples. The two aspects of unity here are inseparable. The disciples did not achieve the perfect measure of this unity though they were consciously striving. The experience of resurrection and the vision of the risen Christ with scars of wounds on his body effected great change in their attitude and behaviour.

In his confrontational conversation with a section of Jews, Jesus explained how he shared the Jewish roots and opened new horizons. He asked them not to be content with enjoying miraculous food but to move on to experience a new kind of food. He went even to the extent of denying that Moses gave bread to their ancestors when they were in the wilderness. To their grumbling he added that he himself was the food from heaven which had lasting effect. This food was his own flesh and blood. 'Verily I tell you, unless you eat the flesh of the Son of Man and drink his blood, you have no life in you' (Jn. 6:53). The language of 'eating the flesh and drinking the blood' belonged to the ordinary labouring folk for indicating close intimacy, as is the case among rural and tribal communities today. No wonder, the elite Jews found it disgusting, sowing the seed for the scandal in the Roman empire that Christians were cannibals. Many disciples found this a hard teaching and left Jesus, while the twelve confessed Jesus as the Holy One of God with words of eternal life (6:60-70).

Connecting with the original Passover meal and covenant, Jesus broke bread and shared wine as his body with his disciples (Mt. 26:26; Mk. 14:22; 22:19). The phrase 'poured out for many' indicates the opening of a new avenue that welcomes all people of any place, race and language. The one word 'many' attached to the covenant makes conversion of non-Jewish communities credible and authentic.

One Body

The image of 'One Body' in the sense of spiritual intimacy, unity and shared concerns was very significant for Paul. We present the following examples:

> For just as each of us has one body with many members, and these
> members do not all have the same function, so in Christ we, though

many, form one body, and each member belongs to all the others (Rom. 12:4-5).

Just as a body, though one, has many parts but all its many parts form one body, so it is with Christ. For we were all baptised by one Spirit so as to form one body – whether Jews or Gentiles, slave or free – and we were all given the one Spirit to drink ... God has put the body together, giving greater honour to the parts that lacked it so that there should be no division in the body, but that its parts should have equal concern for each other. If one part suffers, every part suffers with it; if one part is honoured, every part rejoices with it. Now you are the body of Christ, and each one of you is a part of it (Cor. 12: 12-27).

(The Church) is his body, the fullness of him who fills everything in every way (Eph. 1:23). This mystery is that through the gospel the Gentiles are heirs together with Israel, members together of one body and sharers together in the promise in Christ Jesus (3: 6). There is one body and one Spirit just as you were called to one hope when you were called; one Lord, one faith, one baptism; one God and Father of all who is over all and through all and in all (4: 4-6). To equip his people for works of service, so that the body of Christ may be built up until we all reach unity in the faith and in the knowledge of the Son of God and become mature, attaining to the whole measure of the fulness of Christ (4:12-13) ...Christ is the head of the church, his body, of which he is the Saviour ... for we are members of his body (5:23-30)

And he is the head of the body, the church; he is the beginning and the firstborn from among the dead, so that in everything he might have the supremacy (Col. 1:18). They have lost connection with the head, from whom the whole body, supported and held together by its ligaments and sinews, grows as God causes it to grow (2:19). Let the peace of Christ rule in your hearts, since as members of one body you were called to peace. And be thankful (3:15).

Is not the cup of thanksgiving for which we give thanks a participation in the blood of Christ? And is not the bread that we break a participation in the body of Christ? Because there is one loaf, we, who are many, are one body, for we all share the one loaf (1 Cor.10:16-17).

The Holy Communion, the Lord's Supper or the Eucharist, is the most visible and powerful demonstration of the worldwide community of Christians as parts or members of Christ's living body. It is a great remembrance of Jesus' self-giving of his body for many on the cross and a medium of proclamation (1 Cor. 11:23-26). Those who partake in it affirm the sacramental blood-relation with fellow Christians here and everywhere. Any act of disconnection, segregation or amputation of Christ's body may be viewed as criminal. A repentance and re-joining are the first requisite of preaching the gospel.

At the Pentecostal revolution, the community of disciples were empowered, expanded and organised. It was dramatic that 'Peter stood up with the Eleven, raised his voice and addressed the crowd' (Acts 2:14). Still they were a vulnerable community unwilling to increase their social or military power. They were still called the disciples until the disciples at Antioch were first called Christians (Acts 11:26). However, the name 'disciples' continued (11:29; 13:52 etc). Another name was 'the Nazarene sect' (from Jesus of Nazareth, 24:5). The most fundamental identity was God's children, authorised and adopted (Jn. 1:12; Rom. 8:4-17; 1 Jb. 3:2). Thus, no other identity for Christians was basic and prominent as Jesus' disciples and God's children.

Churches Known by Locations

In the early church, particular congregations were known by the names of the locations of gathering, places and regions. Thus, the apostles addressed in their letters to: 'All in Rome who are loved by God and called to be his holy people' (Rom. 1: 7); 'To the church of God in Corinth, to those sanctified in Christ Jesus and called to be his holy people' (1 Cor. 1: 2; also 2 Cor. 1: 1); 'To the Churches in Galatia' (Gal. 1: 2); 'To God's holy people in Ephesus, the faithful in Christ Jesus' (Eph. 1: 1); 'To all God's holy people in Christ Jesus at Philippi' (Phil. 1: 1:1); 'To God's holy people in Colossae, the faithful brothers and sisters in Christ' (Col. 1: 2); 'To the church of the Thessalonians in God the Father and the Lord Jesus Christ' (1 Thess. 1:1; 2 Thess. 1:1). The names of the seven churches in Asia Minor are listed by their places such as Ephesus and Smyrna (Rev. 2: 1-3; 22). The pro-Jewish James mentions 'To the twelve tribes scattered among the nations' (Jas. 1: 1). Peter notes, 'To God's select, exiles, scattered throughout the provinces of Pontus, Galatia, Cappadocia, Asia and Bithynia. Who have been chosen according to the foreknowledge of God ...' (1 Pet. 1:1f.). But in his second epistle Peter simply mentions, 'To those who through the righteousness of our God and Saviour Jesus Christ have received a faith as precious as ours' (2 Pet. 1:1; cf. Jude 1: 1). It is significant that while in most cases we have quoted the name of the church was defined by the place all of them were given a theological qualifier, more or less the same, and this affirms the oneness of God's or Christ's church.

There were house churches too; that means, believers in a particular locality gathered for worship in the house of an influential person. The apostles in their letters greeted those who met in such house churches. E.g. The church that met in the house of Priscilla and Aquila (Rom. 16:3, 5; 1 Cor. 16:19); church in the house of a woman Nympha (Col. 4:15); the church that met in the home of Philemon (Phil. 2). Faith and fellowship were more important than the building and place of worship. This was within the spirit of Jesus who said he would be present where two or three were gathered.

Is Christ's Body Divided?

If looked at objectively, the nature and structure of Christian faith was very complicated. Not all things were simple and straightforward. The main reasons were two-fold. Although, the Jewish-Christian relationship could be well formulated by the phrase *Common Roots and New Horizons* (the title of Hans Ucko's book, 1994), in the vigorous process of many Gentiles becoming Christians, the Jewish connections were blurred. Even Paul had to undermine the Jewish traditions such as the law in defence of the Gentile converts against the Jewish critics. However, when the Gentiles took advantage and boasted, Paul rushed to return to an affirmation of the Jewish roots of the Christian faith and this could be seen, for example, in Rom. ch. 9-11. Nevertheless, the integration between the Jewish roots of Jesus and his presentation in the Hellenist and Roman world could not be worked out neatly and convincingly. At the same time, it would still make sense if viewed that the Christian faith was not grounded on set of doctrines and strict traditions, but represented a process, an open-ended process as the full significance of Christ was still unfolding. Paul was prepared to consider his prestigious tradition a loss because of the 'surpassing worth of knowing Christ' (Phil. 3:7). This knowing continued, and for true Christians it should continue today, in that the profound insights of the past will assist in the discernment of God's presence, through the 'imagined image' of Christ and power of the Spirit in today's world. In spite of differences in certain matters, if the disciples of Jesus and God's children, wherever they live, come together in the name of the triune God and in fellowship with that divine communion will certainly find a way to live in unity.

There were many kinds of division in the early church. The most common though not dangerous division was not about certain issues such as determining true apostleship, cases of incest and other sexual immorality, concerning celibacy, concerning food sacrificed to idols, on covering the head in worship, concerning spiritual gifts and circumcision which were dealt with by Paul as we find mainly in 1 Corinthians and Galatians. These were mainly pastoral issues of particular congregations. The first Council at Jerusalem, deliberated the issues prayerfully and keeping the scriptures in mind, made a profound affirmation and magnanimous decision. 'The council's letter to Gentile believers' concludes with the following words:

> It seemed good to the Holy Spirit and to us not to burden you with anything beyond the following requirements: You are to abstain from food sacrificed to idols, from blood, from the meat of strangled animals and from sexual immorality. You will do well to avoid these things (Acts 15:28-29).

There is no reason to believe that this resolution put all the divisions and tensions to an end. Continued guidance and instruction were needed, and Paul chose to put forward the nature and requirements of Christian love (1 Cor. 13) in the context of such guidance and instruction. At the same time, he warned the churches against those who caused division:

> I urge you, brothers and sisters, to watch out for those who cause divisions and put obstacles in your way that are contrary to the teaching you have learned. Keep away from them. For such people are not serving our Lord Christ, but their own appetites. By smooth talk and flattery, they deceive the minds of naïve people (Rom. 16:17-18; also read Jude 19).

Another kind of division was on the basis of personalities. The figures who were said to command the following are: Paul, Apollos, Cephas and Christ. Paul advocates 'perfectly united in mind and thought' and the punching questions are 'Is Christ divided? Was Paul crucified for you? Were you baptised in the name of Paul?' (1 Cor. 1: 10-13).

Paul allowed 'differences among you to show which of you have God's approval'; however, he did not tolerate this affecting the sanctity and integrity of celebrating the Lord's Supper by displaying wealth and skipping fellowship with the poor (11:19-26). Unity in diversity is our common knowledge today just as in Paul's time. But the primary implication for him was the integration, cooperation and mutual concern of the parts:

> Just as the body, though one, has many parts, but all its many parts form one body, so it is with Christ. For we were all baptised by one Spirit so as to form one body – whether Jews or Gentiles, slave or free – and we were all given the one Spirit to drink. And so, the body is not made up of one part but of many (12: 12-14).

The integrity and life of a body require each part belonging to the body along with other parts respecting even the weakest part which may be indispensable, sharing the pain of the other parts and using the different goods for common good (12: 15-30).

On the whole, through their own unity, the Christians were supposed to be looking and working for the ultimate fulfilment, 'to bring unity to all things in heaven and on earth under Christ' (Eph. 1: 10). But there have been successive deviations and multiple divisions.

Greater Divisions

Now we have to be trotting forward through several centuries of history. We will snapshot the most decisive moments. To start with, the fundamental cause for misunderstanding and divisions in the early centuries was the failure of clarity about Christianity's relationship with its Hebrew/Jewish traditions. To use Paul's analogy, the Gentile Christians (including ourselves) were the 'wild olive shoot grafted in among the others share the nourishing sap from the olive root' (Rom. 11: 17). He acknowledges that there were some branches which fell off from the root (those Jews who did not believe in Christ). Paul explains further to the Gentile Christians of Rome:

> Do not consider yourself to be superior to those other branches. If you do, consider this: you do not support the root, but the root supports you. You will say then, 'Branches were broken off so that I might be grafted in.' That is true. They were broken off because of unbelief, and you stand by faith. Do not be arrogant, but tremble. For if God did not spare the natural branches, he will not spare you either. Consider therefore the kindness and sternness of God: sternness to those who fell, but kindness to you, provided you continue in his kindness. Otherwise you also will be cut off … God is able to graft them again (11:18-23).

What is known as anti-Semitism has distorted the Christian message and witness. Marcion, a second century ship-builder, rejected the Hebrew scripture as a Christian book. In his canon he accepted the earliest abbreviated version of Luke's Gospel (omitting the birth narrative) and ten edited Pauline epistles (omitting the Pastoral letters). His theological position was based on a sharp contradiction between the Hebrew scriptures and the God they portray and the New Testament and the God that Christ revealed. For him Paul was the only apostle as the twelve were simply Judaic. The leaders of the main churches rejected his teaching, and subsequently Marcion set up a rival church which flourished to be a great church. As he insisted asceticism, he administered baptism only to the unmarried and gave water in the place of wine in communion. He was judged to be a heretic.

There were a few more such heretics, not so radical and extreme as Marcion, but on the questions mainly of who Jesus was. For instance, was he a created being like others? Was he divine, human or divine-human? Further, since the Roman emperor Constantine converted to Christianity in the 4th century and Christianity became the state religion, the nature and structure of the church took a radical turn. Emperors played a role in determining what was the true teaching and what was the correct structure of the Church. Constantine persecuted Jews,[1] and the

---

[1] Constantine's anti-Jewish law in the fourth century forbade the Jews to convert or marry Christians, to have slaves, to take up civil positions where they could judge Christians and to serve in the military. His successors continued such restrictions in and outside Europe. Persecution of the Jews in England was widespread. For example, in 1190 about five hundred Jewish men and women were massacred when they tried to take refuge in York castle. Further, Jews were segregated with badges, and anti-Jewish attitudes were sustained in the following centuries.

vehement anti-Semitic attitude of the Church Fathers complemented this. Thus, the significance of the Church was defined more in religio-political-cultural-linguistic terms and the original identity of the Christians as God's children and Christ's disciples was forgotten. This was true yet peculiar in the case of Nestorius of the 5th century, the Patriarch of Constantinople. He used the term *theotokos* (bearer of God or mother of God) in reference to the Virgin Mary, thus denying the humanity and shared divinity of Christ. Nestorius was condemned to be a heretic after repudiating his views. However, several Eastern bishops defended him and were united to form a separate Nestorian Church, the first church with a person's name. Probably the Nestorians contributed to non-biblical beliefs about Mary, the mother of Jesus (e.g. stories of her remaining immaculate, her ascension into heaven, her position as mediator between God and devotees, and worship of her with icons and statues), though those who consider themselves Nestorians prohibit the designation, 'Mary, the Mother of God'. It is assumed that the frequent condemnation of Jesus as Son of God and Mary, etc., in the Holy Qur'an reflected the prophet Mohamed's encounter with them with indignation in the 7th century. In any case, the early Asian church inherited mainly two traditions of the Western church – the East Syrian or Nestorian tradition and the West Syrian Orthodox Church or 'Jacobite' tradition (named after Jacob Baradeus, a sixth century monk, consecrated secretly, who opposed the definition of Christ by the Western Church, and spread the gospel and established churches). There was persecution of the Eastern Churches by the Western Church with imperial patronage.

Missionary expansion became the obligation of the Western Church as well. Particularly, Pope Gregory sent Augustine of Carthage (in north Africa) in 596 to convert the Anglo-Saxons. In 8th century there was the conversion of Germany by Wilfred of York and others. Ansgari was the first known missionary to Denmark and Sweden (829). In 1000 Christianity reached Ireland. And so on. The parallel great missionary movement was Islam, often with political force.

The Christian Church was greatly weakened by its most decisive schisms. They were two. First, the four-year (863–867) Photian Schism was schism between the episcopal see of Rome and Constantinople, which since the 5th century was the centre of the Eastern Roman Empire. Photius, a powerful patriarch at Constantinople, represented the growing discontent with the papal claim to jurisdiction in the East. Thus, the schism betrayed a struggle for ecclesiastical control of the southern Balkans and a personality clash between the heads of the two sees, the Pope in Rome and the Patriarch in Constantinople, both of whom were elected in the year 858 and both of whose reigns ended in 867!

Connected with the above power-conflict and personality clash, was the famous *filioque* clause. In 589 the Council of Toledo inserted the *filioque* clause into the Nicene creed, changing the procession of the Spirit as 'and from the Son'. Though it irritated the leaders of the Eastern bloc, it was Photius who openly attacked in 867 this Latin aggression of adding the *filioque*. However, the formal 'great schism' was sealed in 1054. Even today the Orthodox version of the Nicene creed has the words 'proceeding from the Father' only. This is a good example of the complex nexus of religion, politics, personality clashes and doctrines. If we proceed with the turn of events in the following centuries, we encounter more conflicts, wars, experiences of Mary's appearance and accumulation of power and wealth around the Pope in Rome.

Reformation and further Shoots

Luther and Lutheranism: Making use of the spirit of renaissance and new initiatives, Martin Luther (1483-1546) posted his 95 theses on the front door of the castle church of Wittenberg (and circulated them around) in Germany on 31 October 1517.[1] This daring act represented an explosion in the history of the Christian Church. The theses were mainly against the exploitative and unbiblical belief in the power and efficacy of the practice of indulgences. In the context of superficial religiosity and pious pursuits for salvation, without losing the positive fruits of his training in scholastic theology, Luther tried to crystallise the foundational Christian truth by presenting the 'three solaces' and the document of 28 articles (Augsburg Confession) that reflected his proposals, written by his colleague Philipp Melanchthon (1497-1560). But all these were rejected by Rome which excommunicated Luther as a heretic, and in turn Luther called Rome 'the seat of the Antichrist'. To stand firm, he had not only the support of a group of likeminded colleagues but also of his prince and nobles. However, he was so pious and humble as to call himself a 'worm' and to reject the suggestion that his name be taken for the new movement or church although there were vested interests both in Germany and Scandinavia to go ahead with the name 'Lutheran.' A re-reading of Luther will redeem us from the deception that he was a demigod and to see his approach to the scripture and theology as the approximation of the absolute truth. The problem is not the 'spirit' but the 'content' of his theology and Reformation. Fundamentally, Luther could not be spared from a murderous anti-Semitism which continued the legacy of certain early Church Fathers. The Jews in Diaspora were charged with deicide and 'blood libel'. We can understand why there was no reference in the Creeds to the Hebrew roots (at least to the Exodus and the prophetic movement) and to the life of Jesus, a Jewish Rabbi and prophet, to start with.

Martin Luther first expected that in the process of Reformation the Jews in Germany would convert to be Christians. When it did not happen, he poured venom on them. He wrote a long article on 'The Jews and their Lies' and asked the local authorities to destroy Jewish homes and synagogues. Luther's attitude

---

[1] This section on Luther is a shortened form of, I. Selvanayagam, 'A Critical Re-appropriation of Martin Luther's Reformation for India', *People's Reporter*, 29/24 Dec. 25-Jan. 10, 2017, 14; 30/3 Feb. 10-25, 2017, 6-7.

influenced the German public and later the missionary movement, and it is difficult to argue that this attitude had nothing to do with Hitler's 'final solution' of exterminating six million Jews in the Second World War. It is not unreasonable to think that Dietrich Bonhoeffer (1906-1945), the greatest Lutheran pastor of the twentieth century, offered atonement for the above atrocities when he became part of a plot to assassinate Hitler but was arrested, imprisoned and executed. His exposition of the 'cheap grace' and 'cost of discipleship' have been a great inspiration for many, who await action in the form of a new Reformation.

One may suppose that since all major Churches including Catholics, Lutherans and Anglicans have offered public apology to the Jewish community, therefore we move on. But it is a stark yet unconscious reality that anti-Semitism continues to dominate our altars and pulpits. Well-informed Jews, while respecting genuine Christians, have produced volumes and point out that much of Christian theology and preaching is underpinned by misuse of the Hebrew scriptures and ignorance of Jewish theology.

We sample the famous three solaces: scripture, grace and faith. First, when Luther emphasised scripture as the sole source for salvation, he had his own bias and selection. In a context where ceremonial actions dominated, he projected Paul's focus on justification by faith as central. Paul starts an exposition of this idea by connecting it with the experience of the Hebrew ancestor Abraham (Rom. 4: 3); however, in his effort to convince the Gentiles of the gospel ('accept that you have been accepted although you are unacceptable'), as we mentioned earlier he undermined the Jewish foundation of the faith as there was a chance that his mission would be misunderstood as the imposition of Jewish culture on the Gentiles (see Acts 16: 20). Also, he had to address the nuisance of some Jews who insisted on circumcision, etc. But there was a tendency among the bubbling new converts to undervalue the Hebrew roots of their faith. Realising this, Paul hastened to reaffirm the indispensable nature of these roots, as we have already pointed out with reference to Romans 9-11. Interestingly, Luther's commentary on these chapters is both misleading and twisting. And he was not able to digest the Christian message as reconstructed on the Hebrew root story and teachings as is evident in the epistle of James and the book of Revelation. He rejected the last book and assessed James as straw. When he highlighted the 'collective priesthood of all believers' from 1 Pet. 2: 9, he did not acknowledge its Hebrew foundation (Ex. 19: 6).

Second, when Luther expounded the idea of grace, he did not give adequate attention to references in the Hebrew scriptures. If God's painful struggle between bestowing grace and demanding justice as presented by the prophets is not acknowledged, grace is bound to become cheap. There is no dearth of ideas of divine grace across the religious traditions. The Judeo-Christian tradition has a unique appeal to all humans as God's grace is primarily manifested in his liberating act of solidarity with victims in Egypt. Repentance and commitment to building up a new community based on justice, peace and love is the authentic response, while constantly relying on God's grace and his unfailing love.

Third, Luther understood and interpreted faith in terms of trusting God and accepting God's prevenient acceptance. But he does not seem to have grasped Jesus' distinctive understanding of faith, i.e. the capacity to transcend, to move on (moving mountains and trees), to experiment with the impossible, and daring to seek alternatives. We will explain this in the fifth chapter. Of course, responding to prevenient acceptance may also be interpreted as faith. But transformative and constructive action alone can be the true fruit of real faith, as James highlights, or else even superficial piety may be mistaken for faith, as he warns. Further, it is challenging that Jesus found this faith in some extraordinary individuals outside his religious fold (a centurion, a Canaanite woman and a Samaritan) which he estimated as greater than that of the 'people of God'. For him outsiders who are involved in acts of liberation 'are not against us but with us'. Luther's favoured passages did not include such texts.

Luther did not have the last word on theology and church polity; bitter theological controversies arose following his death. Seven Lutheran documents based on the three classical/ecumenical creeds formed *The Book of Concord* in 1580 and this long document (about 700 pages in English) has united the Lutherans who regard it as most authoritative. In more recent times, the Lutheran World Federation (a global communion of 145 churches in the Lutheran tradition, representing over 74 million Christians in 98 countries), formed in 1947 and based in Geneva, coordinates programmes and initiates dialogue across the Lutheran world and with other major Churches including the Roman Catholic Church.

Calvin and Zwingli, and Presbyterianism: Luther's Reformation in Germany was not the only reformation in 16th century Europe. We point to two more figures and their movements and church traditions in Switzerland: – John Calvin (1509-1564) and Huldrych Zwingli (1484-1531).[1] They overlapped with Luther's thinking and activities. Calvin's *The Institutes of the Christian Religion* (1536) came to be the most influential and synthetic text of Protestant theology. This was followed by extensive materials on various themes written either by Calvin himself or by others. After living in Paris and Basel he came to Geneva where there were tensions and political conflicts. He supported the Reformation which had just been introduced by a group with evangelical faith. He had to oppose the 'Libertines' who did not have any respect for his idea of godly order. Finally, peace prevailed and gave him an atmosphere conducive for his continuing his reforming activities. The *Institutes* deals with themes such as creation that bears God's glory and witness, it deals with providence, sin, faith as the medium of

---

[1] See for greater detail, I. Selvanayagam, 'Ever Reforming Evangelical Church: An Indian Protestant View', in *Church on Pilgrimage: Trajectories of Intercultural Encounter*, ed. by Kuncheria Pathil, Bengaluru: Dharmaram Publications, 2016, 130ff.

sanctification, redemption and the Church as a godly community. His exposition of the idea of justification by faith shares much with Luther's, but his idea of predestination of the select believers for redemption, which for him is a mystery, appears contradictory, though he modified it later. His idea of the Church is the same as that of the other reformers, i.e. that body where the Word of God is preached and the sacraments are properly administered. In this connection he gave much importance to the office of the pastor. Teachers and deacons had to assist the pastors to preserve and nurture the faith. This 'order' was necessary to establish a godly commonwealth in Geneva. From this centre Calvinism spread all over the world and different new denominations took its ideas, though with different selections and emphases. Calvin's success in Geneva encouraged the Scottish reformer John Knox (1513-1572) who was in exile and claimed that Geneva was the most perfect school of Christ since the days of the early Church. He was ministering to the English-speaking refugee community of the city. There he found true reformation and true preaching with the uncompromising affirmation that Christ, the enfleshment of the eternal Word, was the Head of the Church. However, what came to be known as the Presbyterian Church in Scotland combines the views of Swiss reformation with the salient features of the Reformed family of Churches (including Evangelical, Congregational, Protestant, Presbyterian, and Free Churches in general). Churches with Scottish and Dutch roots are likely to be Calvinist and inter-connected while those with English roots Zwinglian and Congregational. The present-day Presbyterian churches were born of the Scottish appropriation of the Swiss Reformation and the theological articles of the Westminster Confession of Faith (1647) that was the most widely embraced Confession among the Presbyterian churches. The Geneva church's influence on the Scottish Presbyterian church can be seen in the series of documents or Books it produced – *Discipline and the Scots Confession* (1560), *Common Order* (1564), *The Second Book of Discipline* (1581), but it rejected episcopacy and worked out systematically the 'Presbyterian structure' with elders made responsible for various levels, from local to national.

Zwingli, first a chaplain to Swiss mercenaries in Italy and then the priest at the Great Church in Zurich, proved to be more radical than Luther himself. His views of church governance, preaching (one could publicly denounce ecclesiastical and political corruption), baptism (not more than a sign) and Eucharist (no powers without the believer's faith) were more reasonable, egalitarian and decentralized. In the context of two disputations (1523) he wrote '67 Theses', his major work. This work effected the change of the cathedral becoming independent of Episcopal control. Like Luther, he too married. Steps were taken to abolish the Catholic mass. For him church reformation could not be simply a social revolution, but reform required the support of the magistrates. With such support of a couple of key magistrates, a reformed church in Zurich was born at Easter 1525. He shared the view of Erasmus that to create a Christian society education was vital. But in due course he was opposed by Erasmus and Luther. And to bring the Reformation to a full circle, war with the Catholics was inevitable, and unexpectedly he was killed in a battle. Though Zwingli did not write a systematic theology, his theses and sermons stressed the absolute Sovereignty of God and purity of people.

On at least two counts Zwingli differed from Luther. First, while Luther contrasted the gospel with the law, he interpreted law as God's guide for Christian living. Second, in opposition to the traditional Catholic view of transubstantiation, Luther proposed consubstantiation (Christ being present in the bread and wine), but Zwingli emphasized that their effect or significance was in the believers' hearts. Further, though he would have accepted Luther's church-state relationship, Zwingli put it in biblical and local terms. Accordingly, just as prophets and kings worked together in the Old Testament, local authorities and interpreters of the gospel (clergy) should work together.

The Presbyterian Churches: The names can be confusing: those with English speaking origins were called Presbyterians while those of the Continental Europe, Protestant or Reformed. There is further variety from region to region. 'Present-day Presbyterian churches emerged from the Scottish appropriation of the Swiss Reformation and the theology of the Westminster Confession (1647).'[1] Scripture was held to be supreme and no reformation without the basis of the scripture was accepted. The priority of divine grace was affirmed and the idea of double predestination (either for heaven or for hell) was rejected, and the doctrine of election was explained as unmerited divine grace. The Roman Catholic priestly order and clericalism was replaced by the pastoral order of the elders of two sections (or elders and deacons). Now the individual should establish his/her own order but work within the corporate order. Today the Presbyterian Church is a worldwide movement with concentration in Scotland, America and Korea. In India, particularly in the north-eastern state of Mizoram the Presbyterian Church is lively. Governorship of the church was the major concern, though liturgical or free worship, different attitudes towards sacraments, the doctrines for corporate ownership and individual convictions were allowed. It was centred on elders (*presbyters*) and they were of two groups, ministers or teaching elders and governing elders, both elected by the congregations. This is a condensed form of Calvin's four offices: pastors, teachers, elders and deacons. The coordinating structures are synods and assemblies. The Presbyterian theory was originally propounded by the Cambridge theologian Thomas Cartwright (1535-1603), and though his views were outlawed by the Elizabethan regime they continued to live in the form of 'Puritan' radicalism in England. And though Presbyterians differed from Congregationalists in understanding church order, they both shared the theological heritage of Calvin. This will explain their coming together in 1972 as we will see later.

---

[1] Joseph D. Small, 'Presbyterian Churches', in *Christianity, the Complete Guide*, ed. by John Bowden, London: Continuum, 2005, 979.

Henri VIII, the Church of England and Anglicanism: To understand the origin of Anglicanism[1] we need to consult the origin of the Church of England which separated from the Roman Catholic Church in the sixteenth century. On the one hand, the origin was part of the English Renaissance, and the English Reformation was presided over by the king of England, Henry VIII (1491-1547). But on the other hand, the origin was part of an intense political crisis created by the personal muddle of the king in the case of his marriage. He married six wives, and some of them he murdered, and for this and other reasons he may be compared to Herod the Great of the New Testament. His first wife Catherine, the widow of his brother Arthur, was unable to provide a male heir to the throne, and Henry thought it was a divine punishment for the immoral marriage in the first place. He also was infatuated by Anne Boleyn, one of the ladies of the court. He appealed to Pope Clement VII to annul the first marriage. Other political ties contributed to the hardening of hearts that led to the breach with Rome and a revolution in England, under the able command of Thomas Cromwell from 1532 to 1541. Consequently, the English Church was separated from Rome; became effectively a spiritual department of the State under the rule of the king who was regarded as God's deputy on earth; fulfilling his wish, Henry married Ann in January 1533; in May the new Archbishop Thomas Cranmer presided over the formality of a trial that pronounced the first marriage annulled; in September the princess Elizabeth was born; the Pope retaliated with a sentence of ex-communication for Henry who had been called the 'Defender of Faith' for his opposition to the 'Lutheran heresy'. 'It was Henry's Act of Supremacy (1534) that gave the English Church its independence from Rome paving the way for what came to be known as the Church of England.'[2] Cromwell transferred the wealth of the monasteries to the crown after dissolving them within a short period (1536-1540).

One early identity mark of the Church of England was the *Book of Common Prayer*, first authorised for use in 1549 and after three revisions given a permanent place in 1662. Since then, with minor changes, it has continued as the standard liturgy of Anglicans in Britain and around the Anglican Communion. Thirty-nine Articles of faith are appended to the Prayer Book and they in many clauses reflect Luther's Augsburg Confession. The Archbishop of Canterbury, based in Lambeth Palace, London, is the head of the Church of England. He and the diocesan bishops and clergy inherited cathedrals and church buildings with towers, columns and high spires, as well as the liturgical colours and vestments from the Roman Catholic Church. Feast Days of saints and martyrs were retained.

---

[1] This and the following section on Congregationalism are based on I. Selvanayagam, 'From Congregationalism to Anglicanism with a Special Reference to Episcopacy', *Indian Church History Review*, XLI/1, June 2007, pp. 50-79.

[2] Marcus Throup, *All Things Anglican: Who We Are and What We Believe*, Norwich (and London): Canterbury Press, 2018, 4.

Anglican chant was developed in the Church; it was a simple harmonized setting of a melody devised for singing prose versions of the psalms and canticles. When the Oxford Movement began in 1833 in order to promote reorientation towards Roman Catholic liturgy, parish churches turned to choral services formerly confined to cathedrals. With a view to facilitate better singing by lesser trained choirs, a method of printing the psalms first appeared in printed form in 1837 and subsequently a system of signs developed that pointed out how a text was to be fitted to a given chant. Furthermore, Anglican Religious Communities for men and women emerged modelling after the Catholic monastic orders.

Anglican Canon Law recognises the British monarch as the supreme head of the Church of England and is held as the ecclesiastical law of the State. Proposals relating to any matter except dogma are made by a Church Assembly (established in 1919) and presented to for approval to the Ecclesiastical Committee of the Parliament; followed by royal approval, the proposal becomes law. This is applicable to the appointment of a bishop in the Church of England which is preceded by the decision of an electoral college after prolonged and wide-ranging consultation in secret. Finally, two names are presented to the Prime Minister and s/he selects one and sends to the king/queen for approval. In this state church a certain number of bishops sit in the Upper House, the House of Lords. The Archbishop is a sort of chaplain to the monarch and presides over important functions, from weddings to funerals. Parishes are not confined to Christians or Anglican members. The pastoral team includes the Rector and Vicar who are popularly called priests and clergy. As the state Church of England it 'is under the obligation to conduct marriages of all parishioners whether they are actually practising Christians or not, are baptised or not.' Only its unaltered rite may legally be used so that that people marrying in this church do not have to go to the Register Office prior to the ceremony or have a state Registrar present at it.

The ecclesial tradition of the Church of England is called Anglicanism, and this word was coined in the context of the CofE spread around the world through the colonial empire and mission. Earlier, it is often claimed that the word *Anglican* itself has its background in *ecclesia anglicana*, a medieval Latin phrase dating to the 12th century or earlier, which means the 'English Church'. It may simply mean English or England. Those Churches who refused to have the name of this alien language or region described themselves with the adjective *episcopal*, hence the Episcopal Church of USA (ECUSA), the Episcopal Church of Scotland, the Episcopal Church in Jerusalem and the Middle East and so on. There is a small episcopal Free Church of England as well.

The Anglican Communion came into being in 1789 when ECUSA broke its colonial association with the CofE and became the first self-governing Anglican church outside Britain. Such move to independence later spread in other parts of the world including India. The Archbishop of Canterbury is the symbol of unity of the Anglican Communion. He presides over the Lambeth

Conference of the Anglican bishops from all over the world, approximately every ten years since 1867. The purpose is stated as to pray, to worship and to counsel together. 'Although, not able to make binding pronouncements for the Anglican Communion as a whole, the gathering of Anglican bishops from around the world does have significant symbolic power to articulate norms and expectations for beliefs and practices in Anglicanism.'[1] In 1971 a representative assembly of lay people, priests and bishops with the name Anglican Consultative Council started to meet approximately once in three years to pray, to worship and to counsel together for common good of the Communion. And from 1979 a meeting of the Primates (Archbishops or presiding bishops) has been taking place, now every year, for the same purposes as above. Though there is no legislative authority, the Primates' meeting tends to safeguard the Anglican solidarity and to set limits for threatening diversity (in issues such as homosexuality).

It is often pointed out that Anglicanism represents the second most widely distributed body of Christians. The following observation gives a balanced picture:

> At the beginning of the twenty-first century, Anglicans numbered approximately 73 million and were found in 167 countries as members of 38 national or regional churches. Numerically speaking, the largest of the churches in Anglicanism remains the Church of England, with over 20 million members. This number, however, needs to be qualified. Given that the Church of England remains the established church in the country, the national church, individuals are counted as members even if their participation in the life of the church is marginal or non-existent. In reality, the active membership in the Church of England is closer to 1 million, with average Sunday attendance approximately 800, 000. The number of active Anglicans in England can be contrasted with active membership in other churches within the Anglican Communion. The Anglican Church in Nigeria, depending on the statistics quoted, has anywhere from 11 to 17 million active members. The phenomenal growth of Anglicanism in Nigeria in the twentieth century has been replicated across the Anglican churches in Africa. As a result, today more Anglicans (approximately 37 million or close to 50 per cent of the global Anglican community) live in Africa south of the Sahara than in any other part of the world.[2]

Here I want to point out that the united churches (rather organic unions) of South India, North India and Pakistan & Bangladesh are unilaterally included in the Anglican Communion, and the number of communicants of these churches

[1] Ian T. Douglas, 'Anglicanism', in *Christianity, the Complete Guide*, ed. by John Bowden, London: Continuum, 2005, 48.
[2] Ibid., 45.

are added as Anglicans, Reformed and Methodists. We will come back to this issue later.

The History and Tradition of the Congregational Church: The word 'Congregationalists' was given later to those first known 'independents' of the Church of England and who emerged in the late sixteenth and early seventeenth centuries. They emphasised the right and duty of each congregation to make its own decisions about its affairs without dependence on any higher human authority. This they shared with Baptists, Disciples of Christ and other Puritans. The congregational polity of self-government was their primary distinguishing characteristic. Perplexed by the dominant Roman Catholic impact on the structure, liturgy and ethos of the Church of England, they wanted to put into practice the reformist emphasis on the New Testament idea of the priesthood of all believers. They had to struggle against the power of the government and at times suffered persecution. Many fled to Holland and the New World of America. Though active even before the English Civil Wars, the Congregationalists gained prestige when Oliver Cromwell, an Independent, was the Lord Protector of the Commonwealth (1649-1660). But their political influence started to decline when Cromwell died, and the Commonwealth was abolished with the restoration of the Crown in 1661.

The accession of William and Mary in 1689 created a change of mood, and the Toleration Act, passed in the same year, marked an assurance of granting full freedom to the Congregationalists along with all other groups of 'religious dissenters.' The Evangelical Revival of 1750-1815 injected a new vigour, and an important watershed was the formation of the Congregational Union of England and Wales in 1832. On ideological ground it had a tie with the Liberal Party, and when this party won victory in 1906 its influence started to be considerable in the society. Many countries including Sweden and Finland got the presence of the Congregationalists. In the twentieth century, the Church went into trans-confessional church unions in many countries. Most significant were the South India United Church (1908) and the United Reformed Church in England (1972) and Wales in amalgamation with Presbyterians.

The Congregationalists gave more importance to the preaching than the Holy Communion, to the locally gathered church than higher bodies. A summary of their theological position mentions that 'Congregationalism understands the church to be God's gathering of saints, called by the Spirit through the word; as such it is both local and visible, catholic and eternal, and subject in all things to Christ as head. The Holy Communion or Lord's Supper is a memorial feast, to do "in remembrance of me" and this is different from ideas of transubstantiation (Catholics and most Anglicans) and consubstantiation (Lutherans). The local church meeting, comprising professed believers, calls its officers (normally ministers and deacons), orders its worship and witness under the word, and is normally, though not universally, associated with sister churches in regional and international fellowship.'[1] However, like all polities, it is 'so vulnerable in human hands, is prone to defacement. Freedom under Christ can degenerate into "freedom to do and believe as we like".' When the polity is misconstrued as democratic rather than Christocentric, the objective becomes "one person, one vote and one government by the majority", rather than the mind of Christ and unanimity in him. The advocacy of local autonomy can be a pretext for (sometime financially motivated!) isolationism.'[2] However, the pattern developed in different countries and regions where the London Missionary Society (LMS) worked, depending on the local culture and societal structure. One of Congregationalism's finest theologians, P.T. Forsyth (1848-1921) argued that the exercise of Congregationalism was a fusion of Calvinism with the free leading of the Spirit that was characteristic of the Radical Reformation. It was far more eclectic in its origins than Presbyterianism, formed from the radical ground of the left-wing of the reformation which also gave rise to Conrad Grebel and the Swiss Brethren, the Anabaptists and the Mennonites. If Presbyterianism was about 'godly order', Congregationalism was about the freedom of the Spirit and the autonomy of the local congregation under Christ. Echoing earlier traditions of monasticism, Congregationalism emphasised the significance of being gathered 'out of the world' into the fellowship of Christ. Decision for Christ was literally of eternal significance, so confessing the faith, becoming a member of the church and accepting the responsibilities of that membership, were of crucial importance. Believers covenanted together under God to be the church in a particular place. For Congregationalists the local was the catholic.[3] Either still standing alone (e.g. the Congregational Federation in England) or in combination with the Presbyterian Church (URC) or with the World Reform Churches, the congregational movement strives for establishing the spiritual equality of all believers, simplicity, self-government and local mission as locus and starting point.

John Wesley and Methodism: John Wesley (1703-1791), one of the seventeen children of an Anglican priest, who himself became a priest after his studies in Oxford where he along with his brother Charles was a member of the Holy Club, characterised by strict spiritual discipline. Interestingly, from their 'methodic' behaviour of Christian life the nickname 'methodist' came. It was the major evangelical/revivalist movement of 18th century England. The Wesley brothers went to Atlanta as missionaries of the SPG. This was almost a failure and they returned to England rather frustrated. Then came a second conversion, a heart-warming experience of John and assurance that the 'chains fell off' for Charles.

---

[1] Alan P. F. Sell, 'Congregationalism', in *Dictionary of the Ecumenical Movement*, ed. by N. Lossky, et al., Geneva: WCC Publications, 1991, 218.

[2] Ibid., 219.

[3] David Cornick, 'United Reformed Church' in *Christianity, the Complete Guide*, ed. By John Bowden, London: Continuum, 2005, 1216.

John Wesley was a 'reasonable enthusiast'. On the one hand, he and his brother Charles (the hymn writer) experienced God's prior acceptance of sinners by grace in Christ, and the Wesleyan hymns celebrate this. On the other hand, he declared 'the world is my parish' and he travelled more than 250,000 miles on horseback, inviting all people to a new orientation in life. He preached to the miners and pointed out how their drunkenness affected the family economy. He declared slavery inhuman and supported the anti-slavery campaign of William Wilberforce. He was open to use any new device to alleviate physical pain. His first open-air preaching (1739) was based on the Nazareth Manifesto (Lk. 4: 18f), the total liberation offered by Jesus. It was not without reason the following saying became proverbial: 'The labour movement owes more to Methodism than Marxism.'

John Wesley emphasised scriptural holiness over the land, through justification, sanctification and perfect love. He continued to be an Anglican, encouraging his followers to worship in the parish churches and then to come to his chapels for bible study and prayer. However, gradually the break happened. One of his forty-four sermons was on 'The Catholic Spirit' preached in 1749. The punch line of this sermon was 'If your heart is like my heart, give me your hand.' Toleration was the primary characteristic of this spirit. The 'people called Methodists' were encouraged to belong to a church and practice the form of worship, acceptable to the individual conscience. Methodists did not have a set of doctrines, and their primary theological resources were John Wesley's 44 sermons, his Journals, and his Notes on the New Testament. But they had an extraordinary ability to move on ecumenically with wisdom and determination.

Three streams of 'Methodism' (Wesleyans, Bible Christians, and Primitive Methodists) came into one as The Methodist Church in Britain through a Deed of Union in 1932. Methodist mission was very successful in different parts of the world. In its country of origin, the Methodist Church is non-episcopal, being a connexion, with annual presidency, District Chairs, Circuit Superintendents, Ministers and Stewards. However, elsewhere the Methodist Church has taken different forms, including episcopal.

Today the World Methodist Council, founded in 1881, is a consultative body and association of 80 member churches in 133 countries which together represent about 80.5 million people. As far its place of origin is concerned, the Methodist Church is concerned about its steady decline in the country of its origin. It has been noted that in the last four decades there is 35 per cent decline, and the present membership is less than 2 million.

Soon after World War II Anglicans and Methodists started negotiation with a view to forming an organic union. It was hopeful until the end. However, in 1966 Methodists accepted the scheme but Anglicans rejected with a narrow margin.

Imported Shoots to South India Planted by Missionary Societies

When the terrible 'war of religion' around reformation in Europe continued to show its scars, mostly raw, attention was turned to discoveries of the lands, colonialism combined with evangelical revival. The history of these developments and of the emergence of denominations have been overwritten and I do not see it necessary to reproduce it here although it is helpful to understand the descent of the western missions on the non-western world with competing claims and confusing labels. However, the ideal of 'one God, one humanity and one mission' was not there at least to reduce confusion. The church resulting out of western mission also took different shapes and names. For our purpose, we point out the Protestant missions and the churches which entered into negotiation and which constituted the Church of South India, though we will mention the other major churches in South India in passing in order to fill in the background.

The first Protestant (Lutheran) missionary Bartholomaeus Ziegenbalg (1683-1717) along with his friend Heintich Pluetschau (1677-1752), from the pietist movement of Halle in Germany, sponsored by a Danish king, landed in Tranquebar, a south east coastal town of India in 1706. This town is celebrated with a caption that '*We*' (or '*It*') *Began in Tranquebar* as we read in the titles of a few important books. Later it became the centre and meeting place of different denominational mission societies. It is most remarkable that in the beginning there was inter-denominational cooperation in the operation of mission. Joseph G. Muthuraj's thorough and excellent study of this cooperation and the interactions in the beginning of episcopacy has unearthed a wealth of information.[1] For example, he has made the following observation:

> To view this early Protestant mission in India as an exclusive achievement of one nation or a denomination, undervaluing the labours of other participating bodies, would be a distorted and a one-sided history. A royal mandate from Denmark, a pietistic spark from Halle and organisational acumen from England combined together to reveal a truly multi-national identity for the Indian mission.[2]

He points out cases of Danish-Halle missionaries who worked under Anglican supervision. 'Both the English and Danish missionaries were receiving ordinations from the Bishops of Copenhagen even until 1818 in order to be sent as missionaries to India through London. In fact, more than sixty percent of the Danish-Halle-English missionaries were ordained in Copenhagen. Historical sources corroborate the three-sidedness of the mission in most circumstances. There is enough evidence to suggest that Copenhagen, London and Halle

---

[1] J.G. Muthuraj, *We Began at Tranquebar*, Delhi: ISPCK, 2010, Two volumes.

[2] Ibid., xv.

maintained the link throughout, until they reached their final breaking points.'[1] The point was that Tranquebar set the model for inter-denominational missionary cooperation. The major breaking point was when the Society for the Propagation of the Gospel in Foreign Parts (SPG) took over the mission from the Society for the Propagation of Christian Knowledge (SPCK) in 1825 and the formal end was in 1847, when the Dresden (later Leipzig) mission took over the mission property rights and made a fresh start.[2] However, cross-sponsoring of missionaries between different missionary societies continued.

The Anglican mission to India started with chaplains of the British East India Company[3] (which received a Royal Charter from Queen Elizabeth I on 31 December 1600). Of the most notable are: David Brown, an ordained deacon of the CofE who arrived in what is now Kolkata in 1786 and founded the Calcutta Bible Society; and Henry Martyn, an ordained priest who landed in India in 1806. Although the chaplains were not expected to preach, their work had a missionary character. Martyn was even critical of the Empire. Of the many missionary societies that sprang forth from the Church of England, those associated with India were SPCK founded in 1699, followed by the formation of the SPG, founded in1701. While these represented the high church, the Church Missionary Society (founded in 1799) represented the 'low church'. Some missionaries of the SPG, for example, made significant contributions to the development of cultures and languages. For instance, Robert Cardwell (1819-1891) and G.U. Pope (1820-1907; sponsored by the Wesleyans!) are still paid tribute for their contribution to the development of the Tamil language, and this is recognised by their statues on Marina Beach, Chennai along with those of great figures of the Tamil heritage. C.F. Andrews (1871-1940), a SPG missionary to India, an associate of Gandhi and friend of poet Rabindranath Tagore, came to be called *Dheenabandu*, friend of the poor. Andrews was the only European missionary who attended the National Missionary Conference at Delhi in 1912. He advocated the indigenous institutions such as *Ashrams*. In the national front, he 'joined with the forces with the nationalist idealism' and 'wrote a pamphlet in 1920 called *Independence – the Immediate Need*. It is not surprising that Jawaharlal Nehru, who later became independent India's first Prime Minister, commented on Andrews's statement as 'nationalism pure and simple.'[4] The Anglican churches were more positive towards the colonial power, and their structures were mostly the replica of the Church of England though the province was called the Church of India, Pakistan, Burma and Ceylon. In climax, after much thought and observation, Andrews found the approach of his Anglican mission society incompatible with the gospel of Jesus. Therefore,

---

[1] Ibid. xviii.

[2] Ibid., ix.

[3] See Daniel O'Connor, *The Chaplains of the East India Company*, London: Continuum, 2011.

[4] Sundklar, 89.

he left the mission because of its support for the colonial power, and for this and his support for the national movement he was labelled as 'atheist of the Empire'.

The Presbyterian tradition became rooted in South India through different forms. The Arcot Mission of the Reformed Church in America was based in Vellore. The mission was founded by the Scudder family of doctors in1851 in order to provide medical help for the poor and desperate who could be potential converts. The Church of Scotland Mission engaged in overseas mission rather late and worked through small bodies and focused projects. Thus, the Madras Christian College, founded in 1837, has been striving to maintain academic excellence and character building. Of the later missionaries of the Church of Scotland, Lesslie Newbigin (1909-1998), sponsored by the Foreign Mission Committee and assigned to the Madras Mission, was most popular and arrived in Madras in 1936. Since then the 'Church of Scotland Mission' has taken different names and forms.

The Congregational tradition worked in alliance with different denominations yet got particular focus in the LMS (London Missionary Society), founded in 1795. The fundamental principle adopted into the constitution of LMS in 1796 is the following:

> As the union of Christians of various Denominations in carrying on this great Work is a most desirable object, so, to prevent, if possible, any cause of future dissension, it is declared to be a fundamental principle of The Missionary Society that its design is not to send Presbyterianism, Independency, Episcopacy, or any other form of Church Order and Government (about which there may be difference of opinion among serious persons), but the glorious Gospel of the blessed God, to the heathen; and that it shall be left (as it ought to be left) to the minds of the persons whom God may call into the fellowship of His Son from among them to assume for themselves such form of Church Government as to them shall appear most agreeable to the Word of God.[1]

The spirit of generosity and flexibility enshrined in the LMS constitution and the agreeability of particular form of church government to the Word of God deserve a separate study. LMS was open to ally with any denominal mission. David Livingstone (1813-1873), explorer and medical missionary in Africa, was one of the many Scottish missionaries funded by the LMS. In any case, the churches established by the LMS adopted the Congregational model with independence for the local church and a federal structure of regional Council (e.g. Travancore Church Council) and the General Assembly. The Madurai American Mission

---

[1] Quoted, Richard Lovett, *The History of the London Missionary Society, 1795-1895*, London: Oxford University Press, 1899, Vol. I, 49f.

founded in 1841 had a Congregational basis. LMS worked in the Travancore areas, the Coimbatore area, and others.

Wesleyan Missionary Missions among heathens started as early as 1786. Just as the movement evolved gradually into a Church, the missionary movement developed through various stages. Most notably, the WMMS (Wesleyan Methodist Missionary Society) originated in the District Auxiliaries, the first of which was founded in Leeds in October 1813. Then embracing the District Auxiliaries, the General Wesleyan MMS (Methodist Missionary Society) came into being in 1818. In South India some Wesleyan soldiers posted in Madras at the end of the 18th century spread the faith. James Lynch, a missionary (later the WMMS Secretary, 1834-1872), visited them from Jaffna in 1814. He then shunted between Jaffna and Madras through Nagapatnam, developed mission resources in Madras, Mysore, etc. Elijah Hoole who arrived in 1821 became competent in Tamil and translated the basic Wesleyan liturgical resources. He was joined and followed by John Beecham and Thomas Hodson in the same century. Among the influential Methodist missionaries in South India in the latter part of the century were Henry Little (1862-1892), William Burgess (1867-1896), Henry Haigh (1874-1901) and William Holdsworth (1884-1900).

The Basel Mission, which had both Lutheran, Reformed and Free Church traditions in a remarkable mission union, was active from its foundation in 1815 by the German Missionary Society (covering Karnataka, North Kerala and South Maharashtra), to 2001 when it was transferred to 'Mission 21'. Its mission started in India, and it specialised in creating employment opportunities such as printing, tile manufacturing and weaving. The Basel Mission churches made a 'constructive contribution to the faith of our common church. It is through that the CSI comes into direct contact with the life and thought of Churches on the Continent.'[1] In General, all the missions followed almost the same pattern of mission with the components of health care, education, technical education, homes for orphans and direct preaching. Hand-outs included Bible, parts of the Bible and tracts. In terms of the structures (church building and governance), liturgy and pattern of ministry the home church style was replicated.

Membership of the Churches in South India in 1900 (which later constituted the CSI)

Anglicans 150,000
London Missionary Society 51,000
Wesleyan Methodists 12,000
The American Board of Madura Mission 11,000
Dutch Reformed Church in Arcot 6,000
Basel Mission Church 1,400[2]

---

[1] A. Streckeison, 'The Heritage of the C.S.I.', *South India Churchman,* February, 1948, 78.

[2] Sundkler, 28. These figures do not recognise converts of the small missions such as the American Arcot Mission, American Methodist Mission, American Jaffna Mission and Church of

The other churches in South India at that time and now are: Roman Catholics, Lutherans, both American and Continental, the Nestorian Christians (who out of zeal carried the gospel to India), Mar Thoma Church (with the claim that they are the true descendants of the converts of St. Thomas, the apostle of Jesus), and the other Orthodox churches in Kerala and elsewhere.

One question in sensitive minds was: given the amount of resources including personal and financial expended on direct and indirect mission, why have we ended up with a tiny minority of Christians? It was a great challenge for those who regarded the social service (education, health, etc.) as bait on a hook to catch the fish. One may imagine that eating the bait safely the fish have become fattened and swimming around happily? Was it a sharp and strong hook or flattened one or plastic one? A group of people of great faith went to Tranquebar, the first Protestant mission centre, with heavy hearts but open minds.

Scotland Mission. However, these and other such small groups could not present a considerable number.

Chapter 3

Stars in the Dark Clouds of
Denominational Divisions in South India

The world church throughout history has celebrated the life and achievement of a number of leaders. Some of them have been canonised with memorials. Others have been appreciated for their saintly life, intellectual calibre and theological depth. But, have we celebrated the achievers of church unity? In this chapter, we will highlight the background, qualification, ministerial experience and contribution of those who contributed to church unity in South India. One of them has been acclaimed as 'the martyr of church union'.

Unity is not a concept but shared and lived relationship. Even before and after thousands of talks, sermons and writings on unity, we are still a divided church. No protocol speech, political or ecclesial, has missed the word unity. But it required people of true faith who could pray, reflect and move things towards a visible unity however feeble it was. Apart from the general faith in terms of trusting God, relying on God's grace and protection and hope for a glorious future, they had the extraordinary faith spoken by Jesus. We will explain this in greater detail in the fifth chapter. Briefly, in response to the disciples' prayer 'increase our faith', Jesus talked about the little mushroom seed which can germinate and grow, a tree which can be uprooted and moved to the sea or a mountain moved and so on. In Christian life and ministry if we do not have this extraordinary faith there will not be any effect of the ordinary faith which may easily deviate to blind piety.

Those missionaries and Indian leaders who dared to realise what was regarded as impossible were fired by the gospel embodied in Jesus. It is marvellous that the missionaries from the West along with their native colleagues ventured into something unknown in history in their mission field in a foreign land. The native Christian leaders had the unprecedented confidence to work with their missionary colleagues. For prayer and consultation, they went to the first station of

the Protestant mission (Tranquebar, from 1706) on 1 May 1919. They embarked
on a new journey and some of them did not make it to the end to see the fruit of
their labour. It makes sense to believe that 'Those who are wise will shine like the
brightness of the heavens, and those who lead many to righteousness, like the stars
for ever and ever' (Dan. 12: 3). We will introduce the life and witness of the main
participants in the negotiations. At the end we will acknowledge the contribution
of a few who participated through comments, counsel and correction.

Major Players in the Frontline

V.S. Azariah

Samuel Vedanayagam Azariah (1874-1945), son of a covert and pious mother
(by a CMS missionary) and ordained minister of the Anglican church, had his
schooling in his local area in Thirunelveli District of the Madras Province (later
Tamil Nadu). He came to be the first Indian bishop and the first non-white
diocesan bishop anywhere in the Anglican Church. He joined the prestigious
MCC (Madras Christian College) but did not complete his first degree due to
illness, and claimed to have a special BA - 'Born Again'.

During his student days in Madras, Azariah was gripped by the vision of the
YMCA (Young Men's Christian Association), i.e. to evangelize the non-Christians
in preparation for the millennium. And his work as a YMCA secretary (1895-
1909) provided a great opportunity to experiment and broaden this vision. As
YMCA was an international Protestant organization, he had several opportunities
to visit other countries, conferences and conventions. He was determined to work
actively for conversion through Christian institutions, but in institutions such as
MCC it was discouraged.

He married Love (*Anbu*) in 1898, a highly educated and devout Christian,
and they had six children. Not only their names but also the living outreach of the
family was noted by neighbours.

Azariah soon realized that the western ways of doing mission and establishing
church hardly appealed to non-Christians. Therefore he explored the way of doing
mission by Indians, Indian resources and Indian methods. He was instrumental
in founding the NMS (National Missionary Society) in 1903. On similar lines,
the IMS (Indian Missionary Society) was founded in 1905 based in Thirunelveli,
connecting with his own mission field Dornakal and then further afield. Later,
after his ordination, he went to work in the Dornakal area of Andhra Pradesh
where, as bishop, he constructed the famous indigenous cathedral and established
the 'Dornakal Divinity School'. He was responsible for a great mass movement, as
preacher, trainer, teacher and organiser. Though he was not a scholar or properly
trained theologian, his prolific readings equipped him with current thinking. He
produced a series of small booklets and, most remarkably, his book in Tamil on
'Christian Giving' was later republished and translated into fifty languages.

His mentor was Bishop Henry Whitehead, Bishop of Madras, who taught him the basics of Christian faith and theology in his house. Even before he was consecrated as bishop, he was known as a passionate indigenous missionary and a fine representative of the younger churches in international and ecumenical gatherings. He was sent to the first WMC (World Missionary Conference), Edinburgh 1910, where his speech given to a fringe meeting made a big impact. Calling for indigenous forms of church and Indian leadership he concluded the speech with the following words:

> You have given the goods to feed the poor. You have given your bodies
> to be burned. We also ask for *love*. Give us FRIENDS![1]

In the light of later debate on a proper title for missionaries such as 'mission partner' and 'companion in mission', his proposal of the title 'friends' reflects a profound foresight.

Azariah's consecration in 1912 was shrouded with opposition not only by white missionaries but also Indian Christians. However, his mentor Bishop Henry Whitehead was his sustained supporter.

Azariah's exposure to the WMC and to the churches in the West helped him to realise how the continuing divisions were damaging the mission, though this was not realised by the churches concerned. His challenge to the western churches was consistent whenever he was given the chance. For example, he told the western audience at the Lausanne Conference on Faith and Order in 1927:

> Unity may be theoretically a desirable ideal in Europe and America,
> but it is vital to the life of the Church in the mission field. The
> divisions of Christendom may be a source of weakness in Christian
> countries, but in non-Christian lands they are a sin and CSI.[2]

While he was known as the champion of church unity in the West, he was acutely aware of the challenges to mission within India. Hence his courageous initiative and leadership in the union movement towards the formation of the CSI.

Azariah as a missionary was working among the poor Dalits in the Dornakal area of Andhra Pradesh. Gandhi unjustly criticised his work of converting people, but refused Azariah's invitation to go and see for himself the kind of people at the grassroots among whom he was working. At the same time, B.R. Ambedkar (1891-1956), the champion of Dalit liberation and opponent of Gandhi embarrassed 'the Father of Independent India' and caste Hindus by deciding to quit Hinduism

---

[1] V.S. Azariah, 'The Problem of Cooperation between Foreign and Native Workers', World Missionary Conference, Edinburgh, 1910. in *The Ecumenical Movement: An Anthology of Key Texts and Voices*, Ed. by M. Kinnamon and B. Cope, Geneva: WCC Publications, 2002, 330.

[2] Quoted, Susan B. Harper, *In the Shadow of the Mahatma: Bishop V.S. Azariah and the Travails of Christianity in British India*, Cambridge: William B. Eerdmans, 2000, 235.

along with his thousands of followers. He was considering the options for the new religion they should join.

Azariah had a personal interview with Ambedkar in 1936 'which deeply embarrassed and disturbed' him, and 'plunged him back into renewed efforts at ecumenism and reform within the church'. Ambedkar criticised the church for denominational disunity and for the persistence within it of caste prejudice.

> Azariah recalled later that Ambedkar asked him the question: 'If we become Christians can we be all united in one Church wherever we live? And will we be entirely free from all caste prejudice?' To which Azariah responded: 'I have never felt so ashamed in my life because I couldn't say YES to either question – I could only come away in disgrace. Azariah often recalled Ambedkar's criticism of Christianity when seeking support in his later years for the unification of churches in South India.[1]

This is one important example of approaching people outside the church and getting their opinion about it. Otherwise we talk among ourselves without coming to a decision for action. In India, the caste-denomination relationship manifested itself in different ways. There were cases when, at times of division within the congregation of a particular denomination, individuals and groups of a particular caste left and joined another congregation of the same caste but of a different denomination.

Azariah stated very politely, that unity was the ideal and disunity a weakness in the churches of Christendom. If, however, he had seen the West as the most challenging mission field in today's world he would have thundered with words such as 'sin' and 'scandal' for division and disunity. He would not have accepted the western Church as the trend-setter in our ecumenical journey, as exemplified in the formation of different evading councils. For Azariah and his colleagues church unity was aspired not for achieving strong economy and efficiency but in attaining credibility in mission and as the fulfilment of Jesus' prayer 'that they may be one'. He would not have allowed the pursuit of the ultimate goal of becoming one with the Father (or the Triune commune) but bypassing an organic unity in both spirit and form that would have concretely testified to the incarnation. In the ecumenical movement what has obviously been lacking is not thinking and writing and rewriting documents on faith and order, nor planning ecumenical programmes or activities, but the will to become one by faith, the faith which Jesus said can move mountains. In his WMC 1910 message he gave a call for the churches in the 'Christian Lands':

---
[1] Ibid., 313.

God is demanding of us all a new order of life, of a more arduous and self-sacrificing nature than the old.[1]

Whether this language is welcome in the ecclesial climate in the west is doubtful as people prefer soft and soothing messages.

From the first meeting on 1 May 1919 in Tranquebar until his premature death in 1945, Azariah was the stalwart in moving forward the negotiations for the formation of the CSI, overcoming hurdles and steering with grace and wisdom. Though he was not able to be present when the CSI was born, it is observed that he had the vision of it just like Moses had the vision of the Promised Land.

Bishop Whitehead

Henry Whitehead (1863-1947) was the brother of the philosopher Alfred North Whitehead and the father of the mathematician J.H.C. Whitehead. He was educated at Sherborne and Trinity College, Oxford. Ordained in 1879, his first post was as a preacher at St Nicholas, Abingdon, and he became an eminent Anglican priest in the last decade of the 19th century and the first quarter of the 20th. He migrated to India where he was Principal of Bishop's College, Calcutta from 1883 to 1899. On 6 July 1899 he was consecrated as the fifth Bishop of Madras, an office he held for 23 years where, as reported by the paper *Harvest Field*, 'Whitehead had come to play a leading role in the union movement and ... during his service in Madras he had swung over from a rigid Tractarian[2] view-point to large-hearted ecumenicity ... Above all it was a steady growth in the understanding of the other man's point of view, and it was caused by a practical approach to the opportunities which South India seemed to offer.' In 1903 he married Isabel Duncan. He was engaged in unity discussions well ahead of the Tranquebar meeting in 1919. Particularly as energised by the Mott Conference 1912, he shifted his emphasis from comity and cooperation of denominational

---

[1] *World Missionary Conference1910: The History and Records of the Conference together with Addresses Delivered at the Evening Meetings*, Edinburgh: Oliphant, Anderson & Perrier, 109.

[2] The word 'Tractarian' came from a series of *Tracts for the Times* (from 1833 to 1841) produced by a group of Oxford-based high churchmen who argued for incorporation of older traditions into theology and liturgy of the Anglican Church. They formed the Oxford Movement. 'In the Oxford Movement, the figure of the bishop emerged as an alternative sacred symbol to that of the sovereign ... urged the bishops, "Magnify your office"!...Only episcopally ordained clergy, incorporated within the apostolic succession, had the means of saving grace, efficacious sacraments, to dispense. Therefore, it was only within the Church of England that salvation could be assured to English people, vast numbers of whom were by now Nonconformist. This insistence became the keynote of the catholic revival in Anglicanism. The identity of Anglicanism was to be found in its episcopal orders within the historical succession.' Paul Avis, *The Anglican Understanding of the Church*: An Introduction, London: SPCK, 2000, 20; individual bishops' reaction and appropriation of the views of the Tractarians have been varied. Many have struggled to maintain the Protestant character of the CofE as well and in any case the so-called Anglo-Catholics have carried the influence of the Tractarians.

missions to a comprehensive church union scheme. His sermons and pamphlets were geared to drive this vision while encouraging cooperation wherever possible but without compromising on his churchmanship. A noted author on his adopted country, he died on 14 April 1947, five months before the inauguration of the CSI. He had been honoured with a Doctor of Divinity (DD).

Whitehead is undoubtedly the most prominent example of a rule which seems to emerge from the study of the South Indian union movements generally: 'that the situation in the mission field tends to have a broadening effect upon the individual missionary'. Whitehead's change towards a more evangelical conception was to a certain extent conditioned by his cooperation with Canon E. Sell, Secretary of the CMS. But the decisive factor which brought Whitehead over to an attitude of co-operation and interest in union was his recognition of the immense evangelical opportunities of South India.'[3] With experience in higher education, he came to doubt if Christian education had an impact on people's religious life and commitment. For Whitehead, the logical conclusion was co-operation and Christian unity, but not unity by denominationalism. He was against the medieval dictum that the ruler's religion is the people's religion, and the comity approach also may be the same. 'On the other hand, there was an element of truth in the comity approach in that it insisted on "the necessity for abstaining from irritating and uncharitable judgments on our Christian brothermen whose opinions differ from our own".' 'Unity, then, should be reached by prayer and charitable judgments and by looking boldly in the face the real causes and grounds of our divisions.'[4]

To a number of Free Church men Whitehead's passion and analysis was fascinating, and Whitehead found them to be more supportive for the evangelical thrust of the church unity than his Anglican colleagues in England. When Whitehead declared his attitude to be 'to lay hold of what is truly fundamental and then with regard to all else extend a hearty toleration for the utmost variety and freedom', the editor of *Harvest Field*, while appreciating this conciliatory spirit, remarked that he did not suppose that Whitehead would agree with (him) in his definition of fundamentals.'[5] The question, 'What are the Christian fundamentals?' evoked wider discussion. The Anglican position of Apostolic Succession and sacramental system was immediately proclaimed as belonging to the fundamentals, while the reasoned Free Church voice was to aim at federation and return to the formula: 'Unity is sometimes best exhibited amid diversity.' However, Whitehead's theological conviction that 'the Free Church theory that any body of Christians is at liberty to form itself into a Church' was particularly dangerous in India. 'It would lead to an emphasis on caste, separate churches for separate castes. Against this danger there was in his view only one safeguard: that

---

[3] Sundkler, 52.

[4] Ibid., 53.

[5] Ibid., 55.

of the historic episcopate. It was in the interest of the unity that Indian Christians should seriously consider the claims of the historic episcopate as a safeguard of unity and a safeguard against caste.'[1] Also, Whitehead tried to convince his bosses and colleagues in England that the church traditions, liturgies and governing structures could not be transplanted into the Indian soil.

He mentored Azariah (both at home and while on holiday in Kodaikanal) and supported his union efforts. When Azariah was consecrated as bishop in 1912 he was made simply an Assistant Bishop to the Bishop of Madras. Feeling the anomaly, Whitehead commissioned him to exercise direct episcopal authority and supervision in the Telugu area. This was just one week before the conference at Tranquebar 1919, and his enhanced position helped Azariah to organise and engage in negotiations with episcopal authority.

Whitehead was not at the Tranquebar Conference. But he heard about the outcome of hope for forming an independent Indian church, and that enhanced his optimism. He clarified that the episcopacy proposed for the new church would not accept any particular theory. Also, there should be no uniformity nor doctrinal rigidity, but accepting a variety of gifts coming from the Holy Spirit in toleration within the body of Christ. While there were conflicts of persuasion, Whitehead stated his belief 'that the only true road to unity lies in a general recognition of all that is good and true in other churches as well as loyalty to one's own heritage'. It was in this spirit of 'general recognition' that the Madras Diocesan Conference passed its resolution in support of the Tranquebar proposals, based on the Lambeth Quadrilateral.[2] The root for him was that 'Catholicity involves comprehension' and its ever-widening scope. Thus, over the decades Whitehead moved from Tractarianism to a moderate Evangelicalism under the urge to unite the Church in India, and such moves in different directions were many in the current experience of working together for the sake of the gospel.

E.J. Palmer

Edwin James Palmer (1869-1954) served the diocese of Bombay (now Mumbai) as bishop for twenty years. He came from a Tractarian background. He was a nephew of the first Lord Selbourne and thus 'had the type of upbringing typical of eminent Anglican divines of his generation'. However, his father, the Archdeacon of Oxford, was committed to church unity, and probably he influenced his son. He preached a sermon in 1872, 'What can we do for Unity?' For Palmer 'Scholarships at Winchester and Oxford were followed by a "Double First" in Greats and a Fellowship at Balliol, then at the height of its reputation.' He took orders and was Examining Chaplain to various bishops. In 1909 without previous missionary experience, he was appointed Bishop of Bombay where he laboured energetically and successfully for twenty years. He then came home and acted as Assistant

---

[1] Ibid., 55f.

[2] Ibid., 114f.

Bishop of Gloucester, assistant to the redoubtable A.C. Headlam, arguably the ablest Anglican ecumenist bishop and scholar of his era. Palmer's advice was sought by Archbishops of Canterbury and York, and he was used extensively in the negotiations of 1932-4 between the Free Churches and the Church of England. He continued to write on ecumenical themes well into his old age.'[1] He had the rare combination of faithfulness to the Anglo-Catholic heritage and appreciation for the commitment and achievements of the Free Churches. Even in his early life he appreciated the virtues of the Protestants in the Free Church traditions. As early as 1913 he defended them against the Anglo-Catholic accusation that they made no distinction between 'evangelical' and 'catholic'. Next year he wrote a letter to the Anglo-Catholic bishop Charles Gore in connection with the 'Kikuyu Affair' in Kenya where Anglican bishops had given Communion to Free Church missionaries that became controversial and viral. He asserted that depriving the Free Church members of the Holy Communion was against the eucharistic hospitality of Jesus which he extended to sinners, prostitutes and so on.

The mission field experience in India opened Palmer 'to a key reality to which he testified in 1933, in a riposte to traditionalist Anglo-Catholic critics of his ecumenical stance'. He wrote with a spirit of mission in a new key:

> The acid test of a church's life is whether it converts pagans at home or abroad. The non-episcopal churches have (to our knowledge) done as much of this work as the episcopal. Is it credible that they would have been enabled by God to do this if He has regarded their communion services as acts of rebellion, imposter, or self-deception or empty forms?[2]

This realisation of a great truth led him to recognise the equal validity of non-episcopal denominations and their ministries, when that was a controversial issue in the negotiations for the CSI. Palmer was well ahead of his time in understanding church and its ministry. Whether established church or free churches, what mattered for him was fruits.

Palmer was fearless in examining Scripture and Tradition with a view to finding ways around ecumenical problems. His approaches and activities showed a combination of theological boldness and personal humility. For him the biblical and theological facts of the fruitful life and mission of the Free Churches are too irresistible to invalidate.

> A great deal of the advance in sacred knowledge, a great deal of the quickening of social conscience and the victories of Christian morality, and a great deal of the conversion of the heathen are due to the activities of the groups of Christians who are not within the

---

[1] 'Palmer of Bombay: A Forgotten Pioneer?' Unpublished paper by an unknown author.

[2] *Derby Commission Reports*, 16 (originally in his letter to the *Times*?).

historic church or churches. We have been outstripped in the fruits of righteousness by many of them.[1]

As a true Anglican he was opposed to the extremes of the rigidity of Roman Catholics, and the other extreme of Protestant liberals who had no respect for the traditions like the creeds. True Anglicanism for him stood in between these extremes as firm yet flexible. 'Clearly Palmer believed that balanced and comprehensive Christian teaching and practice could only be restored *koinonia* of the entire church; hence his call for a vision of the Great Church which would plead all Christians to realise the essential incompleteness of their present denominations and the need to strive for their transcendence and completion in a great whole.'[2] He advised that we should not cling to views and customs that come from the exaggerations of reaction. In 1933 Palmer wrote to the veteran Methodist scholar, Lofthouse:

> If we want the reunion of Christendom, we must expect the reconciliation of opinion and the attachment of agreement to take place in our children and grandchildren's time, and to take place largely because, unlike us, they will be brought up, they will live and they will work in one body.[3]

On his return to England, Palmer found the CSI union scheme 'under frequent attack, particularly from Anglo-Catholics' who regarded it as a betrayal of catholic principles. Whatever risk involved, he justified it by missionary imperative. However, he could not initiate anything similar in England due to the 'militant Anglo-Catholic opinion' and the failure of the Free Churches, particularly the Methodists, to reconcile Palmer's insights with their earlier leaders' aspirations. For him any unalterable positions and structures are detrimental to missionary exigencies. On the whole, Palmer was a pioneering ecumenist with a passion for mission in the Anglican Communion.

A.M. Hollis

Arthur Michael Hollis (1899-1986), born of a highly placed Priest Vicar of Wells Cathedral in England and his reputed wife, and grown up in the cathedral precinct in Wells and parish in Leeds, was sent to a non-denominational Public Day School and proved to be an outstanding student. He was engaged in the literary and debating society and sports and gained leadership roles. After his national service and a curacy in Huddersfield, Hollis was invited by Hertford College Oxford to be the Chaplain and tutor in church history. In 1926 he was elected a Fellow of the College and Lecturer in Theology. 'We see the emphasis he put on the

---

[1] 'Palmer of Bombay', 4.

[2] Ibid.

[3] Ibid., 6.

intellectual foundations of Christianity. He had little use for a false piety which was largely emotional, but encouraged students to face honestly the problems and the difficulties of the faith. Also, he was already showing the practical side of his nature, the intention of getting things altered if it was possible and beneficial.'[1] In any case, the prestigious position was replaced by a commitment to a mission field in the dry and hot Anglican Thirunelveli area in South India.

As an SPG missionary, Hollis started teaching (1931) in a theological seminary at a place Christianised as Nazareth. Combined with pastoral work, his teaching theology inspired many of his students in ministerial training. His catholic outlook was seen as a spontaneous expression of his spiritual maturity. This rare approach helped him naturally to contribute to the CSI union negotiations which had already completed more than ten years. The negotiations were struck by the refusal of Anglican participants to accept inter-communion and equal validity of all ministries. The SPG was concerned about the position of those who did not believe in the Anglican view of divine ministry and holy sacraments. Taking exception to an article in *Church Times* in 1932 summer, Hollis wrote to the SPG. Noting the purpose of this article was to 'oppose Church Union tooth and nail', he gave his own position without dissembling:

> I don't know how you feel about the last cause of all this bother. I cannot agree with the CHURCH TIMES attitude. We are committed by the Union Scheme, believing that the sacraments of the other united bodies are in a true sense sacraments really bringing man into union with our Lord.[2]

For the SPG, if a non-Anglican was invited to celebrate communion in an Anglican church it was 'a very great blow to Catholic Order.' However, intercommunion did take place in meetings of negotiations for union, and this was a bitter pill to swallow for those belonging to the Anglo-Catholic wing.

Hollis was an inspiring person in a non-assuming way. Later, when he was the bishop elect in Madras, his future successor wrote some of his reminiscences in the *Madras Guardian*:

> In August 1933 I had the privilege of taking part in the S.C.M. Regional Conference in Tranquebar, when Mr. Hollis, with the Revd. R.S. Manuel, was the chief speaker. During the whole Conference he lived with the students, eating Indian foods and dressing simply in *veshti* and *jibba*. He seemed particularly anxious that the Indians present, several friends and students, should take leading parts, and he always kept himself in the background as far as possible. His discourses

---

[1] Constance M. Millington, *Led by the Spirit: A Biography of Bishop Arthur Michael Hollis*, Bangalore: Asian Trading Corporation, 1996, 9.

[2] Quoted, Ibid., 17.

were delivered quietly, were simple, practical and straight forward, obviously the result of much study and thought. His humility in view of his profound learning, and his sincere and unaffected piety were lessons to all who attended the Conference.[1]

In 1934 Hollis announced his engagement to Cordelia Burn, the daughter of the Dean of Salisbury Cathedral, a nurse who worked in the World War I, who after further training went to Ramnad as a SPG missionary in 1925. They met in Kodaikanal, the hill resort for summer for missionaries. They married in 1935, and in the next year they went on furlough and were expected to return to work in South India within a year. However, as Cordelia expected a child, Michael asked for extension until June 1937. Sadly, a male baby was born prematurely and for the sake of his wife's health, on the advice of the doctors, he resigned from SPG. Associates in the seminary he taught including the Bishop of Thirunelveli wrote how gravely was he missed. However, the possibility of the formation of the CSI was in his mind and he pondered over his ministry in Thirunelveli as an open Anglo-Catholic. He took up a position in the CofE as the Rector of Charlton near Cheltenham in Gloucestershire, a beautiful area. But as WWII broke out he was called up to join the forces (he had been in the Officers Training Corps at his school) as the Army Chaplain with the rank of Captain.

However, in 1941 Michael was elected as Bishop of Madras, and as Cordelia was found to be fit for travel, the couple went to the capital of the most important Province of the empire. They were determined to lead a simple life as fitting the scale of the salary of a missionary society, vastly different from the government scale. With reference to sudden shifts in his life and the new era in the formation of the CSI, he expressed succinctly his conviction of divine guidance in unprecedented ways: 'Loyalty to our past can be disloyalty to God's will now.'[2] When Hollis was consecrated as bishop in St. George's Cathedral on 27 September 1942, apart from managing a vast diocese, he had to face the challenges of WWII on the one hand, and the crucial phase of the national movement for independence with the Quit India movement gaining momentum, on the other. He did not cover himself in pious garments but called people to reflect on the issues and share opinions. Through an appeal published in the *Madras Diocesan Magazine* April 1943 he invited contributions with the following words:

> We must make our decisions on Christian grounds, and never consciously or unconsciously allow interests of State or Empire to usurp the place of God. There cannot finally be two right answers, but the possibility of our being led by the Spirit into a fuller truth depends on our unswerving determination to put God first, whatever it may

---

[1] Quoted, Ibid., 51.

[2] Quoted, Ibid., 42.

cost … and also we must determine to understand why we differ, our
duty to 'make prayers and supplications for all men' is unimpaired
even by the greatest war.[1]

Though shy and humble, Hollis had a sharp intellect and profound
spirituality, and his analytical mind facilitated honest thinking and decision
making. He would not allow himself to be addressed as 'Lord' nor his name to
be included in any memorial inscriptions. He shocked his flock in Madras by
'carrying his own bag to the Cathedral or pedalling round the city on a push-bike'
and it took time for them to appreciate his simplicity and friendliness.

As a church historian, theologian and exemplary leader, Hollis's contribution
to the union movement in South India was very significant. For him the turning
point of union was 'in the whole history of the Christian Church not less
momentous in its final effects than Luther's challenge to the medieval system when
he nailed his 95 theses on the church door at Wittenburg. Then the separations
began. Can we begin the re-uniting?'[2] As Anglicans were the majority, their voting
was decisive. But Hollis was keen to get the support of people, not simply leaders.
Therefore, he spoke and wrote in order to convince people. Without rushing,
he postponed the Diocesan Council on the (CSI) Scheme from July 1943 to
September 1944. The October 1943 *Diocesan Magazine* carried the following
message from him.

> Re-union is not likely to come by way of intellectual victory on one
> side and the surrender of the vanquished. If we are absolutely certain
> that we are right and other people wrong, then we have to be loyal to
> truth and leave the consequences to God, whether the body to which
> we belong is large or small is irrelevant. The Scheme on which we have
> to decide is an attempt to find a way of healing the divisions among
> Christians without requiring from anyone what amounts to a denial
> of his previous Christian life and ministry.[3]

Hollis observed that 'existing communal distinctions have succeeded in
perpetuating themselves in the comparative decency of religious principles', 'the
past is in our blood' and 'deep lying irrationalities.' For him the CSI would be a
minimum expression of union, and there may be unanswered questions to explore
further. He called on Anglicans to realise not only the privileged position of the
CofE (Church of England) but also, 'the way psychological and doctrinal matters
are intertwined'. He pointed out that there had never been an 'authoritative
doctrine of the Church and Ministry' as there were anomalies and irregularities
following every schism. He called the Anglican Church which claimed to be

---

[1] Quoted, Ibid., 56.

[2] Quoted, Ibid., 65.

[3] Quoted, Ibid., 66.

both Catholic and Reformed, to go forward in the 'attempt to find God's way to overcome the breaches between His followers here in South India'. Corporate re-union was the work of God, and human responsibility is to pray, hope and act.

The Madras diocesan council in September 1944 was very crucial as it had to decide on the Union Scheme one way or other. Hollis' speech was momentous. After the adoption of the Scheme, a general discussion took place and each speaker was given five minutes. 'They all favoured Union, – no one was bold enough to oppose the principles, but it was to be a union on the basis of an extension of the Anglican Church.' 'Strongly felt opinions were expressed without bitterness and there was an entire absence of pettiness. Many speakers took part in the debate – Indian, European, Anglo-Indian, men and women.'[1] After the presiding bishop's masterly summing up and observance of silence, the scheme was put to vote and was passed with an overwhelming majority. A note in the following *Magazine* recorded:

> ... the admiration which our Bishop received and deserved for his leadership. He was very conscious of the difficulty of his task, but he need not have been anxious. He was firm and patient as a chairman should; his sanity and practical wisdom in dealing with questions raised, his fairness and his humour; above all his ability and sincerity with which the spiritual atmosphere needed for such an occasion was secured, all illustrate his success.[2]

Nevertheless, a complaint reached Lambeth about the way Hollis conducted the election with a long speech in favour of union and summation before the voting, again by show of hands not by ballot paper that would have encouraged the nervous persons to vote against. However, the bishop was positive about the proceedings and even excited about the saving of the union scheme as it had appeared to be dead for two years.

There were still critics around about the CSI union. Hollis' final role was to persuade members theologically and pastorally to ensure the logical conclusion. Hollis, relatively a late entrant in the negotiations, was a persuasive influence in the General Council of the CIBC (Church in India, Burma and Ceylon) in 1945 and took the place of Azariah (who was no more) to be the convener of the Anglican delegation to the committee meetings. J.S.M. Hooper, a Methodist, who was the secretary of the Continuation Committee of the union scheme, commenting on the CIBC meeting and the role of Hollis in a letter mentioned, 'A heavy burden fell on Madras who had to present the Scheme at the last moment, and his handling of the business was said to be masterly. He is a great gift from God

to the Church in India at this time.'[1] Even the last hurdle of the interpretation of
the Pledge (we will come back to it later) in the General Council of CIBC held in
Madras in January 1947 and his role in overcoming it was decisive. Those present
at the Council attributed the success of the motion to 'the obvious sincerity and
integrity of Hollis'. Prominent figures such as Newbigin appreciated his clarity
of mind and courage to remove the last blockade. When some leaders felt the
Anglican element was withdrawn, Hollis and his close associates insisted that the
best of the traditions would live and thrive.

At the same time, 'he commented on the fact that once the united Church
came into being they would cease to be members of the Anglican Communion'.
Yet he said that 'We realize what we are seemingly to lose. We believe that we
shall gain more and pray that through the sacrifice, God will be enabled to bless
the Church not only in South India but throughout the world ... There remain
many problems to be solved and questions to be answered. Only God can solve
them and only God can answer them. May the prayer of all of us be, "Not my
will but Thine be done".' In conversation with his friends Hollis never mentioned
how crucial was his contribution to the CSI union. If pressed hard, he used the
quotation, 'It is surprising how much good can be accomplished if a person does
not mind who receives the praise for it.'[2]

Two days after the inauguration of the CSI (27 Sept., 1947) Hollis was
installed as Bishop *in* Madras diocese. His consecration sermon in Tamil was
moving. In his other addresses to the clergy and diocesan council he defended the
union, realised the reduced boundaries of the diocese and expressed the privilege
of working with colleagues of the non-Anglican traditions. He called people to
rejoice in the new reality of CSI and grow in the sense of organic unity. It was not
surprising that he was elected to be the first Moderator of the new church and
continued for three terms, i.e. six years. Those who came in contact with him were
so impressed by the way he combined genuine prayer, intellectual acumen and
sensible action. George K. Bell, the Bishop of Chichester, a supporter of the CSI
union and chairman of the Joint Committee of the Convocations of Canterbury
and York to discuss CSI matters, visited in 1949 and communicated his positive
impressions about the CSI and its first Moderator with the Metropolitan and
others. For example, he wrote, 'It may truthfully be said that in this short time
substantial progress has been made in the unity and stability of the leaders of the
Church as well as the mutual trust of those comprising the constituent groups ...
I was impressed with the humility of the leaders of the Church. No-one who has
been in touch with the leaders can fail to be conscious of the firm and abiding
vision of unity by which they are possessed ... It was clear that episcopacy is

[1] Quoted Ibid., 76.
[2] Quoted, Ibid., 84f.

deeply valued, that the bishop is looked up to as a Father in God.'[1] In response to a communication, Hollis wrote to the Bells:

> People who come to visit us catch something of this thrill and sense of expectancy which we feel here, it is almost impossible to convey it in writing. It is going to mean everything to us that you have seen it for yourselves.[2]

Whether these testimonies were taken seriously in England was a different matter. We will later give anecdotes of how he was humiliated in Anglican circles in England. Further, to set an example, Hollis resigned not only his Moderator role in 1954 but also his position as Bishop in Madras in 1955. He joined the United Theological College to teach church history.

Hollis was pained that in spite of the positive waves moving around the world about CSI, his home church was not able to recognise that God had done a new thing in the history of Christianity. Humility and clarity of thought were his highest points. His reflection on patronising missionaries and power-mongering Indian Christians led him to do in-depth research. It developed into a thesis which he sent to the Senate of Serampore College (University) for a doctoral award. But because of engaging in creative and didactic writings for many decades he was not able to present the material in academic fashion (i.e. with elaborate references), and therefore the thesis was not accepted. However, a studied merit of what he wrote qualified it to be published by the Oxford University Press entitled *Paternalism in the Church* (1962).

Michael Hollis left India in 1960. A written farewell note by R.D. Paul, a most remarkable civil officer, a lay Christian leader and General Secretary of the CSI Synod, mentioned:

> Such a combination of scholarship and humility, of profession and practice, sincerity and courage of conviction, of clear thinking and administrative ability as was found in Bishop Hollis is rare anywhere and much more so in the Indian Church at the present time.[3]

The author adds Hollis's stress on the role of the laity, unity from experience as brothers and sisters. The Hollises had a round the world tour, and the stay in the USA was used by two theological faculties for teaching for a term each (Vanderbilt, Nashville and Union, New York) in 1961. When they returned to England in the same year there was expectation in the minds of those who knew him that he would be given a significant post, bishop or archbishop, so

---

[1] Quoted, Ibid., 126f.

[2] Quoted, Ibid., 126.

[3] R.D. Paul, 'Bishop Michael Hollis – The Builder of the CSI', *South India Churchman*, May 1960, 5f.

that his South Indian experience and all the reflection therewith could be shared fruitfully. By coincidence, the Anglican-Methodist unity talk was going on, which later narrowly failed by the hardened position of the Anglicans. Actually, there were cases of returned missionaries made bishops in the CofE and obviously the disqualification of Michael was his major role in the CSI union and celebrating communion with members of non-Anglican churches. Nevertheless, in spite of his church's indifference and negligence, as he was determined to serve his church in such a hostile atmosphere, he followed its rules and discipline. After a period of searching, he met the bishop in Sheffield, who appointed him vicar of the parish of Todwick, a mining town on the outskirts of Sheffield. However, his quality of graciousness never diminished. He was called to assist the bishop, particularly for administering confirmations and shared the CSI experience wherever possible. He and Cordelia were regular to CSI Day gatherings in London. Perhaps during this time his book, *The Significance of South India* (1966), was written. After retirement the Hollises moved to care homes in Surrey. Cordelia was ill and towards the end of few years Michael had a difficult time to look after his wife though he did it with his characteristic grace. She died in 1984, and Michael in 1986. Until the end the most refreshing memory and sweet story on his lips was the formation of CSI.

Lesslie Newbigin, who later became bishop in the diocese of Madras observed:

> It was Bishop Hollis who had the courage to cast the decisive casting vote which settled the matter. He earned thereby the deep and lasting displeasure of many and he had to live with this for the rest of his life. But he made possible the Church of South India.

> The same qualities of clarity and courage ensured that he played a decisive part in the early years of the united Church. He did, I think, more than anyone else to create an atmosphere of mutual trust without even the best church constitution cannot work. He understood the feelings of those who came into the united church from other traditions and, more than any other single individual, he made sure that they were never ignored or over-ridden. He had a transparent honesty which, sad to say, is not always the most obvious character of those of us who have to engage in protracted and difficult negotiations on ecclesiastical matters.[1]

The CSI established the Bishop Hollis Memorial Lectures. In the first lecture in 1990, given by Russel Chandran who had been the first Indian young Principal of UTC when Hollis was on the faculty. He was introduced by the newly elected bishop in the diocese of Madras, who claimed that 'Hollis had been a martyr for

---

[1] 'Foreword', Ibid., vii.

the cause of Church Union.'[1] Though exaggerated, it shows the rejection and harassment that Hollis suffered from his own church on the one hand, and the affection and respect he enjoyed from thousands of the CSI members. What is the key for understanding such a great person? The title of his biography has the answer, i.e. *Led by the Spirit.*

J.S.M. Hooper

John Stirling Morley Hooper (1882-1974), was the son of a Methodist Minister and his devout wife, and was born in Stirling, Scotland. After education at the Methodist Kingwood School near Bristol, and graduating from Corpus Christi College, Oxford, achieving both B.A. and M.A. first class honours in Modern History, Hooper went to India in 1905 and stayed in Madras (now Chennai) serving as a minister of the Wesleyan Methodist Church. He married Sarah Rosalind Cooling in 1910, and they had a daughter, Jean. While the couple were serving at the Methodist Girls' Boarding School at Ikkadu, a rural centre west of Madras, Jean died at the age of two in 1924; the parents built a chapel in memory of their daughter. Then Hooper served as Headmaster of the Wesley Higher Secondary School, Madras. His illustrious roles in education qualified him to become the Principal of the Wesley College, 1926-1932.

In 1932 Hooper became the first Secretary of the British and Foreign Bible Society for India, Burma and Ceylon and continued until 1944. In recognition of his remarkable work on the Bible and its translations, the Kaisar-i-Hind gold medal[2] was awarded to him by King George VI in 1938. He became the first General Secretary when the independent Bible Society of India was formed on 1 November 1944, and he held the position until 1947. Most remarkable was Hooper's creative role and efficient leadership in negotiations for the formation of the Church of South India. First, he was interested in only cooperation with other denominations, but 'being loyal to Methodism and suspicious of the Anglicans', he largely kept aloof from contacts with this church, although, in 1906, he preached in St. George's Cathedral on the occasion of a united communion service. In 1928 he was appointed by the Wesleyan Provincial Synod to the JC (Joint Committee) of Negotiation in order to 'guard against sacerdotalism'. For him the CSI Scheme was impossible to achieve. The person who 'converted' Hooper was Bishop E.J. Palmer. For a day and half Hooper presented his objections to the Scheme, and Palmer was not ruffled. More than twenty years later, Hooper exclaimed about 'the patience the old man showed with me!'.

---

[1] Ibid., xiii.

[2] The Kaisar-i-Hind Medal for Public Service in India was a medal awarded by the British monarch between 1900 (when it was established by Queen Victoria) and 1947 (India's Independence), particularly to distinguished service in the advancement of the interests of the British Raj. There were 3 medals: gold, silver and bronze. (ref. Wikipedia as on 22 Aug. 2018).

Hooper was ingenious to remove ignorance and suspicion about persons of other denominations, and when he arranged hospitality, along with Bishop Waller, for the Joint Committee in Madras (1929), 'Everyone was accommodated in the home of someone belonging to a church other than his own: the Anglicans coming to Madras for the meeting were the guests in Methodist or Congregationalist or Presbyterian homes, and *vice versa*. The preachers in the Sunday services were appointed according to the same plan.' He created an atmosphere in the meetings where prayer could be surrounded by humour. He published interesting editorials in *Church Union News and Views* which were of great value for the understanding of the historic development of the union negotiations (1934-1937). With reference to the growth of the CSI scheme with additions, Hooper observed an interesting fact: 'Once something had found its way into the Scheme it proved very difficult to remove it or to alter it without raising disproportionate suspicions on the right wing or the left.' When Anglicans proposed a supplemental ordination for the non-episcopally ordained ministers a controversy arose. A sub-committee was formed of which Hooper, Azariah, Newbigin and Paul Ramaseshan were members. Of course, his position was equal validity of all ministries, and he felt that the attitude of many Anglican bishops was 'likely to kill the South India Scheme'. He and his Methodist colleague C.H. Monahan were greatly concerned when Archbishop William Temple proposed dual ministry which was defended by V.S. Azariah. However, as the Secretary of the Negotiation Committee and friend of Michael Hollis, Hooper tackled the challenge with friendliness and firmness. Simultaneously, he had to gently influence the Methodist Synods. Finally, he was made the Secretary of the Central Body of twelve for the selection of the bishops and there was no complaint about the fairness and wisdom of the selection.

It was not without good reason that Hooper was invited to preach at the inaugural service.

Hooper's responsibility was not over with the inauguration of the CSI; the Administrative Union was yet to be inaugurated. He continued to be the convener of the Coordination Committee until the meeting of the first Synod in March 1948. It was his responsibility to organise this Synod. He was involved in important tasks including the election of the first Moderator; he himself was made the Treasurer of the Synod; he encouraged the Synod on missionary outreach and ecumenical relations. In a desperate situation he was asked to stay on for two years in order to establish the Church of South India Trust Association to which all the properties were attached (except those of ex-Anglicans in some areas).

Hooper returned to England in 1950 and settled in Stratford, the birthplace of Shakespeare, where his father (John H. Hooper) had been a Methodist Minister, 1912-1916. He enjoyed being a preacher, class leader and tutor for local preachers. Though the local church was not able to appreciate his contribution to the formation of the CSI, those who were close to him expressed genuine appreciation for his mature leadership. For example, Michael Hollis, in his book

The Significance of South India makes the following dedicatory note: 'In grateful affection to J.S.M. Hooper to whom both I personally and the whole Church of South India owe more than can be measured or expressed.' Hooper was awarded 'Doctor of Divinity' by the Senate of Serampore College (University) in 1957.

Sarah Hooper died in 1955, and John in his last years became increasingly blind and infirm. He died on 2 May 1974. The *Stratford Upon Avon Herald* (10 May 1974) published a glowing obituary; so also, did the Methodist Church. Significantly, in his scribbling for his own funeral he requested 'Donations in lieu of flowers to the Church of South India Thanksgiving Fund'.

Hooper wrote many booklets and articles on various subjects. He wrote on the Gospels and approaches to them. His mastery of the Tamil language and interest in the study of 'Alvars' (those who perished, i.e. in the love of the Lord Vishnu, the poet-saints of the Vaishnava Hinduism), resulted in the translation with notes and publication of *Hymns of the Alvars* (1929). His addresses to the CSI bishops in a quiet day conference in December 1947 were published, on request, as *The Temptation* (1948). The main focus was the temptation of power. Booklets on the Bible and its translations were many. The last booklet was *The Story of Methodism in Stratford-upon-Avon* (1963), marking his filial piety to Stratford. To mark the 70th anniversary of the CSI there were two ecumenical services (Broadway, August 13 and Stratford, September 24,) in the Circuit of Stratford & Evesham in which tributes were paid to Hooper. Also, arrangements were made for an inscription about him in the Book of Remembrance kept in the Chapel of the Oakley Wood Crematorium. The particular page will be open on 27 September each year!

In the historical notes of the CSI, J.S.M. Hooper was rightly called the 'architect of the new Church'. Until his end he was passionate about the formation of the CSI. 'On February 12, 1953, the CSI Council in Great Britain was formed with Hooper as Chairman to represent and interpret the CSI in the UK and to further its intents.' Later, the formation of the 'Friends of the Church in India' was to function with the same aim.

C.H. Monahan

Charles Henry Monahan (1869-1951) has been regarded as a great gift of Irish Methodism to the World Church, particularly to the Church in South India. A son of the manse (his father was a Methodist minister), he was born at Ballyshannon, Donegal and studied at Kingswood School, where he was the captain of games and an outstanding student. After a brilliant career at Trinity College, Dublin, where he was awarded the gold medal in the B.A. Classical Honours Examination, he continued his training for his life work at Richmond College, and proceeded to India in 1893. He obtained scholarship to Trinity, Cambridge and took Law Tripos (MA) and was designated for the African Administrative Service and awaited his call to the Bar at Gray's Inn. Instead, he was accepted as candidate for the English MA and went to Handsworth College, 1928 which prepared him to be a missionary in South India. He was back and forth between India and England. Many were the activities of this great missionary, yet his simple evangelistic ministry to humble village congregations must rank in many respects first and foremost among them all. He was never happier than when communicating the Christian message to the village folk he loved. Yet he was equally at home among the students and rendered distinguished service in Chennai (Madras) both at Wesley College and in the Guindy Bible School, which he founded and of which he was the first Principal, training evangelists and catechists for the Methodist stations. Throughout the whole of South India and beyond, Monahan exercised an influence which was to be felt for many generations. Pre-eminently it was his contribution to Methodism that is remembered with particular thankfulness. Such offices as Chairman of the Madras District for nearly a quarter of a century, twice called to the Chair of the Provincial Synod, and elected by Conference to the Legal Hundred, are in themselves testimonies to his place within the ranks of the ministry he practised so faithfully. He was a much-respected member of the NCCI (National Christian Council of India), and his outstanding work was recognized by the conferring upon him of the Kaisar-i-Hind Gold Medal. After retiring in 1940, he devoted seven further strenuous years in India to completing the revision of the Tamil Bible. The whole Bible came out in May 1949, and the second edition was published in 1954. It was seen as a great improvement on the previous version, nearly 200 years old. A fortnight before his death he received a beautifully bound edition of this Bible from Madras. It seemed a fitting climax to a great life's work. He died in Surrey.

Fully convinced by the validity of church union in South India for spiritual maturity and effective mission, Monahan missed no opportunity to defend the union scheme both in India and in England. During the hectic period of controversies he regularly visited England and lobbied for the union of CSI in and around the Methodist Conferences. At a meeting of the General Committee of the Methodist Missionary Society, Monahan, defending the Methodist entry into the church union movement, observed that 'there are Indians who were once, as Hindus, united in caste, but now, as Christians, are divided in Christ. To remedy this state of things is a solemn duty, and no effort must be spared to secure that in the future there shall be "one fold and one shepherd"'.

Monahan was made the chairman of the JC from 1938 and, having three of his brothers as Anglican priests including one as the Bishop of Monmouth, he would allow the only personal reference in *Who's Who* as 'Special interest: South Indian Church Union'! Not in least he was in the planning, growth and consummation of the CSI. He was one of the happiest missionaries and ministers to experience the first organic union in the history of Christianity.

Lesslie Newbigin

James Edward Lesslie Newbigin (1909-1998) was born in Newcastle upon Tyne, a city on the England-Scotland border. He was educated at Leighton Park, a Quaker Independent Boarding school in Reading, Berkshire. He went to Queen's College, Cambridge in 1928, during which time he became a committed Christian. Having graduated, he moved to Glasgow to work with the SCM (Student Christian Movement) in 1931. He returned to Cambridge in 1933 to train for the ministry at Westminster College, and in July 1936 he was ordained by the Presbytery of Edinburgh to work as a Church of Scotland missionary at the Madras Mission. A month later he married Helen Henderson, and in September 1936 they both set off for India where they had one son and three daughters. His ministry in the rural areas around Chennai was both challenging and rewarding and equipped him to become a great church leader and mission thinker.

Newbigin was in the thick of the negotiations during the last years before union. In 1942 he was elected convener of the union committee of the Madras Council of the SIUC (South India United Church) and in 1943, of the union committee of the SIUC as a whole. His skill was seen to be 'eminent'. He promoted the debate through the publication of a sixty-page booklet in which five leading participants could develop their arguments for or against the Scheme. His own contribution, entitled 'The Church and the Gospel', contained the results of a good deal of personal 'theological wrestling', which he later described having serious difficulties with.

When Newbigin was on furlough in 1946, the negotiations for the CSI Union were going through a crucial and critical stage. Of his many books *A South India Diary* and *Unfinished Agenda* have important bits of information on the negotiations and inauguration of the CSI. For example, he notes how he defended the CSI scheme against militant opposition from the Church of England. He visited a bookshop in London which stocked 'Catholic' publications and walked away with armful of books and pamphlets.

I was staggered by the violence of their tone and by the misinterpretations of what was happening in South India. Most of them were published by a body called The Council for Defence of Church Principles', in which a leading role was played by my old friend and colleague on the SCM staff, Michael Bruce. From August 1946 until my departure I was involved in almost continuous correspondence and discussion with him. He combined many passionate affirmations of his total dedication to the cause of unity and his love and regard for all of us involved in the scheme, with repeated warnings that if the scheme were accepted by the Church of England disruption and prolonged litigation would follow. Never have dire threats been voiced in accents of such profound and affectionate regret![1]

Advised by Bruce, Newbigin attended the residential meetings at the home of Cowley Fathers,[2] Oxford, with Anglican and non-Anglican representatives. There were vigorous moments of dashing but without losing personal cordiality. Subsequently, Newbigin wrote a theological defence of the union entitled *The Reunion of the Church*. Even before he returned, he was glad about the 'Pledge' proposed by Hollis and accepted by the Joint Committee that led to the voting. Newbigin appreciated Hollis as one among the bishops 'with the clarity of mind to know that the time for decision had come. It was his courage that removed the last block on the road to unity.'

As the youngest, Newbigin was made the note-taker in the pre-inauguration session of bishops-designates. Interestingly, there was the topic of titles such as Archdeacon and Canon which he already scribbled, but as it was decided as 'abolished', with probable amusement he noted the same! He watched the inaugural service with great excitement. When the *Te Deum* (church's ancient song of praise) was sung the near 4,000 strong congregation appeared to burst into liberation and joy. He notes that he could not withhold his tears of joy.

When the CSI was inaugurated in 1947 Newbigin was the youngest of the first batch of bishops, and he was appointed in the Madurai-Ramnad diocese. While Madurai was the popular temple town of South India, its outskirts and Ramnad region were full of remote, dry and poor areas. He already knew the ongoing in-fighting in that diocesan area and it reflected in a major section of people demanding the appointment of someone from them. Finally, what they needed was an efficient administrative boss, and Newbigin clarified that according to the new CSI Constitution a bishop is a pastor, evangelist, teacher and leader of worship. His friends prayed for his courage. However, he got his name inscribed in the memory of the people of that diocese for his humility, efficiency and evangelistic zeal.

Newbigin's engagement with the ecumenical movement and particularly in the mission thinking brought him in 1959 the prestigious post of the General Secretary of the IMC (International Missionary Council). It is significant that IMC merged with the WCC (World Council of Churches) in the third General Assembly of the WCC held in New Delhi, 1961. Also, he was invited to be the

---

[1] *Unfinished Agenda*, 86.

[2] The Society of St John the Evangelist (SSJE) is an Anglican religious order for men. The members live under a rule of life and, at profession, make monastic vows of poverty, celibacy and obedience. SSJE was founded in 1866 at Cowley, Oxford, England, by Richard Meux Benson, a priest in the Church of England, and Charles Chapman Grafton. Known colloquially as the Cowley Fathers, the society was the first stable religious community of men to be established in the Anglican Communion since the English Reformation. For many years the society had houses in England, Scotland, India, South Africa, Japan, and Canada. Ref. Wikipedia as on 8 August 2019.

Associate General Secretary of the WCC. He remained in Geneva until 1965 influencing ecumenical discussions on mission through his speeches and writings. The influencing continued even after he returned to India as Bishop in Madras Diocese, where he stayed until he retired in 1974. In Chennai, apart from all his exemplary acts of leadership, participated in the Tamil Nadu government's programme of slum clearance. Also, he was instrumental in including on Marina beach the statues of three missionaries who had made a significant contribution to the development of the Tamil language. His own proficiency in Tamil amazed Tamil scholars. He promoted the exclusive theological views of his ecumenical colleagues Karl Barth and Hendrik Kraemer, the uncompromising appeal of the Christian message without drifting to conservative-fundamentalist trends.

Newbigin and his wife Helen returned to the UK in 1974, travelling overland using public transport, carrying two suitcases and a rucksack! They settled in Birmingham, where Newbigin was invited to be a Lecturer in Mission at the famous Selly Oak Colleges for five years. Of the British denominations linked with the Church of South India, he chose to join the URC (United Reformed Church), a union of Presbyterian and Congregational Churches (of England Wales) since 1972. 'In retirement he took on the pastorate of Winson Green URC, located opposite the gates of the HM Prison Birmingham, and encouraged people to visit prisoners as he did regularly. He was made the Moderator of the General Assembly of the URC for the year 1978-9. During this time, he preached at Balmoral Prison and continued the prolific writing career that established him as one of the 'most respected and significant theologians of the twentieth century'.

Newbigin was shocked by the state of his country and its emerging culture. He connected the growing mental illness of the youth with hopelessness and recalled the youth in Chennai slums being more hopeful in life. He used strong words and championed the challenge of the Gospel to post-Christian Western culture, which he viewed not as a secular society without gods but as a pagan society with false gods. From Newbigin's perspective, western cultures, particularly modern scientific cultures, had uncritically come to believe in objective knowledge that was unaffected by faith-based axiomatic presuppositions. Newbigin challenged this ideas of neutrality and also the closely related discussion concerning the distinction between facts and values, both of which emerged from the Enlightenment. He was part of a movement called 'Gospel and Contemporary Culture' and published insightful materials.

After retirement in Herne Hill, South London, Newbigin regularly had theology students come over from King's College to read chapters of theological texts to him since his eye vision had diminished. Still he continued to preach from his memory. While he was approaching the end, I had three occasions to see him. First, he received me and a group from India in the Euston station and provided hospitality. Second, in a service of silver jubilee thanksgiving in a Sri Lankan Tamil congregation in London he pronounced the blessing in pure Tamil. Third, in the Friends of Church in India (his last in October 1997) when I asked 'How are you able to speak still in good Tamil?', he answered in Tamil 'It is the celestial language!' He died in West Dulwich, South London, on 30 January 1998 and was cremated at West Norwood Cemetery. Newbigin was normally slim, shy and child-like, but stubborn to hold on what he thought to be the Truth.

Newbigin's reasoned and theologically sound view of the church, unity and mission, is evident in the following words from his *The Household of* God:

> The Church is the pilgrim people of God … It is on the move – hastening to the ends of the earth to beseech all men to be reconciled to God, and hastening to the end of time to meet its Lord who will gather all into one. Therefore, the nature of the Church is never to be finally defined in static terms, but only in terms of that to which it is going. It cannot be understood rightly except in a perspective which is at once missionary and eschatological, and only in that perspective can the deadlock of our present ecumenical debate be resolved. But – and this is of vital importance – it will be a solution in which theory and practice are inseparably related, not one which can be satisfactorily in terms of theory alone … When the Church ceases to be one, or ceases to be missionary, it contradicts its own nature. Yet the Church is not to be defined by what it is, but by that End to which it moves, the power of which now works in the Church, the power of the Holy Spirit, who is the earnest of the inheritance still to be revealed. To say that the ecumenical deadlock in the debate will be resolved in a perspective inseparable from action, and that action must be both in the direction of mission and in that of unity, but these are but two aspects of the one work of the Spirit.[1]

J.J. Banninga

John J. Banninga (1875-1963) was born to Jan and Elizabeth Banninga in 1875 in Muskegon, Michigan, USA. His parents were born in Uithuizen, Groningen Province, the Netherlands, and migrated to America in 1867. John Banninga graduated at from Hope College in 1898, the Western Theological Seminary in 1901, and received an honorary Doctor of Divinity from Hope in 1917. He married Sophia Maria ('Mary' Damson) in 1901, who had been a teacher in the Holland Public School system for seven years. He was the first person to be commissioned at Hope Reformed Church under a new form of service adopted by the Synod of the Reformed Church in America which provided for the commissioning of people for foreign missions. John and Mary left for India in 1901 and served there for forty-two years. In 1917, Banninga (though closely associated since its

---

[1] Quoted, G. Wainwright, *Lesslie Newbigin: A Theological Life*, Oxford: Oxford University Press, 2000, 102.

inception in 1914) became the principal of the Union Theological Seminary at Pasumalai, on the outskirts of Madurai, a position he would hold for 25 years. It should be mentioned that united theological education set a good background for the young generation of ministers and Christian workers to imbibe the spirit of church unity. Earlier in 1910, with a strong Congregational foundation, UTC Bangalore was established to promote the ecumenical spirit. The Seminary at Pasumalai served as a training ground for Indian pastors and evangelists.

Banninga effectively propagated union through seminary education by bringing the SIUC ministerial candidates into contact with Anglicans. For him union represented the great liberty, friendship, friendship of the children of God. He appreciated the 1888 Lambeth Conference's issue of the Quadrilateral which formed the basis of the union in South India and which promised to make the whole world move towards union, and Banninga was instrumental in the drive to create a United Church of India. He served as secretary for the first fifteen years of the SIUC and as a council member until his retirement.

He agreed with the proposal of episcopacy as good form of government if desired by Indians. He approached the Tranquebar proposals with a peace of mind. As the Secretary of SIUC at the time he was the key mover of his church to accept union negotiations. He emphasised the absolute spiritual equality of the ministry and non- re-ordination. This was different from his home situation where according to the US concordat the majority Congregationalists accepted re-ordination which he did not want to happen in India.

With reference to a group giving more importance to (doctrinal) theology than history, Banninga already in 1919 told the readers of the *United Church Herald*: 'There is altogether too much ignorance of the simplest facts of church history. If India ignores church history, she will lay up trouble for the future.'[1] During the last months of 1920 there was a revealing and frank correspondence between Banninga and Azariah. Quite clearly Banninga interpreted the Lambeth proposals of episcopal re-ordination of non-episcopal ministers as ruling the SIUC out of court. He consistently insisted on the 'absolute equality of the ministry and membership of the two churches' and 'their desire to retain communion with the churches with which they were already in fellowship'. He pointed out that the proposal for re-ordination contradicted their agreement that non-episcopal ministries were owned by the Holy Spirit. For him, to be re-ordained by bishops was not much different from being re-baptized by the Baptists.[2] This issue continued to be a vexed one until the end of negotiations. Banninga participated in the Faith and Order of Lausanne in 1927 where Azariah challenged the western churches to move forward in unity for the sake of mission. Banninga, along with Palmer, delivered important addresses on the church's ministry with a South Indian flavour. Next year, he co-drafted with F.J. Western the South

---

[1] Quoted, Sundkler, 127.

[2] Ibid., 133f.

India Scheme of Church Union. When the Scheme was criticised from different angles in the JC meetings, he as a secretary 'effectively contributed to the smooth and rapid progress of the Committee's work'. With reference to him, Palmer recorded that 'the strength of his hope about South India unity and its probable effect on the whole world was one of the formative factors of the meeting.'[1] In response to different opinions shared in meetings and in *Church Union News and Views* (of which Banninga was the Editor, 1930-1933), Banninga, in his unique style stated: I have developed a theory that the further the Church moved from Pentecost the more it forgot the teaching of Jesus and began to follow the example of the Old Testament and the Roman Empire. Therefore, you have in Cyprian the development of the sacerdotal and imperial ideas.[2] Perhaps Banninga was not able to contradict the imperial Roman Empire with the Hebrew visions and ideals of equality, justice and preferential treatment for the victims of injustice. His own stated ideals of Christian brotherhood, comprehension, and spiritual & democratic principle had the foundations in Jesus' religious tradition. He argued for taking the Reformation seriously and not bypassing it in our recession to the past tradition. By sending questionnaires, he collected theological opinions from Britain and USA on issues such as lay celebration of communion. At the same time, as if sharing the view of some South Indian theologians, he held that the doctrinal battles of church union should be fought in Europe, not in South India. However, he was always prepared to face the Anglo-Catholic outcry and himself became a strong supporter of Lay Celebration, which at one point appeared to wreck the union scheme.

Banninga was a member of the ad hoc sub-committee on the 'governing body' to settle the devolution and of the relation between church councils and the highest authority of the church. Also, as the convener of the SIUC committee on union he communicated the decisions of the JC meetings and invited responses. His efficient leadership changed the temperature of enthusiasm among the congregations of SIUC towards the union negotiations. At the same time, he was faithfully loyal to the SIUC position of no assent to a mechanical transmission of the Spirit through episcopacy of the apostolic succession. His own Madura Council favoured a 'service of mutual commission.'

After his retirement in 1942, John and Mary moved to Claremont, California. Mary died in 1949, and John remarried in 1952 Helen Elizabeth Vogleson. John J. Banninga passed away in 1963. Important proceedings of the councils of which he was a member and his own writings are kept in the archives of the Yale University.

---

[1] Quoted, Ibid., 168.
[2] Quoted, Ibid., 180.

Vernon Bartlet

James Vernon Bartlet (1863-1940), a famous Professor in Church History, taught at Mansfield College (Congregational), Oxford. He authored several books on historical and biblical themes. He contributed 16 entries to the 11th edition of *Encyclopaedia Britannica*. As a leading Congregationalist theologian in England, he represented along with others the Congregational Church in the Faith and Order Conferences between Anglicans and Free Churchmen at Mansfield in 1916-1918. Organic union with the Church of England was the main target of some stalwarts, and later Bartlet somehow came into contact with the union negotiations in South India, giving important advice to negotiators such as Banninga at crucial moments.

While the SIUC insisted on the equal validity of both the Episcopal and non-episcopal ministries and Anglicans on re-ordination, Bartlet counselled Banninga with the idea of 'a service of mutual commission' which was accepted by the Madura Council. It was said that Bartlet combined in 'a very striking way a strong Congregational and Free Church loyalty with a genuine ecumenical sympathy.'[1] Sundkler further observed: Barletlet's proposal of 1921 represented an important approach to the unification of church in South India. The proposal was interesting also because this Congregationalist theologian from now on came to be regarded in South India as the authority of the non-Anglicans. For twenty years Bartlet's scholarship in patristics was the arsenal with which to confront E.J. Palmer's arguments. Bartlet seemed to be using Palmer's phraseology in saying that he wanted to promote the 'most equitable and catholic and *inclusive* (Bartet's italics) solution'. He also wanted to safeguard the condition laid down by Banninga from the first in the series of negotiations, viz. absolute equality of the ministry. In accepting episcopacy, Bartlet stressed that no particular interpretation of the fact of the historic episcopate should be demanded from either side. Bartlet's chief contribution to the debate was his suggestion 'to combine in a single rite the forms hitherto distinctive of the ordination of chief pastors in the respective types of church life'. In the consecration of bishops, presbyters of the South India United Church should take part and so also in the ordination of presbyters (ministers). Only by applying the principle of equality to the form of episcopal ordination could that principle be preserved and adequately safeguarded.

In a characteristic phrase, Bartlet suggested that 'those desirous of entering the united church's ministry from outside would gladly accept the joint or twofold form of conferring ordination or ministerial commission of the new or union type – one more fully catholic and constitutional that any already existing – as that proper to the new union type of church organisation which it is the aim of the uniting Churches to inaugurate for India and ultimately modern Christendom.' He regarded his method as 'the simplest and most satisfactory solution … since

---

[1] Quoted, Ibid., 146.

it is one that resolves the difficulties of the transition period'. This general commissioning service, as suggested by Bartlet, would not imply re-ordination or repudiation of previous ordinations. Bartlet was also optimistic enough to believe that it would be generally regarded as not detracting from, but adding to, the authority of the act, because it would combine authority from the two churches. He was sure of the results of his methods: 'If bishops and presbyters (in the first instance those of the SIUC) both cooperate in ordinations alike to the episcopate and the presbyterate of the united church, then there will be such equality of treatment that there will be no room left for "conscientious scruples" arising in any congregation *of either line of tradition* within that church, as regards the exercise of his ministry by any of the ministers, for none will be likely not to "avail himself of the liberty" to receive "a full commission" inclusive of the sort which hitherto he had not received.' While Bartlet did not draw up a particular form of mutual commissioning, he nevertheless claimed that this method 'and it only, can be accepted without scruple by those who hold the most different views.'[1]

Bartlet was aware that some of his Anglican friends were uneasy about denying something special in the episcopal ordination and others (Palmer) suggesting a ceremony 'which will express the addition to every minister of anything that the members of other uniting churches think to be lacking in his ministry'. He was openly asking them, 'What is the special gift which only comes through ordination by a bishop?' However, it could not convince those who had scruples of their tradition but were committed to church union.

In his Birkbeck lectures at Cambridge in 1924, Bartlet staged the interplay of two elements in the life of the early Church: 'the inward, spiritual, and experiential on the one hand, and the external, formal and organisational on the other.'[2] This position reflected in all his statements. In 1932, for example, there was a strong challenge from Palmer (with reference to the modifications made by the JC in June 1932) saying what they now had was 'not the historic episcopate, but a fancy episcopate'. In response, Bartlet called himself 'an old fellow worker in this most representative effort after and experiment in the field of recovering the outward unity of the one Church of Christ, on the basis of sub-apostolic principles of church order — for at least a century after the close of the apostolic age, if not for a good deal longer.'[3] Palmer was pleased with this response. Actually, Bartlet's passion was not only to go back to the Church of early centuries but still further back to a more 'constitutional or well-balanced stage in its relations to the presbyterate and laity'. There is no wonder that along with Palmer, Bartlet has been regarded an eminent theologian, who though physically distant, influenced the church union in South India. He was so glad when 'parity of ministries' was achieved in the negotiations in early 1930s. He saw in it a 'new Catholicism'.

---

[1] Ibid., 147f.

[2] Quoted, Ibid., 179.

[3] Quoted, Ibid., 179.

Sherwood Eddy

George Sherwood Eddy (1871–1963) was a leading American Protestant missionary, administrator and educator. He was a prolific author and indefatigable traveller. His main achievement was to link and finance networks of intellectuals across the globe, especially Christian leaders in Asia and the Middle East. He enabled missionaries to better understand and even think like the people they were serving. His long-term impact on the Protestant communities in the United States, and in the Third World, was long lasting.

George was born to George Alfred Eddy and Margaret Louise Nolan at Leavenworth, Kansas. His father was a leading businessman and civic leader; he and his wife Margaret Norton were of Yankee stock. The son attended Phillips Andover Academy, and graduated at Yale College in engineering in 1891. G.S. Eddy married Alice Maud Harriet Arden in 1898. They were the parents of two children, Margaret and Arden. After his first wife's death, he married Catherine Louise Gates in 1946.

After college, Eddy attended Union Theological Seminary (1891-1893) in New York. He enlisted in the Student Volunteer Movement, which sought to 'evangelize the world in this generation'. He also worked on the staff of a local YMCA. In 1893-1894 he served as a travelling secretary for the Student Volunteer Movement in the United States. Eddy's father died in 1894, leaving him an inheritance that made him financially independent and enabled him to work for the causes he believed in without concern for finances. He attended Princeton Theological Seminary, from which he graduated in 1896.

Eddy was one of the first of sixteen thousand student volunteers who emerged from the leading universities of the U.S. and Europe to serve as Christian missionaries across the world. In 1896, he went to India and worked at the YMCA-organized Indian Student Volunteer Movement. He served as its secretary for the next 15 years. Working among the poor and outcasts of India he mastered the Tamil language and served as a travelling evangelist among the students and masses of southern India beginning in Palayamcottai. In 1911 he was appointed secretary for Asia by the International Committee, and he divided his time between evangelistic campaigns in Asia and fund-raising in North America. He is also known today for his works with the Oxford Group evangelical group, a predecessor to Alcoholics Anonymous.

He spent the next 15 years doing student evangelistic work across Asia – from China, Japan, and the Philippines, through the Near East to Turkey, Palestine, Iraq, Egypt, and then to czarist Russia and made 15 trips to the Soviet Russia. He admired the Soviet system and refused to believe reports of famine; in 1937 he agreed that the victims of Stalin's show trials were traitors as charged. His was criticized as a 'fellow traveller'.

The Fellowship of Socialist Christians was organized in the early 1930s by Reinhold Niebuhr and others on the left. Later it changed its name to Frontier

Fellowship and then to Christian Action. The main supporters of the Fellowship in the early days included Eddy, Eduard Heimann, Paul Tillich and Rose Terlin. In its early days the group thought that capitalist individualism was incompatible with Christian ethics. Although not under Communist control, the group acknowledged Karl Marx's social philosophy

'The war did something to me,' Eddy recalled in 1934; 'I could never be quite the same again.' Emerging as a pacifist and socialist, he promoted a radical social gospel during the years before his retirement from the YMCA in 1931. From 1921 to 1957 he led the influential Fellowship for a Christian Social Order, a liberal organization that hosted travelling seminars for American leaders to England, Europe, and the Soviet Union in search of Christian solutions to the reformation of industrial capitalism. He also helped to organize the Christian Socialist Delta Cooperative Farms in 1936, a project in Mississippi that provided land for families of evicted tenant farmers. His latter-day explorations of psychic evidence for life after death are described in his book *You Will Survive after Death* (1950).[1]

Many of those influenced by the YMCA including V.S. Azariah became actively participating in the South India Union negotiations. Eddy was particularly associated with the Madura-American Mission (Congregational). In both the World Missionary Conference Edinburgh and Madras meeting of the Faith and Order (1910) he addressed with passion pointing out the achievement of the SIUC which he represented, and the scope of greater unity. Further, he was the key mover of discussions on organic union on the basis of the Quadrilateral. Though he was a life-long independent and Congregationalist, Eddy discovered that 'Congregational Church government is not the fittest to survive in the Orient.' Taking up the aim of forming a 'National Church of India', he found the need of episcopacy, but non-hierarchical, simple, constitutional and primitive model. For him mutual recognition of ministries was essential. His wordings enriched the Tranquebar Manifesto. His record of publications, mainly on evangelism and church union, is impressive.

J.H. Wyckoff

J.H. Wyckoff (1857-1914), an American Presbyterian in the Arcot Mission was 'a missionary, leader and stateman', as put in the title of his biography by an Indian author. As a key participant in the Madras Missionary Conference in 1900, he was made the convener of the Committee on Comity and Co-operation which was passed by the next step of union. He came to admire the liturgical tradition of the Anglicans, particularly the *Book of Common Prayer* which he started to use from time to time. He eventually formed the opinion, influenced by the young Indian pastor Meshach Peter, which was the same of his Scottish colleague Maclean, that

---

[1] https://en.wikipedia.org/wiki/Sherwood_Eddy; http://www.bu.edu/missiology/eddy-george-sherwood-1871-1963/ as on 25 April 2018 and slightly modified.

episcopacy was the best form of the church government in India. He was a key person in the formation of the SIUC, constituted first by the Presbyterian groups (1901) and later including the other Free Churches (1908). He presided over the second general Assembly of the SIUC in 1909. He was the chief promotor of the idea of a united theological college which was formed in Bangalore, 1910. All these laid foundations for building on the greater unity, the organic unity of the CSI.

C.K. Jacob

C.K. Jacob (1886-1957) was born at Pallom, Kerala, to Korula Ashan. He graduated from the Madras Christian College and joined the CMS College High School Kottayam as teacher. He studied theology at the CNI Bible College, Calcutta, and was ordained as a priest in 1914. He then went to Oxford for higher education and was appointed Archdeacon at Mavelikkara. He served as the head master at the CNI School. He also served as the Principal of the CNI Bible School for 20 years. He served as Principal at Bishop's College, Calcutta and worked as the secretary to the first three bishops of the 'Travancore-Cochi Diocese' (Anglican) and was made an archdeacon and then bishop in 1945. He was known for his bible knowledge and prayerful life. In acknowledgement of his contributions to the formation of the CSI Church, Wycliffe College of the Toronto University in Canada presented him an Honorary Doctorate.

He succeeded and was surrounded by foreign bishops and priests. With the inauguration of the CSI and reorganisation of boundaries, he was made Bishop of the diocese of Central Travancore, and served until he resigned on 15 March 1957. As wished by Keralites, he combined in himself Syrian-Anglican-CSI – and actively participated in the union negotiations. Most significantly, he was the presiding bishop of the inauguration of CSI who, standing on the highest platform of the St. George's Cathedral, declared the formation of the CSI. His *My Prayer Book* is a testimony that he was a man of meaningful prayer. He won the affection of the people by knowing them and being accessible to them, and at retirement (he resigned in 1957 due to ill health) he undertook writing the history of CMS in South India.[1]

D.M. Devasahayam

D.M. Devasahayam (1883-1957), in an interview recounted his interesting story:

> My parents were Anglicans from Dohnavur and later became L.M.S. members. I was baptized in C.M.S., brought up in L.M.S., brought to light by the Salvation Army (by a sudden conversion in Nagercoil, Travancore, in 1905, in a revival which carried some 150 people with

---

[1] See a short write up in *South India Churchman*, July 1957, 7.

it), sent to Serampore by an S.P.G. missionary, Downes, trained there by Baptists.[1]

He developed into an eminent thinker with the rare qualification of Batchelor of Arts and Batchelor of Divinity (B.A.B.D.). and he was one of the first batch of B.D. graduates at Serampore College (university) in 1915. For a while he was a renouncer (*sannyasi*) but about 1918 he came under the spell of liberal theology through the missionary F. Kingsbury. Inspired by the work of the Baptist missionary William Carey of Serampore (north of Calcutta), who was an indigo planter as well, Devasahayam became a tea planter and claimed, 'So I am in the apostolic succession. I don't believe in any other succession.'[2] This shows the vigour with which he promoted the union scheme by arguing with its opponents. In the 1920s he became a member of the *Christo Samaj* which worked for the indigenization of the Church and was for some time the editor of its weekly *The Christian Patriot*. From 1930s he came to be the most well-known exponent of the union scheme in Nagercoil, a main Congregational mission station of Travancore. Two organizations, the South Travancore Christian Young Men's Retreat and the Bangalore Conference Continuation Group, provided him the platform he needed for pushing his ideas.

Devasahayam's first pamphlets were largely a string of the usual long words such as sacerdotalism, ritualism, exclusivism, resuscitation of medieval forms, formulae and institutions. But his own scheme of 1933 professed to be a 'Basis of Union to Comprehend All Evangelical Christians'. Also, denouncing the traditional creeds as inadequate for the modern requirements of faith and its evangelical appeal, he produced his own creed. It affirms belief in God, the Ultimate Power and Supreme Being and ruler, acceptance of the Holy Scriptures, especially the New Testament as containing all things necessary for salvation, sacraments as symbolic embodiments of religious truth. The (CSI) Joint Committee's acknowledgement of the valuable gifts of lay Christians gave impetus to Devasahayam to develop his idea of paid official ministers and prophetic ministers who could be celibate and sacrificing, and who should be treated with dignity and honour. For him the church organization was to be largely modelled after the Travancore Congregational System, i.e. a union of fully independent local churches or congregations.[3]

Devasahayam was elected in the SIUC General Assembly in 1935 to represent the Travancore Council for the CSI Negotiation Committee. He was initially an opponent of the CSI scheme, particularly because of possible Anglican overbearing. He is noted as the 'Indian theological layman from Travancore'; his 'enthusiastic onslaught on the floor of the Joint Committee was formidable'. He

---

[1] Sundkler, 194.

[2] Ibid.

[3] See, Ibid., 195.

was part of a group who produced a scheme of its own, 'An Evangelical Scheme of Union'.

It is from this angle – a Nagercoil combination of nineteenth century Liberal Protestantism and loyalty to supposedly Congregational ideas with a dash of Indian romanticism – that Devasahayam viewed the efforts of the Joint Committee. In August 1935 he formed an organisation called the South Travancore Evangelical Association, to 'counteract any acceptance or approval of the scheme in its present form by church authorities without radical changes from the evangelical and congregational points of view'. He contrasted the anti-doctrinal 'Tranquebar Manifesto' with the pro-doctrinal scheme of 1929. He also claimed that 'the Indian genius' was pro-Congregationalist and democratic while the above scheme was anti-Congregationalist and undemocratic.[1] Of his publications the book *Unknown Binding* (1938) has been considered remarkable. When he found the Anglican domination persistent, he revived the above association with the new name 'South Indian Evangelical Association'. Its aim was to prevent the acceptance of the Proposed Scheme and promote the union of 'Protestant Evangelical Churches'. More remarkably, he allowed himself in 1943 to be made the President of another grouping by the name 'Travancore Bible Faith Mission', distinct from SIUC although he continued to be a member of the Travancore Council of the SIUC and the Church Union Committee until 1947. Even towards the end of the process of union, Devasahayam opposed the Anglican proposal for supplemental ordination and all the issues around it, and his influence in the Travancore Council was considerable.[2]

John Jacob

John A. Jacob (1872-1959) wasborn in Nagercoil and educated in Scott Christian College, trained in UTC Bangalore and Serampore, worked in the American Arcot Mission in Katpadi, and taught in UTC (Church History and History of Religions). Always smart, he was connected with the Church Union movement for over twenty years, editor of *Desopakari*[3] from 1953 until his death. He edited the year books of the Indian Christian Endeavour, being its president. He retired as District Minister, Nagercoil. Though a Congregationalist, Jacob took a middle stand between the primitive Church and the future Church, particularly the united church in accordance with scripture.[4] He had personal connections with the Anglican churches and some leaders in Thiruneveli, and was untiring in

---

[1] Ibid., 196.

[2] His tombstone in the graveyard of Nagercoil Home Church reads: IN EVER LOVING MEMORY OF OUR DEAR UNCLE, D.M. DEVASAHAYAM B.A., B.D., WHO DIED ON 24TH NOV. 1957 AGED 74 YEARS. 'Your Prayers and your Alms have ascended as a memorial before God' (Acts 10:4).

[3] 'Helper to the Nation' Church Magazine, Nagercoil.

[4] See the Tribute by V.D. Sahayam in *Desopakari*, August 1959, 10.

speaking in favour of union. In the context of not much support for the scheme of union, Jacob was convinced that Travancore ought not to isolate itself but to join the union. When some people argued that any compromise on the lay celebration of Communion would mean being disloyal to the LMS, Jacob asked them not to think in terms of western missionary society but in terms of the Indian Church which badly needed union.

A.J. Appasamy

Aiyadurai Jesudasen Appasamy (1891-1976), with a distinguished PhD from Oxford University for research into Hindu-Christian *bhakti* (devotion) and association with the Cowley Fathers and scholars, in the 1930s was on the staff of the Bishop's College, Calcutta. He came to be known as one of the outstanding Indian Christian theologians. He was the member of the Joint Committee from 1930 and continued until the end. He represented the 'Indian view' and interpreted the bishop as the Christian *guru* balancing the tendency of the Western perspectives. He published in 1930 *Church Union, An Indian View*. He found that the *Christo Samaj* had called the attention of Christians 'away from the externals to the inner core of religion'. He held that tolerance was the Indian genius which was conducive to the Scheme of Union. 'Appasamy's influence was widened when his *Manifesto on Church Union* of 1930 was signed by nearly two hundred Indian Christian leaders'. Here the 'Indian' viewpoint was defined as indifference towards the theological dogmas of the West. 'The Indian has always stressed *bhakti* and feels that through faith in God his highest feelings can best be expressed rather than through dogma.' Unlike Chenchiah and Chakkarai, Appasamy came to a different conclusion from theirs: 'A united church, free from the bonds of the present separate denominations, will provide a congenial atmosphere for the Indian expression of Christianity.'[1] It was significant that Appasamy was sent from the CSI Synod as the first bishop in the Coimbatore diocese which initially refused to accept bishopric. I have witnessed the Appasamy birth centenary celebrations in 1991 in which a senior/retired presbyter confessed with tears and sobbing his regret at being part of a group protesting against the arrival of such a bishop who proved to be saintly.

E.W. Thompson

Edgar Wesley Thompson (1871-1963), son of a Wesleyan Methodist minister, was born in Glastonbury, England, educated in Woodhouse Grove, Kingswood and Aberystwyth, and graduated MA in London with honours in Philosophy. After committing to ministry, he spent a brief period in Richmond College, and was appointed to Mysore District in 1894. He served for twenty-five years in India and fifteen years in the home church as the General Secretary of the Wesleyan Methodist Society. Using his competence in philosophy, he engaged in

---

[1] Sundklar, 206f.

public debate on theosophy both in India and in Britain (with Mrs. Besant, one of the missionaries of the Theosophical Society in Madras). Under his editorship the weekly newspaper, *Vrittanta Patrike*, became an effective instrument of 'the missionary message, of social righteousness, and of political criticism'. At the same time, he was at ease with the congregations of the Dalits (untouchables) and had great influence on the formation and direction of policy in the great Dalit community movements of Hyderabad and Tiruchirappalli. He was admired by his colleagues for clarity of thought and persuasive speech both in English and Kanarese. He and Gulliford did yeoman service for missionary cooperation in South India through their writings, particularly in *The Harvest Field*. He also influenced the 1911 Methodist Conference for modification of the Constitution and administration of the Missionary Society. The same influence with versatility and insight could be seen in changes in the structure and administration of the overseas Methodist Districts of West Africa and West Indies. The Conference Declaration of Racial Policy (1950) was largely his composition. His book *History of India* was used in schools over the sub-continent for more than a generation. His most memorable Fernley Lecture (1932) was on 'The Word of the Gospel to the Hindus'. His thinking and engaging all through his life is summed up in his last saying: 'I always put truth first, but we cannot know the truth unless we love.'

Thompson served on the JC for many years as one of the representatives of the Wesleyan Methodists. His sharp analysis of interaction between churches on policy and structure showed the Free Churches that they had assimilated the defects of the Church of England supplied by Provincial Conferences and Parochial Church Councils. When the issue of supplemental ordination, insisted on by the Anglicans, was still remaining, Thompson took a strong line: 'The cardinal principle of Free Churchmanship is that the Church is a living organism of the Holy Spirit; and as such, is free under His guidance to choose whatever means will do the will of God.'[1] Subsequently, he suggested a draft resolution to be presented to the Methodist conference where supplemental ordination was 'in accord with the letter and spirit of the teaching of the Methodist Church'. Of course, it was too radical for his Methodist colleagues, and the open-minded Anglican colleagues were already finding alternatives to overcome this prolonged hurdle. Thompson wrote several books on Methodist themes, and in relation to CSI union the most remarkable was *The Church, Catholic and Free: Reflections of a Methodist upon the South India Scheme*, London (1944).

W.E. Tomlinson

William Earnest Tomlinson (1877-1944) was a Wesleyan missionary from England. He was born at Hankow and his father was a Methodist minister. Just like the Wesley brothers, at a young age, he had a dramatic spiritual experience of receiving the assurance of forgiveness which he wanted to share with others.

---

[1] Quoted, Ibid., 310.

After training at Didsbury (Manchester) College, Didsbury, he went to India in 1900. After two years of service in Bangalore as Secretary of the Kanarese Evangelical Mission, he spent the whole of his ministry in the Mysore District doing all sorts of Christian work including preaching the gospel. In 1904 he married Dorothea. He claimed that Jesus was his supreme *guru*. He mastered the language (now known as Kannada) and taught at the Union Kanarese Seminary and toured tirelessly throughout the Mysore State as District Evangelist. Towards the end, he was immersed in literature work and most remarkably revised the Kanarese Bible (1916-1934). In his home country he encouraged young people to take up missionary work. He was a great advocate of the CSI union which he found indispensable for propagating the gospel. He was actively involved in the CSI union negotiations (1924-1944), and updated the developments for anxious Wesleyans in his Home Board in London. A 'man of charm, he gave glow and sparkle to the interest in union in the Methodist Church and outside it.'[1] Because of his decisive influence, along with his colleague Gulliford, unlike other District Synods, the Mysore Synod readily accepted the union scheme. On the last Sunday of his life he preached his final sermon in an Anglican church and died in Mysore city on completion of forty-five years of ministry. A memoire of him gave a first-hand testimony of the life and work of Tomlinson.[2]

H. Gulliford

Henry Gulliford (1852-1937), a colleague of Tomlinson in Mysore, was born at Dunster in Somerset. After training in Didsbury College, he joined the staff of the Mysore District in 1877. In the early part of his missionary work he was a highly respected high school teacher. Then he concentrated on literature work, both production and circulation. For nearly twenty years he was the editor of the famous Methodist journal *Harvest Field*. He was also the editor of a local vernacular paper *Vrittanta Patrike*, during the early years of WWI. His literary work won him the prestigious Kaisar-i-Hind medal. After the war he was engaged in church plantation, particularly in the Nilgris, with the support of the Basel Mission. He worked with vision, commitment and patience. Solid and serious, he actively participated in the union negotiations of the CSI with particular attention to the emerging Constitution. He chaired the Joint Committee for several years until his death. His distinctive achievement in promoting the union was acknowledged by all those who worked with him. In few months before his death he laid down the secretary-ship of the Provincial Church Union Committee. His obituary of the home mission board concludes with the words: 'It was said that they "gave him the freedom of the city of God in South India."' In a deeper sense that freedom had long been his; his selflessness, his brotherliness and humility, the reality and

---

[1] Quoted, Ibid., 189.

[2] N.C. Sargant and Marcus Ward, *W.E. Tomlinson: A Memoir and Some Papers*, Madras: CLS, 1952.

reverence of his prayers, marked him out that one of those whose citizenship is heaven.'[1] Gulliford wrote *The Handbook of Wesleyan Methodism*, embodying the laws and usages followed by the Methodist Church in Ceylon and India, prepared in accordance with the resolutions of the first General Synod of that Church, held in Madras.

W.H. Thorp

William Hubert Thorp (1870-1950), the son of a Methodist minister, studied at Kingwood where he became Senior Prefect and took a London Degree. After two years of service as Asst. Master at Rydal School, he was accepted for ministry in 1892 and sent to the Handsworth College as Asst. Tutor in 1893. He went to Mysore and joined the District staff in 1896. In 1902 he started training evangelists in the Mysore Training Institution and then Hardwicke College where he started a commercial class that attracted many young Christians who came to hold high positions in the Mysore Government service. Some of his former students took up ministry, and they include P. Gurushanta, the first bishop in the Mysore diocese of the CSI. Thorp joined the staff of UTC, Bangalore in 1911 and after six years of teaching he was involved in revising the Kanarese Bible. He became the Chairman of the District and 'he administered its affairs with sound judgement and impartiality'. In 1930 he returned to UTC, now as the Principal, and held this position for the remaining six years of his ministry in India.

Thorp was a member of the JC of the CSI union. Initially, he was critical of the intentions of promoting church union by Anglicans by showing generosity of the spirit but not taking seriously the experience and principles of the Free Churches. When spiritual equality was affirmed, and the ministry of the non-Anglican churches was somehow recognised, he joined his Methodist colleagues pushing towards the goal of organic union. His own personality and approach helped in clarifying and persuading. 'Those who knew him will always think of him as the ideal of a perfect Christian gentleman. In him authority was combined with an unusual winsomeness of personality and responsibility with real humility. He inspired the highest ideals in others because his whole life was governed by them.'[2] After his return to England too, people could notice in him the above ideals and dedication to ministry.

Marcus Ward

Arthur Marcus Ward (1906-1978) was born in Sevenoaks as the only son of Arthur Ward, a Wesleyan minister. Educated in Kingswood, university college, Southampton and trained in Wesley House Cambridge with a first class in Theological Tripos, he served two years as asst. tutor in Richmond College. He was ordained and sent to India as a missionary in 1932. After four years of school

---

[1] *Minutes of the Conference*, 1938, 205.

[2] Obituary, *Minutes of the Conference*, 1951, 132.

teaching in the Wesley School Madras, he joined the staff of UTC Bangalore in 1936. His involvement in the CSI negotiations and his inauguration of Christian Students' Library series with the publications of two volumes of on Christian doctrines earned him a Doctor of Divinity from the Senate of Serampore College (University). He was engaged in interreligious dialogue and called Christians to understand what people of other religions believed and practised but without losing pastoral concern and passion for sharing what God in Christ had done for them. He returned to England in 1955 and worked as tutor in New Testament Languages and Literature at Richmond College for nearly twenty years. During this time, he played a leading role in the examining and executive work of the University of London and its Institute of Education. He was also the secretary of the Board of Studies in Divinity and Divinity Lecturer at Southlands College. His interest was varied, and his friendly approach attracted both colleagues and students. His wife Edna fully shared in his friendships. His ecclesiastical contacts and ecumenical commitment made it possible that during his retirement Ward was made a part-time teacher at Heythrop Roman Catholic College. 'Uniquely among Methodist ministers a Requiem Mass was said for him.' At the same time, he remained an enthusiastic Methodist preacher and class leader, loved by friends from all denominations till the end of his life. John Newton's book on him, *A Man for All Churches* (1984) is a detailed account of his extraordinary commitment to ecumenism and Christian unity.

As noted in the above book, Ward makes seven affirmations:

1.   Christian unity is God's will and gift.
2.   It is rooted in the biblical revelation.
3.   In a religion of incarnation, this unity must be made visible.
4.   Work for unity must begin in prayer.
5.   Theological barriers to unity must be faced with integrity – there must be no sacrifice of truth in the course of unity.
6.   The way to unity is through shared Christian mission and service.
7.   To be a good ecumenist, a Christian must be a loyal and committed member of his own denomination, – precisely so that he brings its distinctive treasures into the 'Coming Great Church.'[1]

When Marcus Ward joined the JC of the CSI union in the mid-1930s he and his Wesleyan colleagues were noted as belonging to 'high Methodism', i.e. the Methodist Sacramental Fellowship, based on the Eucharistic hymns of Charles Wesley. He was a member of the committee appointed to study Lay Celebration of Communion as practised in the Congregational church. The sub-committee met in Ward's study in Bangalore in 1940. Ward prepared a statement which was

---

[1] John Newton, *A Man for All Churches*, London: Epworth, 1984, 75.

added to the scheme. It affirmed: 'God is the God of order; it has been His good pleasure to use the visible church and its regularly constituted ministries as the normal means of the operation of Holy Spirit ... But it is not open to any to limit the operation of grace of God to any particular channel.'[1] This helped to clarify a vexed issue in the negotiations and to move on, though it was never accepted by all. He wanted to do justice to both Anglican tendencies of sacerdotalism and the Congregational emphasis on the priesthood of all believers. Ward, along with some of his Methodist colleagues, encouraged by a resolution of the Methodist Church, agreed for supplemental ordination although it was upset by the strong voice against it from certain SIUC representatives (some Anglicans too!). Above all, Ward is greatly credited with his book *The Pilgrim Church: An Account of the first five years in the life of the Church of South India*, Madras (1952).

P. H. Loyd

Philip Henry Loyd (1884-1952) was an eminent Anglo-Catholic bishop and author. Educated at Eton and King's College, Cambridge, he was ordained in 1911. His first post was as a Curate at St Mary of Eton, Hackney Wick after which he was Vice-Principal of Ripon College Cuddesdon. From 1915 to 1944 he served the church in India rising in time to be Bishop of Nasik, after having served Palmer's chaplain in Bombay and later his assistant bishop. After Nasik, transferred to be the Bishop of St. Albans to serve until 1950. He published extensively, mainly on the New Testament and the most popular book was *The Holy Spirit in the Acts* (1952).

Obviously as an outstanding Anglo-Catholic, Loyd became a member of the JC in 1930. 'Many observers have referred to the spiritual quality of the committee meetings. Nobody did more to make the business of negotiations transparent with the presence of God than Bishop Loyd. His position was far from easy. Theologically and by natural disposition he was an Anglo-Catholic. But he held together with this fundamental attitude a passion for the union of the whole Church. There was a strong tension between these two attitudes, but it was resolved on the level of deep personal piety. His testimony to the value and significance of episcopacy — interpreting the bishop as a Father-in-God — did more than intricate theological arguments to overcome opposition to the Scheme, and certainly achieved more than the "barbed remarks" ... the position of the non-episcopal churches.'[2] In the controversy over inter-communion, Loyd along with his colleague bishop Tubbs stressed the spirit rather than form. He felt that the rigidity of the Anglicans had to be overcome by not a formula but 'the Pentecostal Spirit'. This new understanding and affirmation spread a flame of Pentecost and expectancy of the imminent inauguration of the new CSI across the Anglican dioceses. And Bishop Loyd's life and attitude created more positive

[1] Quoted, Sundkler, 294.

[2] Ibid., 184f.

attitude towards episcopacy in the non-episcopate circles. The retreat he led in 1932 before the meeting of the JC exuded conviction because of clarity, simplicity and humility. Further, in the discussion on the parity of ministries, Loyd suggested an amendment to the non-Anglican proposal for participation of the presbyters in all the consecrations of the bishops: 'It shall be permissible for Presbyters to join with the Bishops in the laying on of hands at the consecration of a Bishop; provided that it always be remembered and taught that the true consecrator is God to whom prayer is made.'[1] Unfortunately, the General Council of CIBC, meeting in 1932, did not accept this amendment although it made a significant 'dent in the Anglican defence'.

C.J. Lucas

Representing the Madras Council of the SIUC, this remarkable Indian lay theologian and President of the SIUC in 1927, came to the limelight by his forthright, bold and convincing arguments in the meetings. From 1920 Lucas was appointed as a delegate of the SIUC along with others including Banninga and Maclean to the Joint Committee of negotiations for CSI and he lasted until the end of negotiations and the event of the inauguration of the CSI. It was not without reason that Lucas was a member of the sub-committee of the JC to draft the final document on union. He, along with the above, addressed special meetings such as the first Women's Conference on Church Union held in April 1933. In 1935 he was a party to a decision to change the Lay Celebration of the Holy Communion (practised in Congregational and Methodist Churches by an authorisation and renewal) to by ordination of eligible catechists and evangelists ordained just for this purpose.

He gave an impassioned speech at the Faith and Order Conference of Edinburgh 1937. There he recounted his extraordinary life background: his father was a convert but still Lutheran; mother too a convert but a Congregationalist, but she had become Lutheran; his mother was a woman of prayer, and at her knees he first learned how to pray and worship; he was initiated into the mysteries of Luther's Smaller Catechism by his father, and later Augsburg Confession just before confirmation; he found the family worship very inspiring; at seventeen he was sent to a Puritan College where he was influenced by the Calvinistic Puritanism; his next college was staffed by United Free Church of Scotland; these two contacts helped him to appreciate the worship form of Presbyterian and Reformed Churches; he found worship at Sunday School, Christian Endeavour Society and YMCA intelligible; in the college as a student and then teacher, he was attracted by Methodist hymnology and effective pulpits; his wife belonged to the Anglican Communion, her parents and some relatives Anglo-Catholics, others Roman Catholics, and a brother-in-law Methodist; in this extended family there was no debate on Apostolic Succession, consubstantiation or the doctrine of

---

[1] Quoted, Ibid., 250.

grace; he had no problem of partaking Communion with his parents according to Lutheran rites and, with people of his wife's side, Anglican rites, and currently as administered in the SIUC; one of his children was baptised by a Lutheran minister, others by Free Church ministers; one son was admitted into full membership by a Lutheran minister, others by Free Church ministers, yet another son was confirmed by an Anglican bishop; for him worshipping with God's people and enjoying different gifts was important; he was both listener and preacher in different services; in church union meetings he found worship and joint devotion enjoyable; he found the Roman Catholic churches attractive for kneeling and praying in for a while.[1] He concluded his speech on effective mission and visible church union with the words, 'Pardon me for my ecumenicity.'[2] Further, his contribution to the debate in the Conference was considered very important. C.J. Lucas shared (or influenced) the view of his Council that the historic creeds, particularly the Nicene Creed, were neither sufficient nor necessary as they were not intelligible. At Edinburgh he suggested that the Conference should modify the creed and in 1950 in a personal interview he asked, 'If one council was able to frame a creed, why should not we be able to change it?'[3]

Stephen Neill

Stephen Charles Neill (1900–1984), was born in Edinburgh, Scotland, to Charles Neill and Margaret Penelope ("Daisy") Neill, the daughter of James Munro (for a time Commissioner at Scotland Yard). He was educated at Dean Close School, Cheltenham, England, where he had his conversion, then in 1918 won a scholarship to Trinity College, Cambridge and was elected to a fellowship in 1924. While still in Cambridge he passed the Church of England's General Ordination Examination which qualified him for ordination, but he had decided to go out to India as a layman. He was proficient in a number of languages

Both his parents were missionary doctors in India but spent much of their adult lives in various European countries for reasons of health and for the sake of their children's education. In 1924 Stephen Neill accompanied his parents to South India and the next year moved with them to Dohnavur. While at Dohnavur, a famous orphanage established by Amy Carmichael, he learnt Tamil and was involved in teaching schoolboys. He soon found himself at odds with Carmichael and joined G. T. Selwyn of Thirunelveli instead, learning Tamil and teaching schoolboys, except when travelling with the American Methodist missionary E. Stanley Jones. He joined the CMS in 1928 and was ordained a deacon in Thirunelveli cathedral, and the next year a priest during furlough. After his ordination he moved to Thirunelveli and later led Thomas Ragland's

---

[1] See Ibid., 31ff.

[2] Quoted, Ibid., 207.

[3] Quoted, Ibid., 276.

North Tirunelveli Itineracy evangelism programme. He taught Tamil in the CMS theological college in Palayamkottai where he served as its first Principal.

There as a young Anglican missionary and impressive scholar, Neill became involved in negotiations for the CSI union. Observing the range of visions and commitments the members of the Joint Committee had to keep in mind, Neill wrote: 'The little group of men and women which met year by year in South India knew that they were like performers in the ring, lighted up by powerful searchlights, their every movement watched by a vast and unseen cloud of witnesses in every country of the world.'[1] Himself a member of the JC from 1935 onwards, he stated the Anglican standpoint 'with brilliant lucidity and had a capacity to understand other traditions which was of particular value'. When the question of inter-communion appeared to break the union scheme, Neill told his official Anglican body, 'It was a case of either breaking off the negotiations or of yielding to their pressure.' He did not hesitate to resist one tradition's formula imposed on others. Neill was elected the bishop at Tirunelveli in 1939. There he held the diocese together during the troubled times of the war, resisting encroachments by the state and initiating development projects in publishing, banking among other areas. In 1944 he resigned. In his autobiography, he attributes this to problems of ill health and certain scandal which had dogged him for most of his life.

After his return from India Stephen Neill became the assistant bishop to the Archbishop of Canterbury. Neill worked for the WCC (World Council of Churches) from 1947 to 1954. In 1962 he went to the University of Hamburg as a professor of missions until 1967 and a professor of philosophy and religious studies in Nairobi between 1969 and 1973. On returning to England, he was offered accommodation by the then Principal of Wycliffe Hall, Oxford which for the rest of his life served as a base between lecturing commitments and advocating communion of churches in various parts of the world and for reading and writing. As editor and author, he produced more than hundred publications including the two volume *History of Christianity in India*.

M. Peter

Meshack Peter from an episcopal background Thirunelveli became one of the central figures in the Arcot Mission (Vellore Circle) and his personal connections advocated church unity. He was born at Katpadi in 1867. 'His father was a pastor in the Reformed Church, an uncle was an Anglican, the grandfather a Lutheran, as was his mother, and his wife came from a congregationalist family. "And I love them all. Why should we not get together?" With his steadily growing influence in the affairs of the S.I.U.C. and his old personal friendship with Azariah, M. Peter became a central figure in church union affairs in South India.'[2] He was along with Azariah and others in the resolution on the *Tranquebar Manifesto*. He

---

[1] Quoted, Sundkler, 182.

[2] Ibid., 98f.

was a signatory to it along with his several colleagues from the SIUC delegate in the JC meetings and effectively propagated union. He convinced his church to accept episcopal authority. In the famous joint Communion services in 1932 in Madras Meshack Peter participated in conducting on the third day.

K. T. Paul

Kanakarayan Tiruselvam Paul (1876-1931) from Salem, studied in MCC, was an ardent follower of Mahatma Gandhi. 'He was the first Indian-born National General Secretary of the National Council of YMCAs of India. A Christian himself of the Congregational church established by LMS, he explored the relationship between Christianity and national identity. He held positions such as President of the Governing Council of UTC Bangalore, and Chairman of the NCCI (National Christian Council of India). Paul's lasting legacy was rural reconstruction, which he initiated through the YMCA in India.'[1] He got a job in the government secretariat but resigned after marriage. He taught in few mission schools and a teacher training college before he became a tutor in MCC in the department of History. He supported V.S. Azariah to establish the NMS (1905) and became its Hon. Treasurer, then Organising Secretary and from 1909 to 1914 the General Secretary. He was deeply concerned about the poor among the depressed classes and initiated the foundation of *Prem Sabha* (Society of Love) in northern India. His evangelical idea of unity among missions found expression in his participation in the formation of the SIUC (1908). Paul worked for the transformation of the National Missionary Council of India into National Christian Council of India with all overseas missions as members and he became its first Chairman. His interest in theological education led him to be the president of the UTC Governing Council and convener of the SIUC committee on theological education. His passion for indigenisation found expression in his reform of YMCA both in administration and performance. Though not liked by some missionaries and Indian Christians, Paul became a Christian nationalist and represented the Indian Christian community at the London Round Table Conferences in 1930–1932 along with S. K. Datta. It was not surprising that when he died Gandhi paid an instant tribute saying how much Paul was missed.

In the India National Conference that John Mott organised in Calcutta 1912, K.T. Paul presented a paper titled 'Indian Leadership in Mission and Church' which represented the discontent and dissatisfaction among leaders particularly of SIUC about the lack of equal footing for Indians along with Europeans. Paul pointed out that there existed a 'healthy unrest and discontent' on this score. Quoting Bishop Waller, he described the aim of the mission effort as 'church-centric, not mission-centric'. By this he 'launched a vigorous complaint against the unwilling of the missionaries to have Indian opinion represented in the

---

[1] https://en.wikipedia.org/wiki/K._T._Paul, as on 28 June 2018.

church councils. This, he said, had led to lack of mutual confidence.'[1] Paul got the support of H.A. Popley, an LMS missionary. The mobilisation of this awareness set a strong background for the question of church union in South India. He played an important role in the joint committee of Wesleyans and SIUC that met in in Madras in 1914 in continuation of a series of meetings identifying issues of their union. The same year in August the Executive of the SIUC appointed a committee called the 'Evangelistic Forward Movement'; Paul was a key leader of this group and the same month it met in his house in Salem. He was in the forefront of evangelistic initiative. He advocated the *ashram* model as an effective way to communicate the gospel with its simplicity and life-changing. Further, though he was for church unity for the sake of communicating the gospel, he first envisioned a pan-Indian Protestant Church without the leadership of bishops and later changed his mind for definite experiment in South India. Although, his scholarly expertise was History, in the question of maintaining a past tradition he confessed he was not a lover of history.

G.E. Phillips

Godfrey Edward Phillips (1878-1963) was born in Birmingham, England, and Studied at Mansfield College (Congregational), Oxford. He was appointed to the Pastorate of Davidson St. LMS Church, Madras, and to work among students. Ordained at Mansfield College in1901, he sailed to India the same year. He was married at Madras, to Clarissa May Stevens in 1902 (she came from England the same year). At the end of 1903 Phillips resigned the pastorate of Davidson St. Church and moved to Tripassore. Later he went to Bangalore, having been appointed on the staff of the UTC. During the Great War, he superintended the work of the German Mission at Shiyati for thirteen months (1915-1916). In 1920 he resumed work in the UTC. In 1922 Phillips, as the representative of the SIUC, moved temporarily to Calicut to assist in the work formerly in charge of the Basel Mission. During his second furlough in England (1919-1920) he followed the reports of the Lambeth Conference on the initiative of union movement in South India with great interest and concern. Of his books most notable are: *The Outcastes' Hope* (1912), *Student Volunteer Missionary Union* (1912), *The Ancient Church and Modern India* (1920) and (with F. Kingsbury) *Hymns of the Tamil Saiva* Saints (1921).

Sensing the situation of the mission field in South India, Phillips stressed the cooperation between missions. In the initial years he had to play the role of the agitating ministers and members of the SIUC against the union with pastoral care, missionary appeal and theological acumen. The South India District Committee of the SIUC appointed in 1921 a special sub-committee with him as secretary to study the whole problem. Freedom of worship was accepted as the leading principle at that point. As a secretary of LMS, he encouraged Azariah

---

[1] Sundkler, 47f.

not to lose heart by the opposition from the SIUC. He felt on several occasions that representatives came to meetings with a pre-determined plan to break the union prospects. He attributed the avoidance of a final break and new departure to divine help. Further, Phillips was the secretary of the British Congregational Commission of 1930, and then as the foreign secretary of the LMS he wrote a memorandum and encouraged certain radical modifications of the union scheme. Also, he attracted the Catholic wing by asking a significant question: 'Are there not in the tradition of the church certain Catholic elements 'without which we cannot give to India a full-orbed Christianity and something which possibly is better fitted to Indian conditions than certain features of our twentieth-century Free Church Christianity?'[1] Thus, Phillips set an example for future participants to bring a balance between the Catholic and Free Church elements.

H.A. Popley

Herbert Arthur Popley (1878-1960) was born at Richmond, Surrey, near London, and studied at Hackney College. Appointed to Coimbatore, he was ordained in 1901 and sailed the same year. As an LMS missionary, based in Erode, he married Lizzie Milda Bragg of the Bangalore Mission in 1908. From 1915 he acted as the Secretary of the YMCA with special focus on evangelistic work in South India and, residing in Madras from 1921, he was immersed in literary work in Tamil. He was a leading missionary but sharing the Indian passion for evangelism and indigenisation. Hence, his support for and cooperation with K.T. Paul. For him church union's sole purpose was to be credible and effective in evangelism. He was a prominent leader along with Paul and Eddy of the Evangelistic Forward Movement within the SIUC (1914). With a view to being relevant in evangelism he prepared and published 'Suggestions for Workers'. His contribution to music in the South Indian churches has had a lasting value. With the cooperation of Paul he created lyrical forms of worship and translated the popular Christian songs into Indian classical music in English. His book *The Music of India* (1921) was internationally acclaimed while going through many editions.

It was Popley's suggestion and support for V.S. Azariah to organise the Indian Ministers' conference on church union just after the annual Ministers' meeting at Tranquebar in May 1919. He was one of the only two non-Indian attendees (the other being Eddy) at the conference and both were instrumental in drafting the *Tranquebar Manifesto*. Also, when the issue of re-ordination or supplemental ordination was burning, while warning against the Anglican absorption of the new united church, he expressed a strange view: 'Personally I find no difficulty whatever about all this trouble about ordination. I do not mind how many human ordinations I receive so long as I am clear about my Divine ordination. I believe there are many who feel the same. I am ready to accept anything which means

---

[1] Quoted, Ibid., 274.

for the good of the Church.'[1] Later, while there were radical opinions floating about the relevance and adequacy of the Nicene Creed in the early 1930s, Popley thought that it 'had no relation to realities in the present day'. Popley retired in Ooty, died and was buried there. His interest in indigenous music and church unity continued till the end.

F. Lenwood

Frank Lenwood (1874-1934) was born at Sheffield and studied at Corpus Christi and Mansfield Colleges, Oxford. Married in 1903 to Gertrude Margaret Wilson, he ministered at the George Street Congregational Church, Oxford, was Assistant Minister at Queen St., Wolverhampton, and Tutor at Mansfield College from 1901 to 1906. The couple visited some of the LMS stations in China and India during 1907-8 and was appointed in 1909 to Benares, North India. Ordained in the same year at Mansfield he sailed too. In 1912, Lenwood visited England under medical advice, and in the same year he was appointed one of the Foreign Secretaries of the Society. The Lenwoods visited India in 1913-14, as a Deputation from the Society. In 1915-16, Lenwood visited Australia, the South Seas and Papua, as a Deputation from the Society. Subsequently he was able to relieve the Society of responsibility for his salary. In 1922-23, he again visited India with a Deputation from the Society. He wrote two books on the mission fields of the East.

Though he affirmed the Congregational value of spiritual equality and independence of local church, Lenwood was not happy about the tendency that every member was a law to him/herself. He was instrumental 'in linking the Free Church Fellowship with the younger missionaries in the fields', and this had a significant influence on the union talks in South India. With deep desire for cooperation and unity among missions, in his home country, he decided to approach the Anglican Fellowship and link it to the Free Church Fellowship. At the same time Lenwood opposed a mechanical view of the Church, Sacraments and work of the Spirit and import of the western formulations in India. He was sympathetic to the 'Rethinking Christianity' of Madras which called for dynamic relationship with the living Christ and indigenous form of the Church.

Bernard Lucas

Bernard Lucas (1860-1921) was born in Birmingham, studied at Cheshunt College. Appointed to Ooty, Tamil Nadu, and ordained in 1886, he sailed the same year and settled at his station. In 1890 he was appointed to the Wardlaw Institution at Bellary of Mysore State, while superintending the work in the Penuconda District, which was carried on from Anantapur. Lucas was married, in Madras, to Mary Jane Earp. In 1915 he was transferred to Bangalore. For his services to India during the Great War, he was made a Member of the Order of

---

[1] Quoted, Ibid., 134.

the British Empire. He died at Bournemouth in his 61st year. Among his many books, notable are: *Christ for India* (1910); *Our Task in India* (1914). Lucas was a key figure in the founding of the UTC Bangalore. He famously remarked that the Indian Church had not yet produced a heresy, meaning independent thinking instead of parrot-talking the western ideas.

Lucas was a member of the sub-committee which was to support the District Committee on the issues involved in church union. He joined those who were responding to those who had opposed the consecration of V.S. Azariah, both Anglicans and Free Church members, on the grounds of what they saw as his inadequate training and experience, while at the same time objecting to the fact that the first Indian bishop was consecrated only as an Assistant to a white bishop (Bishop Whitehead of Madras). Also, Bernard Lucas was among those who opposed the proposed 'comity' in missionary cooperation. In the wake of differences of opinion in Anglican ranks, in response to the question about the next step towards unity, he replied, 'There is no next step, for the Anglican cannot advance and the Non-Conformist cannot retreat.' Also, he was convinced by Whitehead's thesis on the historic episcopate as a 'necessary safeguard of unity.'[1] Further, while the War intensified, challenged by an article in the *Harvest Field* which pleaded for a National Church for India, Lucas suggested the inauguration of a 'League of Indian Christians' in order to promote nationalist and catholic ideas, catholic meaning un-denominational, among the Indian Christian community. But it was rejected as an insufficient foundation to build a church. Later, as a representative of the British Congregationalism (which had suffered persecution by the state church) he could not be as positive to the Tranquebar proposals as were the American and Australian Congregationalists. The view of a mechanical succession of grace was for him the most difficult issue. This is not to deny his commitment to achieve viable unity for the sake of mission.

A.H. Legg

Arnold Henry Legg (1899-1980) was born, brought up and schooled in Derby, England. After six years in Derby School and three years of business and military life, he joined the Cheshunt College at Cambridge in 1919. He took the Theological Tripos in 1922 and continued at Cheshunt for his postgraduate studies in 1924. Then he decided to be an LMS missionary and was ordained in 1924 and sent to the Trivandrum District of the SIUC. When LMS decided to put this District's pastoral work under Indian leadership in 1934, Legg was appointed Evangelistic Missionary of the northern area of Travancore to work among the low caste Ezhava community which started to move towards Christianity. He was known as effective preacher in fluent Malayalam with appeal to practical life. Also, he was an able administrator. For several years Legg was the President of the Travancore Church Council (SIUC), Chair of the Travancore Mission Council

---

[1] Sundkler, 70.

(LMS) and Treasurer of both. With regard to the union negotiations, he was the President of the General Assembly of the SIUC in the crucial period of 1937-1939.

Legg was first opposed to the idea of an episcopal united church and slowly developed interest in credible evangelism. When there was the question about the vital element of Congregationalism in reference to the 1929 Scheme, Legg thought that in every normal function of the local church, meeting was taken away from it and distributed amongst the bishop and his central council and the presbyters. The church would become a complex machine in which the individual congregation and the individual member were merely cogs. The SIUC ought to press for 'some real element of local self-government, such as the right to nominate their own pastor'. The bishop must not be thought to constitute a superior grade of the ministry, and should be commissioned by the whole church. He was opposed to the imbalance between Anglicans and members of the Free Churches in the area of power. However, he could not persuade the Travancore Council of the SIUC to oppose the Scheme as the majority wanted the union without delay. In 1946 when the decisive vote for union was taken, Legg was the convener of the SIUC Church Union Committee. He was an outstanding example of one who had begun as a radical Congregationalist opponent of the Scheme but eventually had become a convinced supporter. Then it was not surprising that in the decisive vote for organic union Legg stood in favour.

Legg was consecrated as one of the 14 diocesan bishops at the inauguration of CSI. Later the Diocese of Travancore was divided in the light of the revised state and revenue boundaries. Thus in 1959, the new Kanyakumari Diocese became part of Tamil Nadu, and Legg continued to be the bishop in South Kerala Diocese until 1967 when he retired.

E.H.M. Waller

Edward Harry Mansfield Waller (1871-1942) was an eminent Anglican Clergyman in the first half of the 20th century. Educated at Highgate and Corpus Christi College, Cambridge and ordained in 1894, he was successively Assistant Chaplain and Vice Principal of St Paul's Divinity School, Allahabad, Principal of Jay School, Benares, Secretary of the CMS (Indian Group), Narayan's and Canon of Lucknow before his elevation to the Episcopate as the 3rd Bishop of Thirunelveli. In 1923 he was translated to Madras where he served for a further 18 years. He reformed his diocese by giving power to the laity and applying democratic principles. He was one of the Anglican representatives in the first Joint Committee in 1920. With his experience as a CMS (Evangelical) missionary and secretary he could criticise both the Anglo-Catholics and Evangelicals for their lack of self-confidence. Waller was the convener of the sub-committee on church government, one of the six *ad hoc* sub-committees of the Joint Committee 1921. In order to allay fear, he clarified that the Lambeth Conference was only advisory and not a legislative body, and that at diocesan level, though the bishop had the veto power on certain matters, there was always room for appeal to the provincial synod the decision of which was final. Also, he and members of his sub-committee defined the duties of the diocesan council just as those then assigned to the church councils of the SIUC. When, in the face of Anglican insistence on issues such as intercommunion and apostolic succession the SIUC started to think of being part of the vision of a 'world-wide-union' Waller was particularly anxious to dispel fears that the SIUC would be absorbed into the Anglican Communion. Just like Bishops Temple and Bell, Waller declared that consecration of ministers as bishops of the SIUC was 'emphatically not a reception into the *Anglican* Church. It was a recognition of fellowship with a far greater company of churches', and this view was shared by Whitehead who visualised the formation of an 'independent Indian Church.'[1] Further, after his long efforts to convince the confused, he suggested a way of concelebration of communion, by representatives of the three Churches jointly celebrating, but without saying the consecratory prayer together but each doing it separately, thus bring together three rites. He did not want to be a communicant at non-episcopal hands! But his colleagues did not agree. However, he was a vigorous champion of church union. With his friendly approach he could win over opponents from his own tradition and other traditions. Finally, he was giving leadership for the arrangements of inauguration of the CSI although he did not live to see it.

F. Westcott

Foss Westcott (1863-1949), son of a distinguished bishop (of Durham) and New Testament scholar, Brooke Foss Westcott, was educated at Cheltenham College and Peter house, Cambridge. Ordained in 1887, his first post was as curate of St Peter's Church, Bishop wearmouth. Emigrating to India he was a Missionary with the SPG before ascending to the episcopate as Bishop of Chota Nagpore in 1905. Translated to Calcutta in 1919, he served as Metropolitan of CBCI until 1945. He retired to Darjeeling where he died.

Without foregoing his Anglo-Catholic convictions, Westcott supported the union particularly as it was interpreted by Palmer including respect for the right of members of the churches in negotiation to have communion with those of other churches either before or after union. He ruled that approval of intercommunion was to respect the conviction of the non-episcopal churches that they received the same sacramental grace from different hands. Also, he asserted that non-episcopal ministries could be regarded as 'spiritually efficacious', and that the sacramental grace was conveyed when administered by such ministers. In this connection what he summed up as the attitude of the Episcopal Synod (1932) is a profound reminder for all generations: 'We feared lest we by rigidity might be found to be

---

[1] Sundklar, 115.

fighting against God.'[1] At the same time further compromises had to be made that resulted in the Pledge. Westcott had to do a balancing act when he received representations from the Church of England ('the storm centre' of the church union in South India), Anglican bishops, councils and synods of the CBCI and the Free Churches. Yet he acted with grace and wisdom.

F.J. Western

Frederick James Western (1880-1951) was educated at Marlborough and Trinity College, Cambridge, joined the Cambridge Mission to Delhi in 1904 and was ordained twelve years later becoming its Head in 1918. From 1923 to 1929 he was a Canon Residentiary of the Cathedral Church of the Resurrection, Lahore after which he was appointed to the episcopate as the fifth Anglican Bishop of Thirunelveli. Western came to the Joint Committee in 1928. 'In South India he definitely moved in the direction of Evangelicalism. As a member and leading draftsman of the Joint Committee, this honest and humourless ascetic was conciliatory to all parties and swift to embody into a resolution, and eventually into the Constitution, the decisions of the Committee.'[2] He was particular that the CSI should not be a copy of the Church of England but a local embodiment of the Catholic Church.

Western expressed the hope as early as from 1929 that the CSI bishops (as well as the bishops of Orthodox, Old Catholics etc) would be invited to the Lambeth Conference. In his view (influenced by Palmer) Lambeth was not of the Anglican Communion only but of a wider fellowship of the churches. He was instrumental to replace the word 'consecration of bishops' by 'ordination of bishops' in order to satisfy the Scottish Presbyterians. And this was accepted by the Joint Committee. He was also instrumental in bringing together the Anglican Seminary in Tirunelveli diocese and the Congregational Seminary at Pasumalai near Madurai in 1935. Unfortunately, he was not able to see the consummation of the CSI as he returned to England in 1938.

H.E. Lefever *(Dates not available)*

Served LMS in India from 1934 to 1954. He was born an Anglican and joined a Congregationalist group and became an LMS missionary. He was one of those who supported Lay Celebration; also as one of the two younger missionaries (the other C.B. Firth) to present a report from the SIUC with reference to answers received from about a hundred replies from the western theologians about Lay Celebration. But there was difference of opinion between the two and in the end Lefever signed the report alone reflecting an exclusive Congregationalist view. 'Lefever put the Congregationalist case learnedly, moderately and fairly. He linked Lay Celebration with the conception of the Priesthood of All Believers.' This was

---

[1] Quoted, Ibid., 236.

[2] Ibid., 123.

directed against the apostolic succession theory of episcopacy. He could not accept that the administration of sacrament given to ordained men was a privilege. He recommended ordaining full time catechists working in the villages. For him, 'We cannot give up our separate existence unless we can continue to exercise our vocation in the united church. We believe that the inclusion of provision for Lay Celebration, with all due safeguards, will be one of the greatest contributions we can make to the Ecumenical Church.'[1] In 1954 Lefever left India to take up a post of Professor of Missions at Selly Oak Colleges, Birmingham, England.

C.B. Firth

Colin B. Firth (1905-1997) was an LMS missionary for 35 years of the Kanarese church council, based in Bellary, where he taught theology. Through his writings and speeches, he represented a minority view within the SIUC, moving away from the exclusive position of Congregationalism as represented by his colleague Lefever. Orientated in Cambridge, his theological position was shaken by radical options. His reading of the book *Divine Service* by W.E. Orchard in 1937 moved him towards a catholic position. Invited by some of his Anglican colleagues of the Joint Committee for Union, he along with his Congregationalist colleague F.H. Brown, took evensong in the English Church. Criticising the individualistic and 'everyone as leader' attitudes, he advocated a return to orthodoxy with illumination of the scripture as experienced in the church's tradition. Therefore, in the end, it was not what the scripture told but what the church told that mattered to him. As scripture itself was in the formative process, the tradition which was illumined by it was important, and which was ever-reforming too. Firth pointed out that SIUC was not exclusively Congregationalist where the church councils had monopolised authority, not delegated to the local churches. He suggested in mass movement areas lay persons should be ordained with special training. But he did not agree on linking Lay Celebration to the Protestant principle of the priesthood of all believers. He said he had seen in India people who were 'much more eager to secularize the ministry than to sanctify the laity'. Then he agreed with Azariah on the dictum of 'one priesthood and different functions' though the Anglican position remained that it was only the ordained priest who could conduct worship! In any case, finally, Firth's influence on the Kanarese church council was considerable to accept the union. He wrote several books, of which *An Introduction to Church History* has been the most popular text book on the subject with continuing new editions.

H.V. Martin

Harold Victor Martin (1898-1968) was an LMS missionary who served the Telugu council from 1930 to 1948. He was a member of the Joint Committee representing SIUC. Though he appreciated the Anglican concession, he could not

---

[1] Quoted, Ibid., 297f.

accept the historic episcopacy as the basis of union and asked for the recognition of the ministries of the non-episcopal churches. With regard to the proposal for supplemental ordination, Martin argued that each of the uniting churches should 'commission the ministers (this meant both bishops and presbyters) of the other two uniting churches'. The form of the commission should be by way of laying on of hands, 'unless the minister concerned prefers otherwise.'[1] His vision of extending the jurisdiction to cover other denominations was rejected as it had no concern about the universal validity of episcopacy. He proposed and published a novel scheme which suggested the new name 'the United Church of South India and Ceylon' which would give greater scope for exercising different ministries after mutual ordination. Also, the Congregational principle of democracy (as opposed to autocracy and sacerdotalism) for provided a framework for maintaining the order of the church.

J.H. Maclean

James Hair Maclean (1868-1943) was born in Greenoak, Renfrewshire in Scotland, and studied at the university and Free Church College, Glasgow, and was ordained in 1895. As a Free Church of Scotland missionary, he was sent to Kancheepuram, a rural town, 68 km west of Madras (Chennai). He was married to Jessie (he married again later). In 1903 Maclean was one of the leading younger Presbyterian missionaries of South India. When SIUC was to be formed in 1908 Maclean defended it confidently: 'It is the only church that has actually be formed as a result of the union. And it is not beyond the limits of possibility that were long its boundaries may be so largely extended as to make the name more appropriate.'[2] Maclean could not appreciate the initial aloofness of the Wesleyan Methodists. Further, with regard to the move towards the formation of 'CSI' he was hesitant, and anxious that it should not be a Communion rejected by a higher church authority. At the same time, as one of his fellow committee members observed, 'There is a strong element of high and pure Presbyterianism in Maclean's make-up. The solid Scottish missionary is one of the noblest figures in the company of union makers. He had firm theological principles and stuck to them – but he could also learn and change.' T.M. Lindsay, Scottish patristic scholar was his authority, and Alexander Martin (1857-1946), Principal of New College, Edinburgh (1918-1935), was his advisor. His letters and essays are great resources to understand his opinions and arguments.

In the twenties Maclean represented the opposition against Palmer's Catholic conception of the united church. Parity of the ministry was his Presbyterian standpoint, real equality his demand, and the practice of intercommunion seemed to him to be a first necessary step. He did not gloss over difficulties. He wrote to Palmer: 'It is essential that in contemplating union we should sound the

---

[1] Sundkler, 312.

[2] Ibid., 38.

depths of our differences even if the statement of them should be painful.'[1] There was the burning issue of intercommunion. He found the Lambeth Conference (1930) to be straightforward. 'After that Appeal, the prospect of reunion in South India was not very hopeful.' In his opinion the Lambeth Conference, while aiming at opening the door as wide as possible, 'in reality come pretty near to closing it.'[2] The proposal of re-ordination also was opposed by Maclean and his associates. He accepted the LMS missionary Godfrey Phillips's opinion that dealing with Azariah would be easier but with doctrines and ideas would be misleading. Thus, committed persons were more important than doctrines! But when the Methodists stressed church order (1933-34), Maclean supported them; so also with modifications around this time, as he explained the union along with Weston and Hooper to those who were to be fully convinced. He had to defend the episcopacy against the critical stand of persons like Principal Martin with the affirmation that 'episcopacy in South India was a great blessing but it would not be at all a bad thing to leave the bishop with a veto.' For continuing participation and conversation, Maclean was succeeded by Newbigin who came from the same church.

A. Streckeisen

Adolf Streckeisen (1895-1951) was a missionary of the Basel Mission in South India during 1924-1949. His marriage took place in Palakkad, Kerala, to Ms. Jungck in 1926. He was the principal of the Malabar Christian College during 1930-1935, preceded by Rev. A. Muench and succeeded by F. Melzer. In 1949 he left India, in order to take over the responsibility as the India-Inspector of the Basel Mission. He is said to be the representative and authoritative voice of this mission in India, particularly in the Church Union negotiations.

Streckeisen was the drive behind the Malabar Council voting in favour of the union scheme. But he challenged the ongoing debate on the appeal to the early church Fathers as held by the Anglicans. As a continental missionary, he felt out of place within the framework of the patristic history and theology which was for him an Anglican artefact. He would rather appeal to the period of Reformation, not for comprehension but definiteness and simplicity on the basis of the scriptures. His own theology and direction equipped the Basel Mission representatives to the Joint Committee 1932. In the question of intercommunion, he had the following rather sharp question: 'The refusal of the Anglican Church to have intercommunion is a real offence to me. What then is the Scheme but an absorption into that church? If we can't recognise each other even so much, is there much use in trying for union, while the necessary presuppositions are mission?'[3] He observed that in the current debate there was more preoccupation

---

[1] Ibid., 124f.

[2] Ibid., 135.

[3] Quoted, Ibid., 229.

to 'order' than 'faith' and the Malabar Council agreed to this. With the influence of Streckeisen, members of the council reaffirmed 'Holy Scriptures as the only standard of faith and life and will tolerate only such teaching as is in conformity with them.'[1] The prevailing emphasis on scripture and experience and concern for comprehensiveness was countered with the Reformation's primacy of scriptures with necessary interpretation and the mind of Christ which they point to. Streckeisen's position was shared by the liberal minds of other councils of the SIUC. Streckeisen was influenced by the German-Swiss theologians such as Karl Barth in attaching primacy to the scriptures and safeguarding against syncretism and uncritical pluralism, as they were the challenges in India. It was not to be obsessed by the ancient creeds but to create modern creeds with a view to working for ongoing reformation of the apostolic church. Streckeisen's view was incorporated in the amended scheme of 1939. With regard to Lay Celebration, Streckeisen felt that that bishops might authorise certain persons to celebrate as needed, as was done in the early Church, though the final decision in the Joint Committee was 'to recommend that trusted catechists and evangelists be ordained as "assistant ministers" (whether presbyters or deacons)'. For him, supplemental ordination was only re-ordination. On the whole, Streckeisen infused a continental, Protestant view, which was convincing, into the union scheme in South India.

A.C. Headlam

Arthur Cayley Headlam (1862-1947), born in County Durham, educated at Oxford, ordained in 1888, was Professor of Dogmatic Theology and Principal of King's College London, and Regius Professor of Divinity, Oxford. His 1920 Bampton Lectures showed the theme of ecumenism that would preoccupy him. As Bishop of Gloucester (1923-1945), and with experience of being the Church of England's officer for foreign church relations he provided his expert advice on crucial issues in the ongoing negotiations of church union in South India. In the context of a hot debate on the authority of episcopal ordination and the Free Churches' insistence of presbyters laying hands on the bishops at consecration, Headlam made an important point about the regulation that visiting ministers and missionaries should be recommissioned. 'If all who should join the United Church, whether they have been ordained episcopally or non-episcopally, have to be recommissioned, you have done away with the idea of a ministry recognised by all. The new United Church would have a ministry which recognises no one else. In fact, you would have created a new class of ordination, a new type of ministry, and would have increased the difficulty of union rather than diminished it.'[2] In his book *Christian Unity* (1930) he stated: 'It is only those who have the courage of leadership who can accomplish anything that is worth accomplishing in the

---

[1] Quoted, Ibid., 271.

[2] Ibid., 152f.

world.[1] Azariah underlined these words in his copy and found reassuring his ability to propel the church union movement. Headlam as a recognised theologian and experienced leader of foreign and ecumenical relations had a long correspondence with Banninga on intercommunion, sharing William Temple's view.'[2] This was approved in the Episcopal Synod of the CIBC and Joint Committee of the CSI union. So also, he shared the views of others that lay celebration would wreck the union scheme. In any case, the 'exception' later became a reality when it happened in the Joint Committee in 1932 though some leading Anglicans did not take part. Headlam, though officially defended, wrote to Banninga noting his wish that 'there had been a little more wisdom exercised'. Also, Headlam shared the view of some Anglican scholars in USA and Britain that Lay Celebration of the Holy Communion would wreck the CSI union scheme. On the whole, however, Headlam's interactions added to the theological and ministerial seriousness of the South India scheme.

C. W. Posnett

Charles Walker Posnett (1870-1950) was born in Sheffield, and his father was a Methodist minister. While at school in Kingswood he received the divine call and dedicated himself for service. With a commanding personality and leadership qualities he influenced many during his training in Richmond College. In 1895 Posnett was appointed to Hyderabad and he was based in the nearby rural area Medak. He reached out the 'untouchables', and gave solidarity with the suffering, starving and vulnerable. Many found a new life through his ministry. Until he retired in 1939, he was engaged in what was known as energetic evangelism. As the Chair of the District and then of the Provincial Synod of the Methodist Church in South India, his influence was evident all around of his ministry. He was awarded the Kaisar-i-Hind Medal for his service of the Indian people.

Initially Posnett, just like his junior contemporary Hooper, was hesitant to become involved in the union movement, but was then convinced of its importance for effective mission. Particularly when the Anglicans agreed on inter-communion in 1932 it was reassuring for him, and from then on he became a great defender of the union. He initiated and supported joint Holy Communion between Christians of Medak (Methodist) and of Dornakal (Anglican) regions of Andhra. When the Methodist Conference in England was still not certain, Posnett suggested in 1933 sending a learned lay person to South India to study the situation and bring recommendations. Consequently, Prof. Lofthouse visited and attended some meetings of union. His recommendation and Posnett's support influenced the Conference to observe that the CSI union scheme was

---

[1] Quoted, Ibid., 185.

[2] 'To make an exception in exceptional circumstances is a way of affirming the general rule.' Quoted, Ibid., 234.

not contrary to the Methodist principles. When implementation was delayed, the Methodists expressed their impatience.

F.C. Sackett

Frank Colyer Sackett (1876-1953), a Wesleyan missionary, born in Manchester, trained in Headingly College, was appointed to Hyderabad District in 1901. His performance in many-sided mission, particularly among the rural masses qualified him for the Kaisar-i-Hind Medal. Like his colleague Posnett, Sackett was a member of the JC of the South India union movement. When the Anglican resolution affirmed the right of any of the uniting churches to continue communion with other churches even after union, Sackett commented, 'There is no doubt that the Anglicans have given a way and shown throughout a most magnanimous spirit.'[1] Attending the longest JC meeting, in 1929, where the proposed the scheme of union was published, he observed the meticulous, orderly and sensitive way the meetings were conducted.

V. Santiago

Vethamuthu Santiago (1869-1929), was a grandson of a soldier in the British army and son of Vethamuthu, who was originally a Roman Catholic in Thiruchirappalli and who converted to Protestantism. Harassed by some fanatic Catholics, Vethamuthu migrated to Madurai District and settled in the village Silukkuvarpatti, west of Madurai. He was deeply committed to ministry which he did along with teaching and practise of native health care. His zeal for ministry made him dedicate all his four sons to ministry. Santiago was born as the youngest of the four brothers and he had two sisters as well. He worked for two years in the Basel Mission, otherwise as teacher in different institutions including the Pasumalai Seminary and American College, Madurai. Ordained in 1908, he ministered most of his career in the Vathalakkundu church of the Madurai American Congregational Mission. He was a great poet of lyrics, and a good collection of his lyrics has been included in successive editions of the official Tamil Christian Lyric Book. His were some of the very few lyrics which talk about liberation of the gospel in a holistic sense including serving the nation and redeeming the oppressed. He promoted indigenous forms of worship.

Santiago, with a passion for church union worked closely with V.S. Azariah, Eddy, Meshack Peter and Banninga. It was he who first approached Azariah to act as the convener of the Tranquebar Conference in 1919. He was the first Indian leader of the Madura Home Missionary Society (1904), a President of the SIUC (1917) and its Moderator also (1919-1921). He was among those who worked to bring the Basel Mission closer to the SIUC.

---

[1] Quoted, Ibid., 163.

M.B. Taylor

Maurice Brown Taylor (1894-1947), son of a minister and born in Beverley, Yorks, educated at the Kingswood School, was sent to the Mysore District where he served for 17 years. Most notably, he worked among the labourers and managers of the Kolar Gold mines and of Nilgiri tea estates. He was also responsible for directing the work taken over from the Basel Mission by the Methodist Church. For a considerable time, he was a member of the Joint Committee of the CSI union before he moved to the Gold Coast in 1936.

As early as 1937, Taylor expressed his optimism on behalf of the Methodists: 'Conversation turns now to ways and means by which union, the main principles of which are acceptable to us, may be achieved. For us, for all vital purposes, the day of debate is over.'[1] But this optimism was upset by the Anglicans who continued to stress and perpetuate the difference between bishops and presbyters. He was a member of the Continuation Committee, which in 1935 considered the question of lay celebration of Communion, and with apparent Methodist influence the agreed method recommended was 'to recommend that trusted catechists and evangelists be ordained as "assistant ministers" (whether presbyters or deacons) but would not have independent charge of administrative charge of pastorates.'[2] This was acceptable to the Joint Committee, but Taylor moved on next year thus escaping more shaking challenges.

H. Sumitra

Hospet Sumitra (1888-1970) was born and died in Bellary (Karnataka). Graduated from the Central College of Bangalore, he joined UTC in 1910 as one among the first students and completed his theological education and ministerial training in 1913. He came to be known as an able leader and exemplary pastor. Originally a Congregationalist, representing the Kanarese Council of the SIUC, he was an influential teacher at UTC Bangalore. He attended the fifth Joint Committee meeting in Madras 1925 where the Bangalore report 1920 was discussed paragraph by paragraph, for the benefit and approval of the hesitant latecomers, the Methodists. It was the start of many subsequent committees which he attended. Also, he participated in the debate on church unity with unique reference to the negotiations in South India in the World Conference on Faith and Order at Lausanne, 1927. Finally, Sumitra's influence along with that of Firth worked when the Kanarese council eventually accepted the CSI union scheme in 1939.

While negotiations for the formation of CSI reached fever pitch, with new hurdles put forward mainly from the Anglican side that caused continued delay, Sumitra famously stated in 1942:

---

[1] Sundkler, 187f.

[2] Ibid., 285.

Left to themselves, Indians would have united long ago. But ... this long delay has meant valuable education to us. I think that both the missionaries and Indians now feel that the need for opposition and controversy no longer exists. The time is drawing nigh for a supreme exercise of faith.[1]

At last at the inauguration of the CSI, Sumitra was among the fourteen bishops consecrated being incharge of the Cudappah and Chittoor dioceses which were later combined as the diocese of Rayalaseema, part of Andhra Pradesh since their bifurcation in 2014. As the first Indian Moderator, Sumitra succeeded Michael Hollis. He was honoured with a DD from the Senate of Serampore College (University) in 1958.

R.D. Paul

Rajiah D. Paul (1895-1975) was born in Tiruchirappalli, had his high school education in Salem, passed his Intermediate exam with first class from the SPG College, Trichy, and later passed the B.A. Hon. from MCC in 1917. After working for a year in MCC, he entered the Madras Civil Service as a probationary deputy Thasildar, being the first to be recruited. After a distinguished service of 32 years during which he was promoted to the Indian Civil Service including as Commissioner of Madurai, he retired in 1950. He worked as the first bursar of MCC for a short time. As an honest and disciplined civil servant his Christian witness was attested by many. He bemoaned the lack of spirituality and integrity among many Christians.

While he was the Commissioner of Madurai, on Paul's suggestion the three main groups in Madurai – Anglican, SIUC and Lutheran – arranged united services in their several churches, attended by thousands, which showed that for lay Christians unity was greater than doctrinal differences. In this context, Paul made a strong appeal as he wrote in the *SIUC Herald* as early as 1939:

The problem before the Church is not how to defend itself against the onslaughts of the world, but how to advance. There is no question of the Church returning to the catacombs. In this advance the main result will be unity of the Church in the next generation.[2]

In connection with the debate on lay celebration of Communion on the basis of the priesthood of all believers, Paul clarified that 'It would be ridiculous for anyone, merely on the strength of this phrase, to make a claim of right to perform any priestly functions.'[3] At the inauguration of the CSI, Paul expressed his impatience at the lack of moving forward and growing in unity by asking,

---

[1] Quoted, Ibid., 207.

[2] Quoted, Ibid., 200.

[3] Quoted, Ibid., 289.

'How long are we to persist in thinking and speaking of ourselves as ex-Anglican, ex-Methodist and ex-Congregationalist members of the Church of South India?'[1] After union R.D. Paul worked as Secretary of the Madras Diocesan Council (while Hollis was bishop) and later Hon. General Secretary of the CSI Synod for three terms (1952-1958). He was one of the six official delegates of the CSI at the second General Assembly of the WCC in Evanston (1954) and played a key role. Also, he served on the Executive and Central Committee of the WCC and as the Chair of the Dept. of Laity where he emphasised the vital role of the laity in Christian witnessing. His commitment to CSI and passion for its development found its clearest expression in his books such as *The First Decade, Renewal and Advance* and *Ecumenism in Action.*[2]

Significant Influences, Visitors, Advisors and Supporters

Peter Taylor Forsyth (1848-1921), born in Aberdeen, Scotland, where he also graduated, studied under the German systematic theologian Ritschi at Göttingen and briefly New College, London, where he eventually returned as the Principal. He first served in four Congregational pastorates and from that period to his end he went through changes in his theological position, particularly from humanist ideals to dependence on divine grace. He was a great Congregationalist theologian of his time and influenced the younger generation of missionaries of that tradition. What he said, for example, on ministry was remembered in the story of the CSI: 'If a church wishes to show its self-respect, it will go out of its way to be respectful to its ministry. The church will be what its ministry makes it. That stands to reason.'[3] His re-orientation from Congregational theology to orthodoxy caused organic union on Catholic basis.

John R. Mott (1865-1955), a long-serving leader of the YMCA (Young Men's Christian Association) and the WSCF (World Student Christian Federation), who was honoured with the Nobel Peace Prize, a Methodist layman from America, came to be a great pioneer of the ecumenical movement. He organised the India National Missionary Conference at Calcutta 1912 which stressed: 'Churches and missions should make a real and unmistakable advance by placing Indians on complete equality, in status and responsibility, with Europeans.'[4] Mott tried to bring a comity of Christian missions which was not easy in a context of denominational rigidity, but those fired by his ideas contributed to the church union movement.

---

[1] Quoted, Ibid., 343; the origin and background of R.D. Paul suggests he was an Anglican, but this author notes him here as 'a leading SIUC layman'!

[2] For a detailed obituary see, 'Editorial', *South India Churchman,* January, 1976, 1; he was buried in the cemetery of St. George's Cathedral.

[3] Quoted, Ibid., 304.

[4] Quoted, Ibid., 47.

H. Pakenham-Walsh (1871-1959), a young Anglican priest who was inspired by the NMS (National Missionary Society). As an educator he served as Principal of Bishop Cotton School, Bangalore. He found that interpreting the historic episcopacy was the heart of the problem. While communicating this to the Lambeth Conference he was critical of the Lambeth view on 'valid ministry' in relation to the ministries of the other denominations. At the time of the inauguration of the CSI, Pakenham-Walsh was consecrated as bishop without diocese.

William Paton (1886-1943), an English Presbyterian who was a great ecumenist. An Oxfordian, he converted to a living faith. As a pacifist he was opposed to fascism, racism and anti-Semitism, and to avoid danger, he was ordained hastily in 1916 and dispatched to India as a YMCA secretary. Paton returned from India in 1919 and provided inspiring leadership for the SCM. Recalled to India in 1921, he served from 1922 to 1926 as the first Secretary of the NCCI (National Christian Council of India). He was keen to check tendencies of sacerdotalism in the course of the negotiations for CSI. As a scholar and writer, he encouraged research on evangelism, and in recognition the William Paton Fellowship was established in Selly Oak Colleges.

Prof. W.F. Lofthouse (1871-1965), a Wesleyan belonging to the high church tradition, an Oxfordian, theological teacher, a great scholar and writer, and church leader (e.g. President of the World Methodist Conference, 1929), visited India in 1934. He attended the Joint Committee in February the same year. 'To his satisfaction the meeting agreed that, as a rule, two presbyters should join together with the bishops in consecrations, but the diocesan council concerned could alternatively decide that the bishops should lay on hands alone.'[1] Unlike Hooper and others he agreed on supplemental ordination. At the same time, he was against tendencies towards sacerdotalism.

Francis Kingsbury: A radical Indian pastor of the Northern Council of the SIUC. His initial position was that Jesus was merely a man, for which he was suspended. His teaching influenced people like D.M. Devasahayam. At the same time he pleaded that the SIUC should not obstruct union or hinder its smooth passage before the 1920 Lambeth Conference.

William Temple: (1881-1944), Headmaster of Repton School, lecturer in philosophy at Queen's College Oxford, Bishop of Manchester, Archbishop of York and finally Archbishop of Canterbury, was a great theologian and social thinker. He was a member of the Anglican Fellowship founded in 1912. He advised Azariah on crucial points of the CSI union. Azariah was taken as a member of the Committee on the Unity of the Church formed by the Episcopal Synod of CIBC and chaired by Temple. Temple endorsed the proposed practice of inter-communion as an exceptional allowance in an exceptional circumstance provided that the union was certainly on. On the vexed question of supplemental

---

[1] Ibid., 265.

ordination Temple stated his opinion that this method 'would no doubt make acceptance of the scheme easier for Anglicans'. However, his judgement on the interim period of the Pledge (for 30 years Anglican congregations should have the right to have ministers only with episcopal ordination) for pastoral concern irritated the Free Church leaders, particularly the Methodists. Towards the end, summing up consultations at different levels, Temple wrote a letter to the Metropolitan of India, Foss Westcott, in which there was an affirmation that the formation of the CSI was the will of God over which all concerned will rejoice. And after stating the above mentioned Anglican pastoral concerns, he stated:

> The united Church would not be a Province of the Anglican Communion, and there will not be at this stage be unrestricted intercommunion between it and this Province, but there would be such intercommunion between clergy and laity of the united church and those of this Province as I have stated.[1]

This was the last statement signed by Temple about South India. Further, in his statement to Canterbury Convocation on union in 1944, he affirmed that the formation of the CSI did not represent a schism but a novel method of union. This led to the consummation of decades of negotiations.

George Kennedy Bell (1883-1958), an Oxfordian, theologian, Dean of Canterbury and finally Bishop of Chichester for nearly 40 years, was radical in his views on war, social ethics and church unity. He supported William Temple, the chairman of the 73-bishop committee on the unity of the church, in response to the submission of the CIBC on the question of CSI to the Lambeth Conference. After a spell of tension and opposition two points of clarity eased the situation. First, the responsibility was with the CIBC, not the LC (1930). Second, the CSI would be regional and autonomous, not a new kind of Anglican church. George Bell who drafted the resolution stated that the southern Indian dioceses 'would go forth from the Anglican Communion in order to make their own distinctive contribution to the faith and order of the new united church. Moreover, the church will be itself a distinct province of the Universal Church, with a rule and character of its own ... the suggestion that the united church should form a new province of (the CIBC) is rejected' as this would seem to be absorption into the Anglican Church.[2] Bell's support for Temple was consistent. He carefully watched negotiations of church unity around the world including South India and published different versions of the *Documents on Christian Unity*. As we noted earlier, Bell visited Chennai and encouraged the first Moderator Hollis. He was impressed by the life and witness of the new church and the leadership of Hollis with whom he had lasting friendship.

---

[1] Quoted, Sundkler, 332f.

[2] Ibid., 218. In the following paragraphs the ways in which the CSI should relate to the Anglican Communion and churches are reproduced.

Norman Henry Tubbs (1879-1965) was educated at Highgate School and Gonville and Caius College, Cambridge. He was ordained in 1903 and was curate at Whitechapel Parish Church before going to India as a CMS missionary, eventually becoming Principal of Bishop's College, Calcutta. In 1923, he was ordained to the episcopate as the 4th Bishop of Thirunelveli. He was translated to Rangoon in 1928 and returned to England six years later to be the Archdeacon of Chester and later its Dean. Tubbs observed that no actual scheme of unity attracted so much attention at the World Conference on Faith and Order at Lausanne, 1927 either in formal presentations or in informal conversations as the South Indian union scheme, though he felt 'it was a conference of old men representing old churches of the West'. Though he belonged to the same school, he often defended the union scheme against Anglo-Catholic criticism. Appealing not to form but to the Spirit of the Pentecost, he supported intercommunion and was optimistic about finding solution for the imminent union.

Cuthbert Hamilton Turner (1860-1930), a Professor in Oxford of Ecclesiology and Biblical Studies, was regarded as great authority in this area. He was one of those who received a questionnaire from the Metropolitan of India for his opinion about proposals for the commissioning service and future consecration of bishops put forward by some Free Church scholars. While he was willing to give concessions for the sake of unity, he criticised the idea of spiritual equality which in his view would lead to claim any right without regard for the tradition of the Apostolic Church. Obviously, he was for the episcopal ministry, therefore, for him a joint form of commission was unsatisfactory and inadequate. 'The only and obvious substitute', he said, 'is that of distinct services or at any rate distinct forms in which each side shall use a form sufficient from its own point of view, to convey whatever seems to it lacking in the previous commission or ordination already possessed by the other.'[1] For him, presbyters laying hands on the bishops at consecration would knock at the bottom of the apostolic tradition. Turner's view was taken by both sides seriously, but he did not live longer to face further arguments and final resolutions.

Venkal Chakkarai (1880-1958), a lawyer by profession, and a convert from the high caste Hinduism, was an associate of the National Missionary Society, *Christ Samaj* and the 'Rethinking Christianity' group in Madras. Through these organisations he promoted the ideal of radical discipleship, liberal views and indigenous forms of Christianity. Chakkarai stated that India was not 'a fit scene where to fight out the battle of Western ecclesiasticism. This ought to be transferred to Rome, Canterbury, or Geneva which is their native habitat ... The South India Scheme ... had no Indian origin. It was an importation from Lambeth.'[2] His views were more or less shared by his relative P. Chenchiah who stressed the raw facts of experiencing the living Christ, and by his colleague D.M.

---

[1] Quoted, Ibid., 152.

[2] Quoted, Ibid., 205.

Devasahayam, but not many among the South Indian Christians and missionaries could stomach them.

Canon R.A. Manuel was another outstanding Indian church leader. He joined the Joint Committee in 1935. When ecumenicity was still not appreciated by certain Anglican circles, Manuel appealed to the Episcopal Synod of the CIBC: 'The Indian Church are sick of the whole thing. We in South India consist of 99 per cent of Dravidians. We have in our sub-conscious mind group-consciousness. We are going to give you something Indian and Catholic. Don't curtail our freedom now. Trust us.'[1] As one of the Anglican representatives, Manuel attended the Joint Committee of 1939 where there was discussion on Lay Celebration of Communion.

John Scott Lidgett (1854-1953), son of the first principal of Westminster Training College, educated at Blackheath Proprietary School and then at University College, London, entered the Wesleyan ministry in 1876. He held top posts in the Methodist Church and has been regarded as one of the greatest Methodists since John Wesley; his honours included a Honorary Freeman of the Borough of Bermondsey. He was a noted consultant for ecclesiastical matters, particularly at conferences between Anglicans and members of the Free Churches on church union, and his influence and advice was of the highest value. Lidgett took part in the Faith and Order conferences at Mansfield College, Oxford (1916-1918) where the Anglican and Free Churches' re-union was a major agenda. As a 'high church Wesleyan' his sympathies with South India were well known, and for this reason he was not preferred to a visit to South India in 1934. Yet he was consulted at crucial points by the Methodist leaders, especially Hooper and his colleagues. To the puzzlement of Hooper, however, he defended the sudden new proposal for supplemental ordination.

George Noel Lankester Hall (1891-1962) was educated at Bedford School and St. John's College, Cambridge and was ordained in 1918. After serving at Christ Church, Luton as curate, he became Vice-principal of Ely Theological College, and he went to India in 1919 as an SPG missionary and became Bishop of Chota Nagpur from 1936 to 1957. He was involved in South Indian negotiations through the CBCI. An Anglo-Catholic, he was an expert to be consulted on Church of the Fathers, yet was open to learn about the Protestant ethos but without allowing to weaken his stand. His contribution found an honest admission with profound insights. E.g. 'To be in a state of schism, and to be guilty of the sin of schism, are two quite distinct things. To be still in that state but eagerly desiring to heal the schism is a blameless condition. I fear to be one who prevents union and so be guilty of the sin of schism.'[2] He thought that conceiving episcopacy in terms of only church governance was reducing it to 'the

---

[1] Ibid., 207.
[2] Quoted, Ibid., 184.

most shadowy dimension'. Finally, he contributed to the liturgy of the inaugural service of the CSI.

Short Contributors in Brief

There were a few who passed through quickly or silently, but making some significant contribution. the following are the most notable.

Newman Smyth (1843-1925), an American Congregationalist, suggested the biological category of the 'anticipatory substitution' for the growth of mission and unity of the church. He wrote a book as early as 1908 entitled *Passing Protestantism and Coming Catholicism* which became influential among leaders of different denominations. In 1912 he visited Britain and established contacts with many different groups of church leaders and held important meetings. The resolutions of these meetings were studied with interest in South India in the background of the Anglican-Free Church conference in Tranquebar. Smyth was realistic when he said that any united church in India would have an episcopal element.

Alfred Edward John Rawlinson (1884-1960), Bishop of Derby, was concerned with the initial Anglican reaction to the South India union scheme. His symposium *Foundations* guided discussions on Faith and Order. He was the Chairman of the committee of theologians to report on the South India basis and constitution.

Newton R. Flew (1886-1962), a Methodist theologian based in Cambridge, a colleague and consultant of Hooper, insisted that presbyters must take part in consecration of bishops and challenged the Anglicans for not accepting ministers from the other side. For him the priesthood of all believers was more than lay administration, and supplemental ordination was in effect re-ordination, but he was open to Hollis's suggestion of an extended commission, not retrospective but prospective, and that it would be for all the ministers of all the uniting churches.

Anthony Watson Brough (1861-1936) was born at Leytonstone, studied at Camden College, Sydney and pastored at West Maitland, New South Wales, where he was ordained in 1885 and was married in the same year to Rosetta Jane Jolly. He became an Australian missionary in the LMS and arrived in Coimbatore in 1894 and later settled in Erode so as to be in the centre of the district, doing mainly evangelistic work. He, along with Banninga and Popley, supported episcopacy in order to achieve the union in view of the tremendous opportunities for evangelism among the masses. As new president of SIUC he was asked to visit all the councils and impress upon them the significance of union for mission, as some were still hesitant to make a decision. In the General Assembly he suggested permitting those councils that so wished to leave the SIUC and enter the union on nothing else but the merits of the scheme.

William Thomas Morris Clewes (1891-1984), was born at Lye, Worcestershire, studied at Cheshunt College, Cambridge, was ordained in 1923 and sent as an LMS missionary. He worked in the northern Tamil area and was involved in the union negotiations. Along with Legg and Newell, Clewes published three interesting reports and manifestos with the signed approval of European and Indian leaders in the LMS councils which influenced the northern council at the time of crisis between 1935 and 1941 when questions about intercommunion and true priesthood rocked the boat. He too opposed the denial of equal spiritual validity and sympathised with the view that the Tranquebar Manifesto was European, not Indian.

A.E. Garvie (1861-1945) was a Principal of New College, Hampstead and member of the Board of Theology and the Board of Philosophy, London University. Author of several books, he was a Congregationalist theologian and joined the like-minded persons who supported the suggestion of an interim period of 30 to 40 years which would be necessary 'before uniting churches could be ready to attain the ultimate goal of organic union'.

S.G. Maduram, an Anglican priest from Tirunelveli, attended the Tranquebar meeting in 1919. He stressed the evangelical Walker tradition of his area. Wearingly, Maduram exposed the wide difference between SPG and CMS that existed in the same church. He sounded the note of comprehensiveness as fundamental to the Anglican church.

J.B. Gnanaolivu, an Anglo-Catholic Indian priest was present in Tranquebar 1919. He was a member of the Joint Committee, 1928-1934. He is noted for his impassioned speech in one JC meeting against intercommunion, calling the Holy Communion services of the Free Churches tea parties!

Paul S. Rangaramanujam was a Tamil Methodist leader, eloquent and vehement in JC meetings. Though his critical comments pained the Anglican members such as Bishop Waller, unlike a Methodist speaker in Hyderabad against union, he was deeply committed to church union. In one meeting where the vexed question of apostolic succession and the Anglican insistence on supplemental ordination caused silence, he 'broke the awkward silence with the suggestion that two things were conveyed in ordination, grace and authority, a Free Churchman might well be content to be channels of the grace, if the Anglicans wanted to be transmitters of authority.'[1]

Karl Hartenstein, Director of the Basel Mission, along with K.G. Goetz, was advisor for Strickstein. Following attending the WMC Tambaram 1938, he visited Malabar at the beginning of 1939. Though he supported union he warned against compromise. Even if there was a problem with the Nicene Creed, he insisted that the Apostles' Creed should be taught in a relevant way and a clear line of demarcation be drawn against syncretism!

R. Robertson, a Congregationalist, a representative of the northern council of the SIUC along with K.T. Paul, reported in the committee of 1923 that the ancient creeds represented the belief and formulation of the people of the particular

---

[1] Ibid., 197.

churches, but the candidates for ordination in South India should be permitted to express their faith in other forms, albeit in harmony with the ancient creeds. He along with his colleagues found the Anglican refusal of inter-communion to be offensive, and that unity should be already experienced before the actual union. For him, just as for many including D.M. Devsasahayam, supplemental ordination was in effect re-ordination.

M.J. Sargunam of Coimbatore, northern council of the SIUC, was first critical of the union. In 1931 he threatened saying 'the Christians of India might have to secede if the foreigners place many insurmountable obstacles before them.' But until the end he argued for the significance of the union for the Indian church and her mission.

Besides these, noteworthy are names such as **S. Gnanapragasam**, an Indian Wesleyan who was present in the JC 1925; **P. Gurushanta**, Wesleyan, member of JC from 1925 and one of the first batch of bishops (Mysore, died 1950); **T.E.T. Shore**, an Anglo-Catholic Father of the Oxford Mission to Calcutta, who was present in the first JC 1920, and adjusted with the Protestant atmosphere, was concerned about not diminishing the Lambeth Quadrilateral 1888; **G.M. Parker** of LMS based in Nagercoil represented the SIUC at Lausanne 1927, and attended the special meeting in 1935 that discussed the lay celebration and part of the organising team for the inauguration of CSI; **P. Ramaseshan** ('eloquent Brahmin convert') was part of the Methodist delegation in crucial meetings including that discussed the commissioning of the presbyterate in the united church (where Azariah, Hooper and Newbigin were present); **J.V. Chelliah** from the Jaffna council of the SIUC, teacher, editor, author and preacher who attended the first JC where through contact with Palmer he changed his negative view of bishops; **John Jamieson Willis**, Anglican Bishop of Uganda from 1912 to 1934; in a crucial consultative body of the Lambeth Conference in 1943 he stood with Temple, Headlam and Bell supporting the CSI scheme; and so on.

These were persons of great faith who dared what appeared to be the impossible. Though with limited components – Anglicans, Wesleyan Methodists, Congregationalists, Presbyterians, and people of the Basel Mission – they were instrumental of causing a 'second Pentecost' (Hollis). To copy the pattern of the Epistle to the Hebrews, by faith they transcended what was familiar, being open to know the other and change to the extent of a new conversion; they prayed with integral action, being passionate to make mission effective and credible, and were deeply committed to realise the prayer of Jesus 'that they may be one'. 'Therefore, since we are surrounded by such a cloud of witnesses, let us throw off everything that hinders and the sin (of disunity) that so easily entangles.'

Chapter 4

Venturing into a Faith Journey
towards Organic Union

The story of the negotiations towards the formation of the CSI is exciting at times, sober at other times and frustrating in yet other times. It involved enthusiastic persons, advocates of their denominations, critics, leaders and consultants from a distance and so on. We have already noted the decisive contributions of some outstanding missionaries, scholars, theologians and church leaders in the last chapter. However, in order to present the story simply and lucidly for the sake of those who have no clue of it and those who have no inclination to read the details of a complicated story here we have some snapshots.

It Began at Tranquebar

Bartholomäus Ziegenbalg (1682-1719) was the first Protestant missionary to India. He was a member of the Pietist movement from Halle, Germany and also a royal missionary sponsored by Frederick IV, King of Denmark. He and his colleague Henry Plutschau arrived on 9 July 1706 in Tranquebar, a small harbour town, on the south-east coast, 280km south of Madras (Chennai). Although, the mission had dramatic turns in terms of learning the surprisingly good aspects of local religions and culture and pioneering creative interreligious relations, despite the discouragement, even harassment, of the officials of the Danish colony, and the discontentment of the locals about the 'wild life-style' of the colony people, the mission could not attract any considerable numbers of converts. However, Tranquebar continued to be the hub of missionary arrivals and encounters during the following decades. It was the most popular venue for Christian conferences and it was not insignificant that mission conferences paid tribute to the first missionaries while lamenting the very slow spread of the gospel.

1919 – Tranquebar Conference and the Manifesto

Conferences were not uncommon among the Christians, organised mainly by overseas missionaries. The Tranquebar Conference in 1919 was a double conference. The first was the regular Indian ministers' meeting under the aegis of the Evangelistic Forward Movement, organised by Popley and hosted by Church of Sweden Mission in this Lutheran Centre. Apart from the hosts, the participants were Anglicans, members of the SIUC and Wesleyans. This was held on 29-30 April with the opening devotion by Azariah, the overall leader, in the Jerusalem Lutheran Church.

There was an extended conference on church union on 1-2 May. All the 33 were Indians except Eddy and Popley who drafted the reports and statements in English. Azariah, the convener, already had sent out three questions to concerned leaders of the churches represented:

1. What do you think to be the distinctive features of the organization and the religious teaching and practice of your own church?
2. Should a united Indian church come into being, what do you consider to be features that ought to be your contribution to that church, and which in fairness to your tradition, you ought not to give up, without serious loss to the full life of the church?
3. What is the attitude of your church towards union with other churches?[1]

When Azariah asked for sharing answers, the Wesleyan representatives confessed that they had not been made aware of the questions on church union. The Lutherans asserted that union on any other basis than their doctrines was wrong. Representatives of the SIUC expressed their doubt about episcopacy, which was followed by Eddy's veiled defence stating its benefits. Representatives from the Anglican Church and SIUC were asked to stay on after the above two groups left. Eddy had reasons to be excited about the episcopal and non-episcopal churches to be united first time in history. With the help of Eddy, Popley, Santiago and Meshach Peter, Azariah was able to present a resolution to the conference which was accepted and afterwards became known as the *Tranquebar Manifesto*. Following is a slightly shortened version:

> We believe that the union is the will of God, even as our Lord prayed that we might be one. Union is scriptural. 'There is one body, and one Spirit … called in one hope of our calling; one Lord, one faith, one baptism, one God and Father of all, who is over all, and through all, and in all.' With challenges of the war and situation in India being critical, a visible unity is vital for winning India for Christ. 'Yet, confronted by such an overwhelming responsibility, we find ourselves rendered weak and relatively impotent by our unhappy divisions – divisions for which

---

[1] Sundkler, 99f.

we were not responsible, and which have been, as it were, imposed upon us without; divisions which we did not create, and which we do not desire to perpetuate.

In this Church we believe that three Scriptural elements must be conserved: (1) The *Congregational* element, representing 'the whole Church', with 'every member' having immediate access to God, each exercising his gift for the development of the whole body. (2) We believe it should include the delegated, organized, or *Presbyterian* element, whereby the Church could unite in a General Assembly, Synods or Councils in organized unity. (3) We believe it should include the representative, executive, or *Episcopal* element. Thus, all three elements, no one of which is absolute or sufficient without the others, should be included in the Church of the future, for we aim not at compromise for the sake of peace, but at comprehension for the sake of truth.

While the Anglican reps stand for the one ultimate principle of *the Historic Episcopate* the SIUC members believe *a constitutional form* on the primitive, simple, apostolic model and the basic condition of *spiritual equality* of the universal priesthood of all believers. Upon this common ground, we propose union on the ground of (i) The Holy Scriptures of both OT and NT 'as containing all things necessary to salvation.' (ii) Apostles' Creed and Nicene Creed. (ii) The two sacraments ordained by Christ himself – Baptism and the Lord's Supper. (iv) The Historic Episcopacy, locally adapted. We will not be subject to any particular interpretation of episcopacy nor will we disown our past tradition.

While we do not commit our respective bodies to any action, we agree that if the SIUC desires union, they should choose from its own members men to be consecrated as bishops. In the consecration of these first bishops it is suggested that three or more bishops of the Anglican Church shall lay their hands upon the candidates, together with an equal number of ministers' representatives of the SIUC. As soon as the first bishops are consecrated, the two bodies would be in intercommunion, but the further limitation of existing ministers with regard to celebrating the Communion in the churches of the other body might still remain. In accordance with the principle of spiritual equality we desire to find some means to permit ministers of either body to celebrate the communion in the churches of the other body. As one possible solution, we would suggest that a special Service of *Commission* should be held. All ministers of both bodies desiring authority to officiate Communion throughout the whole Church should present themselves to receive at the hands of all the bishops of the United Churches a commission of such celebration of the

Communion. Ministers of either body not desiring to officiate at the Communion at the other Church would be under no obligation to present themselves. Full liberty would be claimed for individuals on the extreme wing of each body to maintain their present views and practices.

While not committing our respective bodies, we, unofficially and individually, with the blessing of God, agree to work toward union on such a basis.

This *Manifesto* was signed by 7 Anglicans and 26 representatives of the SIUC.

1919 - Immediate Follow Up

There was so much excitement about this unprecedented move for the sake of mission. Some participants in the Tranquebar Conference were enthusiastic to make it widely known. Eddy, for example, after meeting bishops Whitehead and Walter in Madras on 6 May, proceeded to Kodaikanal where he called 30 of the missionaries, enjoying their summer holiday on the hill, to a conference on 15 May. He briefed them about the significance of the momentum and their support for the Indian leaders. Banning was among them and was of the opinion that episcopacy might be a good form of church governance if Indian churches so desired and that it was applicable to the main denominations including Syrians and Catholics. Articles were published in the mission journals such as the *Harvest Field* (Methodist). It was explained that the *Tranquebar Manifesto* was bridging between the Lambeth Quadrilateral and SIUC Quadrilateral.[1] But there were some who were hesitant about these proposals while leaders of the 'Mother Churches' started to air their own opinions and interpretations.

1920 – The first Joint Committee Meeting and Beginning of Negotiations

The first of a long series of JC (Joint Committee) sessions of representatives from the two Churches was held in Bangalore on 18-19 March, 1920. Unlike the Tranquebar meeting this was the official one. There were 5 Anglican and 10 SIUC representatives. Azariah took the initiative for calling the meeting together and explained that the Anglican bishops wanted to have a clear understanding of issues involved before going to the Lambeth Conference.

---

[1] The SIUC Quadrilateral: (1) The principle of spiritual equality. (2) An autonomous Indian Church, free from Lambeth, the Church of England and the State. (3) A Church free to be in intercommunion with such bodies as it may determine. (4) A constitutional episcopacy with a written constitution like that of the Protestant Episcopal Church of America. See Ibid., 107.

1920 – Disturbing Suggestions from the Lambeth Conference

Though the SIUC insisted time and again on the equal validity of ministry between the Anglican and non-episcopal Churches, though Azariah shared this, the 'Encyclical Letter' of the whole conference, largely the creation of bishop Palmer, suggested episcopal re-ordination of the non-episcopal ministers. This caused a flurry of correspondence.

1920 – The Second Joint Committee

This was held in Bangalore on 14-16 December. The issue of re-ordination was contentious. Azariah and Palmer explained that what Lambeth asked for was 'really mutual commission' and that it applied to the Anglicans as well as the others. At the same time, realising the need to be sensitive, Azariah pleaded with his SIUC partners to respect the 'principle of individual and congregational freedom' for the Anglicans also, i.e. freedom for an Anglican congregation to accept Communion at the hands only of episcopally ordained ministers. One Anglican representative commented that within the Anglican Church, the CMS group were never invited by the SPG group to celebrate Communion in their church; then, he asked, 'should not the non-episcopally ordained ministers of the SIUC be able to accept union on similar conditions?' What was obvious was to achieve comprehensiveness with room for great difference of opinions. The committee took a vote for a resolution. 'According to the resolutions, all ministers in the uniting churches should be ministers of all the churches after union; each should be free to seek additional or fresh commission from the bishops of the future church, and thus be enabled to minister in the church to which he did not belong before the union. The principle of individual and congregational freedom should be applied to both sides; each should respect the conscientious scruples of the individuals or the congregation and were thus brought together in this "comprehensive" scheme of "fresh commission."'[1] However, the matter was not settled there, although Whitehead affirmed the ideal of comprehension and toleration, not narrowness and exclusiveness, a vision of true catholicity.

1921 May – Six Ad Hoc Sub-Committees

These were appointed by the JC – on the subjects of the Governing Body (and Devolution), Intercommunion, the Creeds, Confirmation, Freedom of Marriage and the Diaconate. The first one was the most important. As there was some relationship between the Church of Sweden and the CofE (Church of England) representatives of the Lutherans of the Church of Sweden Mission participated in these discussions. It was clarified that the 'LC (Lambeth Conference) was an advisory and not a legislative body' and that each province was 'free to decide its affairs as determined by local conditions'. However, as we will see, the LC continued to be dictating certain crucial issues.

---

[1] Ibid., 136f.

1921 – Third Joint Committee, Madras

Church government was the main issue as the concerned sub-committee had already prepared papers. Division of areas, names of Councils (Diocesan) and powers of bishops (e.g. would they have veto power on certain issues as was the existing practice among the Anglican bishops?) were discussed. The question of equality of ministry was still outstanding as was already a proposal for re-ordination of non-episcopal Church ministers by Anglican bishops. Freedom of worship was accepted so that existing traditions would continue. A number of the negotiators took a definite stand on union while pursuing the vexed questions.

1922 ff. Theological Consultations

This happened in various ways, one of which was corresponding with experts and gathering their opinions. Consultants included the Archbishops of York and Canterbury. Again, the main issue was equality of ministries; while most of the SIUC representatives insisted on mutual commissioning, most of the Anglicans insisted on a supplemental ordination which was construed as re-ordination.

1924-1928 – Methodist Entry

The SIUC's invitation to the 'Lutherans' and Wesleyan Methodists was immediately responded to positively. While the Lutheran Churches could not come up with a common resolution, the Wesleyans started a process of counsel and consultation in 1924. They expressed their cautious response by stressing 'not for negotiations but consultations'. The fifth Joint Committee in Madras, February was 'virtually an information meeting for the Wesleyans'. It was done in the presence of the important leaders of the SIUC and the Anglican Church.

1926 Feb – an Important Meeting at Trichinopoly

It was dramatic as it represented 'a crucial date in the negotiations, because it laid the foundation of what can now be regarded as the characteristically "South Indian" approach to union'. Though the fundamental problem of mutual recognition of ministry was yet to be solved, the Methodist contribution boosted the union movement and made the gathering most remarkable. However, the ambiguity of the proposed commissioning service caused a deadlock at the beginning of the meeting which threatened a breaking down of the negotiations. Palmer wanted that from the beginning of union all the ministers should be recognized by all the churches. In Trichinopoly he was convinced of the necessity of union and of a new departure towards that end. Earlier, there were new questions: when the future CSI had episcopal ordination, what would be the position of new missionaries coming from the Free Churches? Would it be a 'conditional ordination' or a 'supplemental ordination' desirable? Was it a good idea to set a limit of certain years of transition period in which the existing ministers would continue to function in their own denominational churches?

Finally, the JC of 1926 adopted the following statement which reflected a bold step: 'That during the fifty years succeeding the union, ministers ordained in the churches which have planted the missions now connected with the uniting churches may be received as ministers of the United Church, if they are willing to make the same declarations with regards to the Faith and Constitution of the United Church as are required from persons about to be ordained or employed for the first time in the United Church. It is the intention of those who make the union that at the close of that period no one shall minister in the church unless he has received regular episcopal ordination.'

With regard to the non-episcopal Churches' wish to guard their time-honoured prerogative of 'inviting ministers of other churches occasionally to celebrate the Holy Communion' there was a further resolution: 'That it will not be a condition of union that any of the uniting churches, or any ministers or members of them, shall forego any rights of communion with other churches that it or he possessed before the union.' Though Wesleyan and SIUC representatives, after conferring together, said that they did not share the theological views of episcopacy propounded in the above Anglican statement, described the statement itself as 'notable advance' on the second meeting of JC. Particularly, F.C. Sackett, a Hyderabad Methodist missionary commented, 'There is no doubt that the Anglicans have given a way and shown throughout a most magnanimous spirit.'

In order to convince critics about the 'bold step' and allowances of Anglican representatives in England, Palmer said in a sermon (May 13), 'In South India we really *dare not* suspend negotiations, because of the Indian demand for union is so insistent. If we broke off the sessions of our Joint Committees, the Indians themselves would pursue the matter and would, I believe, settle it one way or other.'

1927 – The Significance of the World Conference on Faith and Order at Lausanne (Switzerland), 1927.

A considerable number of representatives from the JC on negotiations for CSI attended. Now the 'Church of England in India' having been de-established and replaced by 'Church of India, Burma and Ceylon', the SIUC stood on the same level. The history of the FO (Faith and Order) movement decisively influenced some of the hesitant leaders of the South India union movement. At the same time leaders from South India found an opportunity to propagate their union movement internationally. The addresses of leaders such as Palmer were both appealing and challenging. It was here that Azariah made his famous statement which we quoted earlier: 'Unity may be theoretically a desirable ideal in Europe and America, but it is vital to the life of the church in the mission field. The divisions of Christendom may be a source of weakness in Christian countries, but in non-Christian lands they are a sin and scandal.' The representatives of the South India union movement returned with renewed confidence and conviction.

1928 Jan – Anglican Opposition to the Trichinopoly Proposals (1926)

In a meeting, other than the JC, in the episcopal Synod of CIBC a few bishops of the Anglo-Catholic wing objected mainly because of their dissatisfaction about the definition of priesthood. Palmer vigorously defended his case against the opposition, seconded by Azariah and Tubb and effectively supported by the Foss Westcott, the Metropolitan, who also drafted the resolution which was unanimously passed by the General Council of CIBC. At the same time there was an appeal for respect of beliefs particularly the grace channelled through Holy Communion; also respect for the conscientious convictions of congregations receiving it from episcopally ordained ministers or others.

1928 June – Joint Committee, Bangalore

In the 1926 JC at Trichinopoly Anglicans seemed to give away their peculiar position, and in 1928 at Bangalore many of their above stated concerns were addressed. The committee affirmed the spiritual unity of all the churches as well as the conscientious convictions of particular members and churches. It was agreed,

(a) arrangements existing at the time of union by which Anglicans in any particular place enjoyed opportunities of receiving communion at the hands of an episcopally ordained minister will not be terminated after union against their will by the church authorities, and

(b) any congregation accustomed to any episcopally ordained ministry will not either temporarily or permanently be placed in charge of a non-episcopally ordained minister unless all the communicant members of the congregation have been informed of the suggested appointment and no one has signified his objection to such an arrangement.

It is the intention of expectation of those who enter into this union that eventually every minister exercising a permanent ministry in the church will be an episcopally ordained minister …

After this period of thirty years, the church will consider and decide the question of such exceptions to the general principle of an episcopal ordained ministry.[1]

The SIUC members largely accepted the interim period, though some of their Councils later questioned it. The resolutions on the interim period spoke of 'respect for beliefs' and referred to 'conscientious convictions'. While these were to be safeguarded, the interim period was to be a *process* of growing together. But how far and how could these be safeguarded and regulated? Irregularity was possible and there was tension between Congregationalists and Anglo-Catholics.

---

[1] Ibid., 165.

This meeting appointed a CC (Continuation Committee) with the remit of preparing a draft for a complete scheme of union with Western and Banninga as draftsmen who spent a week in Bangalore in September 1928.

1929 Feb-March – Eighth Joint Meeting, Madras

For this meeting Bishop Waller and J.S.M. Hooper took care of the hospitality arrangements for the delegates. 'Everyone was accommodated in the home of someone belonging to a church other than their own: the Anglicans coming to Madras for the meeting were the guests in Methodist or Congregationalist or Presbyterian homes, and *vice versa*. The preachers in the Sunday services were appointed according to the same plan ... The atmosphere of the meetings was characterized by humour and by prayer, by patience and eager expectancy.'[1] This atmosphere helped the delegates to overcome divisions and to form personal friendships. This was remembered in the later meetings. The Methodist representatives brought a solution to the above tension commenting upon the consequences of union as a process of growing together. The resolution came to be known as the *Pledge* and it was accepted in the following form:

> They therefore pledge themselves and fully trust each other that in the united church no arrangements with regard to churches, congregations or ministers will knowingly be made, either generally or in particular cases, which will offend the conscientious convictions of any persons directly concerned, or which would hinder the development of complete unity within the church or imperil its subsequent progress towards union with other churches.[2]

Together with the interim period (reduced from 50 to 30 years), the Pledge represented 'the characteristically South India method of union'. Not by letter, it was understood, but by the spirit and trust the Pledge was to be sustained.

Also, in this meeting the proposed *Scheme of Union of 1929* was published. It appeared with a Foreword by Gulliford who stressed comprehension and balance.

Faith: The Scheme starts with the affirmation of the uniting churches holding the faith in Jesus Christ, the Redeemer of mankind, God incarnate, and worshipping one God in Trinity and Trinity and Unity; accepting the Holy Scripture of the two Testaments as containing all things necessary to salvation and as the ultimate standard of faith; accepting the Apostles' and Nicene creeds as witnessing to and safeguarding that faith and containing a sufficient statement for a Basis of Union.

Ministry: It recognizes that the Episcopate, the Council of the Presbyters and the Congregation of the Faithful must all have their appropriate places

---

[1] Ibid., 196f.
[2] Ibid., 166.

in the order of life in the united church. The historic episcopate will be in a constitutional form (as in the *Tranquebar Manifesto*). The consecration of bishops is to be performed by bishops, not less than three taking part; the ordination of the presbyters is to be performed by the laying on of hands of the bishop and presbyters. Apart from a tentative arrangement for consecration of bishops and ordination of presbyters at the inauguration, the uniting churches agree that it is their intention and expectation that eventually every minister exercising a permanent ministry in the united church will be an episcopally ordained minister. For thirty years ministers may be received in the existing churches and after that only the episcopally ordained ministry will be valid.

Membership: Those baptised will become eligible to be communicant members, and the present method of confirmation will continue in the united church.

Worship: There will be wide freedom of worship within 'spirit and truth', either to use the traditional forms or create new ones.

Relations with Other Churches: The united church is to be autonomous without any external control. However, there will be freedom to relate to and have fellowship with the mother churches of the West and 'with other branches of the Catholic Church with which the uniting churches are now in communion. Thus, it was hoped that it would be in full communion with all the parent churches, that its bishops would be invited to the Lambeth Conference and that the delegates would attend the World Presbyterian Conference, the World Union of Congregational and the Ecumenical Methodist Conference.'[1] 'None of the ministers or members of the united church would forgo any of the rights with regard to intercommunion and inter-celebration which they had before the union, and ministers would be at liberty to exercise any ministry in a church outside the area where they were entitled to minister before union and to retain the ecclesiastical status they had before union in the church of their ordination.'[2]

Government: 'There were to be pastorate Committees under the presbyter in charge, Diocesan Councils under the bishop of the diocese, and a Synod, presided over by the Moderator. All the bishops would be *ex officio* members of the Synod, three presbyters and three laymen would be elected by each Diocesan Council (with additional representation for dioceses with a higher proportion of communicants).'[3] The Synod will be the supreme body for faith and doctrine, conditions of membership and functions of ordained ministers including conducting worship. Matters will be brought to the Synod and a process of proposition with discussion and voting will be followed. In this process the bishops will have a special role to play.

---

[1] Sundkler, 171.

[2] Ibid.

[3] Ibid., 171f.

The ***Scheme*** was presented to all the three Churches (CIBC, SIUC and Methodist). Though they had given general approval to the basic principles involved, none of them were able to be committed to any part of the scheme. However, the publication of the first edition of the scheme created a new atmosphere. Further, as expected there were comments on particular clauses of the scheme, and especially some leaders of the SIUC questioned the continued validity of the two ancient creeds. The idea that the bishops represented the apostolic succession were either unclear or unacceptable for some, though the idea was not explicit in the scheme. Freedom to use any form of worship caused many Anglicans to raise their eyebrows as for them using *The Book of Common Prayer* was obligatory.

With lively debates in the twenties and publication of the Scheme in 1929, there was enough reason to anticipate that the consummation and inauguration were within reach. But the prolongation from 1929 to 1947 with the publication of six new editions of the Scheme frustrated many and attracted statements such as 'a decade of deterioration' and 'a case of optical illusion'.

1930 November Joint Committee: Negotiations Prolonged

The year 1930 was most significant in the venturing journey of organic union in South India. The Episcopal Synod of the CIBC had submitted the Scheme to the Lambeth Conference in 1930. The main responsibility for dealing with the problem in this conference belonged to the Committee on Unity of the Church, consisting of 73 bishops under the chairmanship of Archbishop William Temple. Of the Asian members were Azariah, Waller and Palmer. The discussions in the Committee were admirably handled by Temple, supported by Bishop George Bell of Chichester, though for the Archbishop it was the thorniest issue as there was opposition mainly from the Archbishop of the West Indies.[1] Significantly, though the responsibility of action lay with the CIBC, the Lambeth Conference under the leadership of the celebrated Archbishop declared some bold statements as we have earlier referred to

The CSI was to be an autonomous regional church, not a new kind of Anglican church ... Bishop Bell stressed this viewpoint and piloted the scheme through in drafting a clause of great importance: the southern dioceses would go forth from the Anglican Communion in order to make their own distinctive contribution to the faith and order of the new united church. Moreover, the church will be itself a distinct province of the Universal Church, with a rule and character of its own. This implies that the suggestion that the united church should form a new province of (the CIBC) is rejected, as this would seem to be absorption into the Anglican Church.[2]

---

[1] See Ibid., 215f.

[2] Ibid., 218.

At the same time, it was noted that any Anglican, ordained or unordained, could communicate in the CSI and take work of any kind. No Anglican church should establish any Anglican church in the CSI area.

> If communicant members or ordained ministers of the united church should go into any diocese of the Anglican Communion, the church of that diocese should receive them to communion whenever this can be done consistently with the regulations of each Province or extra-Provincial diocese, and episcopally ordained ministers of the united church should be qualified, at the discretion of the bishop, to officiate, subject to the rules of the diocese for its ministers.[1]

Other than these, the Lambeth Conference 1930 gave assent to the main clauses of the South India Scheme such as episcopacy without a defined theory of it, unification of ministry with the Pledge period of 30 years (during which congregations would be allowed to continue their traditional ministry) at the end of which the ordained ministry of CSI only would be valid, and there was no insistence of Confirmation as a prerequisite term of union. But its use was most earnestly recommended. Also, the Conference gave advice on the following specific points. *Intercommunion with non-episcopal churches* was an anomaly, but, as part of a movement towards general and complete union, such an anomaly may be covered by the principle of "economy"; *Consecration of bishops per saltum*, while normally undesirable, was not invalid and in the circumstances of inauguration of the united church it was justifiable; *Confirmation before ordination* was the normal procedure but not absolutely necessary; *Participation of presbyters in consecration of bishops* was "a legitimate symbolism" when referring to the inaugural service of Consecration but in subsequent Consecrations it would tend to confusion and should not be adopted. If adopted it should be fully explained that the presbyters did not take part as Consecrators."[2] On the whole the LC appreciated the CIBC for the 'courage and wisdom which had shown in sanctioning the negotiations at various times' and encouraged them to continue to seek union.

Joining with the Methodists' demands in 1930, the SIUC delegation presented a long list of far-reaching proposals, concerned mostly with delimitation of episcopal authority. More importantly, the burning issue of intercommunion needed further deliberation in the two subsequent meetings. Underneath the controversy of the intercommunion was the question whether the members of the non-episcopal churches were eligible to receive communion from the hands of the bishops or episcopally ordained ministers, and in return if the communion celebrated by ministers of the non-episcopal churches would be received by

---

[1] Ibid., 21.

[2] Ibid., 219; 'the principle of "economy;" *Consecration of bishops per saltum*, literally, "hopping:" the phrase means reaching a position without first going through the usual preliminary steps, here being consecrated as bishop without first being ordained priest.'

Anglicans. On this count from the beginning, delegates of the non-episcopal churches found it an anomaly if the Anglicans were truly committed to be part of an organic union. Already, the SIUC leaders expressed the incomprehensibility of the Anglican position and warned that this might cause the collapse of the negotiations. What Streckeisen of the Basel Mission, a newcomer, expressed represented the views of all the non-Anglican churches.

> The refusal of the Anglican Church to have intercommunion is a real offence to me. What then is the Scheme but an absorption into that church? If we can't recognise each other even so much, is there much use in trying for union, while the necessary presuppositions are missing?[1]

Lambeth 1930 (Resolution 42) had undertaken 'not to question the action of any bishop who would use his dispensing power and sanction as an exception to the general rule in special areas.'[2] This gave Azariah the necessary authority to move forward in this matter. He had persuaded Banninga that this was doing something 'for mere demonstration purposes'. And 'Azariah felt he had the powerful support of Dr. William Temple.'[3] The only condition that Temple put forward was to make sure that the union plan was definite. Nevertheless, there was blockade put forward. In the group meeting of Anglican delegation for the Joint Meeting 1930 there were 'strong opponents of such an impetuous step'. They decided to refer the question to the Metropolitan and Episcopal Synod.

But quite unexpectedly, in the meeting there was a bombshell from an Indian Anglican member! In a letter to Gulliford, Hooper relates the episode: 'Like a bombshell in the full committee came a long and altogether offensive speech from Gnanaolivu against the mere suggestion of intercommunion. In matter and in manner I have never heard anything more dreadful, and the other Anglicans were filled with shame and confusion of face. The speech was beyond description'. Sundkler adds: 'Gnanaolivu's point seems to have been that the non-episcopalians in their desire for intercommunion with the Anglicans were labouring under an illusion with reference to their ministry. He seems to have suggested the Communion services of the non-episcopalians were rather in the nature of tea-parties. The speech acted as a *katharsis*. Leading Anglicans in the Joint Committee emphatically disassociated themselves from the statement. W.E.S. Holland, who for thirty years had struggled with the intercommunion problem declared "with overwhelming feeling" that "a God who would limit himself in the sacraments in the way that Gnanaolivu had suggested was no God for him."'[4]

Sensing the controversies, 'A Manifesto on Church Union' was issued around this time (1930), signed by 107 Indian Christians (including A.J. Appasamy,

[1] Quoted, Ibid., 229.
[2] Quoted, Ibid., 230.
[3] Ibid.
[4] Ibid., 231.

J.A. Jacob, Meshach Peter, C.J. Lucas, K.T. Paul and V.S. Azariah).[1] The short document starts with the equality of ministries and ministers as insisted from the beginning by the SIUC. It mentions, 'Even as early as 1892, Kali Charan Banurji of Calcutta urged in the Decennial Missionary Conference, Bombay, that immediate steps should be taken for Church Union. There was considerable opposition from Missionaries of the Conference and his attempt fell through.' As in other fields, the longing for union was connected with uniting communities composing differences.

The desire of keeping the fundamental unity is vigorously expressed itself in the Indian Church. It may also be said that desire for Union is in keeping with the spirit of tolerance of different forms of belief that has been characteristic of the people of India. Further, Christians in India are free from those memories of historical struggles which the Christians of the West have inherited from their past. The theological dogmas accepted by Western Churches have not dominated the Indian mind as they have not been indigenous, and the attitude of the Indian Christian has been one of indifference towards them. The existence of denominations tends to retard the growth of Christian experience and limits the scope of its expression in those ways of thought and life which are most normal to the peoples.

Noting *bhakti* (devotion) as the highest expression of faith, only being free from the bonds of the present denominations alone would provide a congenial atmosphere for the Indian expression of Christianity. The united Church in South India would be integral to the Universal Church. 'In the absence of any other Scheme', the Manifesto concludes, 'the present Scheme provides ample room for development and also the possibility of union with other Churches, and we urge our fellow-Christians in South India to accept the present Scheme as early as possible for further negotiation. The present Scheme, whether perfect or not, certainly affords a working basis and such changes as are felt to be absolutely necessary can be introduced.' It is important to note that this one-page Manifesto points out the Indian desire for union even before the Tranquebar Manifesto.

The issue of intercommunion continued to be a major concern in the Free Churches. R. Robertson in 1931 suggested that the three churches ought to act 'as if they were already united' and stressed that intercommunion was the surest way of obtaining 'unity before union'.[2] Methodists also expressed in strong terms that the Anglican refusal of intercommunion was a great obstacle and it should be removed at any cost. In the same year (1931) the Free Church spirit found expression in the speeches and writings of persons like D.M. Devasahayam. For example, he wrote an article with a threatening title, 'The Scheme: Its Broken

---

[1] 'A Manifesto on Church Union', typed paper kept in the folder of *Papers of Lesslie Newbigin* (DA 29/2/4/5), available in the Cadbury Research Library, University of Birmingham.

[2] Sundkler, 230f.

Pledges,'[1] in which he showed that he 'had already entrenched himself into the position from which he was to conduct his warfare up to 1947 and beyond. The Scheme of Union with, in his view, its foundations of institutionalism, ritualism, sacerdotalism and the "historical" episcopate, well and truly laid, and with the strong central government vested in the Synod and the Episcopate, would carry the churches nearer to Rome. It was a "resuscitation of medieval forms, formulae and institutions."'[2] However exaggerated with strong words, Devasahayam's influence in the South Travancore LMS area was far reaching. Strong loyalty to the LMS made some to see it as mother and the emerging united church as step-mother, and to lament the departure of missionaries and their resources. Nevertheless, despite some uncertainty about the relevance and benefit of episcopacy, certain other councils of the SIUC (especially Madura and Madras) were definitely for union. In the case of the Methodists there were strong supporters of union but, apart from Mysore, their District Synods were not ready to accept the Scheme of 1929 without modification. Hyderabad was not happy about the term and powers of the bishop. Medak did not want to lose Methodism's great spiritual and administrative power. This concern found expression when a minister Daniel Napoleon rose in the Provincial Synod and shouted in unaccustomed English: 'If union come, Methodism go to dog, India go to dog, world go to dog!'... Voting showed that among the Indian representatives only five were for union, eighteen against, and fifteen neutral.'[3] It is noteworthy that in the JC 1930 most of the modifications suggested were by Methodists.

The Scheme of June 1932

In an important meeting of the Episcopal Synod of the CIBC, Calcutta, February 1932, the decision on intercommunion proved to be a fateful turning point in the negotiations. Bishop Stephen Neill gives a first-hand report. When one of the bishops was asked 'why, in the face of the strong opposition of many Anglican to the proposal for intercommunion, it had been felt necessary to press the matter up to a vote in the Episcopal Synod', he replied, 'It was a case of either breaking off the negotiations or of yielding to their pressure.' Neill adds; 'Here we find the root cause for the embitterment and frustration of the next few years: the negotiators were no longer a company of men, united in spirit, and desiring to find God's will for them – some at least among them were seeking to exercise pressure on others. This was a tragic declension from the high hopes and possibilities of the early days.'[4] This judgment may be one-sided as the members of the Synod were not all of the same mind. With slight modification of the Scheme of 1929 this sought

---

[1] It was included in a *Manifesto on Church Union*, published as a result of a South Travancore Christian Young Men's Retreat in 1931. See Ibid., 226f.

[2] Quoted, Ibid., 226.

[3] Ibid., 227.

[4] Quoted, Ibid., 232.

to clarify the church order. The SIUC delegation presented a long list of far-reaching proposals and they aligned them with the Methodist demands of 1930. 'The modified Scheme obtained in the Joint Committee 1932 was the result of criticism which the Methodists and the SIUC delivered against the provisions for church order in the edition of 1919. As from 1933-34, the Methodists aligned themselves with the Anglicans in defence of the church order as it was then set out in the Scheme, and were supported by Presbyterians, such as J.H. Maclean and Indian leaders of the Presbyterian tradition.

The Methodist representation was dominated by those who adhered to the Methodist Sacramental Fellowship. Earlier in 1932 the Methodist union movement reached a decisive stage when by a Deed of Union (Wesleyans, Primitive Methodists and Bible Christians) the 'Methodist Church in Britain' was born. This development had indirect support for the union movements around the world. In the case of union in South India delegates were appointed by the Provincial Synod and therefore enjoyed backing of a central body with determined goal.

1933 – Retreats and Conferences

In 1932 some thought 'that the Joint Committee achieved the definitive form of the Scheme', but others felt 'our greatest task is yet to come'. Subsequently, local retreats and conferences were organised to reflect and discuss the Scheme. The report from a Pasumalai conference in 1933 has the following summing up: 'The eager participation in the discussion periods was certainly impressive evidence of the longing in the hearts of Christian leaders of a speedy coming of a more full and fruitful fellowship in the Christian life in South India. "Why wait?" "What hinders?" was the constant overtone of what was said.'[1] Special categories of people such as pastors, teachers and women were called to their particular union conferences.

1935-1939

The Congregationalist opposition raised many fundamental problems of church order in 1935 leading to the crisis of that year. Questions on the Faith were raised by the SIUC councils in 1937-39. 'They brought the ferment of the Reformation into a scheme which was professedly built on the broad "comprehensive" foundations of the early Church. There was a modification of the balance between bishops and Synod in 1939, but it was only slightly different from that which was already achieved in 1932.'[2]

'The main contestants in this debate were not to be found in the assemblies of South India. They were sitting in their studies in Oxford and Cheltenham. They were the same two men who in the twenties had put forth the fundamental ideas

---

[1] Ibid., 199.

[2] Ibid., 178.

of the South India scheme: V. Bartlet and E.J. Palmer.'[1] One was trying to recover the original church constitution, and the other that of two centuries. Other voices joined, either defending the two or presenting slightly different views, taking the Reformation, for example. The Anglican leaders 'regarded the Scheme of 1929 as establishing a just equilibrium between the various church traditions. But in the thirties the SIUC challenged this conclusion, and towards the end of the thirties they took the initiative...leading to apparent deadlock. While the Methodists ... held the balance in their hands, the Anglican representatives now found themselves in a position requiring certain aspects of the Scheme to be reshaped – if there was to be any church union at all.'[2] Now Anglican participants in the union were no more to be decided by Canterbury or the Lambeth Conference but the CIBC, and fortunately the Metropolitan, F. Westcott, based in Calcutta, was actively engaged on the side of union. But in 1929 Palmer left India to become assistant bishop in the Diocese of Gloucester. However, along with Westcott the bishops took great interest in the union. Though the Indian representation on the Anglican side was minimal, Azariah continued to be the champion of union, speaking and writing on the significance of unity.

In 1934 the visit of Prof. W.F. Lofthouse and the Methodist Conference boosted the union movement. The Conference declared that 'the Scheme of 1934, taken as a whole, was not contrary to the principles of Methodism.' 'While towards the end of the decade Congregationalist opposition to certain features of the Scheme sharpened, and Anglo-Catholic reaction as a sequence grew more vocal, the Methodists, themselves becoming more "Catholic" and ecumenical, worked steadily towards the goal.'[3] A few Indian Methodists first created noise opposing the union but were won over in due course. At this stage, for the Methodists, 'the day of debate was over'.

The case of the SIUC was a different story. The earlier admission of episcopacy eroded, and the fear of its domination revived. 'The number of SIUC church councils represented on the joint committee was increased to eight when in 1932 the Basel Mission – Malabar, South Kanara and South Maratha – were invited to send delegates. The equality and direction of the theological contribution given by the Basel Missionary, A. Streckeisen, made this decision of particular importance.'[4] There was some concern about sending representative delegates to other councils, particularly Travancore, but explanations were given and minor adjustments made. 'At the SIUC Assembly in 1935 the representation was changed. Appointments were to be on "an elective basis", with the church councils themselves responsible for appointing their own committee members. Due consideration was also given to the relative numerical strength of each

[1] Ibid.
[2] Ibid., 182.
[3] Ibid., 187.
[4] Ibid., 190.

council: Travancore was to appoint four members, the Madura, Madras, North Tamil and Telugu councils three members each, and smaller Jaffna, Kanarese and Malabar church councils two members each. To these twenty-two members the Executive Committee was to add three other members.'[1] This was seen as being in line with Congregational self-determination, though there was the problem of occasional local opinion swaying the balance and affecting the balance within. As representatives were changing, a position could not be sustained.

The Schemes of 1929 with amendments and additions in 1932, 1935 and 1936 (and even the Scheme of 1942) were not simple and direct. There was criticism which the Joint Committee in 1935 decided to address. It decided to publish an English résumé of the Scheme together with translations in Tamil, Telugu, Kanarese and Malayalam. However, there were suggestions to reduce the bulky document and make it an irreducible minimum including 2 Testaments, 2 Creeds, 2 Sacraments and unification of ministries under the episcopate. However, the Joint Committee in 1938 decided to keep an explanation that each church was free and competent to give assent to the Scheme. It stated further that 'A general assent to the Basis of Union, interpreted by the Governing Principles in Part II, chapter II of the Scheme of Union, is quite sufficient as permission for the union to be consummated, and no assent need be asked or given to the reminder of the Scheme or to the details of the constitution of the United Church.'[2] But the negotiating bodies 'would have to give their assent not only to the Basis, but also to the Constitution'. Of course, the western mother churches of these bodies did not restraint from exercising their influence. There were individual theologians and church leaders whose opinions ranged from issuing warnings against the union in South India as it deviated from orthodoxy and long tradition to favouring this great adventure, feeling the shame of unnecessary divisions.

The Congregational practice of Lay celebration, a theory, was gradually accepted by the other (Presbyterian and Basel Mission) constituents of the SIUC but resisted by the Anglicans and Methodists. In 1937-38 Banninga felt that Lay Celebration would act as a unifying factor within the SIUC. 'With one voice they could now impress upon the Anglican leaders the necessity for being more cordial, for showing in practice that fellowship which was necessary to make union a reality, and for allowing a wider scope within the Scheme of Congregationalist practices. He would no longer march far ahead of his church council and his own church. He felt the need of being identified with what he believed were their aspirations.'[3] Subsequently, there was consultation with scholars and theologians in India, Britain and USA. The General Assembly of SIUC in September 1939 expressed the demand (as in 1937) for Lay Celebration in moderate terms as a matter of principle. Though the Methodist delegates in the Joint Committee were

---

[1] Ibid., 192.

[2] Quoted, Ibid., 204.

[3] Ibid., 286.

critical of the SIUC attitude, interestingly, the Methodists in Hyderabad practised it to some extent, but did not want it as a principle!

There was intense discussion among the key leaders. Unexpectedly some councils of SIUC joined the Anglicans and Methodists on the question of Lay Celebration, and there was a suggestion to let them leave the SIUC. The Travancore council in September 1939 voted decidedly against the scheme. Some of their Indian leaders 'almost in despair and felt that union would have to come without the contribution of the Travancore forces'. The options were to wait and persuade such forces or proceed with the union without them. The 'priesthood of all believers' was once again referred to, but informed laymen like R.D. Paul argued that 'It would be ridiculous for anyone, merely on the strength of this phrase, to make a claim of right to perform any priestly functions.'

The discussion in Travancore turned to a polarity between those who stressed their loyalty to LMS and the English missionaries, and those who were deeply committed to create a new church in India. Azariah saw a growing respect for sacraments and felt 'a most sacrilegious thing to make provisions for the performance of a sacramental rite by any person not solemnly set apart to perform the rite'. The Joint Committee in November 1939, with the influence of this Indian opinion but without accepting doctrinal views, 'maintained the rule of the Basis of Union that none except bishops and presbyters were to have the right to celebrate the Holy Communion, although in the event of union exceptional arrangements would have to continue until permanent arrangements could be made by the united church itself. The problem of Lay Celebration was to be studied by a committee of nine members, three from each of the churches. They were an interesting and highly competent group of men.'[1] There was study, sharing views and wide consultation. Though asked to withdraw their demand, the SIUC councils persisted, but the Joint Committee had to decide against their request and accepted the report of the Lay Celebration sub-committee from which the following statement was added to the Scheme:

God is the God of order; it has been His good pleasure to use the visible church and its regularly constituted ministries as the normal means of the operation of His Spirit. But it is not open to any to limit the operation of the grace of God to any particular channel ... All share in the heavenly High Priesthood of the risen and ascended Christ, from which alone the Church derives its character as a royal priesthood. No individual and no order in the Church can claim exclusive possession of this heavenly priesthood.[2]

This statement seems to strike a balance between sacerdotalism and sacrilege. Indirectly it goes beyond apostolic succession through which grace flowed to bishops and by their laying hands to the presbyters. At the same time, though

---

[1] Ibid., 290; for the whole of discussion on Lay Celebration, see 283-295.
[2] Ibid., 294.

there is no direct approval of Lay Celebration, a way is open for its practice at least on special circumstances through special arrangements.

The issue of intercommunion too was a vexed one. It was the Telugu council of the SIUC which pressed for making this rule before union. A resolution to this effect was adopted by the General Assembly of the SIUC in 1937 expressing its conviction that if this request was accepted 'one of the chief obstacles to union would be removed'. Intercommunion was ecumenically stressed as the best demonstration of unity. But what was to be clarified was whether it could happen before union or after. The Joint Committee in February 1938 replied: 'The only true answer to the desire of intercommunion is the consummation of union itself, which it is now the task of the churches to hasten by all means in their power.'[1]

1941 – 1947: Towards Consummation

In the following assemblies (1939, 1941), with the exception of the Madras council, the SIUC pressed further. The Joint Committee (1939) repeated its former decision but yielded so far as to admit that 'full advantage has not yet been taken of the permission granted in the resolution of the Episcopal Synod'. The Joint Committee (1941) took the reconciliatory suggestion of the Madras council that 'general permission should be given when all the three churches had voted in favour of union'. It also prepared 'to extend the permission about intercommunion. This decision was taken when the Methodists decided to proceed to the consummation of the union and the attitude of five SIUC councils was favourable to union.' United services were organised.[2]

The composition and constitution of the (CSI) Synod was prolonged task for the negotiators. Fixing the number of representatives from the dioceses, defining the nature, power and function of the bishop within the equation of power between him and the Synod as desired before required careful scrutiny. However, the exercise did not prove to be controversy free. Much work was done in 1930s.[3]

In the Joint Committee in October 1941 the final Scheme was decided. Since then the churches through their responsible councils took over. 'From the point of view of the Joint Committee this change seemed to bring about a certain centrifugal tendency, shown in the claims of Congregationalists and Anglo-Catholics ... The lessened role of the JC is indicated in that after October 1941 it did not meet until November 1944. This latter meeting had to consider certain proposals on the Pledge, on Supplemental Ordination, etc., but in each case it decided to let the 1942 Scheme stand. This meeting and the following, in December 1946, had mainly to receive resolutions from the three churches, and

[1] Quoted, Ibid., 296.
[2] Ibid.
[3] See Ibid., 298-300.

to prepare for the inauguration.'[1] Also there was large turnover in membership of the JC (e.g. Banninga left in 942; Azariah died in 1945), while a few who started in the 20s still continued. A young group of interesting and highly competent theologians from all three churches (A.J. Appasamy, L. Newbigin and Marcus Ward) joined. The convener of the Anglican delegation for the last two JC meetings was Arthur Michael Hollis, Bishop of Madras and a man witnessed to be 'led by the Spirit'.

Supplemental ordination was meant to be an episcopal ordination of the ordained ministers of the non-episcopal churches, and many saw it as a re-ordination or undermining the ordination they already had in their church. Influenced by an American document published in connection with the unity talk between Protestant Episcopal and Presbyterian Churches (published in 1942), already in 1943 a revised edition of the 'Basic Principles' of the South India union omitted the rite of Supplemental Ordination though it was felt the plans were to be developed more fully. Azariah published his suggestion stressing that:

> … it was not a plea for re-ordination. Upon the consecration of
> bishops at the inauguration service there should follow in the dioceses
> a rite of mutual commissioning of all presbyters and priests already
> ordained before union. The commission would convey to each already
> ordained presbyter authority 'for the wider exercise of the ministry'
> under the new conditions established by union. In the case of non-
> Anglican ministers, the commission was to be given by the bishop
> of the diocese concerned together with presbyters of the Church of
> India, Burma and Ceylon. In the case of Anglican ministers, it was to
> be conveyed by the bishop together with representative presbyters of
> the other churches in the diocese. In order to establish full unity, the
> formula to be used was to be identically the same in all cases.[2]

The proposal came to the Continuation Committee where the question could be discussed in a preparatory way. It observed that Supplemental Ordination was too a radical step and what could be aimed at was some kind of 'commissioning for wider service'. The Committee recommended to the JC that the following change be made in the Scheme: 'All the initial presbyterate of the united church, without the laying on of hands, for the exercise of the ministry of the word and sacraments throughout the united church.'[3] A sub-committee was formed to deal with the problem.

Outside the sub-committee opinions flew here and there and the seriousness of the matter was such that a section in SIUC (1944) demanded removal of

---

[1] Ibid., 301.

[2] Ibid., 306f.

[3] Ibid., 307.

Supplemental Ordination from the Scheme and it had implications for the interpretation of Pledge. A sombre mood set in the key leaders. J.S.M. Hooper went to England in 1946 'depressed and convinced that another five years were needed to achieve union'. Hollis stated that the real union would not reach 'anything like adequacy until the second or third generation. You cannot just add Methodism, Presbyterianism, Congregationalism and Anglicanism together like a series of counters.'[1] Further, Hollis asked his brother bishops in South India to sign with him the following statement:

> After the inauguration of Union we, as Bishops of the Church of South India, shall be ready ourselves to receive communion at the hands of any Bishop or Presbyter of the United Church that all who have the status of Presbyters in the United Church are capable of performing all the functions assigned to Presbyters in the United Church by the Constitution of that Church in every congregation in the United Church; and that no Presbyter of the United Church will exercise his ministry in a congregation where members consciously object to his ministrations, and that no member of the United Church can 'consciously object' (in the sense in which these words are used in the Constitution of the United Church) to the ministrations of any presbyter ordained within the United Church. The suitability of a Presbyter for a particular congregation is another question and will have to be considered in all cases by the appointing authority.[2]

As Sundkler has observed, 'The effect of this statement was astounding. It represents the last decisive heave which made union a reality. It cleared the sky which until then had seemed so dark. It is also an interesting indication of the influence that South India had had on an Anglican leader such as A.M. Hollis.'[3] He was an extraordinary Anglican to concede that episcopal ordination was non-essential to the existence of 'a true ministry and to the celebration of the Eucharist'. Hollis moved the above resolution at the General Council of the CIBC. Suggestions to decline or defer reply until advice was obtained from the Lambeth Conference were lost in the voting. The resolution moved by Hollis obtained a sufficient majority. 'It is significant that the resolution was accepted with an overwhelming majority by the House of Laity (33-1), while less majority in the House of Clergy (30-22) and still less among the Bishops (7-6).'[4] As we have already noted, as early as July 1943 the Methodist Conference in England approved the decision of the South India Provincial Council Synod. With a chequered sequence, the SIUC

---

[1] Ibid., 320.

[2] Quoted, Ibid., 321.

[3] Ibid.

[4] Ibid., 322.

voting in their General Assembly in September 1946 voted 103 in favour, with 10 against and 7 abstentions. Thus, an ecclesiastical battle for a ground-breaking noble cause was won!

Inauguration 1947

It was not insignificant that India's freedom was declared on 15 August and the Church of South India was inaugurated on 27 September 1947. The Continuation Committee had appointed a committee back in 1943 to look after the arrangements for the inauguration. As a matter of course Hooper was the convener. He held different threads in his clear mind and able hands. The service was held at St. George's Cathedral Madras (Chennai), built in 1815. Hollis made sure that everything was in order for the service of inauguration. Five days of retreat (led by the saintly bishop Packenham Walsh, 1871-1959), a conference and two days of shared counsel about 'the multitudinous problems' that faced people when they went back to the new reality of dioceses, preceded the service. Newbigin, the minute taker of the final two days, later remembered, "At one point someone asked: 'what do we do about archdeacons, deans, canons and things like that?" There was a silence … After a moment someone said "abolish". The chairman asked for other views. There were none. I wrote the one word 'Abolished', and we went on to the next business.'[1] Probably the titles Rt. Rev. and Rev. and the clerical uniform were also decided in this meeting. But no record is available.

While there was excitement about the preparation for the inauguration, the sad news came that the Anglo-Catholic missionary society SPG decided to withdraw support to the CSI. Immediately many Indian clergy withdrew their assent to union; they and their congregations were mainly from the deanery of Nandyal and the Dornakal diocese. 'The issue was complicated by local rivalries and the disappointment of those whose candidate for the bishop's office had not been chosen.' However, in the face of apparent disintegration of the church, the Continuation Committee respected their consciences and asked the Metropolitan to provide pastoral care to those who had withdrawn from the union. Also, the SPG decided to stop the grants to dioceses from the end of the year (1947). The missionaries and Indian clergy who became members of the CSI were asked to forego their connection with the Society from the date. Nevertheless, through the intervention of Archbishop G.F. Fisher, a South India Separate Account in aid of former SPG missionaries and work in South India was organised by the Standing Committee of SPG itself.

Now, we follow the first-hand reflective report of bishop Lesslie Newbigin, the youngest of the fourteen bishops consecrated in the service, as recorded in his *A South India Diary* (1951) taking only the highlights.

---

[1] L. Newbigin, *Unfinished Agenda: An Autobiography*, London: S.P.C.K., 1993, 94.

At seven o'clock in the morning everything is still fresh and cool after last night's rain, and the cathedral looks its best in its setting of wide lawns and leafy trees. There is still an hour before the service is due to begin, but the cathedral and the vast *pandal*[1] alongside it are already beginning to fill up. People from all over South India are arriving in a constant stream, and here and there one recognizes one of the delegates from the Churches in other parts of the word. The inevitable photographers are everywhere laying their ambushes.[2]

As the cathedral bell strikes at eight, the service of inauguration opens and the long procession representing the three uniting Churches moves up the centre aisle of the cathedral. We join in prayer and then listen to the reading of the great High Priestly prayer in the power of which alone all these long years of wrestling with our divisions have been possible. Then on our knees we confess afresh that our unity, holiness, truth are in Him alone and not in us. One by one the authorized representatives of the three Churches come to the chancel steps and read out the resolutions of their governing bodies accepting the Union, and then go to the Holy Table and lay thereon signed copies of the Scheme of Union, and the signatures of all the ministers assenting to it. As each one does so he kneels before the Table and he and we together offer up silently to God a life given up that it may be won.

Now the three volumes lie side by side on the Table. There lie our separate selves. We have been proud of them, these great names, great principles, secure traditions of faith and worship, beloved patterns of holiness. We shall sometimes look back, because the flesh is weak. But 'pearls for pearls' is the law of God's kingdom. Lord, receive these goodly pearls which thou gavest! We are praying again …[3]

Bishop C.K. Jacob taking on his feet and voice ringing through the cathedral solemnly uttered the historic words:

'Dearly beloved brethren … I do hereby declare that these three Churches, namely: the Madras, Travancore and Cochin, Tinnevelly, and Dornakal Dioceses of the Church of India, Burma and Ceylon;

'The Madras, Madura, Malabar, Jaffna, Kannada, Telugu and Travancore Church Councils of the South India United Church; and

---

[1] A thatched makeshift extension.

[2] L. Newbigin, *A South India Diary*, London: SCM, 1954, 21.

[3] Ibid., 22f.

'The Methodist Church in South India, comprising the Madras, Trichinopoly, Hyderabad and Mysore Districts;

'are become one CHURCH OF SOUTH INDIA, and that those Bishops, Presbyters, Deacons and Probationers who have assented to the Basis of Union and accepted the Constitution of the Church of South India, whose names are laid upon the Holy Table, are Bishops, Presbyters, Deacons of this Church: In the name of the Father, and of the Son, and of the Holy Spirit. *Amen.*'[1]

A great peal from the organ breaks in upon the words and in a moment four thousand voices burst into the *Te Deum* in one tremendous shout of praise. All the long-frustrated desires of these last painful years have burst through the dam and are flowing in one irresistible flood. We look at each other with a kind of wonder; we are no longer friendly strangers but brothers in one household. With God all things are possible. Is this a dream or is this really true? (the heavenly choir, prophets and all those who have gone before in faith join our singing) ...

We are seated again and ready for the second part of the service, that which concerns 'the unification of the ministry'. Bishops and other ministers whose authority has hitherto extended only to the bounds of separate Churches are commissioned with prayer to exercise that ministry throughout the wider fellowship that is now ours. We sing a hymn that lifts our hearts and minds up to the ascended and regnant Christ, who having led into bright morning sunshine for a brief interval before the second service.[2]

In the second service which witnessed the Catholic-Evangelist integrity, nine presbyters of the CSI were made bishops and the first Communion together with 3,500 communicants partaking and experiencing the true foretaste of the heavenly banquet and season of joy that none of us will forget.[3]

It was not without reason that J.S.M. Hooper, the silent driver as the convener of the Joint Committee, firm and persuasive correspondent, to tackle critical issues, raised particularly from the Anglican side, was invited to preach at the inaugural service. In his sermon Hooper mentioned:

God has matched us with His hour; the Church of South India has an unparalleled opportunity. The reconciliation between our divergent

[1] Sundkler, 343.
[2] Ibid., 22-24.
[3] Newbigin, Op. cit., 23-25.

elements ... enables us with fresh conviction and force to proclaim the Gospel of reconciliation to all the clashing elements in this nation's life.[1]

On that Saturday night there was a great open-air meeting, and on Sunday there were special thanksgivings for the outstanding achievement by the work of the Holy Spirit.

Administrative Union

Following the inauguration of the 'ecclesiastical union' there remained the inauguration of the 'administrative union'. Again J.S.M. Hooper was called back to give the leadership until the first meeting of the CSI Synod in March 1948. 'Hooper as Convener of the Continuation Committee had very wide powers, which he used in close cooperation with the bishops. The election of Bishop A.M. Hollis as the first Moderator ... was important. Of great significance were the decisions by Synod about the ecumenical and missionary outreach of the church. The very fact of the Church of South India was a challenge to the other churches in India.'[2] We will point out in the sixth chapter initiatives to have wider communion with other Churches, especially with the Lutheran Churches. To complete one phase of the union, we have to mention that Hooper was called to stay on to complete the task of the Church of South India Trust Association (mainly to bring all the church/mission properties under one umbrella although Anglican dioceses formed their own trust associations) which was formally established under the Indian Company Act on 26 September, the day prior to the inauguration.

Rejoicing and Recognizing!

The second assembly of the World Council of Churches, held in Evanston 1954, visibly rejoiced at the achievement of organic unity in South India. The CSI Liturgy of the Lord's Supper was used. P.D. Devanandan and Bishop Lesslie Newbigin had the chance to report about the new union.

Carol Graham, a well-known woman missionary observed: 'In spite of all the years of patient negotiation, in spite of the very real growth in mutual knowledge and trust of one another, which had preceded union, the actual birth of the united Church came as the result of a great act of faith on the part of all concerned. It demanded a great act of faith for those born and bred in the Free Church tradition to accept episcopacy; it required an equally great act of faith on the part of Anglicans to recognise the existing ministries of the other uniting

---

[1] Sundkler, 339. (For the full text of the sermon, see Rajiah D. Paul, *The First Decade: An Account of the Church of South India*, Madras: CLS, 1958, 243-249.)

[2] Ibid., 344.

Churches without any question of supplementary ordination.'[1] R.D. Paul, a famous civil servant and lay leader of the CSI noted: 'One of the positive points in the CSI is that the united church affirmed all their previous traditions as the heritage of the whole church. He wrote, 'The denominational heritage of the churches which were coming together, the heritage of the life, experience and thought of the Church Universal and the heritage of India's spiritual past were all to be conserved, used, absorbed and fulfilled in the life of the new united Church. The new church was not going to supersede or supplant or replace anything. It was going to fulfil, to enrich, to perfect the life of each of its components.'[2] Newbigin and others felt that with the achievement of the CSI 'God has made our feet like the feet of a deer; he causes us to stand on the heights' (cf. Ps. 18:33).

Unfinished Task

On the whole, 28 years of patient persistence in faith with passion for making the Christian message credible, was a journey with moments of uncertainty and anxiety. Thorny issues prolonged arresting the attention of the participants in negotiations. Although through discussions in the councils, conferences and conversations the scheme of the CSI was made public and popular, it was impossible to get the opinion of every member of the all negotiating churches. Not many were well versed in the issues involved or competent to put forward their arguments. Women had their own opportunities to share their views through participation in their church councils and special conferences. However, there was no woman able to be a member of the Joint Committee. These were some of the limitations to achieve the fruits of having the collective will of the people and best outcome of democracy.

Moreover, the number and kind of representatives in the Joint Committees were not consistent. 'The total number of different persons attending the Joint Committee meetings from 1920 to 1947 was in the case of Anglicans 49, Methodists 51, and SIUC 71. This made the work in the Joint Committee difficult, particularly as much of the time was spent on debates between the SIUC representatives themselves.'[3] Not only persons of different temperament but also views different of constituent traditions like the Congregational idea and practice of the lay celebration of Communion made the process slow. Also, some prominent leaders who were visionaries of the union had gone.

We have already noted the negative reaction of the Anglican mission agency SPG which caused the withdrawal of a considerable number of priests and congregations of Nandyal and Dornakal areas. They had to be given special pastoral care and brought to the fold. There were jeering voices such as that CSI

---

[1] Carol Graham, *The Church of South India: A Further Stage in Development,* On behalf of the Appeal Committee in CSI, 1960, 5.

[2] Ibid., 6f.

[3] Ibid., 192.

was a mud-horse which would collapse in one stroke! The Anglican churches in Thirunelveli (plus later Tutukudi) and surrounding areas (e.g. Madurai) joined with the condition that they would not join the CSITA but would form the Tirunelveli Diocesan Trust Association (TDTA). Also, influential and wealthy congregations such as St George's and All Saints' in Madurai enjoyed autonomy or semi-autonomy, having a strange relationship with the CSI diocese which has shifted in pace depending on the aptitude of leaders and issues.

Part of SIUC (LMS) in Travancore continued to remain as the LMS Church, and it still continues to be separate, often in conflict with the South Kerala and Kanyakumari dioceses. A major section of the Northern Council of SIUC refused to join the CSI but later formed as Coimbatore Diocese in 1950.

Different segments of the Basel Mission Church had to join in a gradual manner. However, the very fact that most churches joined the CSI in their own time proved that change is always possible with the guidance of the Holy Spirit.

Chapter 5

Clarification of Some Issues

In the last chapter we came across controversial issues such as the importance of episcopal ordination, intercommunion, lay celebration and the creeds. In this chapter we initiate a discussion on these and more, which may throw some light on our understanding of these issues and on the understanding of others. If we deal with issues which were not prominent in the CSI negotiations, the intention is to help understand the foundations and fundamentals of the Christian faith which we want to live with some conviction, and even defending it in the face of other denominations and other religions. Of course, for those who are consciously taking the claim of Jesus that he was the way and truth and life, they cannot avoid getting into the depth of this claim. And if they have the necessary spiritual maturity, they should always believe that if they reflect on this claim along with the new dimensions and insights, that may call for dramatic changes in our practice of faith, the structure of our church and the practice of mission. In discussion on interreligious relations, with a view to avoid superficial slogans and wish-washy ideals, now for some decades a basic *mantra* has been repeated, i.e. 'Commitment and Openness'. This is certainly applicable in local as well as ecumenical discussions on church relations.

Approaching the Bible

The CSI negotiations started on the primacy of the two testaments of the Scripture. Further added was part of the Anglican Article of Faith no. 6 that they contain 'all things necessary to salvation'. But the negotiators never explained their adequacy and meaning of salvation. A detailed treatment of the subject is beyond the scope of this study. We have already noted that going through affirmations and decisions of the Anglican Communion on church union they seem to pay only lip-service to scripture. In the CSI negotiations Jesus' prayer that 'they may be one so that the world will believe' was repeated. It was Adolf

Streckeisen from the Basel Mission Church who brought the Bible as a testing stone of principles and practices. As we noted earlier, he accepted 'Holy Scriptures as the only standard of faith and life and will tolerate only such teaching as is in conformity with them.' Influenced by Karl Barth who stressed the primacy of the Bible, he brought into the discussion the Protestant emphases on issues such as the priesthood of all believers, and when Lay Celebration became controversial, he suggested that the bishop could authorise certain persons and thus strike a balance between tradition (episcopal) and the New Testament message. However, Streckeisen could not provide guidance on the basic approach to the Bible.

The Anglican theologian Richard Hooker (1554-1600), in his *Laws of Ecclesiastical Polity*, suggested the three sources of Scripture, Tradition and Reason, as sources of the Church's authority. Later many applied it to theology and some theologians used the image of 'three-legged stool'. It has become 'four-legged' with the addition of 'experience.' For non-western theologians it is difficult to accept the tradition, reason and experience as developed in the West, although some who have been schooled in theology in the western context continue to hold them uncritically. The recent theologies developed in Asia, Africa and other 'nations' have reclaimed the authenticity of their traditions, reasoning with wisdom and profound experience, often collective and communal. In any case, as his writings suggest, Hooker himself 'regarded Scripture as the highest source of authority', which is consistent with the view put forward in the 39 Articles. Thus, Article 20 concerns the authority of the Church, but delimits this according to a biblical framework when it stipulates: 'It is not lawful for the Church to ordain anything that is contrary to God's Word written ....'[1] The question is: strictly speaking, what is God's Word? The answer, 'it is God's word in human words' is a simple and popular answer. But human interpretations of the human words are too complicated, and the emergence of denominations has made this more complicated.

The problem lies in the very nature, structure and relevance of the Bible. Those who have seen and read some of the other religious scriptures, would realise that the Bible is most complex, inconsistent and in many cases contextual and culture-specific. But today, roughly, we are placed between two extreme developments. On the one extreme, there is the ever-increasing sophistication in the historical and textual study of the Bible which is hardly accessible to ordinary readers. On the other extreme, often in reaction to the above, we have fundamentalist readings and interpretations which source the mushrooming growth of sectarian churches and movements. The magnitude of the contrast may be stated by saying that the Bible has inspired many saints (and those with simple, sacrificial living and service), and the same Bible has motivated manipulative fundamentalists, commercial evangelists, fascists and murderous cult leaders.

---

[1] M. Throup, *All Things Anglican*, 63.

The only way out is to follow Jesus in his approach to his scripture. Jesus knew his scripture well. When he was tested in the wilderness the devil quoted certain verses from the scripture and asked him to act literally. Jesus countered each with alternative citations. He rejected the approach of the devil and condemned the Pharisees and lawyers who gave a tenth of their spices but neglected the more important matters of the law – justice, mercy and faithfulness' (Mt. 23:23). He selected, revised, re-interpreted and so on (Mt. 5:17-48). In his reading of Is. 61:1f. he omitted 'the day of the vengeance of God' (Lk. 4:18). More than everything else he followed the practice found in summarising, crystallising or essentialising. For example, almost at the climax of giving the Law, God said,

> And, now, Israel, what does the Lord your God ask of you but to fear the Lord your God, to walk in obedience to him, to love him, to serve the Lord your God with all your heart and with all your soul, and to observe the Lord's commands and decrees that I am giving you today for your own good? (Deut. 10:12-13).

A similar verse from the Prophets:

> He has shown you, O mortal, what is good. And what does the Lord require of you? To act justly and to love mercy and walk humbly with your God (Hos. 6:8).

In answer to a question, Jesus said that 'The greatest commandment is to love your God with all your heart, mind, soul and strengthen and love your neighbour as yourself.' In addition, he gave his own command: 'Love one another' (Mt. 22:34-40; Mk. 12:28-34; Jn.15:12). The question is whether we follow this pattern of summarising, crystallising or essentialising?

It may be a useful exercise to collect together the doctrines of scripture in different denominations. For example, 6 and 7 of the 39 Articles of Faith mention the scripture in detail. For example, the apocryphal books are listed with the note '... which the Church reads for example of life and instruction of manners; but it does not apply to establish any doctrine'. More significantly, as opposed to the earlier heresies, Article 7 'Of the Old Testament' starts to say, 'The Old Testament is not contrary to the New: for both ... everlasting life is offered to Mankind by Christ ... Although, the Law given from God by Moses, as touching Ceremonies, do not bind Christian men, nor the civil precepts thereof ought of necessity to be received in any commonwealth; yet notwithstanding, no Christian man whatsoever is free from the obedience of the Commandments which are called Moral.' It is often asked if the Anglicans are fully free from those ceremonies and rites and using the title 'priest' (rather than presbyter, minister, pastor, etc). Of course, no one may claim that there is a moral higher than the above-mentioned integrated love. In any discussion on differences – denominations, races, sexual orientation – what matters is not being like-minded but love-minded.

Faith Verses Familiarity

The word 'faith' is most commonly used by Christians, but there seems to be no interest in knowing and expressing its different meanings in the Bible. First of all, we have to distinguish faith from clinging to familiarity. Familiarity is a common phenomenon where even strange things become familiar in due course. This we see in ordinary experiences such as a married life, owning a new house, living in certain surroundings for a long time. In all such cases once we become familiar and find some enjoyment we never want to lose it. Where we are compelled to move on, the new experience is strange and challenging but until we become familiar. Thus, familiarity itself provides a glue or a sense of feeling at home. It is power, a strong sticking power in which we find comfort and say 'This is the way we have done things for ages', and so on.

All theist religions talk about faith. Normally it is to trust God, to seek his/her mercy, guidance and help. For this reason, in the context of interreligious relations and dialogue the word religion is replaced by faith. Hence, interfaith relations and interfaith dialogue. Participants in dialogue often tend to cover all religions in one canvas and they are at ease when they proclaim that all religions are the same or of same essence. If we press on asking what is that essence, answers will be varied. Some are willing to explore to a limited extent but most go with their familiar position. Here there is a challenge for the Christians to define their faith when they say or hear Catholic faith, Anglican faith, Methodist faith, Reformed faith and so on. Interestingly, formed originally by the dying of the above-mentioned Protestant Churches, the Church of South India is not called a faith!

Some biblical insights should enlighten us. Basically, faith means trusting God etc. as noted above. For instance, when shattered by the threats of enemies in the 8th century BCE, King Ahaz was told: 'If you do not stand firm in your faith, you will not stand at all' (Is. 7:9). Faith finding expression in a crisis is very common in the Hebrew religion. But originally this faith was enhanced and enriched by the core story of God in the enigmatic name of Yahweh who manifested showing solidarity with a vulnerable community groaning in slavery in Egypt. He initiated liberation and then all their journey, frustration, celebration, receiving law, moments of deviation, prophetic condemnation, call for repentance and assurance of hope – all these were part of the faith of individuals and community. In many words they were reminded that their mission was to set a model community based on justice, peace and love. In nutshell their faith was shaped by not only God's guidance with compassionate love but also their faithfulness.

Jesus found in his community the lack of faith in a specific sense, inability to transcend and move on for creating something new. He called his disciples 'of little faith' when they were worried about what to eat and drink but not to seek the kingdom of God and its righteousness (Mt. 6:30). He used the word faith for the adventurous act of four men who lowered a paralytic after opening a roof (Mk. 2:5), and for a woman of 12 years of bleeding (Mt. 9:22). In response to requests, Jesus told his disciples: 'You have so little faith; if you have faith as small as a mustard seed, you can say to this mountain, "Move from here to there and it will move".' (Mt. 17:20f; 21:21). Jesus warned: 'When the Son of Man comes, will he find faith on the earth' (Lk. 18:8). At the same time, Jesus found the faith in extraordinary behaviour in certain persons of other religions (Mt. 8:10; 15:28; Lk. 17:19).

Later, Paul acknowledged the 'mountain-moving faith' though greater was love (1 Cor. 13:2). He tells the Roman church: 'do not think of yourself more highly than you ought, but rather think of yourself with sober judgement, in accordance with the faith God has distributed to each of you (Rom. 12:3). Clearly, the measure of faith suggests not belief, trust, etc., but ability move on to change. Further, Paul brought the central dimension of faith to interpreting the gospel to the Gentiles. It is normally called 'justification by faith'. That means, by sending his Son to die, God justified all, irrespective of religious and moral strength. In other words, in Christ God has accepted us though we are unacceptable. Faith here means not to count one's merits but to accept this gracious acceptance with gratitude and to live a new life (see Rom. 1:1; 3:26; 4:5 etc). Here, faith as the ability to shift to a new framework is not different from adventurous acts, persistence and mountain-moving, we have indicated above. When this new framework was taken by some as an easy-going life or complacency, James brings back the faith framework of the Hebrew tradition and advocates a balance of faith and deeds (Js. 2:14-26).

The only place faith is defined openly and comprehensively is Heb. 11:1: 'Now faith is confidence in what we hope for and assurance about what we do not see.' Then a list of the ancient 'heroes of faith' is given. Their faith found different expressions, yet the base line was the capacity to transcend and move on with conviction of truth and assurance of a great future. If this biblical exercise is sensible, what is Christian faith? Those who initiated the movement for CSI and those who participated in negotiation experienced a test of their faith. There were those who clinged to familiarity and tried to be faithful to their church tradition which had been followed for centuries. Others by faith wanted to create something new which could not be believed in the beginning. Anomalies were overcome, hurdles removed, misunderstanding cleared and the first organic unity was achieved by faith.

It is fair to say that the majority of Christians of different denominations are not well aware of the history and doctrines of their church. What matters for them most is an ambience of the church building, ambience of the internal structures (altar, holy table etc.), vestments or other uniforms of their worship leaders, music, liturgy, way of doing things and familiar fellowship. It is often observed that every denomination has created a sub-culture, and individual congregations may have their own specific ethos, and all these form for them 'faith'! The real faith, however, is willingness to be 'led by the Spirit' for what God wants to be new.

Comprehensive Creed

The CSI Scheme accepted the two creeds, Nicene and Apostolic. The Anglican Articles of Faith have taken the Athanasian Creed as well. This creed has a helpful reflection and statement on Trinity, but at the beginning and end it consigns those who are out of the Faith to condemnation and eternal fire. For this reason its use has dwindled, although some congregations use it on Trinity Sunday. As we have noted earlier, the adequacy and relevance of the classical creeds was questioned by South Indian theologians such as K.T. Paul and G. Robertson. We will note studies of the history of the creeds and propose an alternative creed.

The Methodist theologian Frances Young's book, *The Making of the Creeds*, is a good introduction to the subject matter.[1] It is seen as the successor to Alan Richardson's *Creeds in the Making*. The Jewish background of moving on with orthopraxy, right action, is acknowledged. It is also acknowledged the legend of apostles produced an agreed statement, but the later Old Roman and Apostles Creed were not based on it. And they were not used in the Greek Church as they had their own formula.

In the doctrinal controversy which led to the formation and adoption of the Nicene Creed, we find people whose doctrines are being questioned or challenged offering in reply what they call the faith they received from their bishop, and then quoting creeds or creed-like summaries of doctrine. There is clear evidence that what lies behind this is the system of training for baptism and initiation into the church.[2]

From the middle of the fifth century on we have a number of series of Lenten lectures, commentaries on various local creeds, candidates to memorize the creeds, then familiar forms of creed. 'Undoubtedly this is the context in which the familiar creedal form was first framed and used. After the adoption of the Nicene Creed, the local creeds survived, and became Nicene by the insertion of the particular agreed formulae into each: that seems to be the way the creed of Constantinople (the one we now use as the 'Nicene' creed) arose, it then being adopted as the official version at the Council in 381 because it had a more developed clause about the Holy Spirit than the formula agreed at the earlier Nicene Council in 325. Creeds did not originate, then, as 'tests of orthodoxy', but as summaries of faith taught to new Christians by their local bishops, summaries that were traditional to each local church and which in detail varied from place to place. Typical variations can in fact be observed simply by comparing the creeds we know from their continuing usage, for as we have already noted, the 'Nicene' creed is a local Eastern creed adopted by the Council of Constantinople, and the

---

[1] Frances Young, *The Making of the Creeds*, London: SCM Press, 1991.

[2] Ibid., 3.

'Apostles" Creed is a descendent of the Old Roman Creed, the creed in use in the church in Rome at a comparable date.'[1] The author points out that the creeds are not summaries of the scripture so much as vital histories of the life of Israel as God's people and the life and teachings of Jesus who came from that tradition.

The character of the creeds as open and plain statements of the Faith was changed when some early Fathers used the titles such as the *Rule of Faith* or the *Canon of Truth,* although they were diverse and unfixed. For example, 'Irenaeus cites it in several different forms, which use different shapes, different selections of details, different stereotyped phrases, but which cover essentially the same ground, and are most typically used to contrast true Christian teaching with the "knowledge falsely so-called" of the heretics.'[2] At the same time, in many ways the *Rule of Faith* is clearly an important precursor to the creeds. They replaced Jewish affirmations of 'Hear O Israel' (Deut. 5:4) and 'My father was a wandering Aramean' (26:5). 'Such affirmations moulded the identity of the Jews, and similarly the creeds (or their precursors) moulded the identity of the new convert. Such Jewish confessions were embedded in worship, and so at first were the Christian confessions that replaced them. Creeds have their genesis in doxology, and they are not to that extent a surprising or uncharacteristic development from Christianity's Jewish background.'[3]

So, we reach the age of creed-drafting in the fourth century. Few were really happy with the Nicene solution, and when the imperial favour tipped towards the anti-Nicenes, Council after Council tried to do a better job. Each competing party had its own creed, and creed after creed was discussed, modified, accepted, only to be superseded by another. After fifty years, this stage came to an end at Constantinople in 381, when the Nicene Creed was reaffirmed, though, as we have seen, in the form of a slightly different creed which developed the third article more fully, and therefore answered the needs of a new generation more effectively. Seventy years later, when another Council met at Chalcedon to try and settle a rather different controversy, the lesson of this confusing period had clearly been well learned: the Council made no attempt to produce a new creed, reaffirming the creeds of Nicaea and Constantinople, while adding a 'Definition' to explain the right interpretation of the second clause around which controversy had arisen.[4]

We recall that in the Faith and Order Conference Edinburgh 1937, B. Lucas, a LMS missionary in South India, suggested modification of the creed with the argument that 'If one council was able to frame a creed, why should not we be able to change it?'[5] More recently, not only the influence of imperial rulers

---

[1] Ibid.

[2] Ibid., 8f.

[3] Ibid., 12f.

[4] Ibid., 13.

[5] Sundkler, 276.

but also the anti-Semitic attitude of the Fathers contributed to the truncated form of the creed. For example, what is known as the Apostles' Creed starts with creation and glosses over the Hebrew history and experience including the prophetic movement, altogether about three-fourths of the Bible, and jumps to the virgin birth. Again, it glosses over the life, ministry and teaching of Jesus, and jumps to his death and resurrection! The excuse that only the controversial clauses were included in the creeds cannot be valid because creation, crucifixion and resurrection were not controversial.

With a recognition of the above factors, Indian theologians have created their own 'faith affirmations' which are used in services. For example, without radical change, I have experimented with the following in two theological institutions I have served in India.

> We believe in the triune God, Father, Son and the Holy Spirit, who created the universe and all people. We believe in the root story of God who in the mysterious name Yahweh manifested and liberated the Hebrew community from Egyptian slavery, making them God's people through a covenant and guiding them by commandments and teachings of prophets. We believe in Jesus, who was born of Mary, grew in Nazareth of Galilee, ministered among the marginalized, confessed as teacher, prophet, Son of God, Son of Man, and challenged the unjust powers, and consequently was crucified under the governorship of Pilate. He was raised by God and manifested before his friends, and made Christ, Lord and Saviour. He ascended into heaven and is in close intimacy with the Father and Holy Spirit participating in the continued mission. His second coming we await. We believe in the Holy Spirit and the Catholic and Apostolic Church which is being sent to the world as witness. We uphold repentance and forgiveness as the basic components of the gospel and commit ourselves for the ministry of transformation and reconciliation.

Those who believed that the creeds produced in the West were capsules of absolute truth and sacrosanct had difficulty to appreciate this though they could not argue. The ones who were open and understanding found it as more comprehensive than the classical creeds. In negotiations on church union today creeds seem to be no longer controversial.

Doctrines

The worst contribution from the western denominations are doctrines which served as part of their identity. Doctrine is not unconnected with regimentation of military order which is important for the safety and integrity of a society or nation. Doctrine, 'the agreed teaching of the church', is not a precise term but 'one that stands midway between "dogma" (a particular doctrine regarded as fixed and inalienable) and "theology" (less formal accounts of Christian beliefs where a measure of speculation and change are to be expected). The boundaries between the three are not always clearly defined. It is not surprising, therefore, that proposals that doctrine should be subject to critical assessment and to change have neither been readily accepted nor wholly ruled out.[1] There are critical studies of the 'truth and adequacy of doctrinal statements'. Christian doctrines are supposed to be based on the Bible, but different approaches to the Bible and various interpretations and the intrusion of philosophical assumptions complicate them.

George A. Lindbeck, a Roman Catholic scholar, after decades of involvement in the Faith and Order movement, has brought out an influential study of the nature of doctrine. He says that the motivation of this book is more substantially theological than theoretical. He rejects either a cognitive or an experiential expressive approach, as well as a combination of them, and finds the conceptual categories provided by a 'cultural-linguistic' perspective as the only convincing way of understanding the function of doctrine within a tradition, particularly Christianity. He distinguishes the function of doctrine rather sharply from theology and argues that doctrine should be taken as having merely a 'regulative' force in relation to the force found plausible by a community in a given cultural context. He acknowledges that 'As one who is deeply concerned about Christian unity, I would like to believe, as have most theologians down through the ages, that my work is of service to the church and the glory of God. In brief, although the argument of the book is designed to the doctrinally and religiously neutral, it is prompted by convictions about the kind of theological thinking that is most likely to be religiously helpful to Christians and perhaps others in the present situations.'[2] For him, 'Those of postliberal inclinations will be undeterred. They will argue for intertextuality on both religious and nonreligious grounds: the integrity of faith demands it, and the vitality of Western societies may well depend in the long run on the culture forming power of the biblical outlook in its intratextual, untranslatable specificity. Theology should therefore resist clamor of the religiously interested public for what is currently fashionable and immediately intelligible. It should instead prepare for a future when continuing dechristianization will make greater Christian authenticity communally possible.'[3] What finally matters is faithfulness and performance. 'There is much in Scripture and tradition to suggest that preaching the gospel understandably is a necessary part of faithfulness.' Those who are stubborn about doctrines even if they are not

---

[1] Maurice Wiles, 'Doctrinal Criticism' in *Christianity: The Complete Guide*, London: Continuum, 205, 350.

[2] George A. Lindbeck, *The Nature of Doctrine, The Religion and Theology in a Postliberal Age*, Philadelphia: The Westminster Press, 1984, 10.

[3] Ibid., 134.

able to understand and interpret as in the case of Indian Lutherans may be helped by such critical studies of doctrines.

Fortunately, the CSI did not adopt a set of doctrines. Two Testaments, two creeds, two sacraments and historical episcopacy with local adoption were the bases, provided by the Lambeth Quadrilateral. CSI as one of the basic principles of the Constitution authorises every member to interpret the scripture contextually. But conservative and fundamentalist approaches continue to be a challenge. Creeds and sacraments have not been serious issues. The nature and function of episcopacy has been subject to vigorous debates in the negotiations and to some extent they continue unofficially. We will come back to this issue later. Here it may be helpful to point out the doctrinal positions of the Anglican, Methodist and Reformed Churches who constituted the body of CSI while in their home lands they are not even in full communion.

In Anglicanism, it is observed, 'The "historical formularies" – the 39 Articles of Religion, the Book of Common Prayer and the Ordinal – are our common legacy. While Anglicanism allows diversity in all sorts of ways, it strives to preserve *unity* in diversity.'[1] It is often said that the Anglican doctrines are permeated through *The Book of Common Prayer* which is a repository of liturgies, prayers and collects, as well as the Articles of Faith. They represent the artistic craft of great liturgists, the distilled wisdom of deep spiritual minds and the articulation of profound thinkers. As a resource the *Book* has been used for more than five centuries and several editions have been printed. Collects have been incorporated and used by other denominations as well, most notably the collect at the beginning of the 'Lord's Supper.'[2] Particularly, the last section of the '39 Articles of Religion' contains certain affirmations, guidance and principles which come close to what is known as 'doctrines'. We have already noted the principle of using the OT, not its ceremonies and rites but the moral teaching. The 17th Article of 'Of Predestination and Election' is now mostly 'omitted in usage' or reinterpreted after rereading the concerned scriptural passage and about sensitivity in a multi-religious context. It is doubtful if there is any motivation for developing positive attitudes to other Churches. Not only the Churches of Jerusalem, Alexandria and Antioch have erred but also the Church of Rome, 'not only in the living and manner of Ceremonies, but also in matters of faith'. Though the Reformed Traditions appeared later, the definition of church as a congregation of the faithful in which the pure Word is preached and the Sacraments duly administered, should qualify them. There is no mention of episcopal authority but the authority of the princes at whose commandment and will the General Council would meet.

---

[1] M. Throup, op. cit., 16.

[2] 'Almighty God, unto whom all hearts be open, all desires known, and from whom no secrets are hid. Cleanse the thoughts of our hearts by the inspiration of thy Holy Spirit, that we may perfectly love thee, and worthily magnify thy holy name; through Christ our Lord. *Amen.*'

On the whole, in many counts, even many Anglicans would admit, *The Book of Common Prayer* needs to dated and refined.

The United Reformed Church around the UK (from 1972) shares the 'statements of faith' of the World Reformed Churches. Following is a summary of the main clauses stated in a liturgical form of affirmation:

> We believe in one God, Father, Son and Holy Spirit. He is the living God, the only God, ever to be praised. Word and Sacraments are the Spirit's gift received continually for the life of faith. The highest authority is God's Word in the Bible which we appropriate with the help of the Spirit. We accept with thanksgiving to God the witness to the catholic faith in the Apostles' and Nicene Creeds. We acknowledge the declarations made in our own tradition by Congregationalists, Presbyterians and Churches of Christ in which they stated the faith and sought to make its implications clear. On the basis of Union we function and if there is need we make new statements of faith. Held together in the Body of Christ through the freedom of the Spirit, we rejoice in the diversity of the Spirit's gifts and uphold the rights of personal conviction. We commit ourselves to speak the truth in love and grow together in the peace of Christ. We believe that Christ gives his Church a government distinct from and not subordinate to the government of the state. We affirm our intention to go on praying and working, with all our fellow Christians, for the visible unity of the Church in the way Christ chooses so that people and nations may be led to love and serve God and praise him more and more for ever.[1]

Apart from such 'doctrinal statements', does the URC have a distinctive ethos in church life, worship and mission? Observers from outside will be able to answer innocently and objectively.

John Wesley, the founder of Methodism, was a priest of the Church of England, who went to America as an Anglican (SPG) missionary. With failure and frustration he returned and went through a heart-warming experience of 'conversion'. Leaving the CofE, he worked for the new Methodist movement which was growing fast. But even then he was faithful to his original Church. When he established chapels for prayer and bible study, he insisted that his followers should take part in the parish communion, and the time of the 'worship in the chapel' was fixed for the convenience of doing this. When the critical moment came, he came out of the church and declared 'the world is my parish'. He did not have time to think of 'Methodist doctrines'. The Bible apart, John Wesley's Journals, forty-four sermons and Notes on the New Testament are the main sources of

---

[1]   https://urc.org.uk/images/Free-Ebooks/What_is_the_URC_Statement.pdf (as on 23 March, 2019).

'Methodist' theology. Is there really a theology? Are there distinctive Methodist doctrines?

When other main denominations asserted their identity in negotiations of union and outside, recently Methodists have tried to claim some doctrines for themselves and build up a distinctive Methodist theology. In 2004 a group of Methodist theologians in Britain brought out a volume entitled *Unmasking Methodist Theology*[1] which contained articles of twenty-five writers in twenty-two chapters. No other book can be a better example of the variety, style and method of doing theology in British Methodism in its most exciting period of history, from 1932 to 2000. It was the result of a project by the Faith and Order Committee of the Methodist Church in November 2000. The book starts with an admission that 'there is nothing that is so special that Methodism can claim a place above other Christian denominations', but with an affirmation that, 'if, as a theological movement, it fails to go on articulating the theological motifs which drive it forward, then it has lost its soul'.

Articles in the first part of the book 'offer their own interpretations of the theological emphases which underlie different aspects of the Methodist practice'. Those in the second part develop certain chosen themes, although one or two in this part also talk about the practice rather than developing a theological theme. The articles of the third and final part by individual respondents to the writers of the first two parts represent a particular section of British Methodism or different Methodist tradition as well as others from Churches including the Church of England, the Roman Catholic Church and the United Reformed Church. Despite unavoidable overlapping, the way the volume is prepared and structured provides a model for presenting theological (and doctrinal) conversations in today's world.

Undeniably, British Methodism has developed and maintained a distinctive ethos of doing theology with a 'catholic spirit'. Instead of creating a theological system, it has deliberately chosen to discover and present theology through a variety of practical channels such as the Deed of Union (1932), statements, reports, catechisms, conversation at different levels of a connexion, songs, constitutional practice and discipline, and sharing views through memorials and writing articles in *The Methodist Recorder*. As far as the unique emphases are concerned, the original Wesleyan themes like personal experience, scriptural holiness, sanctification, perfection in love, prevenient grace and God's love for all are repeated. But these themes are not interpreted regarding their deep implications and the only exemptions are the articles on experience, the nature of the activity of God and growing in grace and holiness, which stand out as representing the most profound explorations.

Scripture, tradition, reason and experience are stated in general to be the sources for theology. Of these, scripture is primary and central, 'the supreme rule of faith and practice'. But the very nature of the Christian scripture, with

---

[1] Ed. by Brian Beck, Angela Shier-Jones and Helen Wareing, London: Continuum, 2004.

various approaches and interpretations that have given way to the development of different factions within Methodism and of denominations, could be profitably discussed illustrating the contribution of a few Methodist scholars to scriptural hermeneutics and biblical theology. And while most of the Methodist favourites are stated with scriptural evidence, the use of the term 'doctrine' is misleading in the light of the 'doctrines' of two Churches we have seen.

The philosophical dictum that 'he who knows one [religion] knows none', which has been applied to comparative religion, is applicable to theologies also. While there is sufficient acknowledgement of partnership with sister churches, contribution to and learning from the world church and the ecumenical movement, except scanty references in passing to few other traditions, there is no attempt to clarify the Methodist distinctiveness in comparison with that of other churches and traditions. For example, the Methodist emphasis on the New Testament idea of the priesthood of all believers, which has been further interpreted in terms of the ministry of the people of God, is readily acceptable to all the free churches although there may be differences in understanding the levels of order and the meaning of ordination. Therefore, it is not surprising that the URC respondent observes that most of the thinking in this book could have come out his own church. Likewise, the Roman Catholic respondent is justified in his observation that, 'What surprises me most about this intelligent and interesting romp round the corners of Methodism is how much of Methodism is common to Christianity, or at least finds its familiar counterpart in that large portion of Christianity called Roman Catholicism.'

The most pressing need for developing a shared theology or at least comparative theology is the common witness for which the Church is called. Methodist emphasis on mission in appealing for both personal transformation and social change within the framework of the kingdom of God is unquestionable. However, what the URC respondent has observed is remarkable: 'What I missed most in this book was a robust recognition that the Methodist Church, like all the other mainline churches, is in crisis: living at a time in which we must listen for a Word of judgment about our life and witness, but also entering an age when through God's grace we can relearn what it means to be a faithful church'. Also, although some Methodist theologians have made enormous contribution to the theologies of religious pluralism none of them have been allowed to get in to the discussion here. Today, while the theology projects continue, informed Methodists respond with a gracious smile when they are told in interviews that they have no doctrines but emphases of certain biblical themes and above all, in sum, a combination of 'soul gospel' and 'social gospel'.

The above brief discussion on doctrines taking the cases of three Churches may well lead the reader to affirm or confirm the futility of doctrines and their unreasonable obstacles for attaining church union. Obviously, many claim doctrines for their churches and movements without knowing what they are, how they overlap with others, in what way they are distinctive from other and how they relate to the scripture and common sense. Also, we may have the strange feeling that in the end our language and formulas are limited and inadequate. Can there be better ways of speaking the fundamentals of our faith?

Biblical Insights

Any honest mind will acknowledge that the Bible is not easy to read and comprehend as it covers more than 1,200 years of history and contains a variety of literary types such as history, myth, folk song, proverbs, psalm, lamentation, dialogue, parable and apocalypses. It is reasonable to ask why then, when most of other religious scriptures are rather simple and plain (e.g. devotional poetry and moral teaching), the Judeo-Christian scripture is heavy and encyclopaedic, inconsistent and even confusing. We do not adequately recognise that the Hebrew scripture of living Judaism forms three-fourths of the Christian scripture. On the other hand, one can take it positively that the good Lord has given us a complex scripture as a great gift but is expecting us to study, investigate and reread it with patience and prayer. Seminaries and theological colleges have helped the ministers to equip themselves before they engage with their congregation members. But denominations and doctrines have often blinded them, and today it is a call at least in South India to read the scripture with new eyes and openness.

Recently, the word 'insights' has been used considerably in connection with the Bible, perhaps again more in South India. 'Biblical insights' or 'insights from the Bible' are directed to a variety of issues such as interreligious dialogue, environment, poverty, equality of genders and the experience of children. Insight involves a search light which is inbuilt in our person and guiding light of the Spirit. It is participating in a journey which encounters with a bewildering forest in night and enjoyable rays of the rising sun in the morning. If the reading is engaging and selfless with a mindset to inform and transform ourselves, we can be sure of enjoying moments of excitement that will lead to transforming action including action for church unity as well.

Insights with our internal search light and the guiding of the Spirit will not take stories of butchery murders, mass rapes, atrocities, unjust rules, unfair judgements, blessing the rich and despising the poor, etc., to take as models to follow even if they claim divine sanction. As Paul says, we test everything and follow what is good. There may be dilemmas in appreciating the contradictions of whether God willed invasions, kingship, temple building, rejection of people of other religions and cultures. Following the process and outcome would help us to decide. We have to differentiate between the first bright part of the lives of kings David and Solomon and the dark second part with untold ambition, authority and atrocities, and Jesus' judgements on them does assist our thinking. Insights into the problem of undeserved suffering lies imperceptibly in the dialogue between, Job, his wife, his friends and God. There are visions of centralising Jerusalem but counter-visions of focusing on insignificant villages such as Bethlehem and Nazareth which came to be places of the saviour Jesus' birth, life, mission and the great Commission. An insightful investigation into the presentation of Jesus would bring to light his multi-faceted personality and multi-dimensional mission. Even his death on the Cross is interpreted about ten ways in the New Testament. The accounts of Jesus' resurrection and his appearance to his disciples and friends are presented inconsistently. There are four versions of the Great Commission. The changing focus of the meaning of the gospel is evident. There are visions for the future but no blueprints.

It may be helpful to distinguish between primary insights and secondary insights. The secondary insights of all well-meaning, applicable, ennobling, enhancing, helpful, positively influencing, inspiring and challenging activities in God's world may resemble both religious and secular values around. As Paul says, we are all created to do good. But the primary and distinctive insights include:

1. God's solidarity with the vulnerable and victims of all kinds of injustice and liberating them as is evident throughout the Bible, pivotally in the life and ministry of Jesus with the power of the Holy Spirit;
2. God's gradual unfolding of being three in one – Father, Son and the Holy Spirit – in creative, dynamic, loving, sustaining and humbling relationship;
3. Power of powerlessness and the authority of servanthood, the ever-suffering love of God, the climax of its manifestation on the Cross of Christ, the final image of which in the last book of the Bible is lion-turned-lamb with blood marks, a Lamb slain from the foundation of the world;
4. Sacrificial engagement of the Church as a reconciled and reconciling community, manifesting the supreme command of love (as we earlier noted) for transforming the world and being joyous in hope.

When we have such a scripture and its interpretations, even after discussion in groups, each one may take a strange position appealing to her conscience. But now it is widely accepted that conscience need not be always pure but may be deluded and corrupted. One touchstone is whether the person's decision is selfish and action divisive, and based on right understanding. In the history of divisions in the Church and the emergence of denominations it is not difficult to find influential persons with these qualities. In a post-modern, post-liberal and post-truth era this touchstone alone seems to be the valid tool.

Apostolic Succession and Episcopacy

The term Apostolic Succession and its associate terms such as apostolic age and apostolic fathers have been subjected to controversies and ambiguous traditions which have often obstructed organic church unions. Even summary treatments of the topic reveal the complexity and misunderstanding.[1] To understand the controversy over intercommunion, supplemental ordination and Lay Celebration the following notes may be helpful.

Although there are different ministries, in its broadest sense ministry is 'any work done by a member of the Christian community on behalf of that community'. However, a minister in the church is a person who believes to have a call to special sacramental, preaching and pastoral ministry which is tested by the church, and the candidate is sent for training. At this juncture it is important to note that 'priest' is not a title for the above person which is noted in the Bible. The first and direct list of 'ministers' and the purpose of their work comes from 'Paul':

> So Christ himself gave the apostles, the prophets, the evangelists, the pastors and teachers, to equip his people for works of service, so that the body of Christ may be built up until we all reach unity in the faith and in the knowledge of the Son of God and become mature, attaining to the whole measure of the fullness of Christ (Eph. 4:11-13).

This understanding is based on the radical view in the Bible of the collective priesthood of God's people or priesthood of all believers (Ex. 19:6; 1Pet. 2:9). A few verses mention the 'priestly role or duty' but in a completely different sense (Rom. 15:16; Heb. 4:14-16; 10:1ff). Then it should be clear that the 'special ministers' are called to equip all the 'priests or people of God' for service, maturity of unity in the faith and knowledge of Christ and attainment of the fullness of Christ; there are few more lists in different order and with additional titles.[2] Then the responsibility of the 'minister' was to coordinate and regulate them for the common good. There are different reasons stated for the continuation of the title and office of priest in the church, and the most convincing assumption is that the idea of collective priesthood could not be digested by the pagan cults where Christianity spread.

However, in due course the special ordained ministry took various forms. Major Churches (Roman Catholic, Orthodox and Anglican) have adopted and maintained an order based on the offices of bishop, priest and deacon with a claim that it came from the early Church. This three-tier ministry has been adopted by Protestant and united churches, although in the New Testament there is no basis

---

[1] For example, see https://en.wikipedia.org/wiki/Apostolic_succession (as on 26-3-2019); J. Bowden, 'Ministry and Ministers' in *Christianity: The Complete Guide*, 749-756.

[2] 1 Cor. 12:1-11 mentions different gifts of the Spirit, different kinds of service and different kinds of working. Each one is the manifestation of Spirit given for common good. Particularly mentioned are the gift of wisdom, of knowledge, of healing, of miraculous powers, of prophecy, of distinguishing between spirits and of speaking in different tongues. In the church in Antioch there were prophets and teachers (Acts 13:10). There are additions of serving, giving encouragement, giving and showing mercy (Rom. 12:5-8). In 1Cor. 12:28 we read a list of the following order: apostles, prophets, teachers, miracles, gifts of healing, speaking in tongues, interpreting them and eagerly desiring the greater gifts.

for such a structure. In fact, the title 'overseers' (*episcopoi*) and presbyters are one and the same, and the title 'deacon' meant for all sorts of service, and they could not be prevented from preaching (Acts. 6, 7). Paul instructs the overseers and deacons together on their moral and spiritual standing (1Tim. 3:1-13). If that is the case, how the word 'bishop' came to prominence and popularity, we will see later.

The word 'apostle' means 'one who is sent' and Jesus was witnessed as apostle, true and faithful (Heb. 3:1f). Jesus called twelve disciples in order to be with him and participate in his mission. The number twelve which signified the twelve tribes of Israel was given importance, as is evident from the fact that Judas was replaced by Matthias who had been with the Twelve even from the time of Jesus's baptism (Acts 1:21-26). At the same time, though not qualified in the above sense, Paul and Barnabas were called the apostles (14:4, 14). Evidently there was controversy over the qualification of an apostle. Some people could not see Paul as qualified and treated him and his friends as secondary to the Twelve. Such attitude affected the churches he was associated with as well. Thus, he writes to the Corinthians: 'Am I not free? Am I not an apostle? Are you not the result of my work in the Lord? Even though I may not be an apostle to others, surely I am to you! For you are the seal of my apostleship in the Lord' (1Cor. 9:1f; cf. Gal. 1:19). Here we see already a misunderstanding about particular church order and the fruits of credible ministry outside it, and we recall that this argument was put forward by non-episcopal church leaders and their sympathisers in the Anglican fold in South India. Credibility of mission lies in its positive result not in following structures and procedures.

The period from the earliest to the time of the death of the last apostle (unknown) is known as the 'apostolic age'. The contemporaries of the New Testament whose writings were well-known are called the 'apostolic fathers'. What is known as 'apostolic succession' is based on a belief that the bishops come in a long chain transmitting grace and power through laying on of hands, although there is no evidence that the chain started from a particular apostle (Peter or Paul? Both were associated with Rome). It should be noted that while the Roman Catholic Church believes that it started from Peter, whom Jesus called the foundation rock of the church (Mt. 16:18), there is no clue of his laying hands on any successor, though once he and John placed their hands on the new believers in Samaria and they received the Holy Spirit (Acts 8:17). In the case of Paul, the prophets and teachers of the church in Antioch, guided by the Holy Spirit, set apart him and Barnabas for the missionary work among the Gentiles. 'So after they had fasted and prayed, they placed their hands on them and sent them off' (13:3). Later, Paul reminded his god-son Timothy, 'to fan into flame the gift of God, which is in you through the laying on of my hands' (2 Tim. 1:6). Earlier, probably appealing to a commercial and mechanical practice (cf. Acts 8:18f), he advised him 'Do not be hasty in the laying on of hands, and do not share in the sins of others. Keep yourself pure' (1 Tim. 5:22).

In spite of the above evidence and absence of clues, several stages of development and collections of church law, there came to vogue the title 'Apostolic See' which denoted the diocese of Rome and Apostolic Delegate, appointed by the Pope to serve abroad. It will be interesting how and when exactly the title 'priest' came to take the middle position in the three 'holy orders' of ministry – bishop, priest and deacon. Orthodox, Roman Catholic and Anglo-Catholic traditions claim in contrast to one another that these three orders are not only part of the apostolic succession but also they were originally instituted by Jesus himself. How to establish the truth? Bishops are mentioned in the NT in plural (*episkopoi*) and then it is difficult to argue for one bishop in an area (diocese). As we noted earlier, bishop means overseer and there is strong arrangement for oversight in the non-episcopal churches as well. However, the name and office of the bishop gained power and prestige, and in the medieval period their government was regarded as parallel to the monarch. Conflicts between these two powers could lead to gruesome assassinations.[1] Many scholars think that the hierarchy of bishop, priest or presbyter and deacon developed in the second century but not on any verifiable proof. Particularly, though it has created the priestly class attracting honour and reverence, as far as the understanding and propagation of the gospel is concerned, it has been confusing, distorting and misleading. The term pope meaning papa or father, applied to the bishop of Rome in the 11th century, and his pre-eminence evolved slowly combining political and priestly powers.

It is unfortunate that those who set up hierarchies in church and ministry and maintained them claiming divine sanction and apostolic succession did not search deeply for biblical insights. This was true in the approach of the negotiators of the CSI. In the world of an ever-living God, the particular origin of a divine institution is immaterial. The writer to the Hebrews provides a stunning reflection on the origin of Melchizedek comparing it to Jesus:

> Without father and mother, without genealogy, without beginnings of days and end of life, resembling the Son of God, he remains a priest for ever (Heb. 7:3).

---

[1] E.g. Thomas a Becket (1118-1170) was the Archbishop of Canterbury, a genius, and the Chancellor in the court of King Henry II. When vacancy came, with the permission of the Pope, Henry wanted to make Becket the archbishop. Soon he realised that Becket had not yet been ordained. All the short cuts were followed. 'Becket was first invested as a priest. The next day he was ordained a Bishop and that afternoon, June 2, 1162, made Archbishop of Canterbury'. In due course the dark period of conflict on the supremacy of power set in. In some remarkable cases Becket acted against the will of the King. Finally, at his order, four knights approached Becket while worshipping in the Cathedral. 'The knights found him at the altar, drew their swords and began hacking at their victim, finally splitting his skull'. He was buried in the cathedral, and there hangs a suspended guillotine to remember his martyrdom. He was canonised and made a saint.

We have already mentioned the extraordinary idea of a collective priesthood, priesthood of a holy community, with leaders of different functions. Moses, the first leader was not able to understand this priesthood and shared leadership. The advice repeatedly came from outside, his father-in-law of Midian, to delegate. Finally, he allowed his spirit to be shared with seventy chosen leaders. The 'ordination' took place in the tent around which the seventy elders were supposed to be standing. But, for some reason, two remained in their camp. When the sixty-eight received the Spirit and prophesied the two in the camp also had the same experience. The young Joshua asked Moses to stop the two but Moses in his good senses said: 'Are you jealous for my sake? I wish that all the Lord's people were prophets and the Lord would put his Spirit on them!' (Num. 11:29). In a subsequent event Miriam and Aaron questioned the behaviour of their brother Moses. 'Has the Lord spoken only through Moses? Hasn't he also spoken through us?' The angry Moses cursed Miriam with leprosy (12:1-15). Further, the agitation against Moses developed to a massive level. Korah and his company (altogether about 300), being aware of the collective priesthood, went to Moses and Aaron and said to them: 'You have gone too far! The whole community is holy, every one of them, and the Lord is with them. Why then do you set yourselves above the Lord's assembly?' When Moses heard this, he fell face down. His reaction ended with the 'rebels' being swallowed by the earth. God was drawn in favour of this action (16:1-35). This is a chilling example of the refusal to put into practice the ideal of collective priesthood, and the tension between laity and priesthood.

Broken links in the 'messianic succession' or lineage provide some profound insights. Though a tradition of Messiah as David's son was maintained by a section of Israelite/Jewish community for an inflated identity and mistaken promises for a golden age, there are clues to rethink this. It is hard to deny that the first part of David's life and work took a dramatic turn that put blood on his hands and created turmoil after his son's atrocious rule created a questionable legacy. In this light the phrase 'A shoot will come up from the stump of Jesse' (Is. 1:1) can be construed not as continuation from David but a new origin altogether from the original root. And it is very significant to note the acclamation of the Persian ruler Cyrus as the anointed (messiah) one (Is. 45), thus breaking the cherished Davidic lineage. The 'messianic' secret of Jesus needs to be understood in such broken links. In any case Jesus, through a riddle, ridiculed the claim that Messiah was the Son of David (Mt. 22:41-46).

The only positive note about David that Jesus made was with reference to what he did 'when he and his companions were hungry. He entered the house of God, and he and his companions ate the consecrated bread – which was not lawful for them to do, but only for the priests' (Mt. 12:3f; cf.1Sam. 21:3-6). This was in response to those who criticised his disciples for picking some corn and eating on the Sabbath. Jesus, thus, broke the mechanical Sabbath and refused to be domesticated by the sacerdotal structures of the rites and ceremonies. We have already noted that just like Melchizedek Jesus had no proper genealogy. The Holy Spirit filled him without any formal structures of ordination or consecration. He was very clear of the way the Holy Spirit worked:

> The wind blows wherever it pleases. You hear its sound, but you cannot tell where it comes from or where it is going. So, it is with everyone born of the Spirit (Jn. 3:8).

Therefore, when the apostles laid hands on some new believers and Spirit descended, there was no idea of hierarchy. When priesthood became well-structured in Israel with different grades and functions and when it allied with monarchy it completely distorted the original vision of collective priesthood. It also led to corrupt practices as condemned by the prophets. There are texts where the interpolation of the priests is discernible. For instance, in Ps. 51 the psalmist says that God would not delight in sacrifice and burnt offerings but a broken spirit and contrite heart (v.16-17) but subsequently the last verse (19) says that God will delight in the sacrifices of the righteous, in burnt offerings and bulls sacrificed on the altar. Is this not a priestly interpolation? Most important for the serious readers of the scripture is a discerning mind.

Jesus and his apostles tried to restore the original vision, but later developments in the Christendom found every excuse to ignore this, and one excuse was that it was part of an 'old vision' or 'old covenant'. The worst outcome of distorted or forgotten vision was the transformation of the office of the 'overseer' to the channel of power, grace and Holy Spirit. His right hand was the 'wire, cable or pipeline' of the flow and the storage is with him, as the person ordained by him cannot channel it to others. Logically what John Wesley did may be justified. When a bishop was not available to ordain his preachers, as an 'ordained priest', he himself ordained them and one of them latter declared himself a bishop. Since then although the word 'bishop' is not used in its place of Methodist origin and some other Conferences around the world because of misleading baggage it carried, 'oversight' has been given utmost importance. It is interesting that after a few union attempts have failed, the Conference of the Methodist Church (2018), with a view to bring the two Churches in closer communion particularly in the areas of ministry and mission, decided to consider the proposal of episcopal ordination of their President by the Archbishop of Canterbury so that the President's ordination of the Methodist ministers become episcopal. At the same time those ministers already ordained are accredited as 'acceptable anomaly'. The Conference decided to consider the proposal and there are critical voices too. We cannot help asking the question if the CofE had this attitude to ordained ministers of non-episcopal Churches in the negotiations in South India, then the process would have moved faster. Also, the difference of terms 'consecration' for bishops and 'ordination' for presbyters with distinguishable vestments made the position of the former very strong.

Understanding the nature and function of episcopacy in the negotiations of CSI was one of the most difficult issues, and still there is no clarity in that first Church organic union. The phrase 'historic episcopacy locally adopted' was not explained in the 1888 Lambeth Quadrilateral. It was clarified later that it was not subjected to any particular interpretation of episcopacy. But it came to the surface during the negotiations that the Anglican participants were prepared to allow minor adjustments but not compromising on the apostolic succession that was assured by the bishop's ordination of presbyters. Finally, it was a great compromise that presbyters of the non-episcopal churches participated in the consecration of bishops by laying hands.

The nature and function of episcopacy is a continued concern to clarify and reform. The CSI has been expected to contribute to ecumenical discussion on the topic. Notably, as early as 1964 a CSI bishop presented a paper at the Wider Episcopal Conference held at Canterbury.[1] Without touching the question of succession and hierarchy, he starts with the basic affirmation that 'The ministry of the Church is a gift of God to His people through Christ.' Then he expounds, with biblical reference, shepherding of the flock of God's pasture with safeguarding and loving care. Further, he explains episcopacy as a sign of the unification of the ministry of the whole Church. He notes the following pastoral demands on the episcopal office with brief reflection: keeping the purity of the 'doctrine', corporate personality of the ministerial team, administrative responsibilities as part of pastoral ministry of the whole church, discipline as pastoral care and meeting the challenge at the frontiers. Often these ideas are repeated sermonically, and what is needed is refining them and ensuring measures to check any kind of competition, corruption, haughtiness and power-mongering and maintaining the challenging combination of dignity and humility.

Discussion on the apostolic succession between the Anglicans-Catholics-Orthodox is going on. Originally, the CofE was a break-away church from the Roman Catholic Church although Henry VIII lived and died as a Catholic. However, his Act of Supremacy (1534) gave the English Church its independence and it became the Church of England, but the Pope excommunicated it. However, the CofE claimed the link through the bishops who were originally in England, though the Pope latter discredited and declared it invalid. Today the Anglican Communion accepts Roman Catholic and Orthodox ordinations but not vice versa. One could make a revealing study of current Anglican opinions on this issue.

Apart from the succession theory, early Fathers and saints have been taken seriously in the Anglo-Catholic, Roman Catholic and Orthodox Churches. The underlying belief is that they were contemporaneous to the Jesus movement. But, does antiquity carry automatic credibility? Within the band of Jesus' disciples

---

[1] See I.R.H. Gnanadason, 'The Episcopacy as a Pastoral Office', *SICman*, October 1964, 4-6.

there was a progress from 'wholly fools to holy fools.'[1] In the New Testament, following the Hebrew notion, Christians are called saints or those called to be saints (e.g. Rom. 1:7; 8:27; 12:13; 1525, 26, 31; 16:15; 1Cor. 1:2; 6:1). No one claimed they were perfect but called to move towards perfection through transformation.

No one would argue against the fact that many of the early Fathers enormously contributed to the life of the Church as exponents of the faith and as its defenders against heresies. But some of them were mercilessly anti-Semitic with murderous consequences for several centuries. Also, certain interpretations of the scriptural passages they offered distorted the real meaning and intention. For example, the allegorical interpretation of the parable of the Good Samaritan, attributed to St. Augustine and followed by others including Martin Luther, was flawed. Accordingly (rough summary), the traveller from Jerusalem to Jericho was the sinner, the robbers were the band of the devil, the priest and Levite who passed aside represented the Old Testament religion which cannot save, the Good Samaritan was Jesus who took pity on the sinner, bandaged his wounds and poured on the oil and wine (the Spirit) and took him to an inn (the Church) and took care of him; next day he gave the inn-keeper two coins (denarii) which were the two sacraments (or two testaments) and asked him to look after the victim promising that he would reimburse any extra expense when he returned (second coming). Still there are fundamentalist preachers around who broadcast this and similar interpretations. But in the gospel, Jesus told the parable to a lawyer who had asked him 'Who is my neighbour?' following Jesus' teaching of the greatest commandment of loving God with one's whole self and loving one's neighbour as oneself (Lk. 10:25-37). When we think of living, worshipping and ministering together with members of other churches, relying on the concurrent guidance of the Spirit, we have the openness to learn from any one whose teaching is in line with the primary insights of the Bible.

Structures – Church Buildings

What is the nature and meaning of church building? Is it identical with Solomon's temple or similar to a brahmanic Hindu temple, with sanctuary and altar inside? Although, this was not a topic dealt with in the CSI negotiations, when we think of organic union, clarity about the significance of church buildings may be helpful. The CSI was inaugurated on 27 September 1947 in St. George's Cathedral in Madras[2] (Chennai) with temporary extensions (*pandal*). It was one of a few cathedrals, situated in the biggest city of South India, and there are a

---

[1] See I. Selvanayagam, 'Theological Education and Regeneration of the Church in India', in *Communion on the Move: Towards a Relevant Theological Education* (Essays in Honour of Bishop John Sadananda, ed. by Wati Longchar & P. Mohan Larbeer, Bangalore: BTESSC, 2015, 37-49.

[2] It was the capital of the Madras Presidency or the Presidency of Fort St. George, and also known as Madras Province, an administrative subdivision of British India.

few other cathedrals in South India as the remaining hallmarks of the missionary works of the Anglo-Catholics. V.S. Azariah, who was keen to develop indigenous mission, liturgy, architecture etc., during his first and only diocese he served (1912-1945), built a remarkable CSI Cathedral of the Epiphany in Dornakal (Andhra Pradesh) with indigenous and interreligious architecture. Another, similar but with different architecture, semicircular with open windows and stone pillars that bear biblical and Indian symbols, was built in Madurai in the mid-eighties. A cathedral (*cathedra* = the seat of the bishop, parallel to the royal throne) reminds us a complicated past, particularly the power conflict between monarchic power and the power of the Church. Without being aware of this history, there are a few in India who would like to build European model cathedrals as marks of pride and glory!

As the primacy of the Bible is accepted by the major traditions we should start from there. After cleansing the temple which looked marvellous in its finishing at Jerusalem, and when some Jews asked for a sign to prove his authority, Jesus said, 'Destroy this temple, and I will raise it again in three days' and when this puzzled his opponents an explanatory note was given: 'But the temple he had spoken of was his body' (Jn. 2:21). Later, this body was understood as the church in the unity of which lay its sanctity.

When all the other testimonies appeared to be false, Jesus was charged with forecasting the destruction of the temple in Jerusalem and the reconstruction of a different kind of temple. The anger of the conservative Jews was understandable. Perhaps they were not aware of its ambiguous and painful story. Originally David proposed to build a house for the Lord in order to match his magnificent mansion. But the Lord rejected it, saying that while in the wilderness journey of the Israelites he never asked for a house to dwell; rather he was moving about the tents of the people.

A different tradition arose that encouraged King Solomon to build a temple. He had some preparatory resources in store left by his father. It took 13 years to build his own palace, and 7 years the temple. The temple work was tainted by heavy taxation, forced labour, cheating in the supply of timber, etc. At its dedication God said clearly that if there was no justice in Solomon's rule the temple would be destroyed. The 'wise turned wicked' Solomon played the greatest havoc in the history of Israel. Consequently, the kingdom of the united Israel was divided.

In due course, the temple and Jerusalem became the hub of religious, political and commercial power. The Hebrew prophets condemned it and claimed it was the house of prayer for all people. And they forecast its destruction. Accordingly, the Temple was destroyed by the Babylonian army in the early part of the 6th century BCE. When the exiles in Babylon returned after about half a century, a simpler and smaller second temple was built under the leadership of Ezra and Nehemiah.

When the Solomon-like Herod the Great, the '|King of the Jews', came to power in 40 BCE he rebuilt the temple with extension and expansion and even in Jesus' time it was incomplete while all the activities were going on. Jesus cleansed the temple and took the outcast disabled into it. When his disciples showed in awe the beauty of the temple, he forecast its destruction. The indication of 'rebuilding' could not possibly be literal. It was building of human bodies and fellowships after resurrection. Where two or three gathered, Jesus declared that he would be present in their midst. The house groups of the early church demonstrated the fact that the sanctity of the church lied in the unity of the people. In the vision of the new Jerusalem in the new heaven and new earth, as recorded in the last book of the Bible, it is stated that there is no temple, and God and Christ would replace it. As Jesus forecast the Jerusalem temple was destroyed by the Roman army in 70 CE. Since then it has not been rebuilt. The disciples had continued to worship in the temple at Jerusalem until they were cast out. The house churches spread fast. Also, Paul interpreted that our body is the temple ('the holy of holies') and was in contact with the house-churches and he was able to mention individual names of hosts and participants in his letters. But this gospel-based meaningful simplicity of worship place and holiness had to face the onslaught of an imperial power.

The great vision in the new world started to diminish when Constantine, the first Christian emperor of Rome, as mark of his power and glory, built a magnificent basilica.[1] No wonder, he was called the second Solomon. Subsequently, basilicas, cathedrals and huge church buildings were built 'for the glory of God' but in reality, expressing the Babel syndrome, 'to make a name for ourselves'. Magnificent temples or worship places by different names are points of pride in other religions also. It may well be expected that a study of them will reveal the process and pattern as parallel to Solomon's temple. Particularly the economy of such buildings might reveal major contributions of the wealthy who exploited the poor. Does people's giving to buildings match what do they contribute to social engagement, caring for the poor, etc.? The 'Hinduised Christianity' in India with a confused legacy of European Christianity with a distorted understanding of glory, soul, priest and heaven, and a strange combination of pomp and piety, may provide a comfortable position for the priestly minded pastors who continue to resist putting in practice the biblical idea of the priesthood of all believers and 'meeting place' of congregations. But they can hardly witness to the unique gospel of Jesus, who was crucified on the charge of forecasting the destruction of the glorious temple at Jerusalem and replacing it with bodies and fellowships of his disciples. Following the prophets and Jesus there have been theologians who advocate a right understanding of church building with simplicity which is different from temple, and which would symbolise God's dwelling in the midst of the gathered congregation. The early chapels of the Methodists and other free

---

[1] Modelled after an ancient Roman public hall with an apse and colonnades, used as a law court and place of assembly. Later a basilica church had special privileges from the Pope.

churches remain a reminder of the simplicity and modesty of the pre-Constantine early Church.

There is no prescription for the design, structure and symbols of a church building. We have major traditions within Christianity ranging from simple purists to elaborate and extravagant symbolists. The development of icons suggests gradual adaptation in the Roman and Greek worlds. The major iconoclastic controversies in the 8-10 and 16-17 centuries which witnessed distorting, vandalizing and destroying icons (mainly paintings on wood, images and idols of biblical figures, saints and mythical figures such as St. George and the dragon) continue in the painful memory of the affected; so also Henry VIII's destruction of many abbeys and churches. The icons had helped millions to read the bible stories, to feel the beauty of arts and holiness and to experience the ambience of heaven and aroma of the incense. Can the purists appreciate this, and can the symbolists appreciate the simplicity of the purists? With due recognition of the loads of baggage from a long past, is an open and prayerful conversation impossible? Can diversity be maintained creatively in a united church? We have one of the ten commandments which sternly condemns idol worship. How can we distinguish between icons, images, statues and idols? If the spiritual view that that which cannot be moved is idol is acceptable, if there is intense will and intent to come together for the sake of the gospel, we may become heroically creative and open, we can be sure that there will be a way.

Ministerial Uniform

In the pre-CSI era the episcopal churches followed the vestments and liturgical colours used in the Church of England, which more or less came from Roman Catholic Church and originally the formal dress of the Roman nobility. The non-episcopal ministers mostly followed ordinary patterns but in a 'dignified' way. For example, they wore *veshti* (a white piece wrapped around with one end tugged into the waist). Their white under shirt tugged into the *veshti*. Then they had an overcoat. Some had the courage to have their turban as old photographs show.

The CSI presbyters were 'prescribed' an alb (cassock), black girdle, surplice and stole, and there is no evidence of which I am aware that there was any discussion and decision. In the case of bishops, the girdle was purple and the wrist bands of their surplice were in light saffron, a symbol of renunciation. There is dissatisfaction in some minds. For example, D. Chellappa, the bishop in Madras, in his letter to the Editor of the *South India Churchman*, made the following options and comments:

1. White cassock can hardly be worn for more than a day, an expensive burden. White does not signify anything except that it is worn by widows.

2. Cream-coloured cassocks, recently accepted by Synod Executive for experiment – 'in the form of cream-coloured cassocks, shaped in an

elongated *jibba*[1] – one can wear this at least for two days. Again, it does not signify anything, the wearer looks pale, if he happens to be somewhat light-skinned. However, it is calculated to win sympathy for bishops as pale and sickly looking!' It brings nearer to an Indian *sadhu* but not elegant.

3.   Purple. Several bishops sport it. But there are objections: traditionally associated with the west, with royalty, and also in the middle east with wealth. There is prejudice that the United Church 'should not copy slavishly the conventions of any one Mother Church'. It will clash with saffron stole and wrist bands that they are worn over a purple cassock. Purple signifies nothing in India particularly for the rural parts. One redeeming feature is that it is excellent for travel – you can wear it for at least a week running.

4.   Light saffron – already for stole and wrist-bands, it goes well, not so dusty, 'Above all it is associated with religion in India – asceticism – looks pleasing – acceptable to all.' The writer recommends experimentation, yet cautiously – on all occasions, 'or at least for outdoor use.'[2]

For the presbyter, the same white cassock with black girdle and white surplice and stole with seasonal colours came into vogue. Initially surplice and stole were worn only for Holy Communion, but in due course for all services. While what was inherited and prescribed becoming a fixed tradition, there were voices of discontentment as in the case of Chellappa. There was a consultation in 1972 when I.R.H. Gnanadason was the Moderator. When there appeared no consensus Gnanadason concluded that 'all we can say is that there should be some dress!' Unfortunately, no record is available about this significant consultation and the conclusion was personally shared.[3] Subsequently, few boldly chose to be different from the norm. For example, Rev. Joseph John (1905-1998) of Madras Diocese got from his bishop exemption from cassock and he chose to wear simple *veshti* and *jibba*. When the diocese was bifurcated (1976) he came to be a minister of the Vellore diocese, and his down to earth approach made him most exemplary, and people affectionately called him *appa* (father).

It is not uncommon to ask questions about the long robed religious leaders that Jesus criticised and the alb-wearing ministers of Christ. Jesus warned common people saying, 'Watch out for the teachers of the law. They like to walk around in flowing robes and be greeted with respect in the market-places, and have the most important seats in the synagogues and the places of honour at banquets. They devour widows' houses and for a show make lengthy prayers.

---

[1] *Jibba* is collarless (or mini-collared), open about one-fourth with buttons, flows to the bottom up to the knee and long hands or half-hands.

[2] D. Chellappa, in *SICman*, Oct. 1960, 9.

[3] Dr. A.E. Inbanathan (1920-1989), former General Secretary of the Bible Society of India.

These men will be punished most severely' (Mk. 12:38; Lk. 20:46). Elements of this behaviour are certainly evident in many ministers. In seminary, we toyed with the explanation of the typical CSI uniform as symbolising servanthood. That means, above the cassock which was the ordinary dress in the middle east and parts of Europe, the surplice and stole were worn by slaves serving dinners for the purpose of cleanliness and hygiene. But historically, we latter realised that the surplice of British origin, resisted by the Puritans, had no particular meaning. the stole probably derived from 'the scarf worn by Roman officials as a sign of rank'. Similarly, the mitre, the headdress of the Anglican and Catholic bishops probably comes from Roman nobility and is explained as the symbol of the Holy Spirit as flame. Today everywhere, maybe in all religions, the interest or disinterest to maintain traditional symbols and practices does not lead to question their meaning and relevance. Tradition and familiarity triumphs!

How can we express the fact that we are the servants of the servant Lord? We need 'faith' to think and act. In certain theological institutions in South India there have been experiments with the dress of workers (e.g. the scanty cloth of the palmyra climbers, and celebrating communion with the dress of the Dalits, the serving class). At the same time, as criticised by some bishops themselves, the use of purple in ordinary appearance is increasing, 'the amethyst ring grows in size; kissing of the ring, the use of the royal "we" in public, the refraining from the use of first names among friends after consecration – all this indicates that the authority of the episcopal office is carried too far.'[1] There are those who prefer sash to girdle, and its size is widening; and on the whole there is a wholesome development of distortion and deterioration. It may be that those who are committed to communicate the uniqueness of the Christian message should think about alternatives and diverse patterns of symbols and symbolic acts. If change is impossible the power of the gospel is denied.

Unless naïve, we should take the biblical acclamation that God reigns over the whole world, and that the earthly authorities, sovereign and others, operate under him. The church has a role to play through structures of authority for both symbolic presentation and effective action. Paul links the two; after affirming that God created everything, visible and invisible, through and for his Son, whether thrones or powers or rules or authorities, all things have been created in and through him and for him, he writes:

> (Christ) is before all things, and in him all things hold together. And he is the head of the body, the church ... so that in everything he might have the supremacy. For he was pleased to have all his fullness dwell in him, and through him to reconcile to himself all things, whether things on earth or things in heaven, by making peace through his blood, shed on the cross (Col. 1:17-20).

---

[1] Samel Amirtham, 'Reflections on Episcopacy in the CSI', *Pilgrim*, 16, March 2000, 4.

Elsewhere, the apostle writes that it was a mystery of his will revealed according to his good pleasure 'which he purposed in Christ, to put into effect when the times reach their fulfilment – to bring unity to all things in heaven and on earth under Christ' (Eph. 1:9-10). The most important insight in this reflection is that unity in the church and unity in the world require the leadership and authority of someone like Christ. And Paul's appeal to the Church means that we should have the 'mindset of the Christ Jesus' who did not consider equality with God something to be used to his own advantage did the radical dissent to be a slave, to the point of even death on a cross. God exalted him so that every knee should bow and 'every tongue acknowledge that Jesus Christ is Lord, to the glory of God the Father' (Phil. 2:5-11). No doubt, this narrative was subverting and challenging the imperial power of Rome.

How could Jesus have had such a band of dull-headed but power-mongering disciples? They were pre-occupied with occupying the twelve thrones. They proved to be 'wholly fools' when they argued who would be first and greatest in God's kingdom. Jesus showed his extraordinary patience when he asked them to follow the model of a lowly child and a slave (Mt. 18:1-5; Mk. 10:45). Jesus must have meant that the primary and greatest field of evangelization was that of the thrones of powers and channels of authority. The above ideals are not only for preaching but constant practice and experiment. However, we do not have a clear and fixed administrative structure in the New Testament. Later in the history of the Church, particularly when it became the state religion in Rome in the fourth century, the church-state relationship sailed through turbulent waters and we do not dare to give here an outline of this history.

After the Reformation, particular denominations organised themselves in their favoured organizational and administrative structures, claiming their basis in the Bible. The three traditions that came together for organic unity in South India followed more or less the patterns of their mother churches. Thus, Anglicans had a Province-Diocese-General Synod-Bishop model, SIUC General Assembly-Council-General Secretary, the Methodists a Conference-District-President model. All had sub-structures and committees. The CSI chose the pattern of Synod constituted by the bishops and lay and presbyterial representatives. One bishop would be the Moderator or presiding bishop for a period. Certain dioceses have claimed different ratios of lay-presbyterial members for their diocesan councils, and so on. But it is observed that with the exceptions of the majority pious members and leaders, the CSI leadership must grow into maturity. Elections – from PC members-stewards-deacons to the Moderator – are hotly fought with corrupt practices of manipulative campaigns and forming parties, caste solidarities, etc. In administrative practice the effects of elections continue. Opponents and critics are side-lined and denied even a reply to their letters of sharing legitimate concerns. 'Effective leadership and evangelistic administration' has been the call from those who want to reform the CSI.[1] It is such a distorted view to see the remote villages and hills of ancient tribal communities as the primary mission fields for evangelization, but no structures of authority and administration. In churches and institutions, effectiveness and efficiency are measured not by honesty, integrity, theological clarity and spiritual maturity but by manipulative power and the ability for political manoeuvring. Particularly among the leaders, the deterioration of life-style, misplaced emphases on being functionaries, etc., particularly since their appearance in the Lambeth Conference, have alarmed well-respected lay thinkers.[2] But all these are covered up by intense piety and most enthusiastic involvement in evangelistic outreach among remote villagers and hill tribes. The pious Christians are 'Bible Christians' as well, but as far as power and administrative structures are concerned, they are unable to find alternatives to what is justified by freedom and democracy. In the pursuit of further unity a comparative study of the structures and administrative practices is essential.

Prayer for Christian Unity

The Week of Prayer for Christian Unity began in 1908 as the 'Octave of Christian Unity', and was focussed on prayer for church unity. The dates of the week were proposed by Father Paul Wattson, co-founder of the Graymoor Franciscan Friars. Protestant leaders in the mid-1920s also proposed an annual octave of prayer for unity amongst Christians, leading up to Pentecost Sunday (the traditional commemoration of the establishment of the Church). The Week of Prayer for Christian Unity has become very popular in recent times, usually during the week concluding with the Feast of the Conversion of St Paul on 25th January. In the CSI every day of the first week in January there is a service in the evening. In England 'Churches Together' in an area have one joint worship in this or the fourth week. United Churches are also asked to observe the Week of Prayer for Christian Unity, but what is not clear is what kind of unity is prayed for – locally, regionally or universally, and to be together without mingling and merging or organic union? And also, what action is attached to prayer? If prayers are offered with the popular implicit notion that God is the only problem to be solved by our fervent and persistent prayer, they betray a very superstitious aspect of religious behaviour. Even the act of 'intercession' is questionable and with our direct access to the heavenly Father through Christ, a meaningful expression is 'prayer of solidarity'. When Azariah and his colleagues went to Tranquebar for prayer in solidarity with God's longing for his servants and children to live together as brothers and sisters, it was followed by dedicated and persistent action in order to achieve organic unity in response to the prayer of Jesus.

---

[1] See I. Selvanayagam, 'Effective Leadership and Evangelised Administration: Some Reflections', *Asian Journal of Theology*, III/2, 1989, 639-642.

[2] E.g. K.M. George, *Church of South India: Life in Union* (1947-1997),160-184.

Today Christians obsessed with their denominations, traditions and symbols create a 'panicking sensitivity' to talk about coming together to work out more effective forms of unity. It is undeniable that there is a confusion between familiarity and faith.

Chapter 6

Efforts to Widen Union

Consolidation and Challenges

When the Church of South India was inaugurated on 27 September 1947, there was surprise and jubilation around the Christian world. Michael Hollis, the first Moderator of the CSI and himself a church historian, declared it was a miracle next to the Pentecost of Acts 2 as it was the first organic union of the Episcopal and Non-Episcopal Churches. It was not without reason that the second assembly of the World Council of Churches held in Evanston 1954 was well represented by the CSI where the CSI Holy Communion Liturgy was used. The CSI was seen as a beacon of light in the ecumenical journey towards organic union, worldwide. There was hope that other churches in India and elsewhere would be inspired by the achievement of the CSI.

The first and foremost concern of the CSI was to consolidate and keep the house in order. Diehards of denomination, especially Anglicanism, took a long time to be weaned away from their pride of identity with a white, economically powerful, monarchy-connected Church. The Archdeaconry of Nandyal in the Diocese of Dornakal, for this and various other reasons, did not join as a diocese of CSI until 1975. Even this was after the odyssey of being a diocese of the Church of India, Pakistan, Burma and Ceylon from 1963 and then of the Church of North India from 1970. In some dioceses (e.g. Madurai-Ramnad) some ex-Anglican churches have continued to maintain autonomy because of their un-readiness to join fully. If pressed hard, they join or threaten to join the 'Anglican Church of India' which has the blessing of similar separatist groups in USA, though it does not have recognition in what is known as the Anglican Communion based in London. The Anglican block of the Thirunelveli Diocese and Anglican Churches in parts of the Madurai-Ramnad diocese did not join the CSI Trust Association but formed their own.

Basel Mission Churches: First, one of the three ecclesial districts (Malabar) of the Basel Mission Church from the Lutheran-Calvinist background joined the South India United Church on 9 March, 1908 about two months (though the process had begun earlier but was hampered by the Word War I) before the seminal Tranquebar Conference in 1919 that led to the formation of the CSI in 1947. It continued to be a part of the North Kerala Diocese, until that diocese became bifurcated recently. Second, there was some opposition to union in the Basel Mission component in Bombay-Karnataka District, and therefore it could not join the union until 1958. Third, similar opposition was sustained with protracted court cases in the South Kanara and Coorg District, yet finally that component joined the CSI in 1968 in a moving thanksgiving service in Mangalore (June 24, 1968). In Karnataka, there was first only one CSI diocese, called Mysore Diocese. On May 1, 1970, however, it was trifurcated into the Karnataka Southern, Central and Northern Dioceses.

There has been a growing sense of belonging to the CSI among the former Basel Mission churches over the decades. At the same time there has been some dissatisfaction – often not articulated – with the administrative style (lack of transparency) as well as the life and witness of the CSI as a whole. Consequently, in South Kanara and Coorg, several congregations have seceded from the CSI and operate as the United Basel Mission Church congregations, though the CSI appears to be silent about it in its communications. There are court cases in this regard which have lingered on at various levels. 'There ought to be sincere attempts at rapprochement on both sides for the good of the church, its life, including ministry and mission. Historical records show that, on the part of the BM, it had raised valid and tough questions vis-à-vis the Anglican views and ways of doing things in matters relating to the church union with a view to remaining closer to the Biblical vision of ecclesial fellowship, including its pattern of ministry and administration.'[1] As we are going to discuss in detail, the lingering Anglican influence in the CSI with the recent involvement of the Anglican Communion indirectly interrupted the growing together within and further widening of the union.

Attempts within India

With Lutherans: The CSI leaders were committed to maintain the new organic union as united as well as uniting. Immediately they started dialogue with the Lutheran Churches in South India – the Andhra Evangelical Lutheran Church, the South Andhra Lutheran Church, the Tamil Evangelical Lutheran Church, and the Arcot Lutheran Church – some of which had withdrawn from the negotiations, while Tranquebar, as a Lutheran Centre, where the first Protestant missionary arrived in 1706 and where negotiations for the formation of CSI started in 1919, continued to be a popular place for meetings. The Lutherans, the

---

[1] O.V. Jathanna by correspondence. The preceding notes too are a summary of what he sent.

oldest Protestant community in India with about 500,000 members, have been divided into 11 Lutheran Churches, each enjoying the patronage of a particular Lutheran Church in the West which created them through their mission. 'Ten of these groups had come into the Federation of Evangelical Lutheran Churches in 1936. Their aim was to work for an organic union of the Lutheran Churches in India as prelude to be integrated into a united World Church. The Federation … meeting in Ranchi in December 1947, formed a committee on ecumenical relations, and the committee was entrusted with the responsibility to study the situation that had arisen through the formation of the CSI and to represent FELC in any exchange of views with the CSI. This … certainly gave impetus to the first meeting of the Synod of the CSI in March 1948 to send out invitations to the non-Roman Churches in South India for conversations with the CSI with a view to consider the possibility of a wider union.'[1] There was no requirement for prior commitment. Consultations with experts were held within the respective Churches in order to ensure that the constitutional basis of the CSI was adequate for starting the negotiations.

A joint meeting of 11 Lutheran, 9 Baptist and 7 CSI members was held in December, 1948, in Chennai. Position papers were presented and comments shared without any clear commitment. 'At the end of the three-day meeting, the Conference recorded thanks to God "for the very real experience of fellowship in the grace and calling of God through Jesus Christ which during these days we have enjoyed". The group, further, recommended the formation of two bodies, an Inter-Church Group to carry on the conversations of Union and a Theological Commission to study the theological issues involved.'[2] The three groups found no insurmountable difficulty in agreeing on the theological and structural positions of others. They appointed committees/commissions to study them further. Some of the basic theological issues were presented to the second of the Inter-Church Groups in September 1949. It decided to establish a conversation between the three church-groups in order to keep the churches informed of developments of these conversations and for the Theological Commission to pursue its work.

Sadly, however, the Baptists withdrew, with the excuse of the NT pattern of the independent local church, and probably with this extreme congregational pattern they could find competent persons to interpret certain doctrines including baptism. This is not far from the reason for which they had not joined the CSI. Reduced to two Churches, the representatives of the CSI and the Lutheran Churches met in November 1950 and discussed at length the draft Doctrinal Statement proposed for the union of the Lutheran Church in India. The Lutherans were supposed to study the constitution of the CSI and come up with their views for the next meeting. Also, a Joint Theological Commission was set up which

---

[1] K.M. George, *Church of South India (1947-1997)*, Delhi/Thiruvalla: ISPCK/CSS, 1999, 131f.

[2] Ibid., 133.

met six times between 1951-1959. However, the usual and obvious issues were shared and repeated, cooperation emphasised, statements produced and regional conferences held, but there was no clear evidence of enthusiasm, bold commitment or resolution to move forward from the Lutheran side. The CSI Synod 'had hoped that the two Churches might lead into unity, and further reaffirmed the statement made in the 1956 Synod that the CSI was willing to enter into immediate negotiations for the establishment of Pulpit and Altar Fellowship along the lines proposed by the CSI-Lutheran Theological Commission while at the same time affirming that in their (CSI) view, the goal must be full organic union.'[1]

The Joint Theological Commission that met in Bangalore in April 1959 discussed the reports from the regional conferences, the CSI statement on Ministry (1957), the Lutheran reply, further explanations from the CSI, Lutheran papers in relation to the ministry of the church, episcopacy and apostolic succession, and the Lutheran approach to the place of the public ministry. 'The meeting discussed the meaning of mutual recognition of ministries, the place of Order in the Church, the relation between the *function* of the ministry and the *office* of the ministry and the place of episcopacy in the continuing fellowship of the Church. After a very frank exchange of issues in an atmosphere of mutual respect and understanding the Commission finally said in the Agreed Statement:

> Having arrived at an Agreed Statement on the Church and the Ministry, this Joint Commission regards the work as completed and resolves to reiterate its former judgement that the degree of doctrinal agreement is such as to warrant a closer fellowship than now existed between our Churches. We, therefore, earnestly urge the Churches to take action to secure such closer fellowship in practice.[2]

This commission further recommended that the CSI and the Lutheran Churches in India should appoint an Inter-Church Commission.'[3]

Though the CSI did not have fixed doctrines, the Synod (1958) approved the 'Agreed Doctrinal Statements' which had been studied and commented upon most favourably by the dioceses and expressed hope of continued regional conferences that would lead to unity between the two Churches. 'The Synod recorded their gratitude in view of the fact that the Arcot Lutheran Church had already agreed to establish such fellowship with the CSI and hoped that the other churches of the FELC would be able to take similar action in due course.'[4] The following year (1960) the FELC commended the resolution and steps taken by its own Executive to the Joint Theological Commission and requested the

---

[1] Ibid., 139f.

[2] Quoted, Ibid., 140f.

[3] Ibid.

[4] Ibid., 141.

churches of both sides to appoint their own representatives on the Inter-Church Commission as early as possible. On the basis of the agreed position on Altar and Pulpit they asked to take necessary steps for implementation.

Nine of the CSI and 14 of the Lutheran representatives participated in the first meeting of the Inter-Church Commission, held in Bangalore in August 1960. Though there was an opinion around to invite representatives of all the Lutheran Churches in India, for the sake of actual union, they were confined to the Lutheran Churches in South India. However, the group felt that the reports should be sent to all the Lutheran Churches in India. Though not a member, the Indian Evangelical Lutheran Church sent its representatives only to be visitors and observers. One of the responsibilities of the Commission was the drafting of a constitution for the expected new united church, taking into consideration all the agreed statements, doctrines etc. The Lutherans pointed out the inclusion of the Athanasian creed as supplementary which might be used for instruction. A common catechism also was suggested. The Commission appointed a special committee to prepare a common catechism and encouraged study by regional conferences of church and the ministry. In the following ten meetings (1962-1975) issues were repeated and clarified, however the negotiations stopped with an acknowledgement of mutual learning and enrichment, but without any hope for organic unity. The CSI was even ready to accept a change in the event of the development of wider union. Hence, the *Proposed Constitution for the Evangelical Church of Christ in South India* (1969). Nevertheless, all that the Lutheran-CSI negotiations could achieve was that Lutheran and CSI candidates came to be trained together in the United Theological College Bangalore, Gurukul Lutheran Theological College Chennai, Andhra Christian Theological College (Baptists included) Secunderabad, Tamilnadu Theological Seminary, Madurai and Kannanmula United Theological College, Trivandram.

Soon there were attempts to consolidate Lutheran resources and reassert Lutheran identity. Consequently, in 1975 the FELC was reconstituted as the United Evangelical Lutheran Churches (UELC – 11 Churches in India plus one in Nepal) and in 1998 as the United Evangelical Lutheran Church, but interestingly, the small letters '' (written in 'CHURCHes', as conspicuously evident in the name written on the Martin Luther Bhavan, the headquarters of UELC in Gurukul campus) were inserted by those who wanted to show the plurality of names and traditions within this Church and to resist uniformity in the name of unity. The Lutherans do talk about unity but seem to be keen about their identity, and a separate study with empirical research is needed to find out the real reason for their abrupt end of negotiations with CSI. The following questions are pertinent: Did they experience a kind of new confidence after a pause in the post-missionary era? When some of them still use the word 'doctrines' what do they mean in relation to the new confidence and the new reading of the Bible? Do many of them take Martin Luther as a demigod without acknowledging his serious pitfalls as acknowledged ecumenically, particularly in the Lutheran World Federation? And so on. Of course, presumably from the Lutheran side, over and above concerns about the faith and order and liturgy, there were fears of material factors such as securing their property and continuing to get the support from their mother churches. One assumes that finance and property were of the greatest concern as in the case of the American Methodists. Moreover, the confessional bodies such as the Lutheran World Federation tended to encourage denominational ecumenism at the international level in the place of inter-denominational ecumenism, including wider union, at the local levels. More in-depth study is needed to ascertain these assumptions.

New Communions that develop in Europe are not taken into consideration when regional negotiations are encouraged. Unexplainable anomalies are created. For instance, 'The Porvoo Communion is a communion of 15 predominantly northern European, with a couple of far-southwestern European (in the Iberian Peninsula) Anglican and Evangelical Lutheran church bodies. It was established in 1992 by a theological agreement entitled the *Porvoo Common Statement* which establishes full communion between and among these Protestant churches. The agreement was negotiated in the town of Järvenpää in Finland, but the Communion's name comes from the nearby city of Porvoo where there was a joint celebration of the Eucharist (or Holy Communion) in Porvoo Cathedral after the formal signing in Järvenpää.'[1] What are the implications of regional communion between Churches in England and South India and Churches in the Porvoo Communion? A separate study may be worthwhile.

The Church of North India was inaugurated in 1970 and the influence of the CSI on its formation was obvious. The principles and constitutional basis were more or less the same. It had additional churches, i.e. the Baptist Churches of Northern India (these were British Baptists, but in South India they had not joined the CSI!), the Church of the Brethren in India, which withdrew in 2006, the Methodist Church (British and Australian Conferences) and the Disciples of Christ.[2] The American Methodists withdrew at the last moment for non-theological reasons. Apart from being members of the National Council of Churches in India, both CSI and CNI have been sharing new theological insights and working together where possible.

Full Communion of the CSI, CNI and Mar Thoma Churches.[3] The full communion of the said three churches was initiated in 1978 with the intention of moving towards an all India organic union of the Protestant Churches with

---

[1] https://en.wikipedia.org/wiki/Porvoo_Communion (as on 26 Dec. 2018).

[2] https://en.wikipedia.org/wiki/Church_of_North_India (as on 4 April 2019).

[3] Mar Thoma Church comes from the Syrian Orthodox background and emerged as a result of the reforms effected under the Anglican (CMS) influence in Kerala in the 19th century – name shortened from Malankara Mar Thoma Syrian Church, which was enthusiastic about the CSI union though could not join.

the desired name *The Bharat Christian Church*. The 16th meeting of the Executive Committee of the Joint Council held in Bombay in June 1982 took the main actions: 1. Festival of Unity, 2. Joint projects, 3. Eucharistic Liturgies. The proposed name had to be reviewed, and after consulting churches the following three names were suggested for consideration: 1. Uniting Church in India, 2. The Church of India, 3. Bharat Christian Church. There was joint response to national issues such as the widening gap between rich and poor and the erosion of moral values.[1] The Joint Council of the CNI, CSI and Mar Thoma, fourth meeting, on Nov. 29th-1st Dec., 1985, appeared to be a setback. 'At the beginning of the deliberations there were misgivings on the part of some of the delegates about the worthwhileness of continuing the Joint Council because of the failure of the three Churches to agree on a common name for the Church in which the 3 Churches belong together as they had earlier affirmed ... consensus emerged ... as going back to the commitment towards organic oneness ...following this affirmation it was decided that the question of adoption of a common name be kept open for further study in the light of growing experience in unity.'[2] The activities of 8 regional councils had to be revived; so also the festival of unity; and information booklets to be published in the vernacular. Above all, the manifestation of visible unity was reaffirmed. 'On the morning of Sunday 1st Dec., 1985 the members of the JC joined the special Eucharistic Service at the Cathedral Church of Redemption New Delhi, which was part of the celebration of the 15th anniversary of the inauguration of CNI, by the Delhi Diocese.'[3] Since then there have been meetings, but an all India united church seems to be a distant dream.

Although, the first step of training together the ministers of these churches was immediately implemented, there was no move further towards realising the dream. Does it prove the comment that without the missionaries from overseas the Indian Christian leaders are not able to achieve new forms of church union? On the positive side, following the meetings of a joint CSI, CNI and Mar Thoma theological commission, the Joint Council of these three churches (formed in 1978) developed into a Communion of Churches in India in 2000 with joint programmes. However, a misunderstanding lingers on about the shape of organic oneness. The Mar Thoma Church never meant a merger but has been ready to maintain communion with the CSI and CNI even if they formed an organic union. Also, the exact nature of the organic union of the CSI and the CNI may require reassessment. The CCI might look to different models of unity. Is there a unity possible on the basis of agreed principles of faith and order, but not necessarily unifying structures and resources? However, we need to resist the models introduced by the ecclesiastical trend setters of the developed world who

---

[1] Ref. J.R. Chandran, '*Joint Council of CNI, CSI and Marthoma Church*', *SICman*, Sept. 1982, 13f; 3rd meeting of the Joint Council, 22-24, Jan, 1983; Ref. *SICman, Feb. 83, 3*

[2] Pritam Santram, Hon. Sec, CNI-CSI-Marthoma Joint Council, *SICman*, Jan. 1986, 15

[3] Ibid.

are unwilling to consider models of the small churches such as those in India. The formation of the CSI was not only in response to Jesus' prayer 'that all may be one' but also in response to challenges from the multi-religious and competing secular ideologies in India. Any form of union may be tentative and experimental but it is significant if worked out with prayer, clarity and commitment to mission.

After discussion, the above council resolved that the CSI could enter into bilateral negotiations with churches wanting to enter into union, while continuing fellowship with the CNI and the MTC and provide whatever help was necessary. The General Secretary of CSI reported in 2002: 'Many smaller groups and para church groups have been expressing their eagerness to become part of CSI. Efforts also have been on to initiate a dialogue with the American Methodist Church and the United Evangelical Lutheran Church.'[1] The earlier vision of moving towards a single 'Bharat Christian Church' is still kept alive with different approaches and interpretations.

Partnership with Ecumenical Councils and Churches in the West

The CSI soon became a member of the World Council of Churches and the East Asia Conference (later, the Christian Conference of Asia). It is significant to note that some CSI presbyters and theologians, both as staff and members of advisory committees, have made significant contributions, particularly in the areas of unity, contextual theological education and interreligious dialogue.

Invited to be a member, the CSI had enjoyed the privilege of a unique presence in the World Methodist Council (founded in 1881),[2] the Anglican Communion (1867)[3] and the World Alliance of the Reformed Churches (1867).[4] These organisations have gone through changes in name and form. Here we need to comment on being a member. It looks as if each body has embraced the CSI as the choicest prize but without openly appreciating its tedious journey towards the pioneering organic unity. And one needs to consult the definitions of these bodies if at all there are such things. For example, each body mentions in their publicity (including the websites) the membership of CSI (about 3 million but with inconsistent count!). Interestingly, the membership of CSI has thus been added in thrice to the total of these world bodies. This is amusing, but very worrying is the CSI's relationship with the Anglican Communion, the outcome of which is an ecumenical tragedy. We will explain the process and consequence in the next chapter.

---

[1] *CSI Life*, Jan., 2002, 4.

[2] The World Methodist Council (WMC), founded in 1881, is a consultative body and association of churches in the Methodist tradition. It comprises 80 member denominations in 138 countries which together represent about 80 million people. Ref. website (as on 5-4-2019).

[3] 46 Churches and Extra Provinces; Ref. websites (as on 5-4-2019).

[4] 218 member churches in 107 countries around the world, with some 75 million members. Ref. websites (as on 5-4-2019).

Chapter 7

Distortion of Organic Union by Absorption into the Anglican Communion

The Distinctiveness of the Anglican Communion's Treatment of the CSI

As I have stated in the Preface, the question 'Is the CSI Anglican?' was the stimulus for undertaking this study. At the level of world councils of the Reformed Churches and the Methodist Church, as we have noted in the last chapter, the Church of South India is a member. At the same time, they have maintained full communion and mutual recognition of ministers and presbyters of the CSI without conditions. This is different in the case of the Anglican Churches. It was stated in the beginning that the CSI bishops would be attending the Lambeth Conference. But they were not invited until 1988 when six of them attended as guests and the CSI was unilaterally declared as a province of the AC; all of them were invited to the LC in 1998 with full membership. However, the ministry of the CSI presbyters was not automatically recognised and regarded in Anglican Churches. Moreover, the URC (United Reformed Church) has welcomed presbyters to work in their churches and theological institutions, and it has never thought of the CSI as an extended URC Synod. The Methodists' initiative to invite and use the CSI resource persons came even earlier. In the 1990s they pioneered the World Church in Britain Partnership by which they brought members of their partner churches and encouraged them to bring new expressions of faith and liturgies as well as to take leadership positions. But the Methodist Church has never suggested that the CSI should be an overseas Methodist Conference. Then we might ask what was the intention of absorbing the CSI as a province of the AC without any consultation with representatives of the CSI (or URC and Methodist Church either) while the great Archbishop William Temple emphatically stated that such thing should never happen.

On the CSI side, one can lament lack of leadership with sufficient knowledge of the history of CSI and theological backbone. Is it not the expression of a colonised psyche to accept uncritically the church of the former colony? Why did they have no respect for the heroes of faith who achieved the CSI as the first organic union despite great difficulty coming from the Anglican side? In any case, since the tragedy happened, the Anglicanization of the CSI and its congregations was intensified. To start with we notice in the signature lines of a recent letterhead of the CSI 'Province of the Wider Anglican Communion', 'Anglican-Protestant' and 'Association.'[1] Do they match? The AC website uses words 'Provincial Secretary' and 'Provincial Treasurer' instead of 'Synodical ...' One can be amused as well as pained by the confusing terms and figures reflecting a distortion in the CSI-Anglican relationships. To understand the dynamics of this aberration we have to outline the whole story.

The Saga of a Development

As we pointed out in the fourth chapter, the formation of the CSI was an Anglican initiative based on the 1888 Lambeth Quadrilateral which was responded to positively by some free Churches in South India. The first Anglican bishop in India and the first non-white diocesan bishop in the Anglican Communion, V.S. Azariah, provided outstanding leadership. Some of the Anglican participants in the negotiations were noted for their saintliness and generosity of spirit. The Metropolitan of India, Foss Westcott, gave wise guidance. From a distance some leaders, particularly Archbishop William Temple played a remarkable role at the end with the support of Bishop George Bell. However, even towards the end of 1946 there was no indication that the negotiations would reach the goal of achieving union because of the Anglican slowdown and continuing influence.

It is understandable that those Anglicans (for that matter others too) who identified faith with familiarity and denied the primacy of the Bible over tradition found it difficult to affirm the spiritual equality of all committed Christians, to participate in inter-communion and accept equal validity of the ministries. However, when the organic union was consummated, all thought that the matter was almost over. But an influential section of the Anglo-Catholics reacted with a jeering voice that the CSI was a mud-horse which would crumble by one stroke. It was their successful efforts which caused the Anglican SPG to stop financial support for the CSI, though alternative support was arranged by Archbishop Fisher. The sudden loss was mitigated by the CofE 'making belated atonement, by encouraging its members to work in CSI and support CSI with funds and prayers'. In any case, about 50% of CSI members were formerly Anglicans, but they could not easily internalise the fact that they were part of a new organic union, not just a 'communion of churches'.

---

[1] In the list of 'Associations' the Anglican Communion is noted before WCC and other bodies. The membership quoted is 3.8 million.

The unexpected hostile reaction of a section of Anglicans upset those who were still celebrating 'the second miracle of organic union'. Some of the stories have been transmitted. For example, in the context of a burning question about the relationship between the CSI and the Church of England a former Moderator recalled: 'CSI bishops were not invited to the Lambeth Conference, SPG withdrew support, ... though it set up a special fund for this, and some churches in England put up notices that CSI members were not welcome to Holy Communion. The first Moderator, Michael Hollis, told of a visit to Ridley Hall, Cambridge, where he was not allowed to celebrate the Holy Communion Service because he would not give an undertaking that he would not do so also in non-Anglican churches during his visit to England. These were some of the prices the CSI paid for the union scheme itself, with its '30-year clause', by which non-episcopally ordained presbyters were recognized, for this period, without being 're-ordained.'[1]

However, there was enough support among the CSI leaders to stand upright. Particularly, the first Moderator Michael Hollis stood as a tower of strength, and he had already won the affection of the people of his Madras Diocese and his colleagues of other traditions in the negotiations. He did all he could to correct misinformation and clarify issues such as the historic episcopacy within a constitutional framework (that bothered some members of the Church of England) through publications and correspondence.

There was an embarrassment when Lambeth 1958 said: 'The inauguration of the union brought about a situation without precedent in the history of the Christian Church.' Bishop Hollis, the Moderator, speaking at the second synod of the CSI, observed: 'The obvious irritation with which the CSI is regarded in certain quarters is a proof of the disquiet which we have caused by uniting among those who prefer church union to remain as an item on the agenda of a long series of conferences ... more and more it must become clear that it is not we in our union who are the anomaly, but the disunited churches here and abroad which still too largely look upon a divided church as the normal condition of those who profess their faith in the same God, the same Saviour and the Holy Spirit. It is not our uniting which needs to be justified but their separation.'[2] L. Newbigin put the point in a striking metaphor. 'It may possibly be that the existence of the CSI, awkward as it must be, could be the grit in the ecumenical oyster without which the pearl of unity could not form.'[3] Marcus Ward has stated it vividly: 'Three churches died that one must live.'[4] There were many such

---

[1] P. Victor Premasagar, 'Anglicanism and the Church of South India' in *Anglicanism: A Global Communion*, Ed. By Andrew Wingate, Kevin Ward, Carrie Peberto and Wilson Sitshebo, London: Mowbray, 1998, 178f; another version was 'This church is not in communion with the CSI.'

[2] Quoted, Douglas Webster, *What is the Church of South India?* London: The Highway Press, 1964, 6f.

[3] Ibid., 7.

[4] Ibid.

comments made. Further, no one was more concerned about the full catholicity
of the CSI than Bishop Palmer. He did not allow that non-episcopal ministries
were *equal* to episcopal ministries but he did insist on regarding them as *real*.
In one of his letters he describes them as 'in the nature of emergency measures;
they were God's second thoughts about the ministry, not superior not equivalent
to the first thoughts but yet His ... But the difference between episcopacy and
Presbyterianism is not the former has a ministry of the form which God designed
as the best permanent ministry for the church, and the latter has a ministry, which
is, in the main, a prophetic ministry used for some purposes for which it was
not intended. But when God has once actually used a particular man for those
purposes, it is not my business to question that action of His.'[1]

The strange case of both approval and disapproval of CSI by Anglicans
created an unhappy scene particularly in England, the founding centre of
Anglicanism. As we have already noted, during the negotiations it was stated
that the CSI bishops would be invited to the Lambeth Conference irrespective
of the Pledge Period of thirty years from 1947. This was not respected, and the
manner in which they were invited was very interesting. In 1978 the Moderator
and deputy Moderator were invited as guests. In 1988 six bishops with their
wives were invited as guests and observers. Furthermore, there is a minute from
the Primates' Meeting of July 1988 which resolved to add the Church of South
India to the Schedule of Membership of the Anglican Consultative Council.
Consequently the CSI was declared as a province of the AC. The Moderator from
the CSI was present at Primates' Meetings from 1989 onwards.[2] In 1998 all the
bishops were invited with right of membership. In 2008 all of them were invited
as members, but now they came with their spouses. The 'forced membership'
and the process in which it was accorded was gossiped with great concern. I had
an experience. It was the Anglican Consultative Council in Dundee Scotland
(1999) where the CSI & CNI Moderators and lay representatives were present.
I was there to give a presentation on interfaith dialogue. One morning in our
conversation over breakfast Vinod Peter (1939-2000), the Moderator of CNI,
said that it had been a mistake that we had agreed to be members of the Lambeth
Conference and that representatives from the organic union should remain as
guests. Sadly he was killed in a road accident next year. At this juncture, Hollis's
caveat published in 1966 is worth noting:

It has yet to be decided whether bishops of united churches shall be
invited to attend the next Lambeth Conference as members. The other
World Denominational bodies concerned have invited CSI to send
delegates to their meetings. The matter was given careful consideration
and the policy adopted by CSI is that *it cannot accept full membership*

[1] Ibid., 15.

[2] Correspondence from the Record Centre of the Anglican Communion.

of bodies which are in their constitution denominational, for that might involve its representatives in decisions which spring from the common acceptance of certain denominational principles, which are not those of CSI and might seem to bind CSI to accept them. It is ready to send *fraternal delegates* to take the fullest possible part in all the deliberations of such bodies.[1] (*italics added*)

In the meantime, one important development was the 'official' visits of the Archbishops of Canterbury and York to South India (whether on free or forced invitation, was not clear). Robert Runcie visited the CSI in 1986. He was personally concerned about the fact that the Church of England was not yet in full communion with the CSI. It is assumed that he had discussion with the leaders of the CSI. But there is no record of the nature of his visit and discussions with the CSI leaders. In any case, he was followed by his successor George Carey. They were given a pompous welcome with platitudes and seen by many as the Queen's representatives. For example, a former Moderator of CSI, best known theologian and Bible scholar who had done his doctoral research in Scotland, wrote: 'Both Robert Runcie and George Carey have visited the CSI and been welcomed by thousands, including people of other religions, who saw them as 'Jagadgurus' (world spiritual leaders). Archbishop David Hope preached at the Golden Jubilee Eucharist in 1997.'[2] It is embarrassing to note such an inflated projection of church leaders from a former colony, 'high priests or primary chaplains' of the British monarch, exposing a colonised psyche. Interestingly, the revivalist Hindus around that time claimed that Hinduism was the *Jagadguru*. When Rowan Williams visited the CSI in 2010 the welcome was with flexiboards and cut-outs, and the title accorded to him was 'the Chief Shepherd of the CSI' though personally he would have no interest in such titles. Sadly, such a visit was never reciprocated, and no leader from the non-episcopal mother Churches, constituent of the organic union of CSI, visited to receive such a welcome.

What were the dynamics operating behind the screen? The Anglican Consultative Council (Singapore 1987), probably with the influence of Runcie, had recommended full membership of the CSI bishops to the Lambeth Conference. As his secretary notes, 'Resolution 17 resolved that at meetings of the Council in future there should be normal membership for the United Churches and requested the forthcoming Lambeth Conference, of the next year, also to consider full membership. This recommendation Archbishop Runcie acted on very happily. The specifically Church of England position was rectified to 'full communion' at General Synod under the Ecumenical Relation Measure, 1988 and an earlier debate on the CSI specifically after which the Archbishops of Canterbury (and

---

[1] Hollis, *The Significance of the South India*, 79.

[2] V. Premasagar, 'Anglicanism and the Church of South India', 179.

York) canonically declared the CSI to be in (full) communion.'[1] The question is whether it was a unilateral declaration or the outcome of negotiations involving the CSI leaders and lay representatives of her people!

What was going on between the Anglican Communion and the Church of South India since the second half of the 1980s raised alarm bells. The 'Friends of the Church in India' had as one of its aims to follow the line of the CSI Council in Britain established in 1953 with Hooper as the President, to promote organic union and raise financial support for the CSI. The FCI consists of returned missionaries from India, visitors to India and Indian Christians living in the UK. Their quarterly magazine *Pilgrim* started to arrange for articles on the question of the CSI identity in relation to the CofE and the Anglican Communion.

The then Moderator of CSI narrates with interest his attendance for the first time in the Primates' meeting (the apex body of the Anglican Communion) in Cyprus, following the Lambeth Conference 1998. Amusingly, the Archbishop in his welcome address called the audience Primates. The CSI Moderator protested saying that he and his colleagues from the United Churches in South Asia should be addressed as Moderators. He also informs that there was a proposal to replace 'historic episcopacy locally adopted' (as in the *Tranquebar Manifesto* and *CSI Constitution*) by 'apostolic succession', then, after argument, the former was retained. He believed that the term 'apostolic succession' would make any future unions almost impossible.[2] On the positive side, he mentions mutual learning on the following issues:

Power and authority in the Church.

1. Usefulness of learning centres such as CEFACS (Centre for Anglican Communion Studies which operated in the College of the Ascension, Selly Oak, Birmingham) in CSI.
2. New patterns of ministry.
3. 'The locally adapted episcopate meant a new and simpler style of life and dress. These were indicated by the saffron robes and stole, which were a reminder of the renunciation pledge made by the ancient sages of India. But in recent years, purple has become fashionable again, and some of the style of life associated with the regal orientation and wealth of the Western Church, and indeed of secular officials in India.'[3]
4. Democratic elections with competitive and manipulative practices, etc., have discredited mission. We may learn from Anglican ways.
5. In the area of mission, with reference to the 1982 consultation on priorities of mission in CSI attended by overseas partners he states: 'As Moderator, I often asked our partners "You are generous in the sharing

---

[1] Extract from his letter to Owain Bell, 6 Dec. 2018.

[2] V. Premasahar, 'Anglicanism and the Church of South India', 179.

[3] Ibid., 180.

of your resources, but you never share with us your mission priorities and invite us to assist you. I am sure that God has endowed the Indian Church with gifts which may be of help to you in your mission. To receive such would be a sign of mature partnership.'"[1]

6.   In the area of worship there is a great Anglican heritage. In the 1946 Derby Commission, concern was expressed that the CSI should be more indigenous in worship and life. The 1950 CSI worship was short and meaningful. 'The recent new liturgy of Eucharist (*created by Eric Lott, a Methodist mission partner to CSI*) has drawn from Indian heritage but is not used in India while USPG has incorporated in its collection of Liturgies.

7.   Anglicization of former non-episcopal churches which are part of organic union is a serious concern. Different traditions need to interact and choose the best.

8.   CSI union has inspired the CNI and the Church of Pakistan and Bangladesh. Many other union movements are taking place. 'We long to see the day when the Churches who brought the Gospel to India would also be united as one Church. We believe that the unity of the Church is a foretaste of the unity of all people and harmony in the whole of creation.'[2]

The ambivalent and ambiguous nature of the CSI Moderator's position is obvious. It may be a valid question on what basis he accepted the invitation to sit in the Primates' meeting. Some of the above points are suggestive of mutual learning and growing together. However, when he advocated the exclusive Anglican Communion Studies, as an ex-Methodist he was not bold enough to advocate the Methodist and Reformed Studies with whom Anglicans have not been in full communion. Also, there is no evidence that he and his CSI colleagues and successors made any effort to inform the people of the CSI about the significance of the new relationship with the Anglican Communion and the Church of England.

'By 1860 there was an Anglican Communion called, though not yet widely called, by that new name of independent Churches, worshipping in the tradition of the Anglican Prayer Book, with a ministry of bishops, priests and deacons, and in communion with the See of Canterbury. It was inevitable that the heads of the various provinces should wish to meet. It was also inevitable that some of those heads should wish for some kind of the supreme government for the Anglican Communion, so that it should not be split apart as the provinces develop their own life, or as controversial questions received different answers according to local

---

[1] Ibid.

[2] Ibid., 181.

circumstances.'[1] A historical note is that under an Anglican Episcopal Council, the first Anglican Communion gathering was held in 1867 but amidst opposition including from the Archbishop of York and the Bishop of Durham.

A Closer and Interactive Study

I spent an extended Indian summer vacation (March-June, 2015) staying with my family in Birmingham. One of the pieces of research I was doing was to find out if partners of CSI have been aware of what has been going on at the ecumenical front. I contacted a few known to me to find out the history of the process of the CSI having become a Province of the Anglican Communion, but no one had any clue. In an informal conversation I shared the concern with a former colleague of mine, an Anglican priest, who was working as an Ecumenical Officer. Initially, he said, 'I want to ask, why should the CSI not be a Province of the Anglican Communion? If the partnership between the Churches who remain part of the CSI is to have long term meaning, then I would expect the CSI to be fully Anglican, fully Methodist and fully congregational. I would expect CSI to be also full members and participants of the World Methodist Council and the World Communion of Reformed Churches. Any other approach to the CSI would mean the United Church has become a new denomination in its own right, rather than an expression of unity between those traditions who are committed in covenant together through the CSI.' Being unconvinced by my friend's argument I raised a few questions to which he replied: 'From your comments, this has been a sticking point, especially around mutual recognition of ministry. Still, I ask the question, why shouldn't the CSI be a Province of the Anglican Communion?'

Finally, I raised three precise questions:

1. What made the Anglican Communion to recognise CSI as a province while in the past it (at least certain official bodies therein) did not recognise it?
2. If there was a change of heart in due course, why has this not been reflected in the Anglican Communion initiating or promoting similar union movements?
3. What and when was the arrangement made to arrive at the above action? Is there any record of discussion and decision, especially from the side of the CSI?

My friend promised to continue the conversation.

In the meantime, I requested some non-Anglican partners of CSI to share their views with me. Some of them were unaware of the whole episode and others were not interested. I felt producing a 'White Paper', would be a great help to historians and local 'mission partners' in South India. Some of us think that a new

---

[1] Coleman, *Resolutions*, iv.

style of partnership should emerge that goes beyond 'sterile protocol courtesy', but speaks the truth in love, and develops a critical partnership with openness to mutual correction. Of course, some may feel this is not their immediate concern as, in the face of priority of mission in a crying world, identity and belonging does not seem to matter, though such a position comes close to uncritical affirmation of 'equal respect for all religions' which we repeatedly encounter in interreligious dialogue.

My above-mentioned colleague wrote to me in May 2015:

I have begun to reflect on your question about the relationship between CSI and the Anglican Communion. All the Provinces of the Anglican Communion are autonomous and the member churches listed include a number of the United Churches – North and South India, Pakistan, Bangladesh. Surely this is how the ecumenical trust is built upon, if at the same time the United Churches are also participating in the world-wide bodies representing the other traditions/denominations who are partners within the United Church.

In Birmingham there is one congregation that has a partnership between the United Reformed Church, Methodists and CofE. If the congregations are not receiving and participating in the life of each of the 3 denominations, then it is in danger of being regarded as a new type of denomination, ceasing to be either reformed, Methodist or Anglican. Perhaps I have missed something from your argument ...'

Obviously my colleague, an Anglican priest and ecumenical officer, did not have any knowledge of the struggle for 28 years to achieve the miraculous organic unity, the CSI. When I pointed out a few decisive moments in that struggle he wrote the following:

Clearly your level of understanding the history is far greater than mine. I can only comment on the principles of the broader relationships between the partner Churches who are part of CSI. I disagree with your phrase 'absorb'. This is not the way that the Anglican Communion works. Each province is autonomous and the communion is a fellowship of Churches/Provinces. As a Province of the Anglican Communion, the CSI is not absorbed into anything. However, it does lead to mutual recognition of partnership and relationships. Surely this is desirable? From my point of view, anything less than being a Province implies a paternal relationship between the Anglican Communion and the United Churches. The principle of mutuality between equal partners is at the heart of the self-understanding of the Anglican Communion and goes back to reports of the 1960s – but after the formation of the CSI in 1947.'

In response, I said: 'I hope this is partly a learning experience for both of us who are committed to the unity of churches for the sake of the gospel. I will comment on your observations in three points:

1. 'The public knowledge of the process of CSI having become a province of the Anglican Communion we should establish. I came to know about this when the "Friends of Church in India" based in UK initiated around 1998 a discussion on the question "Is the CSI Anglican?" Some pertinent articles were published in their magazine *Pilgrim*. After a period of non-welcome the CSI entry into the Lambeth Conference had a chequered history.

2. 'As I told you, though it was an Anglican initiative, towards the end the Church of England was putting hurdles on the issues of inter-communion and equal validity of ministries. From the CSI side there was written expectation that the British Churches would become one like the CSI as most of the missionaries who participated in the Union negotiation were British. Later, there was a process of Anglicanization in the CSI particularly in non-conformist mission areas. Then CSI became full member of Anglican communion. But the relationship of the CSI with the Methodist and Reformed Churches was entirely different.

3. 'From the Anglican perspective, it is unfair to "absorb" the united churches while Anglicans continue to be hesitant to move on forming similar united Churches in their strongholds. You know what has been happening in England. What effect there is of the Anglican-Methodist unity talks and Covenant? (As you know) when the United College of the Ascension closed and its mission studies and training moved to the Queen's College, at the last service we suggested con-celebration of Holy Communion with Methodist, Anglican and CSI celebrants. Anglican response was a stout "no" and it was left with CSI, that is me. As such, tell me whether Anglicans have a face with absorbing CSI as one of their provinces. Is it to display their worldwide strength at a time when the Communion itself was at a breaking point due mainly to the issue of homosexuality? In any case, was there a discussion in any committee to absorb the United Churches of South Asia?' The above conversation increased my interest to know the truth.'

I used a few contacts to air my concern and research. My greeting letter to a friend from CSI who joined an Anglican parish in Australia, wished him to be an ambassador of the CSI and not to be absorbed by the host denomination. It connected with some of our mutual friends. For example, an Anglican woman lay theologian, wrote:

I went on to be the Manager of the 2008 Lambeth Conference. Re the issues you raised about the CSI relationships with the Anglican Communion. I don't think the process was nearly so formal as you intimate, which is why you can find no reference to it.

My understanding, and various people told me the same story, was that after the formation of CSI the Indian bishops were not invited to the Lambeth Conference, the assumption being they were no longer 'Anglican'. After some years many complained about this, saying that the Anglican Church had been subsumed into the CSI, so they still had an Anglican identity and should not be cast off, and so it was agreed to invite them to attend – following this CSI/CNI were recognized as members of the Anglican Communion, just as, I understand, they are members of the World Methodist Conference. It is still an opt-in, as the bishops are invited to the Lambeth Conference, members of CSI & CNI from time to time represent at Anglican world bodies and are open to participate in the life of the commissions and the Anglican Communion. There is also the mutual recognition of ministries – you would not have been recognized as an Anglican priest in the UK, nor … in Australia, nor … in the US were it not for the fact that the CSI belongs to the Anglican Communion.

I am sure people like … will have a much better explanation than this – however, that was how I understood the situation came into being.'

One of the referents in this letter wrote in support of me. He was one of the best-known theologians of the CSI, now based in a Methodist seminary in USA who was invited to lead bible study in the 2008 Lambeth Conference. Recognizing the ambivalence in the relationship and the story of his father being one of the six bishops from CSI who attended the Lambeth Conference 1988, he wrote:

I think Israel is correct to open up the relationship of CSI (and other ecumenical so-called united provinces) to the Anglican Communion. We, as CSI, are really post-Anglican and organically a new creation. Many of our CSI bishops may act like Lord Bishops but they have very little connection to the theology and the ethos of Anglicanism.

This brings up another issue that Israel rightly hints at with regard to CSI Bishops being participants at Lambeth. I think for many of our lay, ordained and episcopate members of the CSI there is very little sense of belonging to the Anglican family. Perhaps they are distant relatives being politely present in a reunion of an intimate family gathering. I was at Lambeth 2008 and have observed this close at hand.

I am more inclined to suggesting that CSI participate as select delegates from ecumenical partners rather than members of the Communion.

In the US I have noticed that the CSI, much along the lines of the Mar Thoma Church, is establishing itself as a denominational church, especially if they have the numbers. This is now endorsed by the Synod with the Moderator being their Bishop-at-large. I myself have taken on a position to seek a license from the local diocesan Episcopal Bishop to work as a CSI presbyter through an Episcopal Church parish. In a strange way I am a post-Anglican priest moving sideways (backwards!) into the Anglican family.

The CSI bishops appear to be excited about the privilege to be in the colourful company of the Anglican bishops worldwide. Most of them wear the full clerical vestments. More than anything, it is a spectacular show of Anglican identity and glamour. Some of them may think that their critics in the CSI are jealous of this privilege. Serious issues such as homosexuality and gay marriage might rock the Conference, and the CSI participants may chuckle and fume but they did not contribute to the discussion. On return, normally the reporting is confined to publishing photographs in the magazine(s).

Let us turn to South India for a while. I wrote a common letter to all the bishops of the CSI giving a summary of the above historical outline and issues involved. Among other things I mentioned an Indian opinion that Anglicanism was the last vestige of British colonialism in India. Of course, I did not expect replies from all. But I was disappointed that some of the bishops were my former favourite and promising students in theological education and ministerial training, who never cared to drop a line. I mentioned in passing my earlier contact with the Synod office and stated that the prevailing norm was that if there was no political clout, no reply. For stating this the CSI Synod office chided me and wrote that I was irresponsible. However, I persisted and met the General Secretary and persuaded him to write about the question of the CSI having been absorbed by the Anglican Communion. Following is part of his letter:

> Your thesis, CSI=Anglican, is unfortunately not the right one. CSI is Anglican, Reformed, Methodist and United and Uniting! As you are well aware that CSI is member of all these church families, ACC, WCRC, WMC, UUC. We are not only considered as a province of Anglican Communion, but also considered equally full members of Reformed Communion (sic), Methodist Council and the family of United and Uniting Churches. Your friend in URC (sic) is right: "'… then I would expect the CSI to be fully Anglican, fully Methodist and fully congregational … Any other approach to the CSI would mean the United Church has become a new denomination in its own right,

rather than an expression of unity between those traditions who are committed in covenant together through the CSI.

The United and Uniting Churches conference (meets once in every six years) will this time around be in Chennai in November-December.)

I have not tried to irritate him by pointing out the inconsistent equations in his statement in the light of what I have observed. Politely I pointed out certain issues for the sake of clarity.

Later he wrote:

As I have already communicated to you orally and through email 2015, CSI continues to be member not only of Anglican Communion but also of WCRC and WMC, and the forum of United and uniting Churches.

We are a uniting Church, with Anglican, Reformed, Presbyterian, Congregationalist and Methodist backgrounds, yet we are not only Anglican, Presbyterian, Congregationalist, Methodist, we do have a hybrid identity. We do still continue to have relationship with the roots, yet we are more than Anglicans, Methodists, and so on.

The Anglican Communion website clearly states that we are a united and uniting Church.

The Church was inaugurated in 1947 by the union of the South India United Church (itself a union of Congregational and Presbyterian/ Reformed traditions), the southern Anglican diocese of the Church of India, Burma, Ceylon, and the Methodist Church in South India. It is one of the four United Churches in the Anglican Communion.

It was a decision of the Anglican Communion to invite 4 United and uniting Churches as members of the Communion and it is pertinent to note all these are South Asian Churches. We are members of the Communion.

Every confessional family accept us as their own, yet they do know that we are different, we do have a different ecclesiology, and ecclesiological structure.

Why then, the same communions do not have communion with the constituent Churches of the united and uniting Churches of South Asia in other parts of the world is a question that needs to be addressed by those regional churches themselves. We have overcome the denominations the western Churches need to find their models.

But we remain by the grace of God, a parable of unity for all the Churches, open to many interpretations and exegesis, even occasions for mockery and misunderstanding, but also a mystery to be explored and experienced, as parables of Jesus do.

It is our calling to be a united and uniting Church, to strengthen communion among Anglicans, Reformed, Methodists and united and uniting Churches, for renewal and transformation.

You are always welcome to research on the 'mystery of the communion' we experience among Anglicans, Reformed and Methodists, not always found in papers and resolutions but in the experience and practice of the Church in the world wide *oikumene* in the libraries of the Church as well as in the theological Colleges in India.

Unfortunately, we do not have the space to discuss and clarify this in a dialogical spirit of commitment and openness. However, this communication reveals a lopsided view of the nature and history of the CSI from those in highest ranks in the Synod. Of course, one can argue that it is the Anglican Communion's strategic approach to absorb CSI after four decades of opposition and non-recognition which created such a confusion. The main confusion is that the Anglican Communion with the immediate instruction of the Church of England has imposed their own structures without realising that they cannot fit the CSI. I cite two examples. First, in the CofE, the parish is more than the worshipping congregation and in a way a political unit covering all people irrespective of their religious affiliations. This may be an arrangement and understanding in a state church. And the diocese is the 'local church' 'through the one bishop acting in council with his or her assistant bishops, together with the priests, deacons and lay persons, in one synod'. This 'bishop-centred local church' is irrelevant to the CSI where the bishop is the symbol of unity of individual self-governing congregations who relate to him/her through intermediate bodies such as pastorates and districts or areas. Moreover, as a Socio-Democratic Republic, India recognises the independent identity of every religious community, locally and nationally.

Secondly, the word and structure of 'province' has specific meaning in the CofE. A well-known commentator of the Anglicanism writes:

> There are *provinces*, usually national churches, of which the CoE (though actually made up of two provinces, those of Canterbury and York), for example, is one. A province is a national church when it is coterminous with national boundaries. It deserves the name 'national church' when it is committed to offering its ministry to the whole national community and seeks to project its message at every level of national life. The significance that Anglicans give to provinces derives from ancient catholic usage, where dioceses are gathered into provinces

under a primate or metropolitan (usually an archbishop). The importance of national churches derives not only from the growing importance of national aspirations at the times of the Reformation, but also from the incarnational emphasis of Anglican theology. The incarnation represents and establishes the involvement of God with humanity in all its particularity. Anglicanism is therefore predisposed, for theological as well as historical reasons, to work with the grain of the given contours of human and social identity, expressed through geography, political structures, cultural traditions, and the shared history of a people. The role of particular or national churches has evolved within Anglicanism into an affirmation of the principle of inculturation.[1]

Those who take pride in or tolerate the use of the name and structure of an Anglican province for the CSI situated in a specific region within the secular nation of India needs to be aware of this distinctiveness. And those who see the Anglican absorption of the CSI as part of trying to bring back colonialism in some form cannot be ignored.

Reports and Resolutions

Referring to the key resolutions and reports of the Anglican bodies gives the most direct, chronological and authentic positions and opinions, not only specifically concerning South India but also church union in general.

Lambeth Conference 1888, Resolution 11:

'That, in the opinion of this Conference, the following articles supply a basis on which approach may be by God's blessing made towards home reunion:

(a) The Holy Scriptures of the Old and New Testaments, as 'containing all things necessary to salvation', and as being the rule and ultimate standard of faith.

(b) The Apostles' Creed, as the baptismal symbol; and the Nicene Creed, as the sufficient statement of the Christian faith.

(c) The two sacraments ordained by Christ himself – Baptism and Supper of the Lord – ministered with unfailing use of Christ's words of institution, and of the elements ordained by him.

(d) The historic episcopate, locally adopted in the methods of its administration to the various needs of the nations and the peoples called of God into the unity of his Church.'[2]

---

[1] Avis, op.cit', 63.

[2] Quoted, Roger Coleman (ed.), *Resolutions of the Twelve Lambeth Conferences, 1867-1988,* Toronto: Anglican Book Centre, 1992, 13.

Resolution 58:

'The Conference reaffirms the Resolution of the Conference of 1867 that "every opportunity should be taken to emphasise the divine purpose of visible unity amongst Christians as a fact of revelation." It desires further to affirm that in all partial projects of reunion and inter-communion the final attainment of the divine purpose should be kept in view as our object; and that care should be taken to do what will advance the reunion of the whole of Christendom, and to abstain from doing anything that will retard or prevent it.'[1]

Lambeth Conference 1920, Resolution 9:

Following an elaborate description of 'Reunion of Christendom', 'The times call us to a new outlook and new measures. The faith cannot be adequately apprehended and the battle of the Kingdom cannot be worthily fought while the body is divided, and is thus unable to grow up into the fullness of the life of Christ. The time has come, we believe, for all the separated groups of Christians to agree in forgetting the things which are behind and reaching out towards the goal of a united Catholic Church. The removal of the barriers which have arisen between them will only be brought about by a new comradeship of those whose faces are definitely set this way.'[2]

Lambeth Conference 1930

'When the South India scheme was presented to the Conference for the first time, it was decided that the proposed church would not be a member of the AC but would be regarded as a province of the Universal Church with only a restricted relationship with Anglicanism. Temple's report on the scheme was credited with dispersing what serious opposition there might have been at that critical moment.'[3]

Resolution 31:

Expressing satisfaction about union movements following the above appeal. Resolution 40 on South India, referring to the scheme, satisfaction about development and doctrinal understanding and authorised the bishops of the region to monitor the progress.[4] In 1946 the Archbishop of Canterbury appointed a commission known as 'Derby Commission' to study the CSI scheme. While affirming the work of the Holy Spirit it made two searching comments:

---

[1] Ibid., 39.

[2] Ibid., 46.

[3] James B. Simpson and Edward M. Story, *The Long Shadows of Lambeth X*, New York: McGraw-Hill Book Company, 1969, 314f.

[4] Ibid., 79f.

i.   that it could have been more authentic expression of a truly Indian Christianity.

ii.   that it could have been more radical and not simply a synthesis of the divergent post-Reformation traditions of the West.[1]

It is surprising that such patronising statements were made without any explanation. What was practised for a long time cannot be changed overnight. Quite apart from the indigenous expression, as Hollis noted, the Anglican liturgy in the Thirunelveli area was sung very poorly! Further, experience has shown that the 'The Anglican, the Methodist, the Presbyterian and the Congregational elements were harmoniously blended together in the formation of the CSI. The Anglican heritage of episcopacy, worship and liturgy, the ministerial fraternity and enthusiasms of the Methodists, the diaconate and lay leadership of the Presbyterians and the Congregational emphasis on the importance of the congregation and the Priesthood of all believers have left a lasting impression on the CSI.'[2] But, whether former defects, particularly in liturgy have been rectified, is a different question.

In any case, the official reply of the CSI to the question formulated by the Derby Committee and put by the LC of 1948 on the subject of the future relations of the CSI with other Churches was bold and outstanding. Following is a paragraph:

> We are united in one Church; our parent Churches are divided. If it is now insisted that we state what our permanent relation with them is to be, we can only say that we can be content with nothing except that they should be united as we are. So, long as they remain divided our position must remain anomalous from the point of view of any one of the divided Churches. But from the point of view of the historic faith of the Church we must surely judge that the real anomaly, the real scandal, is that the Church should be divided. We have promised at the end of thirty years to give equal weight to two principles; that our ministry shall be one and that we shall maintain and extend full communion with our parent Churches. As things stand, these two principles are irreconcilable. They can only be reconciled when the parent Churches now divided are united. Our act of union is an act of faith in the Holy Spirit that he will bring this about. We cannot therefore say more than the Constitution has said about what our successors will do in circumstances which we pray may be profoundly different from those in which we now are.[3]

---

[1] Quoted, Victor Premasagar, 'Is CSI Anglican?', 7.

[2] Ibid.

[3] Quoted, L. Newbigin, *The Reunion of the Church*, London, SCM, 1960 (first edition 1948), xxxv.

Lambeth Conference 1948, Resolution 52:

... general satisfaction of report about CSI, pledge to pray for even more development to fulfil the will of God and look forward hopefully and with longing to the day when there shall be full communion between the CSI and the Churches of the Anglican Communion.[1] *Resolution 53:* 'The Conference expresses the hope that, so soon as it may appear to the authorities of the Church of South India to be expedient to take up the matter, such provisions of the Constitution of that Church and such statements contained therein as are known to have given rise either to uncertainty or to grave anxiety in the minds of many, may be reconsidered with a view to their amendment. The Conference would call special attention to the six points specified in the Report of its committee on Unity.'[2]

Resolution 54:

In the sphere of immediate and practical action, the Conference recommended:

(a) That former Anglicans, clerical or lay, who are now members of the CSI, and also Anglicans who hereafter join should be accepted and allowed full privileges of ministry and communion in any Church, province, or diocese of the Anglican Communion, subject to the regulations of the area concerned.'

(b) Such members who may go to South India, 'should not be subject to any censure if they join the CSI and take work of any kind in it'.

(c) '... so also if they accept or receive hospitality of the Church for the performance of the priestly functions or the receiving of Holy Communion subject to the regulations of the Churches, provinces or dioceses to which they belong.'

(c) (But) '*Ministers of the CSI who have not been episcopally ordained should not be regarded as having acquired any new rights or status in relation to the Anglican Communion as a whole solely by reason of the fact that they are ministers of that Church.*' (italics added)

(d) 'In regard to the bishops, presbyters and deacons consecrated or ordained in the CSI as or after the inauguration of that Church, the Conference is unable to make one recommendation agreed to by all. It therefore records the following two views:

  (i)   The majority view is that they should be accepted in every part of the Anglican Communion 'subject only to such regulations as are normally made in all such cases by the responsible authorities in each area.'

  (ii) Another view by 'substantial minority' is that it is not yet possible to pass any definite judgement upon the precise status of them or in the Church of Christ or recommend to the Anglican Communion.'

---

[1] See Coleman, *Resolutions*, 102.

[2] Quoted, Ibid.

However, though there was no outright condemnation there was recognition of the difference in the attitude of churches, 'but it expresses the unanimous hope that such differences may never in any part of the Anglican Communion be made as a ground of condemnation of any action taken by any Church, Province or diocese.'

(a) Lay members of CSI who have received episcopal confirmation should be received as communicants in Anglican churches 'subject to the approval of responsible authority, but should not thereby acquire any new status or rights in relation to the Anglican Communion as a whole'.

(b) Any such regulations as may locally obtain, should 'be admissible to communion by any exercise of the principle of economy'.

Resolution 56 is a statement of Church Union in general.

'The Conference calls upon all the Churches of the Anglican Communion to seek earnestly by prayer and by conference the fulfilment of the vision of a Church, a genuinely Catholic, loyal to all truth, and gathering into the fellowship "all who profess and call themselves Christians" within whose visible unity all the treasures of faith and order bequeathed as heritage from the past to the present, shall be possessed in common and made serviceable to the whole Body of Christ.' It recognises that 'within this unity Christian Communion now separated from one another would retain much that has long been distinctive in their methods of worship and service.' Theological issues concerning Church and Ministry should be faced at the outset.

Resolution 57 on organic union:

'The Conference has heard with satisfaction and hope of proposals for organic union in various areas, and, while calling the attention of those concerned in such schemes to the warnings contained in the Report of the Committee on Unity, believes that schemes of this type have undoubted advantages.'[1] In all these resolutions the authenticating authority is implicitly claimed by the Anglican authority without caring to represent the positions of the CSI.

A Joint Committee of the Convocations, 1950

Two CSI bishops (Jacob and Newbigin) spoke. The Convocation found the CSI positions to be less satisfactory than presented before. There was 'grave and deepening anxiety'. The CSI statement on Sacrament was found to be misleading and should be freed from misleading ambiguities; there should be modification of rules of Synodical procedure and proper safeguarding of the position of the

---

[1] See Ibid., 102-105. For a summary by a historian, see, Roger Lloyd, *The Church of England 1900-1965*, London: SCM, 1966, 494.

bishops; there should be reconsideration of relationship with non-episcopal churches.[1] More significantly, it was noted: Amazing ... that a spirit of mutual misunderstanding of the contentious difficulties and principles of different individuals, a spirit of Christian deference, should have been among them the whole of the time.[2]

On the whole, while continuing to show a patronising and evaluating role, the Convocation gave general endorsement, thanked God, and looked for the day when there would be a full communion, while anxieties/ambiguities still needed addressing. The above meeting agreed that CSI ministers could exercise ministry in other churches where they had relations. While concluding our Report, it was mentioned that 'We wish to reaffirm our strong desire for a steady growth of fellowship between the CofE and the CSI, and to assure its bishops, presbyters and all its members of our prayers ... for full communion, not yet come, pray ... will come.' 'Exchange of views on the six points, between CSI Synod representatives and Church of England representatives.' This expression preceded a number of meetings and exchanges between the two sides.[3] The responses and explanations by CSI representatives were outstanding. They did not give up the position and emphasis of their respective traditions. For example, A. Streckeisen of the former Basel Mission Church based his arguments on the position of Karl Barth. The main position of the meetings of Convocation and the further exchanges of views reflected the position of the Lambeth Conference and still asked (CSI) for 'amendments.'[4]

A Joint Committee of the Convocation appointed in 1955 by the Convocations of Canterbury and York (old structure preceding the present Synod) to study the subject of inter-communion with the CSI. It prepared certain resolutions which reached the headquarters of the CSI.[5] Those who stand in the Anglican tradition feel that these reveal openness of mind and generosity. The resolution reflects the resolution of the above Lambeth Conference but with the tint of the Church of England. Following are the main points:

I.   This House feels no longer need to defer resolutions with regard to the status of those consecrated *at the Union* (italics added) and acknowledge 'such bishops, presbyters and deacons as the true bishops ... in the Church of God.'

II.   That this House further resolves that

---

[1] See, *The Church of South India: Being the United Report of the Joint Committees of the Convocations of Canterbury and York*, Westminster: The Church Information Board, 1950, 6.

[2] Ibid., 7.

[3] See, Ibid. 28ff.

[4] See, Ibid., 69-71.

[5] *SICMan*, Aug. 1955, 'From the Editor', 1-3.

(a) Members of the CSI who are communicants in that Church may, when in England, can receive Communion in the Church of England.

(b) Members of the CSI who become permanently resident in England and desire to be habitual communicants in CofE shall be required to conform to the regular discipline of the CofE.

(c) Bishops, Presbyters and Deacons of the CSI may be invited to preach in churches of the CofE with the permission of the bishop of the diocese.

(d) Any bishop or episcopally ordained presbyter of the CSI may be free to celebrate the Holy Communion in a church of the CofE at the invitation of the incumbent, with the permission of the bishop of the diocese, subject to his willingness, while in England, to celebrate in Anglican churches only, and, where these apply, to the provisions of the Colonial Clergy Act.

(e) The bishop of a diocese may at his discretion authorise the loan of a parish church in his diocese from time to time for the celebration of the liturgy of the CSI by a bishop or episcopally ordained presbyter of that Church.

(f) A bishop or episcopally ordained presbyter or deacon of the CSI who desires to officiate as a bishop, presbyter or deacon of the CofE, whether a limited period or permanently, may be allowed to do so, provided that he has received such permission as may be required under the Colonial Clergy Act. Such bishop, presbyter or deacon becomes subject in all respects to the rules and regulations of the CofE.

(g) Other ministers of CSI who desire to enter the ministry of the CofE who visit the territory of the CSI may accept the hospitality of that Church for receiving the Holy Communion within it.

III. That this House respectfully requests his Grace the President to take appropriate action to give effect to this Report and Recommendations concerning practical help to CSI with a view to paramount importance to persistent and informed prayer for the church. No more limitations imposed formerly. 'But the important thing for us to realise is the genuine willingness on the part of the Anglican Church to maintain fraternal relationship with the CSI … we need not go behind the details of this desire which itself is enough for having inter-communion. The present disabilities are due to certain historical circumstances and if we understand them we shall be less patient at the caution exercised by the Convocations in their approaches to the CSI.'

... The CofE stands in the Catholic tradition. The Reformation ideas undoubtedly affected its life, both in its political as well as religious aspects, but they did not succeed in shifting its centre of gravity. The living tradition of the past is still a potent factor giving it both its outward form and its inner stability. The Anglican Church, unlike the RC, has not tried to buttress its authority by doctrines, which are un-scriptural, nor has it tried to override conscience of the individual by an assertion of infallibility. There is unity within it which is more than static uniformity. At one extreme it is evangelical and at the other, liturgical but both held together in a unity and interact upon each other in live synthesis. The Anglican Church has ever been willing to define its attitude to new knowledge whether it be the Enlightenment of a former century, or the historical and critical study of the scripture or the discoveries of science of the present-day. If it be said that it is so inextricably bound up with national life, it can also be maintained with equal truth that every national question (we may not define it narrowly) is of vital concern to the Church. In short, it takes seriously the 'Visible Church'.

... The CSI owes a great debt to the Anglican Church, for the tradition of catholicity that has come to it through one of its constituent bodies, the Diocese of the Church of India, Burma and Ceylon that have now become an integral part of the new Church. This is not to belittle the other traditions that have merged into it. The Protestant tradition is not really that of Sectarians. The evangelistic zeal of the Sectarians is proverbial. A passionate adherence to the scriptures, the guide book to truth, accompanies their sense of missionary responsibility. But Sectarianism is not really the product of Reformation. Individualism is rather an aberration from the Reformation doctrines, just as much as the magical notions of the ministry and sacraments would be perversions of the Catholic insistence on the form and order of the Church. No one has any right to decry Anglican sacramentalism because of its possible degeneration into magic. Neither may one condemn Protestantism because of its possible, and sometimes actual degeneration into arbitrary individualism ...

The Union of Churches is not an indiscriminate mixture of traditions. We would do well not to make hasty judgements on what we may imagine to be 'ecclesiastical pretensions' of others or 'mere' matters of Church order and discipline. True cohesion in our ranks comes through a sympathetic understanding and not through doctrinal rigidity. The Convocations have taken a real step forward in their approach to the CSI. It is taken with caution but in a generous spirit. Not all the 'limitations' to inter-communion are removed but they look forward to a time when inter-communion would be unhindered and free.

The CSI has rightly decided that there should be no interruption of communion with any of the parent Churches – whether episcopal or non-episcopal. It has also resolved that in the course of thirty years, its ministry shall have become unified. The first is a truly Christian decision. The second might be a measure of expediency. It is apparent that these decisions are mutually contradictory. This anomaly can only be resolved, says the report, 'in the unification of the Church of God in every part of the world, not least in England'.

To defer a decision on the question of inter-communion till such a time would be to evade the challenge that the event of the Union in South India presents to existing institutions. The CSI is not an unrelated event. It is in continuity with all the institutions and traditions that had existed before. To disregard them would make the CSI a new denomination or sect. It is the interaction between the institution and the event, the old and the new, that makes for that fulfilment which is true Catholicity.

The above document on 'Inter-Communion and Catholicity' received many positive comments both in England and South India. For example, the Bishop of Exeter said that he was specially impressed by the fact that the Synod of the CSI, faced with the urgent need of countless small isolated congregations for the Sacrament, had not even considered permitting lay catechists to celebrate Holy Communion, but had decided to ordain such men for ministry in their own areas only. Similarly, the assurance of the CSI that they have orthodox intentions together with the fact that the Creeds must be used in the Liturgy and Baptism services, was held to remove any possible doubt about their credal orthodoxy. However, the implicit assumption that Anglicanism alone is truly Catholic is exposed here. In actual fact, the classical creeds accepted by the CSI are accepted by the Anglican Communion. The non-episcopal churches also have a sense of catholicity but refuse to be defined by episcopacy and Anglican structures. The Roman Catholics claim that they are the only truly Catholic church. It will be rewarding to do a comparative analysis and go deeper into the profound meaning of being Catholic.

The debate in fact made it quite clear that there were only two remaining obstacles to full inter-communion: 1. The fact that there were still non-episcopal ministers in the CSI. This obstacle, it is assumed, would automatically disappear with time, and in any case it was hoped that it would not arise at all in North India and Ceylon where there were plans for initial unification of the ministry. 2. The doubts still remaining in the minds of some theologians whether the Constitution of CSI sufficiently safeguards the Faith for the future. The CSI

Synod had made it clear that it was willing in due course to consider amendments which might satisfy these doubts. But at the same time the CSI must be clear and even confident enough with world standard theologians in her membership, to consider amendments not to satisfy certain overseas Churches but to be a relevant and effective organic union in mission in South India.

The Editor of the *South India Churchman* who was to become a bishop in the Madras diocese of the CSI and who chose to publish the above document in his 'Editorial'wrote a concluding note: 'Compared to the 1950 Report, which had restrictions for CSI, now after 5 years – and more – the CofE is at last convinced that the CSI 'has grown in its inner unity and cohesion and in its sacramental life' and in the appreciation of the office of the bishop in the Church of God.'[1] He further added a note that still there is no loaning of Anglican church buildings for CSI liturgy and no full inter-communion between Laity. Also, it should be noted that the Anglican participants in the negotiations for the CSI and members of the CBCI who voted in favour of the union did not expect further scrutiny in such detail by the Lambeth Conference and Convocations of the Church of England. What was neglected was the cutting edge of the achievement of CSI for the CofE and other provinces of the Anglican Communion to speed up initiatives of similar organic union.

There were CSI reflections on the convocation debate. One such reflection points out the problem of continued division between the CofE and the Free Churches including Methodist and the Reformed Churches (other bodies of the organic union of CSI). 'It was emphasised that the CSI was asked to accept this limitation out of respect for the pastoral needs of the CofE and that we on our side accept it as a challenge to face with penitence and resolution of our own divisions.'[2] But divisions within one Church and with other Churches are not the same. It may well be expected that increasing unity among Churches will help to heal divisions within.

R.D. Paul, one of the greatest lay theologians of the time, wrote a chapter on the CSI and Anglican Communion in his remarkable assessment of the first decade of the CSI. He noted developments in the above Convocations, Lambeth Conferences and further visits and reflections of the life, growth and witness of the CSI. With a full independent spirit with conviction, he stressed that any attitude of the AC and the CofE as superior or totally distinctive was unreasonable and unbiblical. He quoted Hollis, Fisher and Bell in his support and wished unity of the AC within and without. For the attention of all those concerned he wrote the following testimony.

What needs to be made clear is that so far as we in the CSI have gone in our life and experience – whatever we may have been taught previously

[1] DCB, D. Chellappa.
[2] Campbell Milford, 'C.S.I. Reflections on the Convocation Debate', Ibid., 4.

by our spiritual progenitors – we have not found it necessary to accept that only an episcopally ordained ministry is valid and competent effectively to celebrate Holy Communion, and perform other priestly functions. We cannot believe that God withholds His blessing to His people because the one who mediates and dispenses God's grace is not episcopally ordained. That would belie all our experience as a united Church. Some of us ex-Anglicans are now accustomed to receive communion at the hands of non-episcopally ordained presbyters of our Church. We have been able to do so without any qualms of our theological consciences, and without any trace of feeling that we have received only the second best. The Lord has been present among us at every celebration of the Holy Sacrament and has not withheld from us 'the benefits of His passion'. The pre-union ecclesiastical status of the celebrant did not make the slightest difference. We have in the CSI the spectacle of our bishops receiving communion from the hands of non-episcopally ordained ministers. We ex-Anglican laymen, if we err, err in good company![1]

He continues to state that 1.3 million lay members of the CSI 'are not unduly worried about what the Churches of the Anglican Communion or the Roman Catholic Church or the Orthodox Churches are thinking of us. What we are really anxious about is that, in the circumstances in which we Christians in this country find ourselves, we must be and become one, if our Christian claims are to be justified in the eyes of the people among whom we live. We are therefore more anxious to do all that is necessary to make such a unity in our country possible than that we should be given some status and recognition when we visit Britain and the United States or any other country of the West.'[2] Whatever may be the consequences, anxieties and concerns about the CSI in the AC and other Western churches, he asserts, we must be allowed 'to do things in our country in obedience to what we think is God's will for us' and 'to rethink Christian Doctrine in the light of the revealed Word of God in relation to the situation in which we find ourselves'.

There were some Anglican missionaries living in India at that time, deeply committed to promote unity by watching developments in the CofE and Anglican Communion. For example, Sister Carol Graham (1898-1989) who was an SPG missionary to South India, became passionate about the Church of South India. She was the key for founding the CSI order of Women in Bangalore. When she returned to England she founded in 1964 Farncombe Community, Surrey, an ecumenical community of women, to work and pray for the unity of Christian denominations. While being in South India, she made the following observation:

---

[1] Rajaiah D. Paul, *The Fist Decade*, 190.

[2] Ibid., 190f

'The outstanding new fact in the relationship of the CofE to the Church of S. India is the decision taken by the Convocations of the Canterbury and York in July 1955, with an almost unanimous vote, to acknowledge the bishops, presbyters and deacons consecrated or ordained in the CSI at or after the inauguration of that church as "true bishops, priests and deacons in the Church of God."[1] She underlines the importance of unification of ministry for the full communion of churches. But the unclear attitude and new strictures in connection with the churches of organic union were not encouraging.

Lambeth Conference 1968, Resolution 43 – The 39 Articles:

The Conference accepts the main conclusion of the Report of the Archbishop's Commission on Christian Doctrine entitled *Subscription and Assent to the Thirty-nine Articles (1968) and in furtherance of its recommendation*:

(a) Suggests that each Church of our Communion consider whether the Articles need be bound up with its Prayer Book;
(b) Suggests to the Churches of the Anglican Communion that assent to the 39 Articles be no longer required of ordinands;
(c) Suggests that, when subscription is required to the Articles or other elements in the Anglican Tradition, it should be required, and given, only in the context of a statement which gives the full range of our inheritance of faith and sets the Articles in their historical context.'[2] (Following a voting this was adopted, with 37 dissentients.)

Resolution 47 – Reciprocal Acts of Intercommunion

While union talks are in progress a Church of Anglican Communion is free to allow reciprocal acts of intercommunion under the general direction of the bishop. Each Province concerned to determine when the negotiations for union in which it is engaged have reached the stage which allows this intercommunion.[3]

Resolution 48 – on CSI

The Conference recommended, while the CSI Moderator P. Solomon and two other CSI observers (Russell Chandran, Newbigin) were watching from the gallery:

(a) That when a bishop or episcopally ordained minister of the CSI visits a diocese of the Anglican Communion and exercises his ministry in

---

[1] Carol Graham, *The Church of South India*, on behalf of the Appeal Committee for Women's Work in the CSI, 1960, 22.

[2] Quoted, Coleman, *Resolutions*, 165.

[3] Ibid., 167.

Anglican churches there should now be no restriction on the exercise of his ministry in other Churches with which the CSI is in communion.

(b) That Churches and provinces of the AC re-examine their relation to the CSI with a view to entering into full communion with that Church.[1]

A small group of Lambeth bishops dissented, withholding their approval apparently because some CSI ministers (about 10 percent) still lacked episcopal ordination.

'The CSI is no longer on trial, we are on trial', said (S. Falkner) Allison of Winchester in proposing Resolution no. 48 for full communion; 'it is no longer an experiment.'[2]

Yet there were restrictions such as that 'any bishop or priest of CSI who desired to officiate in Anglican Provinces could not officiate at other than Anglican altars ... Lambeth X urged that those restrictions be dropped and it asked that every province take steps to establish full CSI Communion'[3]

Michael Hollis while an assistant bishop [4] in the Diocese of St Edmundsbury and Ipswich, spoke of the Lambeth Conference in a high-pitched voice:

Every organization has in some way a vested interest against change ... we can't be part of a united church and the Anglican Communion at the same time ... Anglicans as much as other bodies do engage in doubletalk, speaking of unity and the Anglican Communion at the same time.[5]

On the whole the mindset of the Anglican Communion appeared to be that of a teacher correcting and re-correcting the paper of a student until s/he was fully satisfied but without realising that his/her own knowledge and articulation needed improvement and attitude change. At last, whether fully satisfied or not, as if showing a gracious embrace of those excluded and remained in isolation, a new status was accorded.

Anglican Consultative Council 7

Resolution 17: United Churches in Full Communion

THAT this Council:

---

[1] Ibid.

[2] *The Long Shadows of Lambeth X*, 219; 20 years earlier the same bishop – then Principal of Ridley Hall – spoke in Church House).

[3] Ibid., 220.

[4] 'In the established Church of England, assistant bishops are usually retired (diocesan or suffragan) bishops – in which case they are *honorary assistant bishops*. Occasionally active bishops are appointed to be assistant bishops – however, unlike a diocesan or suffragan bishop they do not hold a title: they are not the 'Bishop of Somewhere'.

[5] Ibid., 257.

(a) resolves that the ACC should now move towards normal membership of the Council for all united Churches with which the Churches of the Anglican Communion are in full communion (i.e. the Church of South India, the Church of North India, the Church of Pakistan and the Church of Bangladesh);

(b) requests the Lambeth Conference of 1988 and the Primates' Meeting of 1989 similarly to consider full membership of those bodies for united Churches in full communion.

Lambeth Conference 1988 Resolution 12 – United Churches in Full Communion

This conference

1. Expresses its gratitude for the presence of bishops from the Church of South India ... acknowledging their presence reminds us that our commitment as Anglicans is to the wider unity of the Church.

2. Affirms the request of the ACC-7 (Res. 17) that all United Churches of the Anglican Communion are in full communion be invited to accept full membership in the Lambeth Conference and the Primates Meeting (as is already the case with the ACC)

3. Welcomes the proposals entitled 'Ministry in a Uniting Church' of the Covenanted Churches in Wales, and insofar as the Welsh proposals are similar to the North India and Pakistan Scheme, sees no difficulties in relation to the question of full communion if such proposals are brought to fruition.

4. Encourages the development of similar proposals in other parts of the world: Church of Bangladesh, Church of North India, Church of Pakistan, Church of South India. The term "united Churches in full communion" is used of those Churches where Anglicans have entered into union with Christians of other traditions. These Churches are in full communion with the Churches of the Anglican Communion.

5. Encourages the development of similar proposals in other parts of the world.[1]

    Explanatory Note: The term 'united churches in Full Communion' is used of those churches where Anglicans have entered into union with churches of the AC.[2] The Reports, Resolutions and Pastoral Letters from the bishops were entitled *The Truth Shall Set You Free*.[3] The misunderstanding persists that the CSI was a communion of Churches into which Anglican Churches entered. Is it a deliberate propaganda

---

[1] See Ibid., 205.

[2] Coleman, 214.

[3] London: ACC, 1988.

in order to conceal the fact of organic union? Whether deliberately or unwittingly that the CSI was an organic union ('dying to denominations and rising to a new reality') was not acknowledged.

Six bishops from the CSI with their spouses were invited as guests at the Lambeth Conference 1988. It was notified that the wives of the bishops would be accommodated in the LC sites and have 3 weeks' conference of their own. The first group experience of a CSI team attending the LC was both exciting and perplexing. Archbishop Robert Runcie, in his opening address said, 'A Church will never learn from its mistakes unless it is ready to risk making some.' What is risk or mistake here? Moreover, Stanley Samartha as a special invitee addressed the group on interreligious issues stressing women's ordination as a broader issue.[1]

Two other interesting matters in 1988 Lambeth were: a) Barbara Harris of ECUSA was consecrated as the first Anglican woman bishop (suffragan); b) It was reaffirmed that the use of unfermented grape juice (in Free Churches) was unwarranted as Jesus and the Roman Catholic Church used fermented wine).[2]

The Anglican Consultative Council which brought together representatives from all 38 Provinces of the Anglican Communion once in 3 years met in Cardiff, Wales, from July 22 to August 4, 1990. This was the first meeting after the CSI was accepted as a full member of the Council. There were three CSI representatives. 'Archbishop Robert Runcie in his opening address said how happy he was to welcome the united Churches of the Indian Sub-Continent as full members, and on our part, we told the delegates that we hoped that our participation would be a source of inspiration for further unity between Anglicans and others.' The reporter adds that 'The Archbishop who lays down office in Jan 1991, sends his greetings to all the members of the CSI.'[3] No doubt, such exposures to the Anglican circles gave the visitors a sense of pride and privilege as well as greater attraction to Anglicanism, the religion of England.

In the centenary year of the Lambeth Conference in 1998 (it was in the first, in 1888, that the Quadrilateral was issued) there was a debate on changing the clause 'Historic Episcopacy Locally Adapted' into 'Apostolic Succession', and after arguments 'Historic Episcopate' was retained. 'The term "locally adapted" was taken seriously when the CSI was formed. It divested the episcopacy of all its royal connotations of power and authority from the office of Bishop. Hence, the simple uniform prescribed for the bishop of the CSI. Further, it was pointed out that in the CSI the Bishops in the Diocesan Councils and the Moderator in the Synod are the Chairs. Except on matters of faith and doctrine, the Bishops do not

---

[1] See 'Reflection' by C.D. Jathanna, *SICMan*, Oct. 1988, 6-8; Total: 525 bishops and 425 wives. Ref. Sarojini Jathanna, ''88 Wives Conference' *SICMan*, Nov. 1988.

[2] See Nicola Currie, 'Twelve Firsts for the Twelfth Lambeth Conference', *SICMan*, July 1988, 13f.

[3] George Koshy, in *SICman*, Aug. 1990, 14.

have separate authority in the church, especially not in financial administration. There is no house of Bishops in the CSI.'[1] However, the very name 'bishop' gives them certain power to assert and manipulate because of its political power and glamour it assumed in Europe and which to some extent continued in the Anglican Communion, particularly the Church of England. It should be studied at what levels and in what circumstances this happens in every diocese.

We skip a few important conferences and resolutions. The Anglican Consultative Council (2009):

(a) thanks the members and staff of the Inter-Anglican Standing Commission for Ecumenical Affairs ... for their fruitful labours over the last ten years, and commends the Report "The Vision Before Us", compiled on behalf of the Commission by the Revd Sarah Rowland Jones, for study as a benchmark ecumenical volume in the Provinces of the Anglican Communion;

(b) endorses the "Four Principles of Anglican Engagement in Ecumenism" set out in that Report as a key description of the Anglican approach towards ecumenical activity and goals, adopts the following shorthand to describe them, and commends them to the Churches of the Communion:

1. The Goal: the full organic unity of the Church.
2. The Task: recognising and receiving the Church of one another.
3. The Process: unity by stages
4. The Content: common faith, sacraments and ministry.

One recalls that there is a marked shift from the 1888 Quadrilateral of two Testaments, two Creeds, two Sacraments and historic episcopacy locally adapted, which was taken as the basis of CSI. The new 'Quadrilateral' is vague and abstract, and there is no wonder that the AC will go on interpreting, repeating, re-interpreting and so on. Further, voices of different Anglican provinces are recorded, but not the CSI's and those of other organic unions. There are many missives, documents with request for action. This raises curiosity to know if they bind CSI, and whether the CSI has acted on them.

Incidentally, there is reference to the 'Windsor Report' which affirms the Archbishop of Canterbury as the focus of unity. This is fitting for the leader of a state church, the high priest of the monarchy, member of the House of the Lords in the selection of whom both the monarch and state are involved. Can it have any implication for an independent church as the CSI and the secular polity of the sub-Continent?

One question repeatedly asked by those who are involved in this conversation is, why did the CSI leadership not collect the opinion of the Synod and members

---

[1] See, Victor Premasagar, "Is CSI Anglican?", 7.

of the Theological Commission? Did their excitement about a trip to London overtake their reasoning? Were they treated as gullible by Lambeth? In crucial discussions on unity in Anglican circles how many of them had the courage to challenge their hosts about their complacency which continue to be the same as in 1927 when Azariah openly challenged and called the disunity a sin and scandal in mission field?

Some Current Anglican Voices

As there is so much ignorance in church circles about the nature of the CSI and its relationship with the CofE (on behalf of the Anglican Communion), with the help of Owain Bell I contacted select leaders of the CofE. Those who were informed of the matter expressed their frank opinions. A senior clergyman, now the chaplain of a bishop, has observed: 'Contrary to the supplementary to the Canons, the latest Church of England Year Book lists the CSI as a Province of the Anglican Communion. Looks like neo-colonialism, but I have asked questions to people who should know.' With reference to the invitation extended to the CSI to become a full member and Province of the Anglican Communion, he rightly asks: What was the response from CSI etc. to this invitation? I add: How was this invitation communicated to CSI and other united Churches? What was the process followed to accept (or reject this invitation)? What was the implication of this resolution for the CofE to have full communion with the URC and Methodist Churches in England and the Reformed churches in the USA, leave alone the non-conformist Churches in the whole of the areas of the AC? Most significantly, by what process and on what conditions was the CSI adopted into the AC as a Province? There is no record of the CSI becoming a Province, even in the Record Library of the Communion nor in the CSI Archives! The whole episode exposes the typical Anglican attitude, particularly that of its centre of gravity, the Church of England. All were unilateral declarations without appeal or response from the other end and without wider consultation.

A retired bishop said: 'I would not be surprised if no formal decision was made (by whom would it be made?) other than a decision by the Archbishop of Canterbury, whose role it is to invite bishops to Lambeth conferences, simply to include bishops of the CSI as members rather than as "guests". Remember too that the status of "guest" also applied to ecumenical representatives from the Roman Catholic and other churches with whom we are not in full communion but who are invited to be present and take part, but of course not to vote. A "guest" is not a member of the family, whereas we do see the CSI as part of our extended family. If a conscious decision was made, I suspect that it was intended not as an act of annexation but rather as a reversal of the rather sniffy attitudes of the mid-20th century, which arose out of Anglo-Catholic suspicions about the orders of CSI ministers and bishops. I also imagine that any decision about the status of CSI bishops at Lambeth would also have applied to the bishops of the other United Churches.'

A woman theologian and biblical scholar with wide ecumenical experience holding high rank in the WCC and honours of the State points out, crucially, 'There was no intention to detach the United Churches from other, non-Anglican roots and relationships. It doesn't read like aggressive Anglican appropriation! If CSI has become more Anglican over the last 25 years could it be by choice? Apart from what I called the possible seductions of Anglican style episcopacy (19th century style!) there might be other factors at work within the local context. It looks as if we need to know more about the story from a South Indian perspective.

'In haste. One of the early issues when I joined … was the status of CSI. (Archbishop) was asked about it in the General Synod. The background was that there had been ministers not ordained in succession after CSI came into being. There was even a church in deepest East Anglia that had a notice in its church porch to say that no minister from South India was welcome! As a result of that, and the belief that all such ministers had by then died, the 1988 Lambeth Conference, at the request of the ACC, passed a resolution … (to invite CSI to be a full member).'

Another retired bishop, after initial remarks, goes on to say: 'My guess is that this is some kind of well-meaning fudge undertaken without really thinking through the implications. A kind interpretation of what Anglican authorities did is that it came from a desire to extend a full welcome to united churches that include a previously Anglican province – and perhaps even in some minds to 'repent' of the years of Anglican hostility to CSI … without thinking through the inevitably patronising impression that would give. And we might imagine what would have been said if the Anglican Communion had refused membership to churches that had previously been part Anglican … ecumenical institutional advance is often messy, and fails to honour both the unity and the separate identity of the various previously separated denominations. It is entirely appropriate, in my view, that Israel should raise the questions he does.'

Another senior bishop confessed succinctly saying, 'First we opposed, then patronised.'

A former Archbishop informed that it had been suggested that the united Churches with Anglican component should be recognised as a different category but it was not accepted.

Among those who have not responded to my letter, despite many reminders, are the present Archbishop of Canterbury and the Moderator of the CSI.[1] The

---

[1] A hard copy was handed to him by an Anglican colleague and friend of mine in Nov. 2018. The last letter sent by post was in April 2019 in which it was mentioned that non-response would be taken as his consent to note it in this book. Similarly, letters have been sent to the Moderator of the CSI. As these two leaders have taken most drastic steps to declare the CSI as a true successor

renewed reclamation of the former Anglican identity has been vigorous following CSI's entry into the AC. For example, The Anglican Cycle of Prayer for Sunday 29 Oct 2017 *Pentecost 22 mentions by name two bishops of the bifurcated dioceses who used to be Anglican before 1947. An analogy could be at least in theory a very late post-mortem of a united body to crab a denominational bit which was decomposed then and there!*

Ecumenical Developments in Britain and the Question of Organic Unions

Though there are other Churches in Britain such as the Methodist Church, United Reformed Church, Baptist Union, Church of Scotland, Episcopal Church of Scotland, the Church of England and its episcopal associates are the major players in attempting or experimenting with forging ecumenical relations and partnerships. Our treatment of the subject is introductory and brief. While the Free Church of Scotland (1843) and the Free Church of England (1844) are not prominent in union negotiations there were a number of federations, councils and alliances of the Free Churches.[1]

British Council of Churches: Following many regional and issue-based councils, while World War II was ravaging, the British Council of (Protestant) Churches was created in 1942. A service was held in St. Paul's Cathedral at which Archbishop William Temple of Canterbury preached. He said: 'Today we inaugurate the British Council of Churches, the counterpart in our country of the World Council, combining in a single organisation the chief agencies of the interdenominational co-operation which has marked the last five years ... Our differences remain ... but we take our stand on the common faith of Christendom, faith in God, Creator, Redeemer, Sanctifier.' The business sessions on 23rd and 24th September were held in the Baptist Church House, Southampton Row. Though all usual slogans were repeated there was no sign of moving towards organic unity. But at the same time there were opportunities for colleagues from different denominational churches to work together in areas such as, racial justice, relief and development and interreligious relationship.

Local Ecumenical Partnership: This is a partnership between different denominations (selected Protestant Churches such as Anglican, Methodist, URC and Baptist) which was piloted in 1964 in the context of renewed effort

---

of the Church of England in India, their comments would have been helpful. The author realises that, despite about 50 years of ministry in both South India and England, he has no influence nor political clout to deserve a reply to his letters concerning unity, mission and truth.

[1] E.g. the Free Church Federal Council was formed in 1940 by the union of the National Council of the Evangelical Free Churches (1896) and the Federal Council of the Evangelical Free Church (1919) for the purpose of 'cooperating in matters of mutual concern'; Free Church Federation (1892); Baptist Union (1891), constituted by General Baptists and Particular Baptists; by a Deed of the Union of the Methodist groups the Methodist Church was formed in 1932.

to give credible witness and the need of sharing resources. It is estimated that at present there are over 800 LEPs. The initiative is local but their link to the mother churches is maintained. There is a legal process and agreement which can be tedious. There are six categories of LEP: 1. Single Congregation Partnerships are based on shared ministry and resources. 2. Congregations in Covenanted Partnerships mean almost the same as the above but some denominations may not share ministry and sacrament. 3. Shared Building Partnerships under the Sharing of Church Building Act 1969, but there may be cases of informal sharing. 4. Chaplaincy Partnerships in educational institutions, prisons and hospitals – working together ecumenically. 5. Mission Partnerships include a variety of contexts including industry, community and media. 6. Education Partnerships focus on training, lay and ministerial, as well as joint or shared schools.[1] If a particular LEP does not work well it is dismantled. In recent years there have been 'Ecumenical Church Centres' which involve a different registration. An LEP provides an opportunity for members of different denominational churches to come together, know one another and become liberated from the fear of others. In most cases, particular denominations' liturgy and hymns are used in worship services in turn. We hear of occasional tensions as well. However, more difficult is to maintain the legality of the partnership and having to be under the authority of different mother churches. At the same time, LEPs have proved that there is no theological or spiritual problem to worship and witness. There is no problem in using different resources in one common worship. As different denominations demonstrate different ecclesiastical cultures (ambience, aroma and accustomed patterns of working – which may appear to be ridiculous to outsiders that it happens within a small country with same colour and race (?) and with the same language). And it has shown the spiritual maturity of those who have chosen to worship and work together with members of other denominations. But it has exposed that the key is to deal with powers and authorities which hardly move especially in the case of a state church.

Council of Churches in Britain and Ireland, and Churches Together in Britain and Ireland: This replaced the BCC. In 1987, at a meeting in Swanwick, the churches adopted a declaration on Christian unity. It acknowledged that the churches are of different traditions and theologies, but were nonetheless committing themselves to a shared journey towards full visible unity in Christ. The membership was expanded to cover different Churches ranging from Pentecostals to the Roman Catholics as well as Churches in Ireland. It was founded in 1990 and renamed as Churches Together in Britain and Ireland in 1999. In every page of the major document there are phrases like shared belief in God, Christ and the Holy Spirit, pictures of rainbows, shared pilgrimage or journey, shared commitment, unity in mission and so on. 'Churches Together' is

[1] https://www.cte.org.uk/Groups/314544/Home/Resources/Local_Ecumenical_Partnerships/Different_types_of/Different_types_of.aspx as on 22 Dec. 2018.

seen as an 'instrument' by which the churches journey towards full visible unity. It has its national (Churches Together in England) regional (CTE Midlands) and local (CTE Cambridge) forms. In my limited experience, I have not been able to understand the nature of CTE at least in its two local expressions. In the former case we were led to do some charity work and have some conversation about the local churches. In the present case, eight churches present in the extended area; apart from doing at least two charity works, we worship together twice a year (the Week of Prayer for Christian Unity and the Day of Pentecost) and we have the witness walk on Good Friday. I suggested sharing of the unique vision and history of each church so that we could learn and move forward towards organic unity as the CTE has envisaged; let us have more joint worship services. There has been no outright rejection but no implementation so far. I have tried to excite them with the story of the CSI but there is no interest at all. One suspects that it has all sorts of interests (including vested interests), as opposed to genuinely moving forward to the set goal of organic unity.

Absence of solid unity leaves the local mission truncated. For example, one of the two major charities our 'churches together' have undertaken is 'street pastors' helping drunken young women of night life on one or two week-ends in a month. Some have asked if this token act leads the victims to regain their self-dignity and self-reliance. The other is supporting a food bank from which the poverty-stricken and homeless people (and drunkards) benefit. Britain being the fifth world economy, some well-informed people ask, should we need to maintain such charities permanently? But so far such questions have not been entertained. One understands that with limited resources of the local congregations and financial assistance from trust funds, agencies and local councils they are not able do more than this. No doubt, however, an organic unity in a so-called Christian country, will place us on a stable platform to analyse deeply the forces that push the hapless victims onto the streets and challenge them in solidarity with the victims.

Churches Together in England (CTE) has been studied critically. 'Theos', the UK's leading religion and society think tank and research agency, has brought a comprehensive research report. Following are the key points of the Executive Summary':

> The contemporary ecumenical landscape in England is complex and continues to shift on account of the following factors: the general climate of church decline; a national trend of falling church attendance and Christian affiliation; economic and financial pressures faced by all Churches; the huge diversity of Christian expression in the country; the variety of views on Christian unity.
>
> Significant number of churches maintain a healthy relationship; there is vibrancy about ecumenical relations. 'Correlated with this is a diminishing interest in pursuing the 'full visible unity' of the

Church – one of the traditional aspirations of ecumenism.' CTE plays a vital role in developing and brokering relationships between Churches, particularly at the national level; provides a space for open conversations; with 44 member Churches (in 2017, it was 16 in 1990), reflects the diversity of Christianity in England; provides a number of practical benefits, including access to faith schools and chaplaincy

The following are weaknesses or areas of concern in CTE that came up across a broad range of interviews: lack of clear vision and purpose: what is CTE for? What does it do uniquely? This was the fundamental weakness found to impinge on most aspects of its work; disproportionality in appeal to different Churches; lack of visibility and public profile; lack of clarity on funding: which members should fund (more)? How much? What are they in fact funding?; difficulties around 'speaking with one voice': on what issues? How can CTE best 'get the word out'?; some confusion about how Intermediate Bodies work and relate to CTE; relative absence of young people from ecumenism; a number of member Churches do not divide themselves along national lines. This constrains their participation in ecumenism in important ways.

Orthodox and Catholic interviewees expressed concern about the predominance of a Protestant style of worship and Bible study in CTE meetings; there is no common mind between liberal Protestant Churches and theologically conservative Churches on key ethical questions (e.g. human sexuality, gay marriage); some members want CTE to broaden its agenda and engage more in inter-faith work; the relationship with and participation of black and ethnic minority Churches remains a challenge, notwithstanding the important progress that has been made on this front

The relationship between CTE and CTBI (Churches Together in Britain and Ireland) needs to be clarified; clarify and 'thicken' vision as a matter of urgency: all weaknesses and areas of concern correlate strongly with the absence of a clear vision; continue brokering new relationships and strengthening existing ones; 'Speak with one voice!'; take on the challenge of discerning issues to speak on and the best processes to do so effectively.[1]

Though it is a small country with a tiny minority of Christians (sometimes with a majority complex!), it is head-spinning to read, connect and understand the complex history and complicated structures and developments. It does not

[1] Mladin, N. et. al., *That They All May Be One: Insights into Churches Together in England and Contemporary Ecumenism*, Theos, London, 2017, 8-12.

give any glimpses into a faith journey towards organic unity for which Jesus prayed, and the CSI was born as a positive response in a simple way with common minimum principles. Although, the Anglican hurdles caused delay, the journey took only 28 years. Fortunately, the South Indian Churches that constituted the CSI had a group of leaders from all the Churches who had a rare combination of spiritual maturity, theological clarity, evangelistic zeal and determined mind to achieve with a definite plan.[1]

It is not unreasonable to think that Methodism and Anglicanism in their country of origin (England) represent two kinds of 'middle path'. Anglicanism is often referred to as a middle path between Roman Catholicism and Free Churches. Methodism is known for its moderation and its middle path between Anglicanism and the other Free Churches. Methodism was an offshoot of the Church of England in the 18th century in preference for spreading the gospel and opposition to complicated structures under episcopal control. John Wesley claimed that as an ordained Anglican priest he had the right to ordain others some of who later declared themselves bishops. Again, for them preaching the gospel of transformation and demonstration of its power in action, personal and social, was more important than analysing which pipelines or cables the Holy Spirit of the Apostles was passing through. This irritated or infuriated the informed Anglicans who still believe that the right hand of an *episcopos* (overseer) is the only instrument of the direct flow of the Spirit while it is discredited by the original promoters of this belief (Roman Catholics). In any case, after the successful experiment of the CSI, the Methodists became more serious about union with the Church of England. Proposals for union between them was worked on from the 1950s onwards, but were narrowly defeated by the General Synod in 1972. After a period of frustration and weariness, in 1979 formal conversations between the two churches recommenced, leading to the adoption of the *Anglo-Methodist Covenant* in 2003.[2]

'Mission and Ministry in Covenant' was prepared by the Joint Implementation Commission, set up by the two churches in response to the Covenant, to progress the journey towards visible unity. Nevertheless, as we have already noted, some church leaders openly confessed that their feeling was as if the Covenant never existed. As far as my acquaintance is concerned several priests and ministers were not aware of it, leave alone implementing some of the key points such as inter-communion and ministerial exchange. To date, last year (2018) both in the General Synod of the CofE and the Methodist Conference a report was presented the basis of which was consecration of the Conference President by an episcopal authority as a major step towards organic unity.

---

[1] Ibid.

[2] See, *An Anglican-Methodist Covenant: Common Statement of the Formal Conversations Between the Methodist Church of Great Britain and the Church of England*, Peterborough: Methodist Publishing House and Church House Publishing, 2001.

The President in turn will ordain the Methodist ministers. The present Methodist ministers ordained by the non-episcopal President will be acceptable to Anglicans as a 'temporary anomaly'. This was noted in the General Synod of the CofE as one of the 'bearable anomalies' the others being the 'biblical and dominical anomaly', the 'historical and theological anomaly' and the 'ecclesiological anomaly'. The Methodist Conference in June-July 2019 was expected to discuss and decide on the proposal but, to the frustration of many, the General Synod of the CofE in July, while backing the proposals and recommendations, requested the 'Faith and Order Commission to work with the Methodist Church's Faith and Order Committee on drafting texts for the 'formal declaration', the inaugural service or services and the service of welcome referred to in the recommendations in the final paragraph of the report on further work, and for the guidelines for the practice of presbyters/priests from one church being received to serve in the other referred to in paragraph 142, with full draft texts being made available to the Synod'; and also requested 'the House of Bishops to report during the next quinquennium on the progress made on the work described in the previous paragraph, together with proposals for implementation.'[1] Whether a momentum was lost once again or the required further work will pave a solid and clear way towards full organic union, we have to wait and see.

Some Methodists, conscious of the unique history, principles and calling of their Church, have already expressed their misgivings about the proposed unity scheme. They do not have any problem in accepting 'bishop' in the biblical sense (overseer), but realise that over the centuries the term has acquired a heavy baggage with political overtones and cultural overbearing such as the pompous vestments. From the Anglican side the overall attitude is the continuation with little adjustment of 'come back and join us'.

The United Reformed Church (URC) resulted in 1972 from the union of the Presbyterian Church of England and the Congregational Church in England and Wales. But a considerable block of Congregationalists remain independent in three groups.[2] The URC was further united with the Reformed Association of the Churches of Christ in 1981 and the Congregational Union of Scotland. In 1982, the United Reformed Church voted in favour of a covenant with the Church of England, the Methodist Church and the Moravian Church, which would have meant remodelling its moderators as bishops and incorporating its ministry into the apostolic succession. However, the Church of England rejected the covenant. The Church of England's attitude in all the above unions, both achieved and proposed, is typical, and the repeated words in their documents such as affirmation

---

[1] bit.ly/MaMiC-gui; '*Conference Business Digest, Methodist Conference, 2018*'; https://www.churchofengland.org/more/media-centre/news/synod-backs-further-steps-towards-communion-methodist-church

[2] 1. The Congregational Federation; 2. The Evangelical Fellowship of Congregational Churches; 3. Fellowship of Independent Evangelical Churches.

of unity, 'not now but later', 'further journey towards organic union' and 'when the time comes' expose its integrity deficit and indifference in the face of urgent challenges for mission in unity. In theological terms its commitment persistently remains as Word but is unwilling to become flesh, to come down to be a servant, the tangible expression of Christ's incarnational mindset (Jn. 1:1-5; Phil. 2:1-5).

It may not be totally untrue to say that Anglicanism at least in England will crumble if detached from the monarchy and privileges accorded by the State. Its monarchic origins, more than haphazard connection with Catholicism and complex traditions make a unique structure and identity. It is a religion of its own kind with both noble and sacerdotal but divisive aspects inbuilt like any other religion, but colonizing is its inherent trait which once found expression in commercial and political colonization. It is hardly far-fetched to suggest that the Anglican Church is trying to absorb the Church of South India which is an entirely new constitution and a unique independent reality. Only those in the CSI who are ignorant of its history, principles agreed and promises made at its beginning, who are not confident to interpret the Bible contextually as encouraged in the constitution and those who have least priority for theological reflection and spiritual maturity, can fall a prey to a devouring force with political and economic power.

Reasserting Identities: The Lambeth Conference 1998 saw an explosion over the hotly debated issue of homosexuality to a breaking point. It led to the emergence of the 'Anglican Realignment Movement' and some provinces became independent of the Anglican Communion including the Episcopal Church of USA. Subsequently, there were attempts to assert the Anglican identity and clarify the core issues. We have already quoted from Paul Avis' book *The Anglican Understanding of the Church* (2000). He starts with stating the context as the market place of religions and Christian denominations and as the purpose of his book he notes: 'While the relationship between the churches is generally excellent and practical cooperation is strong, the existence of a plurality of faiths has the effect of relativizing the claims of each.' 'Secularization and pluralization mean that as English Anglicans we can no longer take our church for granted. We know that our message will not be heard, our ministry will not be received, our values will not survive, unless we grasp the challenge of mission with both hands. To do that we need, among other things, an understanding of our message, our ministry, our values. The competitive situation in which ... now we find ourselves means that we cannot assume that people either inside or outside the church know what we stand for'. (ix). There may be those who will not accept his observation of positive relationship between churches. Further, he mentions in passing Anglican involvement in ecumenical partnerships and united churches including the CSI. But there is no mention of the struggle to achieve the first organic union of the CSI nor its unilateral incorporation into the AC.

Avis commends his Anglican church's distinctiveness in terms of 'homely picture of a parish church with its kindly but somewhat harassed vicar. It is, however, worth emphasizing in passing that Anglicanism, like all the many and varied forms of Christianity, is inescapably a way of salvation. Its liturgy, in the tradition of the Book of Common Prayer, is profoundly and seriously soteriological. Anglican worship arises from a heartfelt sense of human need and a thankful acceptance of the remedy provided by the grace of God. Anglicanism is one of the humanly, historically conditioned institutional forms taken by that gracious saving action of God, through the ministry of the word, sacrament and pastoral care, and our human response to it in faith and discipleship. This fact suggests that the Church is actually inextricably involved in the Anglican way of salvation and we are not far out, after all, if it is the church, rather than an individualistic image of salvation, that first springs to mind when Anglicanism is mentioned.'[1] However, for outsiders the validity of this self-understanding can be authenticated by comparing with similar claims and interpretations by theologians of other denominations.

Then he identifies three historical models of Anglicanism: the nation as church model, the episcopal succession model and the communion through baptism model. At the same time, he claims that Anglican identity and basic Christian identity is almost the same. 'Our fundamental Christian identity must be one that shares with our fellow baptized Christians throughout the world and the history of the Church. It would indeed be retrograde if, as Anglicans becoming more conscious of our historical distinctiveness and of the resources of our heritage, we were to attempt to define ourselves in a way that distanced us from Christians of other communions. It is solely on the basis of our solidarity with all Christ's people in his universal body that we can then be free to pursue our distinctive Anglican way. Our fundamental identity is that given in Christ; confessional identities are secondary and require continual conversion to Christ and the gospel.'[2] Then what is the problem of joining with other churches with some practical understanding?

Yet he points out remarkable features to define Anglican identity and distinctiveness. For example, the central feature is its approach to questions of authority which is threefold: 'scripture, reason and tradition; combination of episcopal pastoral leadership and oversight with conciliar, synodical church government in which laity and clergy are not merely consulted but have constitutional roles; concentration on essentials, on central abiding truths, on fundamentals, that coexists with much latitude in their interpretation; tolerance and comprehensiveness of a range of internal traditions – catholic, evangelical and central – each touched by a spectrum of stances from conservative to radical;

---

[1] Ibid., 9f.

[2] Ibid., 25.

and the weight that is placed on the corporate celebration of the liturgy and the lightness of touch with which juridical sanctions are invoked.'[1]

Appealing to the historical continuities in the life, worship and ministry of the Church and to the authority of the undivided Church of the early centuries including the pre-Augustine presence of Celtic Christianity which was represented in Arles Council 314, he clarifies that 'the principles of the Reformation, grounded in a return to scripture and a recovery of the liberating gospel of justification by faith, consequences of these for the reformation of the church – Anglicans being apologetic to Reformation.' 'They cannot help feeling rather sheepish about the political manipulation, the dubious motives of Henry VIII, the wholesale dissolution of the monasteries, the compliance of Cranmer, the iconoclasm, the inadequate theology of the 1552 Prayer Book, followed by the astute compromise of the Elizabethan settlement. The apparent lack of principle is disturbing. Of course there is much to be ashamed of in what took place then. It must have seemed to many of the faithful that Christianity itself was being obliterated. But we need equally to remember that there is much to embarrass Christians of other traditions in their particular histories. It must be even more difficult for a devout Roman Catholic to come to terms with the corruption, ruthlessness and immorality of the pre-Reformation papacy because of the exalted claims that concurrently were being made for the "Vicar of Christ".'[2]

Avis lists the distinctive sources of Anglican ecclesiology: Bible, tradition, the historical formularies (39 Articles, the Book of Common Prayer, the Ordinal, the Canons, the Lambeth Quadrilateral, other notable statements of the various Lambeth Conferences and the classical Anglican theologians). Anglicans affirm the credal formula about the church as holy, catholic and apostolic and adds the famous title 'Church of Christ'. This calls for an understanding of and attitude to other Churches. The author presents a positive Anglican voice: 'We are the Church. You also are the Church. But none of us is the Church as it should be.' This acknowledgement of the incompleteness of one's own church and recognition of the ecclesial reality of other churches generates the commitment to the quest for Christian unity. Anglicans have been in the forefront of leadership of the ecumenical movement. Here again we glimpse something of the distinctive ethos of Anglican ecclesiology. Anglicans believe that the Church on earth is united with the Church in heaven, in the communion of saints (*sanctorum communion*). They speak of 'the Church Militant here on earth' and the Church triumphant in heaven. They worship God together with 'Angels and Archangels, and with all the company of heaven'.[3] But most uncompromising is the historical episcopate in apostolic succession. Referring to few well-known writers he points out that 'ordination in the historical episcopal succession enhances and contributes to

---

[1] Ibid., 25f

[2] Ibid., 37.

[3] Ibid., 62.

the catholicity of the Church'; 'episcopacy is constitutive with sacraments and proclamation of the word of God…And the episcopal ministry in due succession and apostolic commission is the immemorial tradition of the catholic church… and therefore is also a providential instrument of the true marks of the church a visible society in history.'[1]

On the whole, Paul Avis' introduction to the Anglican understanding of the Church is commendable for historical facts, beliefs and interpretations. What is lacking, however, is that while mentioning other churches there is no effort to present their position with empathy and theological openness. As we noted earlier, bishop E.J. Palmer affirmed that God has used the non-episcopal churches in mission. The CSI accepted historical episcopacy locally adopted without realising that the adoption would not be accepted as existential but connecting with a link to Canterbury though the Catholics will argue that it was broken. It is repeatedly noted by well-informed persons of non-episcopal churches that they have no problem in accepting the role of 'overseer' (*episkopas*) as directed by the New Testament but not 'bishop' as it has been historically tainted. If primacy to the scripture is truly given, the idea of corporate priesthood and servanthood of leadership cannot be compromised and individual leaders are 'ordained' to keep the order and to coordinate gifts and graces. One may wish that Anglicans will display their tolerance, catholicity etc when they discuss with non-episcopal churches the term and connotations of 'bishop' and go for alternative terms. The CSI's attempt in this regard we will point out in the next chapter. Finally, he has not explained the implications of the legacy of 'political manipulation, the dubious motives of Henry VIII' in the glamorous and expensive establishment. There are many Christians who find it difficult to sing the English national anthem (included in many hymn books) which extols the glory, victory and health of a single person, the monarch.

When Rowan Williams was enthroned as Archbishop of Canterbury in 2002 there was optimism in the air about movement forward in the 'faith journey or pilgrimage towards organic union'. In 2003 he signed the *Anglican Methodist Covenant*. But in 2004 his booklet *Anglican Identities* appeared. The booklet starts with 'The question of what if anything holds together the Anglican Communion has recently become a painfully immediate one.' The highly respected theologian has taken the word 'Anglican' 'as referring to the sort of Reformed Christian thinking that was done by those in Britain at first, then far more widely, who were content to settle with a church order grounded in the ministry of bishops, priests and deacons, and with the early Christian formulations of doctrine about God and Jesus Christ – the Nicene Creed and the Definition of Chalcedon. It is certainly *Reformed* thinking, and we should not let the deep and pervasive echoes of the Middle Ages mislead us: it assumes the governing authority of the Bible, made available in the vernacular, and repudiates the necessity of a central

---

[1] Ibid., 69.

executive authority.'[1] There are comprehensive definitions such as the most recent one, highlighting the variety of the understanding of faith and practices, the slippery nature of the word 'Anglicanism' meaning different things to different people, the confusing things within, foundational reference to King Henry VIII's Act of Supremacy (1534) that gave the English Church its independence from Rome and the geographical reference (*Angle* = like Anglo-Saxon) and the historic formularies (the 39 Articles of Religion, the *Book of Common Prayer* and the Ordinal).[2] Compared to this, William's definition is limited and misleading, to say the least. A researcher may come to surprising conclusions after doing an analytical study of the assumptions of his booklet relating to Anglican structures and practices, not only in having the monarch as the 'defender of faith' but also supporting the British Empire. In the last chapter we argued the futility of doctrines, the limitation of the classic creeds and the lip service accorded to the primacy of the Bible.

Here we briefly point out the lack of awareness of 'the credible representatives of Anglicanism over the centuries' (seven thinkers in detail and four in brief) who and whose ideas could be claimed by other denominations as well. William Tyndale (c1494-1536), who pioneered translating the Bible in English amidst fierce opposition and who died in a burning fire praying 'Lord, open the King of England's eyes' was almost the contemporary of Henry VIII (1491-1547), the founder of the Church of England, and it is reasonable that the Reformed Churches claim Tyndale to be a great forerunner of Reformation. The classical Anglican philosopher Richard Hooker (1554-1600) is introduced in detail. Hooker's exposition of the doctrines of God, Holy Spirit, grace, sacraments, fallibility etc can be shared to a great extent by any perceptive Christian in general but with an awareness of his particular political, geographical and ecclesiastical context. In Paul Avis' view Hooker was 'a class of his own here as the prime architect of Anglican ecclesiology and the most effective defender of the Elizabethan settlement of religion which established the principle of comprehension or toleration that is intrinsic to Anglicanism'.[3] Hooker's certain sermons had a bearing on the rhetoric and spiritual poems of George Herbert (1593-1633) which have inspirational insights for all Christians of all generations. The contribution of B.F. Westcott (1825-1901) to textual criticism of the Bible which led to new translations has been appreciated and appropriated by students of the Bible beyond denominational boundaries. However, the theology of the church and significance of the historical episcopacy by Michael Ramsey (1904-1988) helped Anglicans to have a grip of their distinctiveness as we have already noted. J.A.T. Robinson's (1919-1983) ground breaking book *Honest to God* is noted to have set a decisive moment in the history of the theology of Methodism as well. Robinson was a Johannine scholar

---

[1] R. William, *Anglican Identities*, London: Darton. Longman & Todd, 2004, 2.

[2] See Marcus Throup, *All Tings Anglican*, 16.

[3] Avis, op.cit., 59.

to be paralleled by Methodist contribution to the study of the fourth Gospel. The Reformed Churches may well go with the reflections of these studies. And it is hard to believe that those who researched and wrote on the fourth Gospel were writing with the acute awareness as Anglicans, Methodists and Reformed but free thinkers leaving their thinking for all Christians. My final note is that Rowan Williams has deeply studied Orthodox (particularly Russian) theologies, and his lectures have fascinated a young generation of theologians. Therefore, he may have written on Anglican identities under certain compulsion or pressure as he was already aware of the similar reasserting of identities in other denominations as well. The question is: while we are in the journey towards organic union, can we claim that theologians, hymn writers, etc., were boosting the identity of a denomination? Conspicuously, the identities asserted are secondary, and no one has dared to point out the primary identity of Christians as 'the children of God and disciples of Jesus'.

Mission and Unity in Britain: The Significance of South India

Soon we will consult Hollis's passionate book *The Significance of South India.*[1] In the meantime, let me make a few observations. I don't want to repeat again and again that the prime motive of organic union in South India was to be effective in evangelistic mission on the basis of Jesus' prayer 'that they may be one as we are one that the world may believe' (Jn. 17:21). There is no doubt that British Churches have made a great contribution to world mission and the establishment of churches. However, recent experiences have raised new questions. If the majority of Christians in Britain were genuinely committed to mission here and everywhere and sacrificially gave financial support, why then when those 'foreigners' (our targets of mission) came to this country were not welcomed but shown an indifferent or hostile face? Why did many choose to move to new residences instead making use of a great opportunity to share the gospel with their strange neighbours of other religions? Is there an element of racism, and if so, can it be challenged by simple morals and preaching the gospel of 'repentance for forgiveness'? If one establishes a thesis that the people of the missionary period were committed to mission, what was its impact on the successive generations? Was the primary motivation not sharing the gospel but civilizing the world by identifying the gospel with British culture?

Perhaps outsiders are able to perceive the church-culture-mission situation in Britain more clearly. After being a mission partner in South India including being bishop in two dioceses of the CSI, Lesslie Newbigin returned to the UK in 1974. Seeing the decadence and degradation of the culture of his country he used such a strong word 'pagan' and started a movement called 'Gospel and Culture'. Particularly he was concerned about growing juvenile mental health problems. He

[1] M. Hollis, *The Significance of South India: Ecumenical Studies in History*, London: Lutterworth, 1966.

compared the hope that the young people have in the slums of Chennai (Madras) and the hopelessness here. Of course, since Newbigin's death the situation has become worse. Today we hear reports of studies that children of broken families are vulnerable to hopelessness and in turn mental illness. Further, increasing crime, overcrowded prisons with smuggling of drugs, etc., and deteriorating discipline of school children which is so stressful for the teachers are alarming. Increasing number of people are taking their own lives, including celebrities. It seems that the characteristic British attitude of uncritical positivity is not visibly challenged.

Now we have a few mission partners from the world church in Britain, but their experience and expertise are not adequately used for getting fresh insights from the Bible and initiating new experiments. Average bible knowledge in this 'Christian country' is dismal compared to that among members of the CSI where there is a passion for knowing the Bible and discussing passages. Most Christians seem to think that being relatively affluent and doing some trickling charity within and without is a substitute for emphasising a new orientation in life, and such a position makes them complacent and self-righteous. What we hear most from the pulpits is a kind of love-lullaby (God loves, embraces, forgives, accepts, etc.) and grace is once again made cheap! At the same time there is no dearth of mission thinking and experiment among the churches in Britain. But the present trend is predominantly charity, giving money, food, etc., but not solidarity in which sustained companionship and conversation take place that may help people regain their dignity and independence. The approach in CSI is different, and although charity work is regarded as a bait in the hook, there is emphasis in new life. The culture of community provides the opportunity to share faith. The membership of the CSI has grown about four-fold since its formation in 1947. But there are factors in the background such as the growth of the population and a charismatic/fundamentalist manipulative approach in 'evangelism' that may benefit CSI congregations. It is important to ask if all conversions are genuine, if they lead to a new quality of life with integrity and sharing, and if a humble, servant-styled leadership is evident.

By an ever-complicating muddle of ecumenical relations, do the churches in Britain have the humility to look at the CSI as a model which may be modified or work out a similar organizational unity? The negotiators in South India did express such a hope. After all, their missionaries in South India achieved the first organic union with the cooperation of the Indian leaders. Have they moved considerably further from their complacency which was pointed out by Azariah as early as 1927? It is pitiable that the experience and expertise of Michael Hollis (theological educator, bishop and the first Moderator of the CSI) was not recognised by his Church of England, and he was placed as a parish priest in an obscure place. The elderly parishioners of that church still tell us how passionate he was about the CSI which he shared not only in meetings but also in conversations. When he reflected from the viewpoint of the CSI his own country's true condition became strikingly clear. Consequently, he wrote the thought-provoking book *The Significance of South India* (1966). He sums up his feelings about the CSI. 'First, there is the release from the bondage of the past. It is not that history ceases to matter, but that it ceases to dominate.'[1] He points out the Anglican obsessiveness with the historic episcopacy which became the criterion for entering into communion with churches like the CSI as the report for the Lambeth Conference 1948 noted. The CSI movement was open to the lead of the Holy Spirit for new ways of understanding episcopacy. Hollis states:

> My comment after experience of CSI is two-fold. First, no one knows the power of the Holy Spirit to guide into deeper understanding until he has taken part in really serious seeking of God's way to unity built upon a certainty that unity is what God wants. The west has become so accustomed to our present denominations, which is beyond any question not what our Lord prays for, that it forgets who prayed that those who believe on Him may be one as He and the Father one, that the world may believe that the Father has sent him ...

> Secondly, if preserving the Church of England, or the Anglican Communion, is to be taken in practice the final aim, when it may be that it has in its present form done what it can do and is even right to disappear, then it has ceased to be an instrument in God's hands and become an idol. No denomination has final validity.[2]

He reasoned that 'Yet if disunity is really contrary to the known will of God and a serious hindrance to His purpose of reconciliation for the world, it ought to call out our full energies with compelling urgency, so that the search for God's way to the kind of unity for which Christ prayed takes a major place in our prayers, our thinking and planning and in all use of our resources in personal and fund.'[3]

There is in much of western Christianity a strange absence of any sense of urgency. It is too easily assumed that, if union comes, it will come so slowly that few if any alive today will see it. The policies of all the major denominations unconsciously presuppose that they have a congregation or more of separate existence to plan for it. They build up institutions, they debate problems, in an isolation which makes no sense if disunity is to be overcome ... Yet, if disunity is really contrary to the known will of God and a serious hindrance to this purpose of reconciliation for the world, it ought to call out our full energies, so that the search for God's way to the kind of unity for which Christ prayed takes a major

---

[1] Hollis, *The Significance*, 8.

[2] Ibid., 8f.

[3] Ibid., 9.

place in our prayers, our thinking and planning and in all use of our resources in personnel and funds.[1]

The word unity in today's political and ecclesial parlance is most often used in sermonic and protocol forms. If not simply a face saving gesture, one body may come forward to make some minor adjustments. Hollis insists that 'Unity is not a minor adjustment which leaves the foundation unshaken. It permeates all thinking and living. The denominationalist will inevitably find the Christian who has experienced even a partial unity unreliable. Where disunity still reigns, so much of the time, energy and material resources of any denominations are taken up with keeping the denominational machine running. There are a vast number of vested interests which make any radical change difficult, however devoted and admirable the individuals concerned may be.'[2] If one church continues to be stubborn, claiming that its denomination is the repository of all truth and not willing to dare a fundamental change, it is in its own right. But it must respect the united churches and organic unions without meddling with their identity and integrity.

If mission is the common focus of all Christians, all practical difficulties of managing and coordinating in the setting of a united church become easy. For Hollis there was no difference in God's working as he had worked as bishop of the united church where out of 93 presbyters barely one third had been episcopally ordained. He realised that somehow the quest for close ecumenical relationship was not inherent in the British psyche. To show the lack of knowledge of ecumenical relations, he pointed out, there was no centre or library in UK for unity and church union as in the Union Seminary, New York.

The very fact of the formation of the CSI, for Hollis, was significant for all Christians in all places. As a renowned church historian, he claimed:

> The most important event in church history since Pentecost. Exaggeration, sentimentality, near-blasphemy, illumination – so different people will judge this remark. What matters now is that it could have been made.[3]

Hollis recalled the jeering voices which were more Anglican than others: 'Some believed that it was a house built in such defiance of all sound ecclesiastical principles that it would inevitably fall to pieces. There were even those who asserted that they prayed for its collapse. If so, that prayer shows no sign of being answered.'[4] He also observed: 'It took Anglicans, first in India, and then at the Lambeth Conference of 1930 a considerable time to realise that the Church of

---

[1] Ibid.
[2] Ibid., 79.
[3] Ibid., 15.
[4] Ibid., 16.

South India would not, and could not, be a part of the Anglican Communion. Even in England today there is far too much talk on both sides of Methodists "returning" to the Church of England. One of the greatest contributions which Bishop Palmer made, both to South India and the whole movement for Christian unity, was his insistence that dying to live is as true of the separate denominations as it is of the individual Christian.'[1] Anglicans had no problem in affirming enthusiastically the importance of unity, but they insisted that it should be in their own terms. Though some of their own comrades out in India were active participants they were not open to learn and change. For example, it is observed that 'Had more Anglo-Catholics imbibed the lessons he (Palmer) strove to teach, unity with at least the Methodists and Presbyterians might have come in the 1950s or 60's instead of being stymied partly by Anglo-Catholic intransigence, and partly by Free Church suspicions which, in their turn, owed something to their unsympathetic perceptions of Anglo-Catholicism.'

Gospel of Unity from the Margins

Though late, there is an important opportunity to re-view the significance of the CSI with commitment and openness. The ecclesiastically proud and even snobbish should learn a fundamental lesson that in the whole of the Bible God has chosen the low in order to challenge the high. the gospel in its power has always come from the margins. For example, God tells the Hebrew community that he had chosen and set his affection on them to be a model community, not because they were numerically stronger than others, but smaller (Deut. 7:7). It was an anonymous slave girl who guided her master Naaman, an army captain of Aram, for healing from leprosy (2 Kgs. 5:2-4). Jesus chose a little flock of ordinary fisher folk and sent them to be workers to be in solidarity with the victim community on whose behalf they had the sole right to forgive or not forgive the culprits (Lk. 12:32; Jn. 20:22). When Jerusalem or Mount Zion was expected to be the centre of receiving God's word (Is. 2:3 Mic. 4:2), Jesus' birth was connected with the forgotten little village of Bethlehem (Mic. 5:2; Lk. 2:4) and his settlement with the remote village Nazareth of Galilee from where, it was thought, no good could come (Jn. 1:46). According to Matthew, the Great Commission was given on an unknown mountain in Galilee (Mt. 28:16). Paul tells the Corinthians that many of them were not wise by human standards, influential or of noble birth (1 Cor. 1: 26). 'But God chose the foolish things of the world to shame the wise; God chose the weak things of the world to shame the strong' (1:27). All such instances are based on the one who was crucified, risen and continued to suffer, whose most dramatic image is a Lion-turned-Lamb standing at the centre of the universe, with perfect authority and presence yet having with blood marks, a Lamb slain from the creation of the world' (Rev. 5:5; 13:8). If it is reasonable to connect this with

---

[1] Ibid., 21.

the achievement of organic union for the sake of mission in India, it has a lesson for the churches in Britain, including the Church of England.

Absorbing the Small: The Parallel in India

If the leaders and members of the CSI were aware of the history and significance of their identity, they could be both a challenge and even judgement for denominations who are stubborn in being strongly glued to familiarity and a particular memory of history. They could not even think about the event of the prophetic movements neutralised and absorbed by the dominant tradition in India. Instead of looking to the model of the CSI, after a period of rejection, and non-recognition, half-recognition, etc., judging a thriving and vibrant united Church as suffering from isolation, in a chequered process the Anglican Communion invited the bishops of the CSI, first as guests and observers, and later declared it unilaterally a Province of the Anglican Communion. If this is a kind of absorption it is worth mentioning a similar process in India. The Vedic-Sanskritic-Brahmanic religion, centred in elaborate rituals which were considered as generating sacred power that would sustain life in all its aspects including that of gods, and handled by a structured priests of various grades and order, corresponding to the universal order and social order of the caste system, faced a great challenge. Around the 7th century BCE there arose a movement of wandering renouncers. They challenged the Vedic beliefs by presenting alternative spiritual power within, affirming equality of all people and preaching the virtues of non-violence, truthfulness, compassion and so on. The most successful movements came to be known as Buddhism and Jainism which attracted great following. Buddhism and Jainism exerted great influence on certain rulers of the Maurian dynasty, the most popular of which was Ashoka (304-232 BCE). He was a covert to Buddhism, denounced war, remained probably a lay Buddhist and promoted the faith and propagated the teachings through edicts. Consequently, the Vedic religion experienced a period of decline. At the same time simplified forms of rituals were maintained, and rituals were sneaked into the Buddhist and Jain movements through converts from Brahmanism which in turn incorporated certain virtues and waiting for a chance to revive.

But in 185 BCE a Brahmanic dynasty came to power which persecuted Buddhists and Jains and drove out the former out of the country. There was a revival of the Vedic-Sanskritic-Brahmanic religion: epics celebrated victory and revival, ritual manuals were produced, law codes were written. Most of the good values of the renouncers were absorbed but without affecting the core of ritual power, priestly power and royal power. When Brahmanic Hinduism expanded, absorption and assimilation continued. Independent traditions and their popular deities (e.g. Krishna) were assimilated and *avatara* (descent of the divine in a particular form) and wedding (god-goddess) were instruments of absorption, not without tension in some cases.[1] Even today under the influence of political Hinduism, small and popular cults are incorporated into Brahmanic Hinduism with conspiracy and strategy.[2] Sometimes such a process creates tensions. For instance, in a village called Swamithoppu, near Cape Comorin on the southern tip of India, a cult in the 19th century (Ayya Vazhi) developed with a combination of Christian-Hindu ideas and practices. In the Christian mission context it represented 'a counter-liberation and cult formation.'[3] It was anti-brahmanic, casteless, prophetic, simple, emphasising human dignity and self-respect. In recent years brahmanic champions came in, built huge towers and established elaborate rituals performed by brahmin priests. The leaders of the cult and local community awoke late and there has been agitation, and the matter is in the court signalling a prolonged battle.

My intention here is not to make a comparison between the CSI-Anglican relationship and all devouring Brahmanic-Ayya Vazhi relationship. However, it may shed light to understand the religious phenomena of powerful, history-bound, ritual-priest-oriented traditions not being able to appreciate new movement or new reality but trying to absorb, thus strengthening its own position and neutralizing the new force. In the case of the Anglican Communion it has been a long-held anomaly, first to reject the CSI and then to absorb it without consulting the members of this historic independent Church and without consulting the other constituents of the CSI with whom they do not have full communion. It is a pity that the CSI leaders have not been aware of this or, if aware, did not act promptly to set it right. This is not to say that there have been no changes in the CofE in key issues such as woman priests, woman bishops and the approval of gay relationships. If such a change does not happen in moving to organic union one may guess that even if the whole world church becomes one, the Anglican Communion will remain separate, and even if the rest of the AC joins the world church, the Church of England will remain in isolation probably as long as monarchy lives and state connection and support continues. At the same time they will continue to appear to be honourable with the slogans of 'embrace', 'catholic spirit' and 'spirit of hospitality'. Distorting the unique identity of the most challenging first organic unity is a stark act of contradiction. Of course my Anglican friends are right in asking why the leaders of the CSI cooperated.

---

[1] For details, see I. Selvanayagam, *Vedic Sacrifice: Challenge and Response*, Delhi: Manohar, 1996.

[2] B. Kolappan, 'Bringing folk deities into Vedic fold: Structure and rituals of temples for Sudalaimadan, Mutharamman in Vedic tradition', *The Hindu*, 14 July 2015.

[3] I. Selvanayagam, 'Counter-Liberation and Cult-Formation: The Case of a Socio-Religious Movement in Southern India', *Black Theology: An International Journal*, 13/3, Nov., 2015, 247-257.

Towards a True Partnership

Partnership is now a popular term indicating inter-church relationship and ecumenical cooperation. Sometimes visits of leaders of different Churches are known as partnership visits. We have already pointed out the difficulty to appreciate the visits to the Church of South India of the Archbishops of Canterbury without reciprocation of inviting the Moderator of the CSI as an official guest of the Church of England and of openly recognising the Methodist and Reformed Churches who in India came to be willing to die with Anglicans for creating a new-first organic union.

The word partnership has different connotations. The most usual meaning is that two or more persons enter into a business relationship by mutually investing and sharing the assets and the liabilities. To use a western analogy, there can be a dance partner whose role is momentary. A couple, married or unmarried, can be life partners. There were partners in work such as fishing (Lk. 5:7,10). Paul commends Titus for the Corinthian church saying, 'he is my partner and fellow worker among you; as for our brothers, they are representatives of the churches and an honour to Christ' (2 Cor. 8:23). He appreciates the Philippian church's partnership in the gospel and mentions its operation of giving and receiving (Phil. 1:5; 4:15). While commending Onesimus he tells Philemon that his partnership in faith may be effective in deepening his understanding 'of every good thing they shared for the sake of Christ' (Philemon 1:5,17). John in prison introduced himself as a partner in the suffering of the persecuted Christians of Asia Minor (Rev.1:9). These ideas may help us to understand Christian partnership in terms of being bound by the gospel, for the honour of Christ, for deepening the understanding of faith, sharing of resources and solidarity in suffering.

True and genuine partnership will move away from the normal pattern of diplomacy, one-sidedness and protocol. It is based on shared discipleship and mission. Can we not engage openly with commitment and openness 'speaking the truth in love'? Empathy is the key for redeeming ourselves from ignorance and prejudice. Our landscapes, weather pattern, history, political structure, etc., are different, and if we affirm God that has created the universe with diversity, one culture or life-style cannot be the norm. At the same time, we need to cherish the freedom to evaluate any culture with the scale of the core gospel values: God in solidarity with the victims of all forms of oppression and seeking justice and equality, response to the loving presence around us, repentance and forgiveness, openness to the ongoing transformation of life and being joyous in hope.

In the 1990s there was a slogan propagated by the mission agencies in UK: *From Everywhere to Every*where. The thinking behind was that, wherever carried out and in whatever form, God's mission is one. There are mission bases and mission fields everywhere. Also, phrases such as holistic mission and mission in Christ's way represented the distilled wisdom of mission thinkers and practitioners. However, it has not been implemented to any considerable extent. Trickling charity out of relative affluence (UK) and sending missionaries to overseas (in limited number) continue to be popular. Partnership in mission needs to be grounded in partnership in Christ and in the gospel. We have the primary biblical insight of loving God with all our heart, mind, soul and strength (passion, intellect, spiritual force and liberating action), and they may multiply with changing combinations in particular contexts. Basically, in a partnership the participants maintain solidarity in mission, understand one another's specific situation, learn and enrich one another, share resources as per the need and support one another in their struggle. Mutual placements would greatly help to do these with understanding and integrity. In sum, creative partnership goes beyond the sterile slogans of unity, protocol speeches and honourable receptions.

Chapter 8

Towards an Ever-Reforming
Evangelistic Organic Union

Some Shattering Challenges

At the beginning, in the life of the new church of organic unity there was anxiety about the post-missionary leadership, administration and new initiatives in theological education and church renewal. The Church of South India Trust Association that owns all CSI (non-Anglican) property became a heavy burden to manage expediently. While the new independent India was in a stage of consolidation of power, construction of confidence and integration of the communities of caste and ideologies and reduction of poverty, churches like the CSI had a great opportunity to make a contribution. But the CSI became less and less credible for the following reasons.

First, there was always a possibility for denominational obsession to continue. Particularly, Anglican influence on sacerdotal tendencies was visible. The process of Anglicanization, the unilateral declaration in 1988 of the CSI as a province of the Anglican Communion and since then the protocol visits of the Archbishops of the Canterbury with titles such as chief shepherd and world spiritual leader (accorded by unknown Indians) distorted the unique identity of CSI as the first organic union with selfhood and independence. The Anglican Communion's attempts to resurrect the (decomposed) body of former Anglicans while the Methodist and Reformed Churches respected the integrity and independence of the CSI was confusing the minds of people. Those who were supposed to be the teachers and guardians of the people and their faith were not confident about the story of their church. Rather they considered attendance in Lambeth Conference and other bodies as a great privilege. Their return from England created euphoria as evident in photographs, etc., in their magazines.

Second, biblical ideas such as crucified power and servant-style leadership were slogans without substance. Elections, including bishop elections, are fought in a fierce and aggressive manner with party formations and caste solidarities. Instead of being undergirded by a theological vision and a strong sense of integrity, bishops have allowed themselves to be co-opted into party politics and authoritarian leadership with an eye on personal gains and vested interests.[1] Piety is often used to cover up political conflicts. Further, it is observed that those who represent churches and councils have a long way to go to gain spiritual maturity and civility and participate in discussions with wisdom and selflessness. Once one becomes a bishop, s/he regards himself as an authority on the bible, theology, history, etc., and many have gone to the extent of having some sort of 'Dr.' in their title. That means they have no respect for the earned doctorates of specialists, who mainly teach in seminaries and who are hardly consulted by the bishops and other leaders placed in high ranks. In actual fact, if they were humble to learn the full history of the CSI they would not have fallen into the trap of the Anglican Communion. Hence, the blind were led by the blind.

Third, the western mission model of running institutions for health, education and training has almost lost its original ethos. Instead of refocusing on the emerging needs (e.g. from general hospital to institute of mental health, HIV Hospice, model school, etc.) some dioceses compete with private institutions, forgetting their commitment to the poor and victims of society. Preaching, planning and church planting is the pattern. Azariah's vision for mission for Indians, by Indians and using Indian resources and methods has never been taken seriously. A consultation held in 1981 between representatives of overseas mission boards and CSI leaders on 'The Priorities of Mission' did not reflect the current ecumenical thinking. Rather, the majority of presentations focused on the needs (vans, tracts, etc.) having an eye on overseas support. While the number of 'missionaries' sponsored by churches and individuals has been increasing, local mission or living outreach is dismal. With the support of the Council on World Mission, the CSI introduced a novel model called 'Vision for Equipping the Local Congregation for Mission' (VELCOM) in the mid-1980s. Regular bible study, prayer, agape and engagement in local issues risking the social (caste) and familial solidarity were supposed to be features. A presbyter was appointed as coordinator in each diocese. But it seems to have died long ago without any review, study or report. With pressure from some quarters, the CSI Centre for Interfaith Dialogue was opened in the CSI Centre in Chennai. Obviously, the major interest was getting the names of the then Moderator and Deputy Moderator etched in the inaugural plaque. This is rather typical. (Just like the 'Constantine Trap' here one finds the 'Babel Trap'.) But there has been no programme!

---

[1] For a short article that reflects heart-searching observation of an enlightened bishop, see, Samuel Amirtham, 'Reflections on Episcopacy in CSI', *Pilgrim: No. 16, March 2000, 2-5.*

Fourth, the multi-headed monster of corruption at different levels seems to have devoured the greater part of the CSI. In a sense it is understandable for, on the whole, Indian society is marred by corruption. A recent international study has revealed that India stands among the highest in corruption and bribery.[1] Two in three persons give bribes. It can happen directly or indirectly, in cash and kind with imperceptible reciprocal influence. If the church in India is not an exception to the national trend one will understand. But the church must confess that it has failed to be counter-cultural, swimming like a fish against the current (or it proves dead as noted by Sadhu Sundar Singh), and this has severely damaged its witness. From the beginning, corruption was noted in the CSI. However, as allegations and counter allegations confuse outsiders, we do not know the magnitude and reality. However, what a recent Tribunal National Law Tribunal Chennai has ordered is shocking.[2]

Fifth, conservatism persists in most churches. Regarding (particularly Anglican) missionaries as demi-gods their legacy in the area of church building with sky-soaring spires, liturgy and music is kept intact with a sense of pride. What is reflected is a 'colonised psyche.'[3] Even if the translation of the Bible in use is outdated and a new translation is available there is no acceptance, though everyone knows that to have pace with linguistic renaissance is indispensable for communicating the Christian message. This is true of the liturgy as well. A former bishop in an ex-Anglican diocese forced a rule that he would not visit a congregation which did not use the *CSI Book of Common Worship*. I am painfully aware that the largest and most educated cathedral churches still use the SIUC liturgy without change of even an iota. Liturgical renewal has been a slogan and the bishops and presbyters do not feel competent to revise and provide options. But at the same time there is openness to the fundamentalist revival meetings, and fundamentalist groups manage to sing with loud music at the beginning of the worship. It is an irony that the Anglican Communion, particularly the CofE, is not able to make a dent in the CSI, their province, with their experience of liturgical revisions and renewals.

---

[1] Bribery and corruption continue to pose a significant challenge in India. The 2012 Transparency International Corruption Perceptions and Bribe Payers Indices rank India 94 (out of 176) and 19 (out of 28), respectively, indicating the severity of the issue. http://www.ey.com/in/en/services/assurance/fraud-investigation---dispute-services/bribery-and-corruption-ground-reality-in-india; accessed on 2 June 2017.

[2] According to the order of 29 September 2016 concerning misappropriation of the several lakhs crores worth of properties of all types with the CSITA, the Tribunal pointed out 27 irregularities and 43 criminal cases, and recommended action against the company and its office bearers through the Serious Fraud Investigation Office. It also dismissed the existing office bearers and members and appointed a retired High Court judge to administer the CSITA with the help of new members of his own choice while further investigations and hearings are going on. A formal Moderator was in prison.

[3] See, I. Selvanayagam, 'Colonized Psyche', *People's Reporter*, 28/18, 25 Sept. - 10 Oct. 2015, 3, 6.

Sixth, fundamentalism has damaged the Christian witness. Around the time of the American 'murderous messiah' Jim Jones,[1] some popular and fundamentalist preachers were flourishing in South India. One can see the pattern of Jones in preaching with emotional manipulation, a particular dress code, hair-style and style of holding the Bible, running magazines, having a catchy name for their ministry and broadcasts, buying radio and TV time. They select favoured verses and interpret them with unreasonable twists. 'Blessing' is their selling phrase which means wealth, health, progeny, assurance of forgiveness and promise of heaven. Those frustrated with them are judged to have no faith. Some amass wealth and start institutions for additional wealth. A few have managed to settle in the West while operating their ministry through agents. Bishops and presbyters use them for revival meetings in order to satisfy the pious people, but it is often alleged that it is to cover up their political sewage. Their influence is everywhere including on the newly emerging independent churches with less glamorous preachers or pastors. A kind of superficial liveliness in the main line churches is evident. 'Come, Give and Protect' is the repeated dominant content of the prayers. Prominent in the popular Christianity is a Jesus cult which made the Hindu members see Jesus as the personal and communal deity of Christians as they have such deities of their own. But they say the Christians are aggressive and triumphalist when they claim their Jesus to be the most powerful deity. Similarly, many identify Christians' pneumonism (Spirit-oneness) with the ecstatic outburst of their popular cults. The unique Christian vision of a Trinitarian God who embodies unity and diversity in dynamic balance by the bond of love has been forgotten.

Seventh, although theological education was given utmost importance in the missionary era, later its impact dwindled. Seminaries that tried to promote an integrated spirituality of passion, reflection and action appeared to be a challenge to conservative churches and fundamentalist groups. There are signs of fundamentalist views and approaches affecting the theological institutions as well. Theological education & ministerial training are regarded as the professional qualification of ministry. Paper degrees are regarded as more important than the degrees of spiritual maturity, intellectual clarity and credible mission. Many church leaders openly say to their candidates, 'Return with your original faith, and bundle up and leave all you have learned from four years in the seminary campus.' But at the same time, apart from paper degrees, there are easy pursuits of honorary titles such as Dr.[2] If these matters are pointed out, theologians face reprisal, ridicule and pressure. Consequently, the most creative institutions suffer from financial constraints.

---

[1] Jim Jones of USA, a popular preacher and self-proclaimed Messiah, became a cult leader promising utopia. On 18 Nov. 1978 in Guyana he led to the mass suicide of 900 of his followers including 276 children.

[2] See, I. Selvanayagam, 'Theological Education and Regeneration'.

Commissions, Cautions and Recommendations

As we mentioned earlier, Marcus Ward, a Methodist missionary, theologian and educator, who emphasised the formation of the CSI as dying to denominations and rising to a new reality of organic union, observed closely the development of the CSI from an early phase. His book *The Pilgrim Church*[1] presents the exciting development of the honeymoon period of the first five years. He acknowledges the Indian interest and insistence on the consummation of the CSI union as it appeared to fold up at many points. At the same time, he points out the need for the CSI to develop as an indigenous church and for vigilance against the evils of corruption and litigation. He observes the immaturity of Indian leaders:

> In committees and councils where both nationals and non-nationals are present, it is becoming increasingly difficult to get nationals elected to responsible positions. Very often the missionary is better qualified and possesses better facilities to do the work in question. The Indian members are rarely united in their choice, because they are generally swayed by family, caste and party feelings. Too often the choice of a missionary seems to put an end to the rivalries that are destructive.[2]

Rajiah D. Paul, a noted Christian civil servant and past General Secretary of the Synod, published *The First Decade*.[3] While the 'pilgrim mood' is retained there are warnings in this book against certain trends that would hinder the growth and distort the image of the united church. The trends include power mongering, indecent ways of electioneering, lack of transparency and accountability and corruption. Subsequently, a Commission was set up by the Synod in 1961 with R. D. Paul as convener to produce an 'honest critique'. The Report[4] confesses that 'all is not well with our Church today' and is concerned with presenting the real situation calling 'attention to its weaknesses, defects and opportunities and to the need *for* action to make it more worthy and more effective'. Factors of both honour and shame are described in detail. While the suggestions of this report were not sufficiently acted upon by the Church, there was a period of 'lull marked by a steady drift towards open power conflicts'. R.D. Paul published another book[5] reminding the church about the need for self-assessment, penitence and moving to a renewed life. On completion of thirty years, the Synod appointed a Commission with M. Abel, the former Principal of the Madras Christian

---

[1] M. Ward, *The Pilgrim Church,* Madras: Christian Literature Society, 1952.

[2] Ibid., 24.

[3] *An Account of the Church of South India*, Madras: CLS, 1958.

[4] R.D. Paul, *Renewal and Advance – Report of the CSI Commission in Integration and Joint Action*, Madras: CSI Synod & CLS, 1963.

[5] R.D. Paul, *Ecumenism in Action: The Church of South India, An Assessment*, Madras: CLS, 1972.

College and well-known Christian educationalist, as convener, to study thirty years of the CSI's life. Known as the 'Abel Commission Report,'[1] it boldly points out the pitfalls and suggests radical steps towards a reformation. Although, the Synod received the report it was seen as too radical for patient discussion and implementation. Hence, it was shelved along with several other paper resolutions of CSI that still await full implementation. All these and other documents are important sources for a thorough study of the CSI as a 'pilgrim Church'. The Moderator devoted the central section of his address to the third Synod to emphasising the obligation of Christians as minorities in the State to set a higher standard of public duty and greater unselfishness rising above divisions. This was felt to be important in a nation which was struggling hard to match its excellent constitution with enlightened people. But over the years the scale of litigation in civil courts has escalated. In his 'Speaking the truth in Love' Victor Premasagar, a former Moderator, with reference to elections in CSI, observes:

> Democracy tends to become undemocratic when one party captures power and uses it for selfish ends. Political electoral practices influence church elections. Elections are won by promises made beforehand to supporters and then fulfilled. Job opportunities and other church resources are controlled by the 'party' in power so that others are frustrated. This breaks the fellowship so that every election alienates the majority through the influence of the few. This happens right from the Pastorate Committee to the Diocesan Council and the Synod. This is the plight of the Bishop's election also where one is appointed and the other three nominees are frustrated, their supporters sometimes taking the issue to a civil court. Episcopacy is no check against this kind of manipulation as Bishops themselves are in danger of being co-opted or controlled by the party in power. Such pressures create untold trouble throughout the church; and such strife damages witness to those outside the Church and of other faiths.[2]

In any case, the saving factor is a section of 'upright with aching hearts' who have been consistent in their criticism and constructive in their call for change. The Abel Commission Report, for instance, mentions the need for a radical restructuring of leadership in the CSI. Realising the misunderstood word 'bishop', it suggests the Indian name 'Pradhana Sevak' (chief servant) for bishops and 'Sangh Sevek' (servants of the community) for presbyters emphasising the biblical meaning of power and authority for serving others. It is very important for people of the CSI who are up on their feet to evangelise others, to realise

---

[1] *The Church of South India After Thirty Years – Report of the Special Committee Appointed by the CSI Synod to Study the Life and Work of the Church*, Madras: CSI Synod & CLS, 1978.

[2] V. Premasagar, 'Speaking the Truth in Love': The CSI - A Movement for Christian Unity, *Pilgrim*, No. 9 August, 1996, 5.

that the first field to evangelise is that of leadership and administration, and that the primary tool of evangelistic witness is servant-style administration and management.

Reform Movements

The word 'reform' was not strange for the CSI. As one of the governing principles of the Church the CSI constitution, affirming the Bible as 'the supreme and decisive standard of faith', acknowledges that the Church must always be ready to correct and reform itself in accordance with the teaching of those scriptures as the Holy Spirit shall reveal it.[1] As early as the second Synod in the context of a discussion on some Christians returning to Hinduism for economic benefits, the Moderator declared: 'It is not just more Christians that we want. We first need better Christians, a purified Church.'[2] Further, commissions were constituted for the periodic review of the life and work of the CSI with a proclaimed view to initiate reform. But there was hardly anyone among the leaders who could work out an appropriation of Martin Luther's Reformation for the Indian church.

The shelving of the Abel Commission Report irritated and frustrated many. Those of the 'aching hearts of the upright' formed the 'People's Movement Towards the Reformation of the Church of South India' in their first meeting held in Chennai, 1982. Their objectives included applying pressure for the implementation of the Abel Commission Report, recapturing the original vision of the CSI, promoting de-centralised structures and people's participation in decision-making at all levels and finding solutions for the pending problems of the dioceses. The key members of this movement included Russel Chandran, a former Principal of the United Theological College Bangalore, theologian and churchman; Ananda Rao Samuel, a former Moderator of the CSI; Abel, Joseph John, a greatly respected senior presbyter of Vellore; B.J. Premiah, a young and dynamic pastor in Chennai; and Sara Chanda, a noted Christian. They held a number of consultations and organised branches in diocesan areas. They had definite plans to work towards a great movement for mobilizing the awareness of people of highest integrity, found everywhere in the CSI, towards a steady and progressive reformation. They had hope to work for clearer formulations of the Christian faith in the Indian context as guaranteed in the CSI Constitution, and to realise the ideas of the Church as stated in Reports.

There were streams of external support for the efforts of PMR-CSI. Journals like the *People's Reporter,* the *CSI Laity Focus* and several other regional publications, carried important information and inspiring articles. The efforts of all those involved in and associated with the PMR-CSI were not appreciated by

---

[1] *The Constitution of the Church of South India*-with amendments up to and approved by the Synod of January 1972 together with the Basis of Union as adopted by the Governing Bodies of the Uniting Churches in India and elsewhere, Madras: CLS, 1972, 5.

[2] Quoted, Ward, *Pilgrim Church,* 24.

the CSI hierarchy. Some saw the movement as a great threat, while others watched it thoughtfully while the demands of the 'reformers' through open letters irritated them. As the reformers decided to fight while remaining in the united church it was not easy to ignore them. As the movement gained momentum, members of the group were subjected to different perceptions ranging from 'loyal rebels within the Church' to 'cynics' and, in between, as irritants, dissenters, people of self-righteousness, unresolved anger and with vested interests. Yet some leaders in the CSI who are 'not happy with the Church as it is now' have started to extend open support.[1]

The passion of those associated with the PMR-CSI was clearly evident in a consultation organised by the CSI Theological Commission in Bangalore in April 1995, under the leadership of its chairman Samuel Amirtham (1932-2017), a theologian, the first Principal of the Tamilnadu Theological Seminary Madurai, former Director of the Programme on Theological Education of the WCC and bishop in South Kerala Diocese. There were great voices demanding the CSI 'Jubilee' to be centred around its meaning of 'restoration of an equity in power and possession, solution for the present character crisis of leadership and transparency in administration'. Whatever may be the self-interest of some of those associated with the reform movement, there is no reason to deny that a good number of people had genuine commitment, clear vision and readiness to sacrifice. Those who loved the CSI could not but associate with the PMR-CSI through support and prayer. State and area level conferences were held and statements issued.

The impact of this movement appeared to bear fruit. For example, two of the recommendations of the Synod in 1996 were for constitutional amendment for limiting the term of the Bishop's office to ten years or retirement at 65, whichever is earlier, and for appointing an Administrator in each diocese thereby relieving the Bishop to enable him to spend time on 'spiritual matters'. While a few bishops opposed these, some other members asked for the optimum period of 7 or 5 years. Developments in the aftermath were so complex that they require a separate study. In any case, the original vigour of the PMR-CSI has wasted away. One or two individuals in their areas continue to create awareness about the need of the reformation of the CSI. In the meantime, new movements have emerged.

In 2000, Gnana Robinson (1935-2019) had retired from about four decades of the ministry of theological education, especially as a Principal of TTS Madurai and of UTC Bangalore. He was the founder of the Peace Trust in Kanyakumari. He decided to take forward the concerns of the PMR-CSI with a special focus on the corruption-free church, servant-style leadership and social justice. First, he created awareness and gathered support through meetings and writings. Along with a group of friends and colleagues he formed 'The Prophetic Forum for the

---

[1] See, for example S. Amirtham, *'Loyal Rebels within the Church'*, <u>South India Churchman,</u> April, 1993, 4.

Life and Witness of Churches' (PFLWC). The first conference was held in May 2003 which was inaugurated and presided over by I. Jesudason (1925-2013), a former bishop in the South Kerala Diocese and Moderator of the CSI. More conferences followed in the following years. Two conferences held in 2007 and 2009 had the theme 'Towards the Second Reformation of the Churches in India.'[1] Due to their campaign the 25th Quadrennial assembly of the National Council of Churches in India (2004) acknowledged that 'corruption which is rampant in society has penetrated the life of the churches undermining truth, justice and peace, disturbing the community and destroying the credibility of the institution and of the life and mission of the churches ... the root cause of corruption lies in the misuse and abuse of power and privilege and therefore corruption is an unethical act leading to moral crisis and conflicts.'[2] Subsequently, after the great Tsunami Scandal that shocked the overseas mission partners, many of whom suspended funds, the CNI/CSI Relations Committee wrote in 2006 to the CSI officers the following:

> In the context of court cases, reports of allegations and counter-allegations; lack of transparency and nepotism; of division and tension between Synod and some Dioceses; ongoing vacancies in many Dioceses; we as supporting partners are currently losing confidence that the CSI is upholding those constitutional principles that we value.[3]

In addition, on behalf of the PFLWC appeals were sent as well as presented in person. All such developments made some of the sensitive leaders angry and restless, but some culprits are said to be still elusive.

Some years later, in March 2012, representatives of the PFLWC met in the Kanyakumari Diocesan Hall, again under the leadership of Bishop Jesudason. It was at this point that the leaders 'wanted a more inclusive name, since already many regional groups have been working under different names for the common purpose of the renewal and reformation of the CSI from different perspectives'. The new name was 'The Movement for the Renewal and Reformation of Churches' (MRRC), and the movement was 'to include all regional initiatives with the common objective of renewal and reformation of all churches.'[4] Holding meetings and conferences has been a regular feature. The core group of the MRRC submitted a detailed 'Memorandum for Renewal and Reformation of Churches' to the Moderator in March 2012. It covered a wide range of concerns

---

[1] For details, see *Tremble at the Word of God: The Church of South India on the Way Towards Reformation*, by Gnana Robinson, Jeyakaran Isaac, C.L. Furtado, Jacob Belly and Siga Arles, Bangalore: National Printing Press for MRRC, 2012,5ff.

[2] Quoted, Ibid., 6f.

[3] Ibid., 7.

[4] Ibid., 13.

including rethinking episcopacy (nature, power, new mode of election, and term of office), corruption, structure of the Synod, functioning of the CSITA, improved transparency and accountability in governance, vigilance, right to information, comprehensive theological focus and healthy spirituality.[1]

Jeyakaran Isaac, a former Principal of the Voorhees College and Secretary of the Vellore Diocese, is a key member of the MRRC, playing the role of contributing to meetings and disseminating reports by publishing periodic papers. As the founder-president of the Abundant Life Movement, A Lay Movement for Service, Training and Development (2005), he has already been engaged in insisting on transparency and accountability in church administration, a simplified and spiritual episcopacy, and equipping the young generation to be credible witnesses to the gospel of God's kingdom. Further, he and his associates launched in March 2015 'People's Synod', 'a new initiative which will be a platform for the members of the CSI to freely articulate their ideas and hopes for the renewal of Church'. The Coordination Committee presented Resolutions at the Special Session of the CSI Synod held in April which included new amendments to the Constitution that would help the church recover from the crisis of management, safeguard the properties held by the CSITA, and restore trust and confidence of the people in the leadership. The theme of a one day consultation in August 2016 was 'CSI Towards a New Dawn', and the invitation mentions a 22-point objective of the CSIPS. Recent court orders have justified all these movements' assessments, although anxiety for the full establishment of justice is not yet removed. While the fighting is on, it may be important to consolidate efforts and mobilise people with genuine commitment, basic understanding of the Christian faith and integrated spirituality, for a single and strong movement for reform.

Individual Biblical-Theological Contributions

Both in association with the above movements and independently, some individuals have made remarkable contribution. Most notable is Joseph Muthuraj, a presbyter of the CSI and former professor of the New Testament at UTC. He has made an extensive study of the nature and development of episcopacy in India and published the findings in several volumes. When the CSI leadership went from bad to worse, he had the audacity to challenge it through his letters, biblical reflections and other publications. Fully aware of the history and degradation of the episcopacy in the CSI, his admonitions bear the marks of both a pastor and prophet. *Speaking Truth to Power* is the title of his book (2015) which brings together his reflections and letters.[2] More recently, he has written an in-depth

---

[1] Ibid., 18f.

[2] J.G. Muthuraj, *Speaking Truth to Power: A Critique of the Church of South India Episcopacy (Governance) of the 21ˢᵗ Century*, Focus 31, Geneva: Globethics. net, 2015.

study of the CSITA and published a very useful documentary.[1] Currently he
has been writing an online series with the title "Stones Cry Out" updating the
CSITA investigations, reminding of exemplary bishops, filling with important
historical facts and commenting on Anglican-CSI relationship including the
pronouncement of the Archbishop of Canterbury on the CSI and his visits. He
has been popularising 'the most punitive judgement the CSI has ever received at
the hands of the courts in India' with reference to the order delivered before the
Madurai Bench of the Madras High Court on 5th August 2019. He is asking
the bishops to wake up and act![2] Unlike the Pope of Luther, the CSI leaders have
chosen to ignore such communication because they know that public rejection
and refutation of such communication will popularise the concerns.

In such a situation the unjust and strategic act of the Anglican Communion
in absorbing the CSI as one of the provinces does not help. It is often said that
neither the Lambeth Conference nor any other organs are legal bodies to interfere
in the provinces. The so-called partnership meetings and visits do not touch
critical issues such as the ones we have pointed out in the case of CSI. They
remain at the level of adding to the numerical strength of the AC, protocol visits
and speeches of their president. It is difficult to deny persons like Jeyakaran Isaac
who have observed greater arrogance and indifference to voices of the lay thinkers
in the behaviour of the CSI bishops after they started to attend the meetings of
the AC including the LC. The Moderators of the CSI not only sit in the highest
Primates meetings as if it was a great honour given mercifully but without guts
to challenge the AC in their dodgy behaviour with regard to organic union, but
naively allow themselves to be pawns in the hands of the Archbishop of Canterbury
who does not show any knowledge of the history and nature of the CSI. During
the Primates meeting in October 2018, flanked by the Moderators of the CSI and
CNI, he solemnly declared that the CSI and CNI are the true successors of the
Church of England in India. How to interpret this? Most probably, it exposed the
ignorance about the unique nature and history of the CSI which included in its
tissues and veins Wesleyan Methodists and Reformed Churches of Europe and
USA; or the neo-colonial aggression through ecclesial garb. But it is more difficult
to interpret the compliance of the two Moderators! All the three never cared to
respond to J. Muthuraj's detailed critical comments.[3]

Reformation in the Indian Church and many other denominational
churches is a far cry from those who are committed to evangelise the whole

---

[1] J.G. Muthuraj, *Corporate Governance for Churches: Towards a Legal Reform Church of South India Trust Association*, Geneva: Globethics. net., 2019.

[2] https://virtueonline.org/processing-anglican-history-india- and-archbishops-canterbury

[3] Muthuraj has asked for a meeting with Archbishop Welby during his visit to India in September 2019; the author has also written to the General Secretary and Moderator of the CSI Synod asking for a meeting with a group of theologians and church historians. But as the final proof of this book is being completed (end of August) there is no sign of a response!

world including the power structures and administrative fields. Certainly, Martin Luther did not have the last word for stating the gospel and administrative structures based on the core insights of the Bible. The slogan of 'continued reformation' has been proclaimed by some leaders of the West. But there seems to no concrete expression which should not avoid the question of organic unity. Through speeches, writings, even songs and bringing into the voice and perceptions people of other religions from the ministry of interreligious dialogue, I have been advocating for an 'ever reforming evangelical church.'[1] In connection with the 500th anniversary of Luther's beginning of Reformation in 2017, *People's Reporter* brought out a special issue. A good number of writers reflected on the greatness and appeal of that Reformation. My article starts with an appreciation of Luther's decisive act of initiating a Reformation which had far reaching significance. But his circumstance was very different: church sharing power with the state; mono-religious and mono-scriptural; the Indian circumstance is very different: multireligious and multi-scriptural, and Christians are a tiny minority. I presented a critical appropriation of Luther for the Indian Church.[2] I am aware of vigorous Luther research continuing with fierce critics of Luther's attitude to and connection with certain issues such as farmers' agitation, support of princes & nobles, Jews, and women on the one hand, and the defendants on the other.[3]

If we do not venerate Luther as a demi-god we need to recognise his continuous legacy in Christian attitudes to the Jewish people and their religion. Although it was five centuries ago that Luther published the tract 'Jews and their Lies' which had murderous consequences and continued impact on Hitler's determination of the 'final annihilation' of the Jews during the Second World War, we should be aware of its theological impact in India. Though the Lutheran and Anglican Churches have offered a public apology, Luther's distorting effect on understanding the Bible and fundamentals of the faith remain unrevised. For example, was the ideal of 'collective priesthood' (i.e. the priesthood of all believers) not Hebrew? Were all the Jews enemies and killers of Jesus? Is not the Epistle of James a gospel of balancing between grace and justice? Do we affirm and share our common roots with the Jewish community? Do we acknowledge that Jesus' last supper was a Jewish Passover meal? We need not hide or deny the new horizons and meanings which are important for us. 'The Judeo-Christian tradition has a unique appeal to all humans as God's grace is primarily manifested

---

[1] I. Selvanayagam, 'Ever Reforming Evangelical Church: An Indian Protestant View' in *Church on Pilgrimage: Trajectories of Intercultural Encounter*, Ed. Kuncheria Pathil, Bengaluru: Dharmaram Publications, 2016, 129-150.

[2] 'A Critical Re-appropriation of Martin Luther's Reformation for India', *People's Reporter*, 29/24 Dec. 25-Jan. 10, 2017, 14; 30/3 Feb. 10-25, 2017, 6-7.

[3] See R. Sahayadhas, 'Luther on Two Realms of God's Activity: Contemporary Reflections' in *Church Reformed: Always Reforming*, ed. By Vincent Rajkumar, Bangalore: Christian Institute for the Study of Religion and Society', 2017, 31-49.

in his liberating act of solidarity with victims, starting from the Hebrew slaves in Egypt. Repentance and commitment to building up a new community based on justice, peace and love is the authentic response, while constantly relying on God's grace and unfailing love.' Following is the final part of my article with an Action Plan:

'Imbibing the spirit of Reformation, relying on the "Eternal I am" and ever moving closer to the unity of the Father, Son and Holy Spirit, we may start with the following:

1. Taking the Bible as the record of a long process of divine disclosures and dialogues with humanity, not using it to support or justify denominations and doctrines, and grasping the distilled wisdom of re-readings of the Bible in India, we should identify its basic insights, both primary and secondary. If the Bible has primacy over tradition and experience, its primary insights can guide discussions on any aspect of difference between the different church traditions.

2. Rework the creed(s) incorporating the Hebrew experience of liberation from Egypt, the prophetic movement with focus on justice, and the Jewish background of Jesus connecting with the Hebrew prophecy of seeking the lost sheep.

3. Crystalize the gospel with its basic dimensions and its common human appeal: 'Irrespective of your condition God has already accepted you in Christ. Accept this with gratitude and work for God's reign and glory.'

4. Replace the terms 'soul' with life-force, 'temple' with church building, 'invocation' with awakening to the presence of God, 'intercession' with prayers of solidarity and 'priest' with servant (minister). This will help to communicate the uniqueness of the Christian message to Indians.

5. Allot a considerable amount of the church's budget for social engagement, taking the local context very seriously.

6. With prayer and consultation evolve a process for election for leadership with decency, civility and order. Define the leadership in terms of educating and coordinating for realising the vision, a servanthood with limited powers (following the example of the Crucified).

We cannot expect a better response from our own Church than what Luther received: ridicule, rejection and humiliation. Cynicism is one of the killers of reform. Opposing indulgence was central for Luther. We have mini-popes in the forms of fundamentalist preachers and sectarian leaders who promise forgiveness and healing, security, prosperity and peace of mind, while the present, broad-minded Pope in Rome is calling for further reform, boosting the most wide-ranging reforms in the Catholic Church including in India since Vatican II (1962-65).

In the Indian context there should be a collective will for a new and unique Reformation. We do not have political support as Luther had. Yet he has given the concluding words: 'Here I stand … God help me.'

There is nothing wrong in reclaiming that South India achieved the first organic union. There is scope to widen it to includethe Lutheran, Mar Thoma and other traditions, but not repeating the mistakes, nor thinking that only the missionaries and their Indian colleagues can do it. Of course as a church, the CSI is neither complete not perfect. But incompleteness and imperfection need not be a hindrance if God's guidance is completely relied on for moving towards perfection. The CSI's unique identity has been distorted by the Anglican Communion on the one hand and sectarian-fundamentalist groups on the other. It is a significant irony that the Anglican Communion's one-sided embrace of the CSI as a Province has given sacerdotal honour to the CSI bishops while leaving them unable to learn from the progressive wing of modern Anglicanism. As piety is the weapon of the leaders and preachers they seem to be confident of evading any kind of scrutiny. If the struggling Spirit is successful, it may be expected that there will be a multi-pronged conversation with genuine openness to change.

Epilogue

When the Anglicans, Methodists and Reformists in Britain and America could not see each other eye to eye, could not stand shoulder to shoulder, and could not share a song book, in a remote corner of an insignificant region of undeveloped India a miracle happened. The Church of South India, the first organic union comprising non-episcopal and episcopal Churches was born in 1947. A group of 71 churchmen, missionaries and theologians at different times with different levels of involvement achieved this. They had the faith to think of the unthinkable but all for the sake of the glory of God, fulfilling in a small way the prayer of Jesus 'that they be one that the world will believe' and greater credibility and effectiveness of mission in a multi-religious India with a Hindu majority. They approached the unprecedented form of church union with commitment and openness, having the rare capacity ('faith') to transcend what was familiar for centuries. In their untiring pursuit, overcoming many hurdles with patience, almost all of them, realised that faith had the fundamental dimension of moving on from familiarity with long history.

For 28 years, God in his grace and pattern of action, as evident in his Word, chose a tiny Christian community in a corner of the globe in order to challenge and inspire the larger churches in more influential lands. However, the negotiators never claimed that the CSI was the only model, though it was not negligible. To be sure, the CSI was not a monolithic church as it covered four states of South India and one region of Sri Lanka and at least five languages.

It is difficult for politically and economically influential churches in the West, to stomach the fact that the 'miracle' of first organic union happened elsewhere in a mission field with a tiny minority of younger churches but with the contribution of their own missionaries and illustrious Indian leaders. One response could be to attempt a similar model or even a better model. But as has happened, what the Church of England and the Anglican Communion have done is that, after some decades of ridicule, opposition, and non-recognition, after about two generations, worked out a plan to absorb the CSI. There was no sensitivity towards the Methodist and Reformed Churches who had been constituent parts of CSI but with whom the Church of England has yet to share full communion. To illustrate, Dr. S. Radhakrishnan, the Spalding Professor of Comparative Religion in Oxford and later the President of India, in the context of writing about the relationship between the Vedic/Brahmanic/Hinduism and the great Protestant movement of Buddhism, mentions: 'Buddhism was the baby of Hinduism and the maternal embrace killed the baby.' Of course, he was not unaware of the history that the baby slipped away from the mother's embrace as Buddhism spread fast to become a world religion. It might stimulate the leaders and members of the CSI to regain their selfhood and independence not only to widen their union but also to challenge the Anglican Communion who appear to have treated them as ignorant and gullible.

V.S. Azariah, the first Indian bishop, who championed the formation of the CSI, challenged the western Churches in 1927 saying that in the mission field Christian disunity was sin and scandal. Pope Francis now repeatedly says that division in the church is the greatest sin. Azariah categorised Christian and non-Christian lands, and since then we have come to affirm that Christian bases are everywhere and that mission fields are everywhere, and that God's mission is one wherever and in whatever form it operates. If disunity and division are declared as sin but there is no effort to overcome it, many non-Christians in India (elsewhere as well) will continue to ridicule seeking forgiveness while remaining in that sin! The greatest spot of this sinning is the Holy Communion which bonds a new blood relationship by sharing the same body and blood of Jesus Christ. Any denomination which refuses to be in full communion and welcomes others (on the basis of non-biblical) objections despises Christ's body. Compared to most temples of other religions, members of Christian denominations and sects appear to be silly, fussy and stubborn, claiming an imaginary or false truth. Also, there is no sense of shame which could be the last redeeming straw as in the case of Adam and Eve. The Spirit told the church in Laodicea: 'You say "I am rich; I have acquired wealth and do not need a thing." But you do not realise that you are wretched, pitiful, poor, blind and naked' (Rev. 3:17).

There have been informal questions asked: Is the CSI the only model? Those who ask this question have not moved an inch further towards alternative models of organic union! Then, theologically, there are few who question about the organizational-organic-union to be the most valid response to Jesus' prayer that 'they may be one'. But if they come up with proposals for more valid responses they must be considered. We have to wait and see whether it is possible to achieve a visible organic unity, moving beyond the existing costly and confusing denominations and names, without some kind of organization. In all such proposals the heresy of spirit without matter and faith without form should be avoided. What the champions of the formation of the CSI achieved in 1947 was remarkable because with providence and for the first time the episcopal and a group of non-episcopal churches came together foregoing their denominational names and forms for the sake of mission. No one claims that what they achieved was ideal and absolute.

World mission faces greater challenges than ever before. Commercial domination makes the rich entrepreneurs and industrialists to be ever richer. The 'casual imperialism' of growing tourism with expensive holidays gains respect while the poor are frustrated. The politics and foreign policy of the wealthy nations and their impact on the world politics push the poor nations to escalate the possession of weapons. In recent years there have been devastating wars under false pretence which were later found to be illegal and immoral. Conflicts, crimes and rapes can be simply the topics of routine prayers and protocol declarations, which are easily done. In such contexts, unity of the church in an appropriate form will boost collective action against all the above evils and demonstrate that it is without doubt one body of Christ. Such acts of great faith alone can capture the attention of the world including unchurched people. Refusal to initiate new forms of unity, moving forward with determination that there should be no more division, does indirectly contribute to all forms of evil.

We have spent so much time, papers of protocol statements and costly media coverage on world peace and unity and have taken some credit, but remain complacent. The world does not need any more sermons and speeches on peace and unity. but concrete forms. As the preacher at the inaugural service of the CSI emphasised, 'God has matched us with His hour; the Church of South India has an unparalleled opportunity. The reconciliation between our divergent elements ... enables us with fresh conviction and force to proclaim the Gospel of reconciliation to all the clashing elements in this nation's life.' Everywhere in the world churches can play a role showing the authentic and concrete form of reconciliation if they are willing to move away from simple familiarity which may become an idol. Church councils at world, continental and national levels may match the secular organizations, but there is no substitute for a community of God's children and Christ's disciples to live as symbols of organic unity in each region and local area.

While scholarship, to a large extent, is based on the experience, articulation and quotes of others, the acts and words of people who have passionately talked about and worked on concrete form of post-denominal Christian unity deserve recognition. The following words of grace and wisdom were shared in the context of the formation of the Church of South India.

'Loyalty to our past can be disloyalty to God's will now' (Hollis).

'There is altogether too much ignorance of the simplest facts of church history' and there is 'No mechanical transmission of the Spirit through episcopacy of the apostolic succession' (Banninga).

Let me add: The belief that the Holy Spirit of power, grace, and love flow through the wire and cable of the right hand of a bishop denies the biblical witness of her filling in groups and even crowds just as in the pouring of the Pentecost.

'I always put truth first, but we cannot know the truth unless we love' (E.W. Thompson).

'We feared lest we by rigidity might be found to be fighting against God' (Foss Westcott).

'Committed persons were more important than doctrines' (Maclean).

'Holy Scriptures is the only standard of faith and life' (Streckeison).

'It is only those who have the courage of leadership who can accomplish anything that is worth accomplishing in the world' (A.C. Headlam).

'All our problems are the caricatures of our own past selves' (Bishop Whitehead).

No one should believe that organic unity in the form of a common name and coherent structure is the ultimate. Jesus prayed that 'they may be one as you, Father, and I are one, and they may be one in us'. The Holy Spirit who is anonymous here is part of the trinitarian form of unity. Just as the Father, Son and the Holy Spirit are constantly one and different, loving and glorifying one another, yet together in working out the salvation and directing the mission, Christians are called to share in the life of the Triune God. As Jesus and Paul have indicated, in an ever-maturing Christian life with reverence and prayer we move towards the perfection of the heavenly Father or all the fullness of God (Mt. 5:48; Eph. 3:19). The question is not whether we can achieve this goal but whether we are consciously and constantly trying on the way. Organic unity certainly helps to move towards this profound spirituality and, moreover, it can lead to many other more inspiring forms of unity.

Denominational Churches in different parts of the world are in fast decline; perhaps the situation in the United Kingdom is fastest. The story of the Church of South India has been forgotten. The Anglican Communion declaring it unilaterally as one of its provinces and using it for adding to their numerical strength and perpetuation of one-sided honour has distorted its true nature of the first organic union. The silence of the other constituent parts of the CSI, the Methodists and Reformed Churches, is mysterious! The leaders and members of the CSI who are also ignorant of the background have sold their birthright for a few trips to London, and have lost their selfhood. What the anonymous apostle wrote to the Hebrews has a warning and advice: 'See that no one is … godless like Esau, who for a single meal sold his inheritance rights' (Heb. 12:16).

Finally, Martin Luther King Jr. (1929-1968), a black American Baptist pastor, champion of human rights and racial justice, a martyr whose statue is installed in Westminster Abbey London, at the heat of his struggle with the nexus of evil forces, declared: 'We, the Roman Catholics, Orthodox and the Protestants, either come together as brothers and sisters or die as fools.'

'I will sing with my spirit, but I will also sing with my understanding' –
St. Paul.

Elect from every nation,
Yet one o'er all the earth,
Her charter of salvation
One Lord, one faith, one birth;
One holy name she blesses,
Partakes one holy food,
And to one hope she presses
With every grace endued.

Samuel John Stone (1839-1900)

Your hand, O God, has guided
Your flock from age to age;
The wondrous tale is written,
Full clear, on every page;
Our forebears owned your goodness,
And we their deeds record;
And both of this bear witness:
one Church, one faith, one Lord.

Edward Hayes Plumptre (1821-1891)

1. Thank God for his leading to union;
We shout out and sing with elation.
United we join in God's great new creation;
Bless Father, Son and the Spirit.
Refrain: Ha-Ha-Ha Hallelujah (7) A...men

2. Committed to travel together,
We seek inner strength for our journey;
In fellowship closer, with life in Christ fuller,
Bless Father, Son and the Spirit.

3. We offer ourselves for your service;
Lord, grant us a vision of splendour;
We'll work for your kingdom of justice and mercy,
Bless Father, Son and the Spirit.
(CSI Jubilee Song-Samuel Amirtham and modified by Eric J. Lott)

Bibliography

(Short articles, reflections, comments and web references are not reproduced from the footnotes)

Books

Abel, M. (ed.), *The Church of South India After Thirty Years – Report of the Special Committee Appointed by the CSI Synod to Study the Life and Work of the Church*, Madras: CSI Synod-CLS, 1978.

Arangadan, A.J., *Church Union in South India: A History of its Progress*, Calicut: Basel Mission Press, 1943.

Avis, Pal, *The Anglican Understanding of the Church: An Introduction*, London: ISPCK, 2000.

Babu, Dass, (ed.), *Priorities for the Mission of the Church – CSI*, Madras: CSI Synod, 1982

Beck, Brian, Angela Shier-Jones and Helen Wareing (ed.) *Unmasking Methodist Theology*, London: Continuum, 2004.

Bowden, John (ed.), *Christianity: The Complete Guide*, London: Continuum, 2005.

Chandran, J.R. (Ed.), *Theological Conversation (1948-1959): A Selection of Papers Read together with the Agreed Statements and an Introduction*, Madras: CLS, 1964.

Coleman, Roger (ed.), *Resolutions of the Twelve Lambeth Conferences, 1867-1988*, Toronto: Anglican Book Centre, 1992.

Cracknell, Kenneth, *Our Doctrines: Methodist Theology as Classical Christianity*, Hope Valley: Cliff College Publishing, 1998.

Dalton, E., *Who Thee by faith – A Biography of Bishop Jacob*, Kottayam: CMS Press.

Devanesan, Chandran (ed.), *Rajaiah D. Paul: Layman Extraordinary*, Madras: CLS, 1982.

Ferguson, Sinclair B. and David F. Wright (ed.), *New Dictionary of Theology*, Leicester: Inter-Varsity Press, 1988.

Garrett, T.S., *The Liturgy of the Church of South India – An Introduction to and Commentary on 'The Lord's Supper'*, Madras: Oxford University Press, 1952.

George, K.M., *The Church of South India: Negotiations Towards Union (1919-1947)*, Mallappally, 1997.

George, K.M., *Church of South India – Life in Union (1947-1997)*, New Delhi: ISPCK and Tiruvalla: C.S.S., 1999.

Gibbard, Mark, *Unity is not Enough – Reflections after a visit to CSI*, London: AR. Mowbray, 1965.

Gibbs, M.E., *The Anglican Church in India 1600-1970*, Delhi: ISPCK, 1972.

Gladstone, J.W. (ed.), *United to Unite: History of South India, 1947-1997*, Chennai: CSI Synod, 1997.

Graham, Carol, *The Church of South India: A Further Stage in Development*, on behalf of the Appeal Committee for Women's Work in the CSI, 1960.

Hanson, Anthony, *Should the Anglicans Support the Church of South India? Seven Objections Considered*, London: Church Missionary Society 1951.

Harper, Susan Willington, *In the Shadow of the Mahatma: Bishop V.S. Azariah and the Travails of Christianity in British India*, Richmond: Curzon, 2000.

Hollis, A.M., *The Fellowship of the Holy Spirit*, Madras: CLS, 1952.

_____ (ed.) *Ten Years Young* (addresses, bible studies and sermon delivered to the CSI), Madras: CLS, 1958.

_____*The Significance of South India. Ecumenical Studies in History*, London: Lutterworth, 1966.

_____ *Paternalism in the Church*, Oxford: Oxford University Press, 1962.

_____*Mission, Unity and Truth*, London: Lutterworth, 1967.

_____*Unity – Hope and Experience* (Carey Lecture), Calcutta: Council of Serampore College, 1960.

Johnson, Y. Gnana Chandra, *Christian Lyrics Poets* (Tamil), Chennai: Keerthana, 2009.

Lloyd, Roger, *The Church of England 1900-1965*, London: SCM, 1966.

Lindbeck, George A., *The Nature of Doctrine, The Religion and Theology in a Postliberal Age*, Philadelphia: The Westminster Press, 1984.

Lovett, Richard, *The History of the London Missionary Society, 1795-1895*, London: Oxford University Press, 1899, Vol. I.

Mackinnon, Donald, *The Stripping of the Altars*, London: Collins (The Fontana Library), 1969.

Mladin, N. et al., *That they all may be one: Insights into Churches Together in England and Contemporary Ecumenism*, Theos, London, 2017.

Moses, Vinay and C. Sugden, *Lambeth: A View from the Two Thirds World*, London: SPCK, 1989.

Muthuraj, Joseph G., *We Began at Tranquebar*, New Delhi: ISPCK, 2010, 2 volumes.

_____*Speaking Truth to Power: A Critique of the Church of South India Episcopacy (Governance) of the 21st Century*, Globethics.net Focus No. 31, 2015.

_____*Corporate Governance for Churches: Towards a Legal Reform Church of South India Trust Association*, Geneva: Globethics.net., 2019.

Neill, Stephen, *Church Union in South India: Towards a United Church, 1913-1947*, London: SCM, 1947.

Newbigin, Lesslie, 'The Church and the Gospel' in *The Church and Union*, ed. by J.E.L Newbigin, Madras: CLS (for the Committee on Church Union, South India United Church), 1944, 46 -59.

_____*The Reunion of the Church*, London: SCM, 1948.

_____ *A South India Diary*, London: Edinburgh House Press, 1951.

_____*Unfinished Agenda: An Autobiography*, London: S.P.C.K., 1993.

(*Bibliography of Lesslie Newbigin's published and unpublished writings, from 1926 to 2006, mainly on mission and church union, are now available in the Cadbury Research Library, University of Birmingham, UK*).

Newton, John A., *A Man for All Churches: Marcus Ward 1906-1978*, London: Epworth Press,1984.

Pathil, Kuncheria (ed.), *Church on Pilgrimage: Trajectories of Intercultural Encounter*, Bengaluru: Dharmaram Publications, 2016, 129-150.

Paul, R.D., *The First Decade – An Account of the Church of South India,* Madras: CLS, 1958.

Paul, R.D. & J. Karunakaran, *Church of South India – Lutheran Conversations,* Madras: CLS, 1970.

Paul, R.D., *Ecumenism in Action, The Church of South India: An Assessment, Madras: CLS, 1972.*

Priestly, Eber, *The Church of South India – Adventure in Union*, London: Church of South India Council in Great Britain, 1970.

Rajkumar, Vincent (ed.), *Church Reformed: Always Reforming*, Bangalore: Christian Institute for the Study of Religion and Society, 2017.

Rawlinson, A.E.J., *The Church of South India*, London: Hodder and Stoughton, 1951.

Rea, Donald, *The Church of South India and the Church*, Oxford: Baxter's Press, 1956.

Robinson, Gnana et al. (Comp.), *Tremble at the Word of God: The Church of South India on the Way Towards Reformation,* Bangalore: Globethics.net, 2012.

Rosenthal, James M. *et al.* (Comp.), *The Communion We Share: Anglican Consultative Council XI, Scotland*, Morehouse Publishing (for the AC Office), 2000.

Selvanayagam, Israel, *Samuel Amirtham's Living Theology*, Bangalore: SATHRI, 2007.

Sibree, James, *A Register of Missionaries, Deputations Etc., From 1796 to 1923*, London: London Missionary Society, 1923.

Simpson, James B. and Edward M. Story, *The Long Shadows of Lambeth X*, New York: McGraw-Hill Book Company, 1969.

Sundkler, Bengt, *Church of South India: The Movement Towards Union, 1900-1947*, London: Lutterworth Press, 1954. (The 'Select Bibliography' in this book shows the wealth of resources produced earlier).

The Book of Common Prayer, Cambridge: Cambridge University Press, 1968.

Throup, Marcus, *All Things Anglican: Who We Are and What We Believe*, Norwich (and London): Canterbury Press, 2018.

Wainwright, Geoffrey, *Lesslie Newbigin: A Theological Life*, Oxford: Oxford University Press, 2000.

Walpole, Beth, *Venture of Faith* (ed. By P.C. Dass Babu), Chennai: CLS, 1993.

Ward, Marcus, *The Pilgrim Church: An Account of the First Five Years in the Life of the Church of South India*, Madras: CLS, 1952.

Webster, Douglas, *What is the Church of South India?* London: The Highway Press, 1964.

Welsby, Paul A., *A History of the Church of England 1945-1980*, Oxford University Press 1984.

Williams, Rowan, *Anglican Identities*, London: Darton, Longman and Todd Ltd., 2004.

Wingate, Andrew et al. (Eds.), *Anglicanism: A Global Communion*, London: Mowbray, 1998.

Young, Frances, *The Making of the Creeds*, London: SCM *Press*, 1991.

Essays and Articles

Amirtham, Samuel, 'Loyal Rebels within the Church', *South India Churchman*, April, 1993, 4ff.

_____ 'Reflections on Episcopacy in the CSI', *Pilgrim*, No. 16, March 2000, 2-5.

Howells, George, 'Church Union in South India', *Baptist Quarterly*, 5/4 1930, 151-167.

Premasagar, Victor, 'Speaking the Truth in Love: The CSI – A Movement for Christian Unity', *Pilgrim*, No. 9, August, 1996, 2-5.

_____ 'Is the Church of South India Anglican?', *Pilgrim*, No. 20, March-April, 2002, 5-7.

Reardon, John, '25th Synod of the CSI', *Pilgrim, No. 8, March 1996, 7f.*

Sargant, N.C., 'Some Problems and Tensions of the Ministry in England', *South India Churchman*, January, 1975, 5f.

Selvanayagam ..., 'The Catholic Spirit in Action! – Methodists and the Formation of the Church of South India', *Indian Church History Review*, XLI/ 2, Dec., 06, 127-148.

_____ 'From Congregationalism to Anglicanism with a Special Reference to Episcopacy', *Indian Church History Review*, XLI/1, June 2007, 50-79.

_____ 'Jewish-Christian Relationship from a Third World Perspective', *Current Dialogue*, No. 25, Dec. 1993, 20-31.

_____ (With C.R.W. David), 'Liturgy and Symbols: Reflections in View of Liturgical Renewal in the Church of South India', *Arasaradi Journal of Theological Reflection*, VI/2, July-Dec., 1993, 19-28.

_____ 'Mission in a Pluralist Society', *Greater Peace, Closer Fellowship, Fuller Life*, Ed. by Lily & Sam Amirtham, CSI Golden Jubilee Publication, Madras, 1997, 310-322.

_____ 'Anglicans and Inter-faith Relations - a Historical Retrospect' in *Anglicanism - A Global Communion*, Ed. by Andrew Wingate et al., London: Mowbray, 1998, 341-346.

_____ 'From Church of South India to Bharat Church of Christ: A Forgotten Vision', *NCC Review*, CXXXIII/8, September, 2013, 42-45.

_____ 'Unequal Partnership in Mission', *Pilgrim*, 42, Feb. 2013, 28-35.

_____ 'Theological Education and Regeneration of the Church in India', in *'Communion on the Move: Towards a Relevant Theological Education'* (Essays in Honour of Bishop John Sadananda, ed. by Wati Longchar & P. Mohan Larbeer, Bangalore: BTESSC, 2015, 37-49.

_____ 'Leadership and Power', in *The Christian Imperative and a Moral Challenge: National Ecumenical Campaign for Transparency, Accountability and Responsibility*, ed. Roger Gaikward et al., Nagpur: NCCI and Delhi: ISPCK, 2016, 51-61.

_____ 'Ever Reforming Evangelical Church: An Indian Protestant View' in *Church on Pilgrimage: Trajectories of Intercultural Encounter*, Ed. Kuncheria Pathil, Bengaluru: Dharmaram Publications, 2016, 129-150.

_____ 'A Critical Re-appropriation of Martin Luther's Reformation for India', *People's Reporter*, 29/24 Dec. 25-Jan. 10, 2017, 14; 30/3 Feb. 10-25, 2017, 6-7.

_____ Collective Priesthood", People's Reporter, 28/3 Feb. 10-25, 2015, 2, 6.

_____ "Anniversary of Organic Unity in South India" in Methodist Recorder, 21October 2016, 8.

_____ "A dying and resurrection in India: (IS) reflects on the first 'United Church, 70 years after its inauguration", Church Times, No. 8062, London, 22 September 2017, 15.

_____ "70th Anniversary of The First Organic Unity", Christians Aware Magazine, Autumn 2017, 4-5.

_____ "From our Minister 5: Genuine Unity, Indispensable for Revival", Evesham Methodist Church Magazine, No. 87, December 2017, 4-6.

_____ "The Great Miracle of Organic Unity in South India", Evesham Parish News, Nov., 2018, 10.

_____ "Archbishop Visits India Amidst Significant Questions", Church Times, July 2019.

_____ "One in Christ: The Forgotten Miracle of the first Organic Union", Methodist Recorder, Issue 8434, 16 August, 2019, 11.

Documents and Unpublished Papers

Proposed Constitution of the Church of Christ in South India, Madras: CLS for CSI-Lutheran Commission, 1920.

Inauguration of Church Union in South India, St. George's Cathedral, September 27, 1947, Madras: CLS, 1947.

G.K.A. Bell (ed.), *Documents on Christian Unity*, 2nd series, 1920-1930, London: Oxford University Press, 1930.

G.K.A. Bell (ed.), *Documents on Christian Unity*, 3rd series, 1930-1948, London: Oxford University Press, 1949.

The Church of South India – Being the United Report of the Joint Committees of the Convocations of the Canterbury and York, 1950.

Newbigin, J.E., 'Statement on the Ministry of the Church – Ordained and Unordained, Paid and Unpaid', Report presented to Executive Committee of the Synod, 1953.

Renewal and Advance: Report of the Church of South India on Integration and Joint Action 1963 (R.D. Paul), Madras: CSI Synod and CLS, 1963.

CSI Theme Papers – Survey on Mission, presented at the 10th Synod, Kottayam, 1966.

The Constitution of the Church of South India – with amendments up to and approved by the Synod of January 1972 together with the Basis of Union as adopted by the Governing Bodies of the United Churches in India and elsewhere, Madras: CLS, 1972 (Reprinted, 1993).

The Church of South India after Thirty Years: Report of the Special Committee Appointed by the Church of South India Synod to Study the Life and Work of the Church, Chennai: CLS, 1978.

The Truth Shall Set You Free: The Lambeth Conference 1988 – The Reports and Resolutions and Pastoral Letters from the Bishops, London: Anglican Consultative Council, 1988.

St. Thomas of India Unity Lecture, 1990 by Thomas Thangaraj, 'Is Full Church Unity Possible or Desirable?' (copies for close circulation).

St. Thomas of India Unity Lecture, 1997 by Israel Selvanayagam, 'A Mission Spirituality for a United Church – Reflections from Fifty Years of Experience of the Church of South India' (copies for close circulation).

Anglican-Methodist Covenant, Peterborough: Methodist Publishing House, 2001 (signed on 2003; final report debated and approved in 2014).

'Palmer of Bombay – A Forgotten Pioneer?' (unpublished paper, author unknown).

'Inter-Communion and Catholicity', *South India Churchman*, August, 1955, Editorial, 1-3; with a supplement entitled 'C.S.I. Reflections on the Convocation Debate', by Campbell Milford, 3-4.

'"That they all may be one": Insights into Churches Together in England and Contemporary Ecumenism', *Theos*, London, 2017.

Index